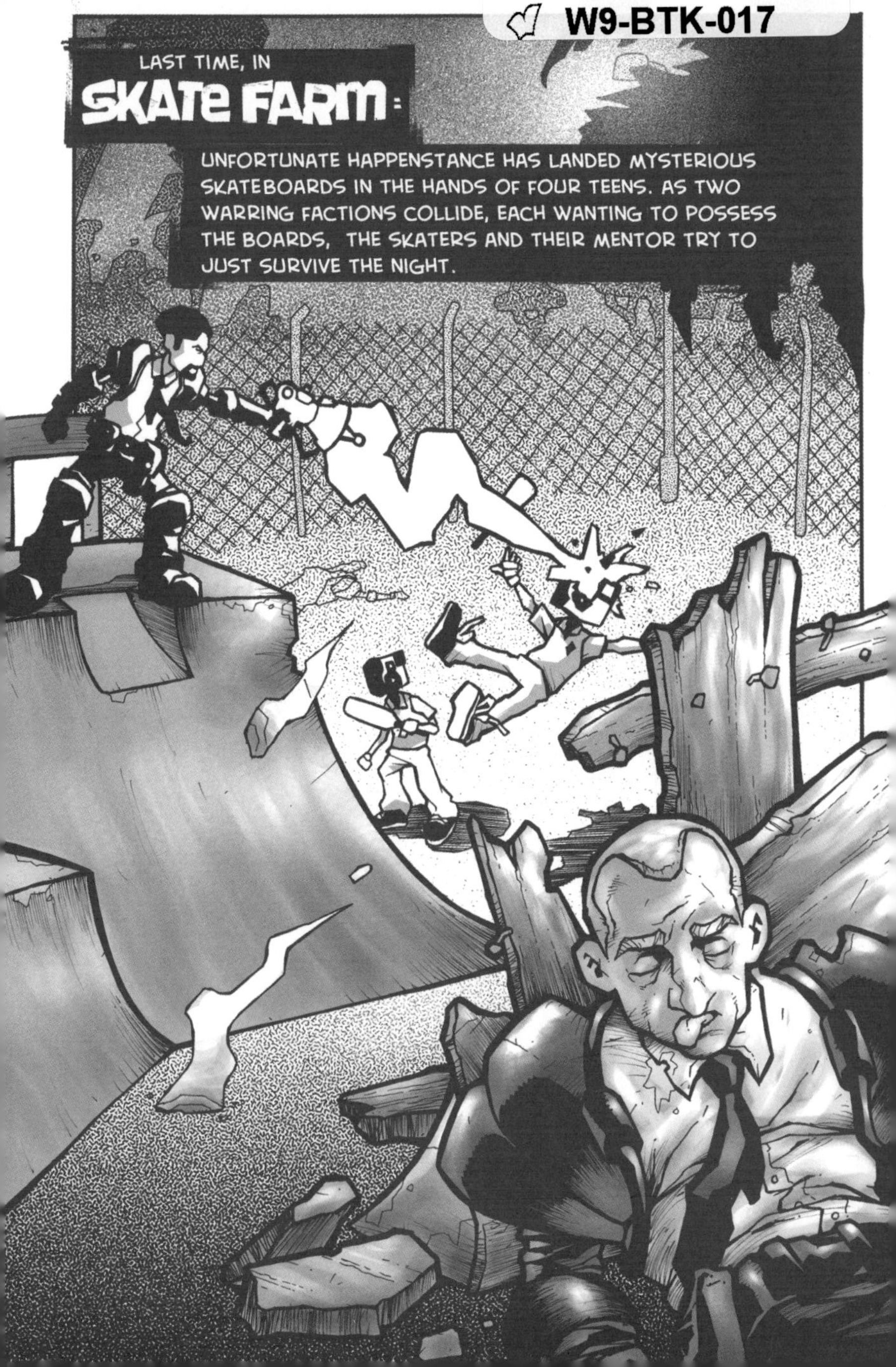
LAST TIME, IN
SKATE FARM:
UNFORTUNATE HAPPENSTANCE HAS LANDED MYSTERIOUS SKATEBOARDS IN THE HANDS OF FOUR TEENS. AS TWO WARRING FACTIONS COLLIDE, EACH WANTING TO POSSESS THE BOARDS, THE SKATERS AND THEIR MENTOR TRY TO JUST SURVIVE THE NIGHT.

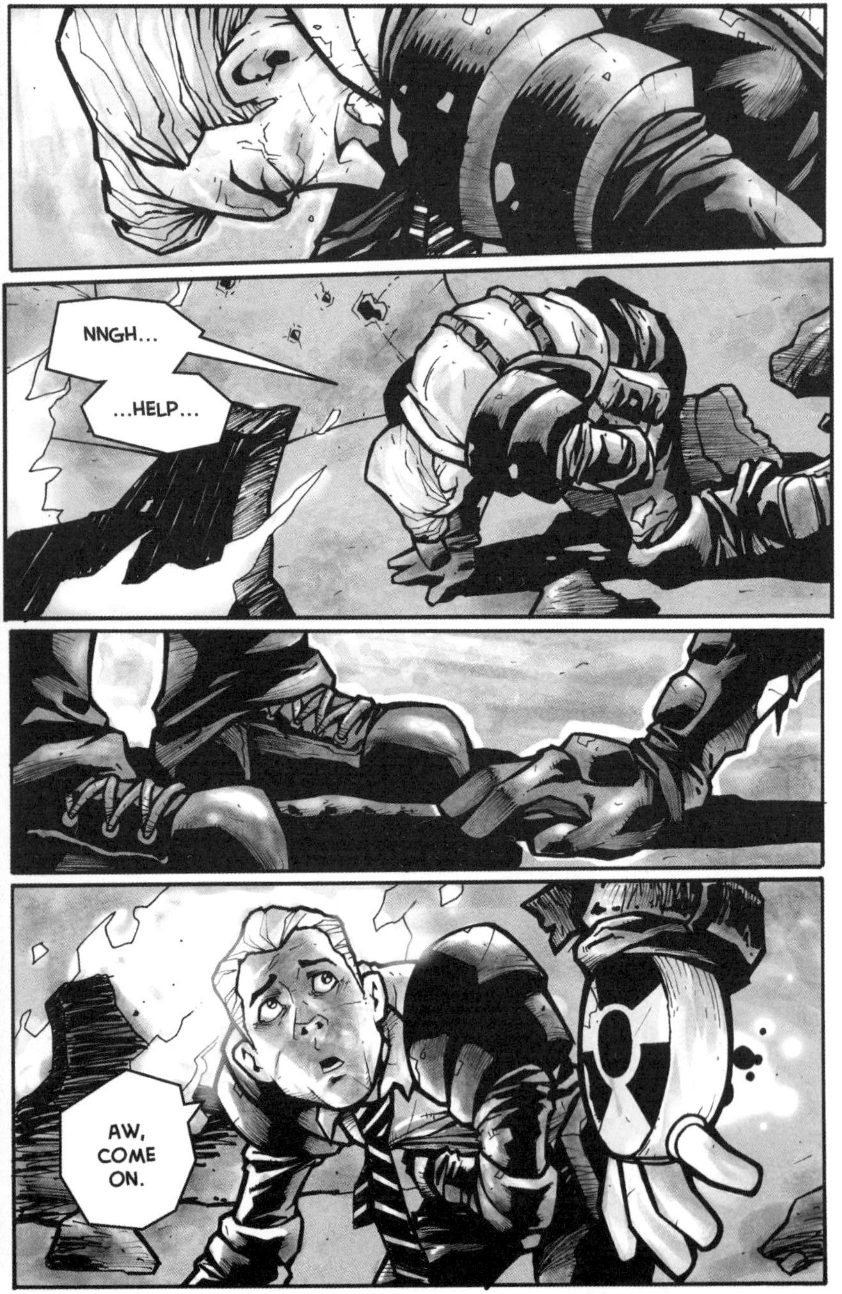
NNGH...
...HELP...
AW, COME ON.

SKATE FARM

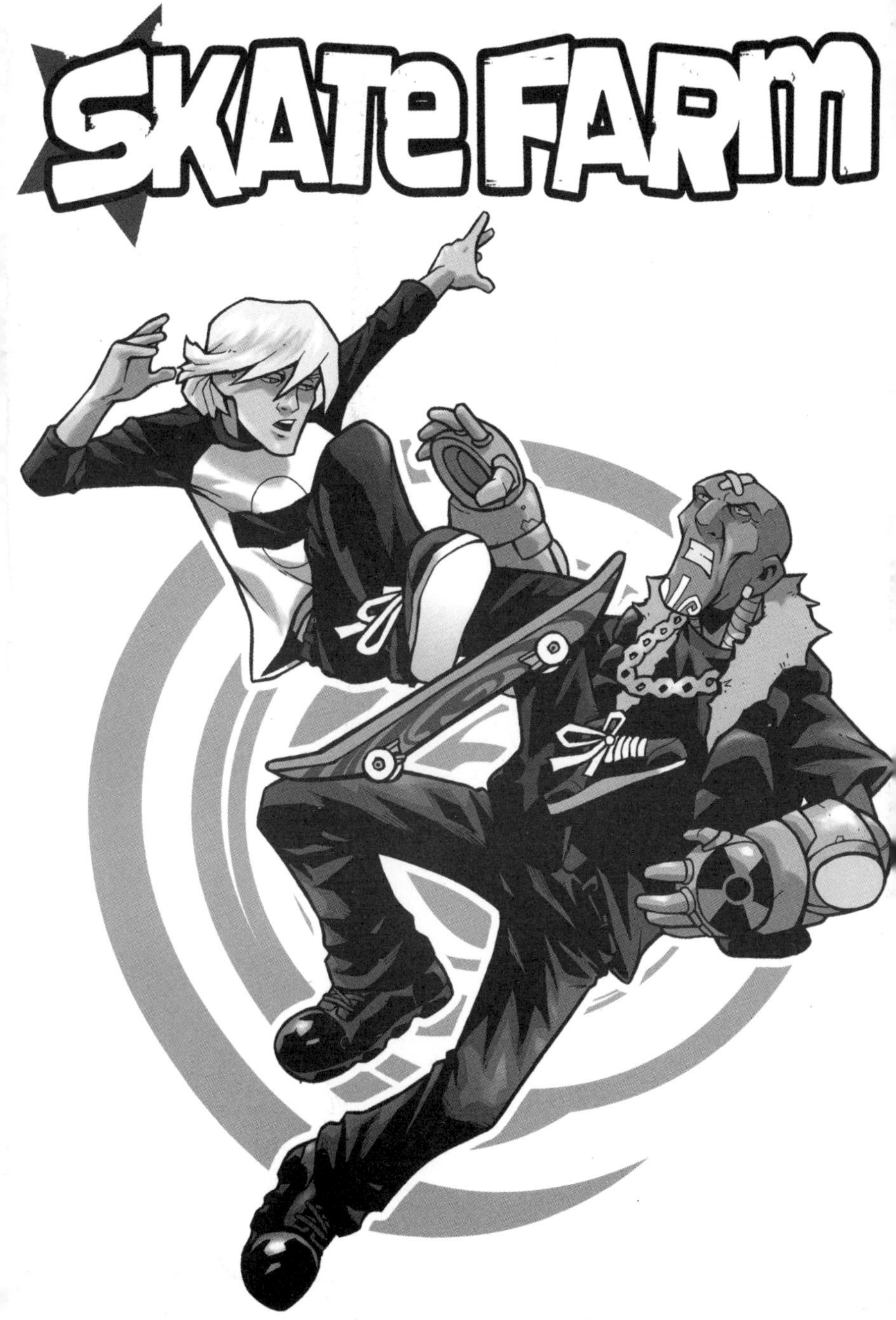

WWW.SKATEFARMCOMICS.COM

CREATED BY
DANNY NEIMAN, JOHN STAUFFER, AND BARZAK

WRITTEN AND ILLUSTRATED BY
BARZAK

EDITS BY
JUSTIN EISINGER

ISBN: 978-1-60010-409-1

11 10 09 08 1 2 3 4

www.idwpublishing.com

In Conjunction With SBK Publishing, LLC
SBK Publishing, LLC is:
Richard E. Johnson, Publisher and Editor
rej@skatefarmcomics.com

Members Include:
John S. Dalton • Peter "PT" Townend • Tosh Townend

IDW Publishing is: **Operations**: Moshe Berger, Chairman • Ted Adams, Chief Executive Officer • Greg Goldstein, Chief Operating Officer • Matthew Ruzicka, CPA, Chief Financial Officer • Alan Payne, VP of Sales • Lorelei Bunjes, Dir. of Digital Services • Marci Hubbard, Executive Assistant • Alonzo Simon, Shipping Manager • **Editorial**: Chris Ryall, Publisher/Editor-in-Chief • Scott Dunbier, Editor, Special Projects • Andy Schmidt, Senior Editor • Justin Eisinger, Editor • Kris Oprisko, Editor/Foreign Lic. • Denton J. Tipton, Editor • Tom Waltz, Editor • Mariah Huehner, Assistant Editor • **Design**: Robbie Robbins, EVP/Sr. Graphic Artist • Ben Templesmith, Artist/Designer • Neil Uyetake, Art Director • Chris Mowry, Graphic Artist • Amauri Osorio, Graphic Artist

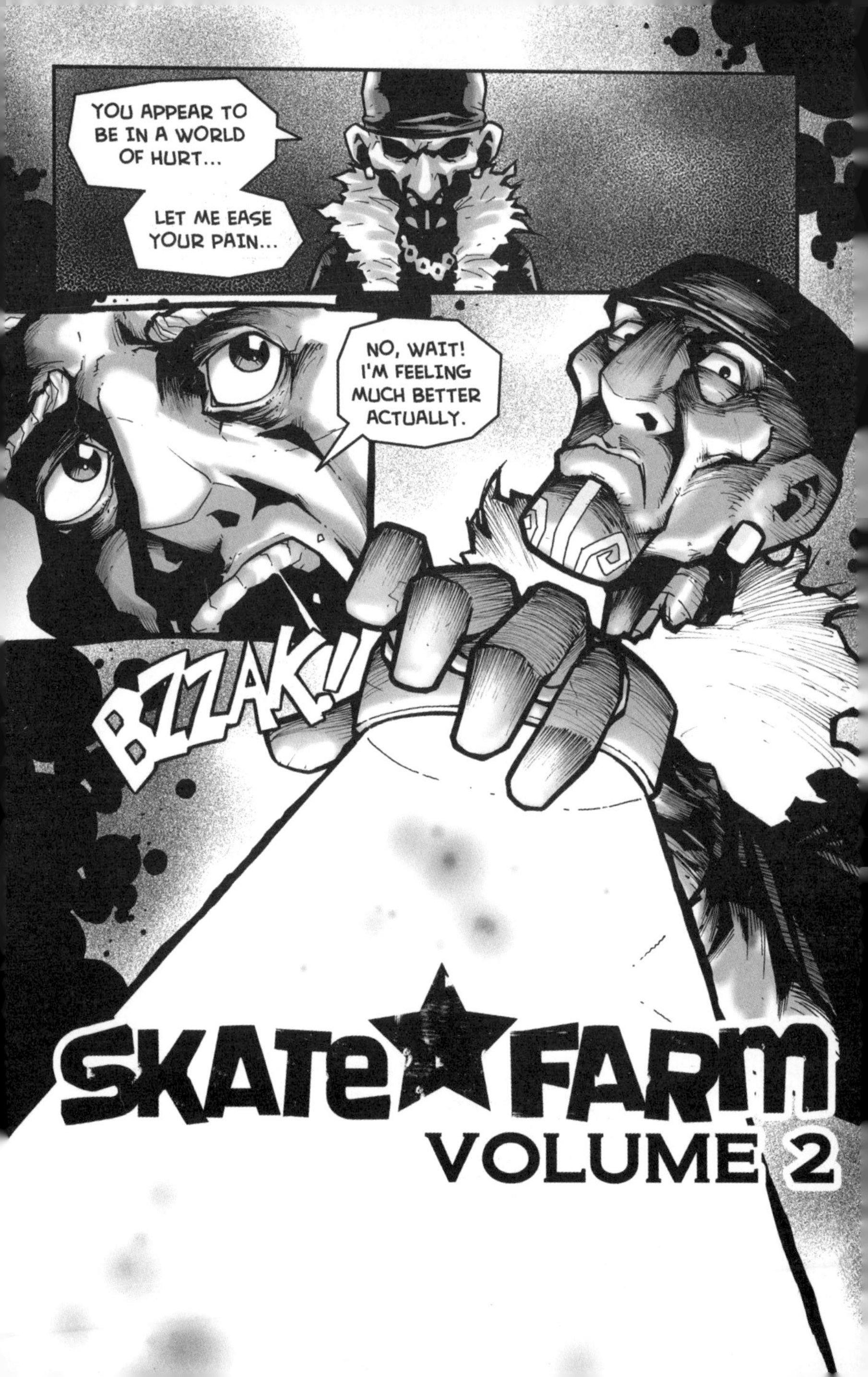
YOU APPEAR TO BE IN A WORLD OF HURT...
LET ME EASE YOUR PAIN...
NO, WAIT! I'M FEELING MUCH BETTER ACTUALLY.
BZZZAK!!
SKATE FARM
VOLUME 2

chapter one

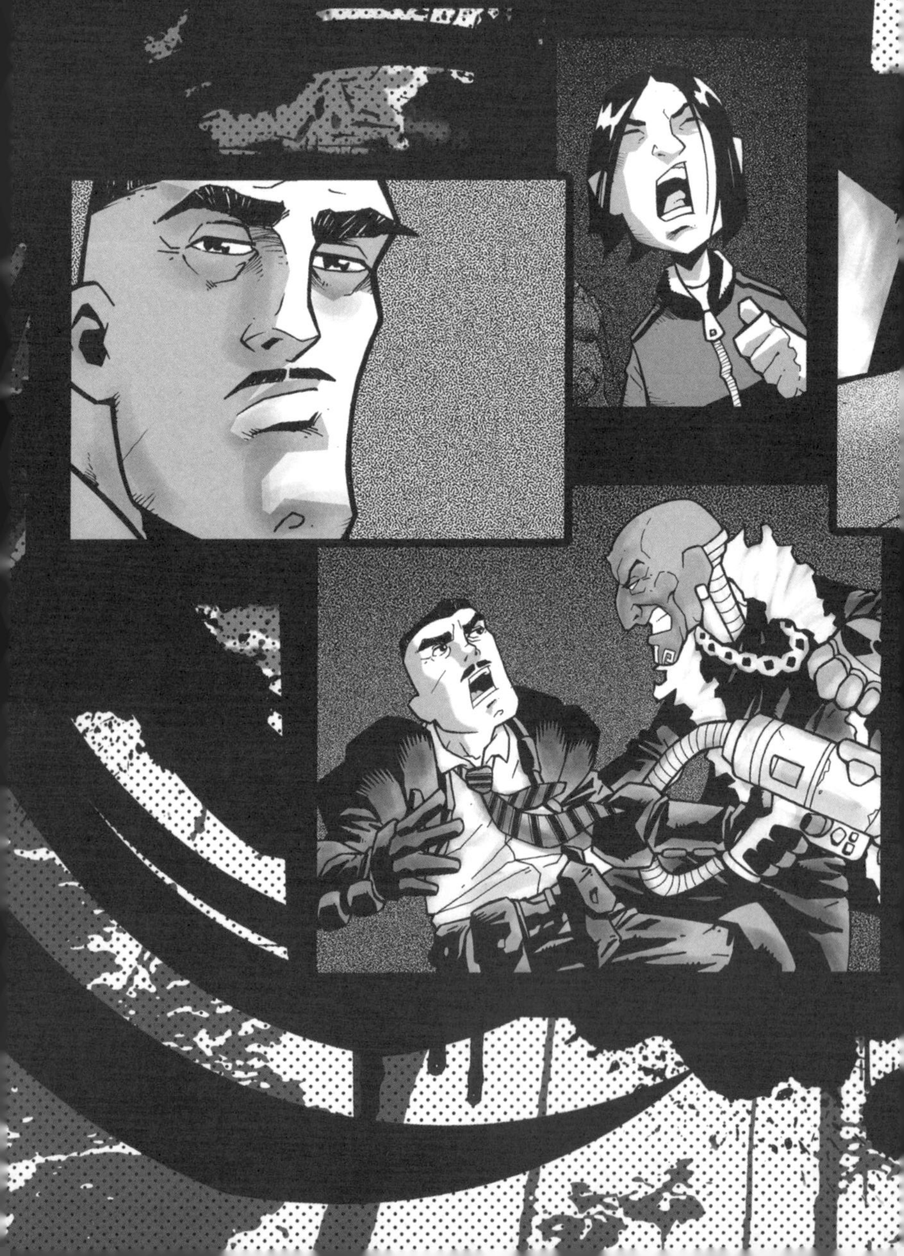

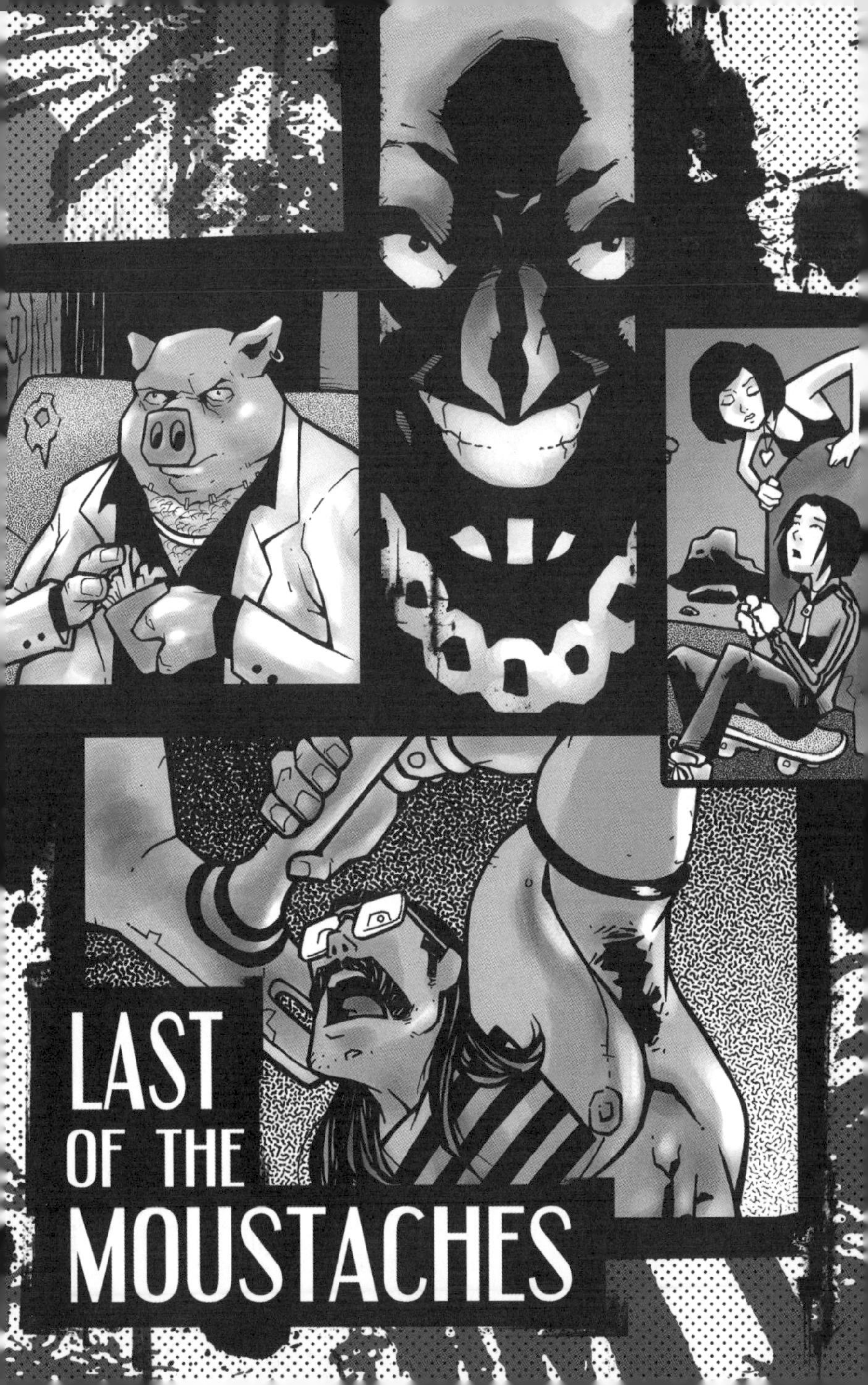
LAST
OF THE
MOUSTACHES

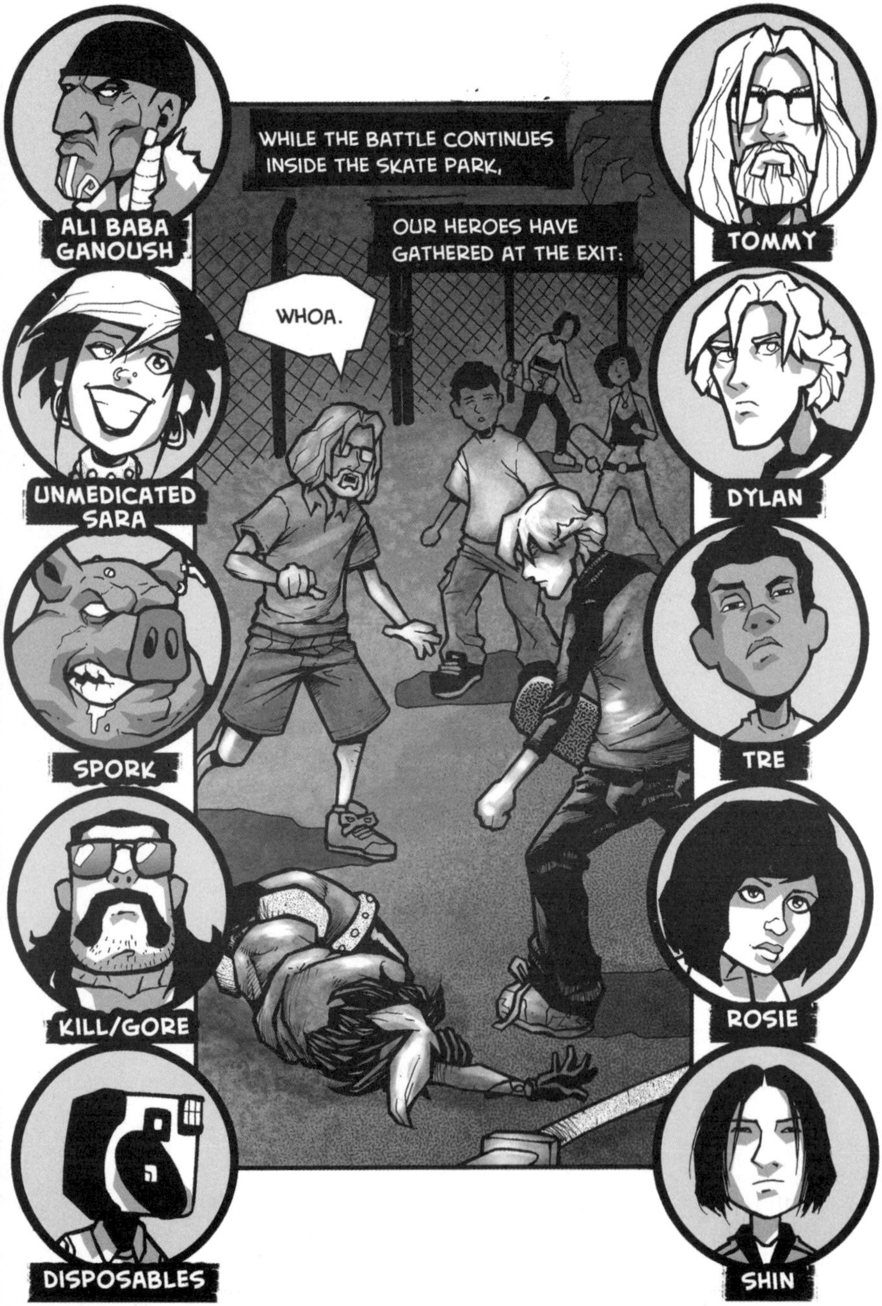
ALI BABA GANOUSH
UNMEDICATED SARA
SPORK
KILL/GORE
DISPOSABLES
WHILE THE BATTLE CONTINUES INSIDE THE SKATE PARK,
OUR HEROES HAVE GATHERED AT THE EXIT:
WHOA.
TOMMY
DYLAN
TRE
ROSIE
SHIN

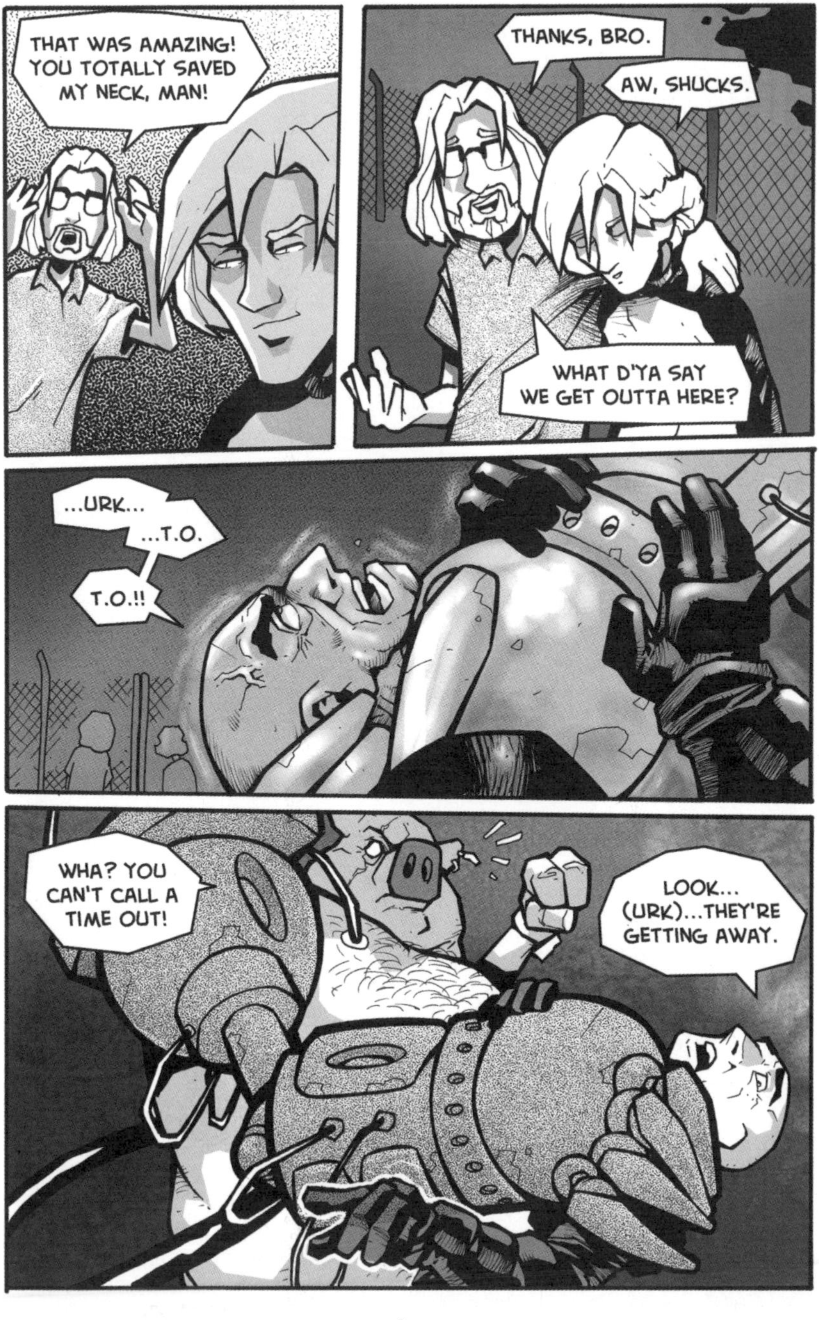
THAT WAS AMAZING! YOU TOTALLY SAVED MY NECK, MAN!
THANKS, BRO.
AW, SHUCKS.
WHAT D'YA SAY WE GET OUTTA HERE?
...URK...
...T.O.
T.O.!!
WHA? YOU CAN'T CALL A TIME OUT!
LOOK... (URK)...THEY'RE GETTING AWAY.

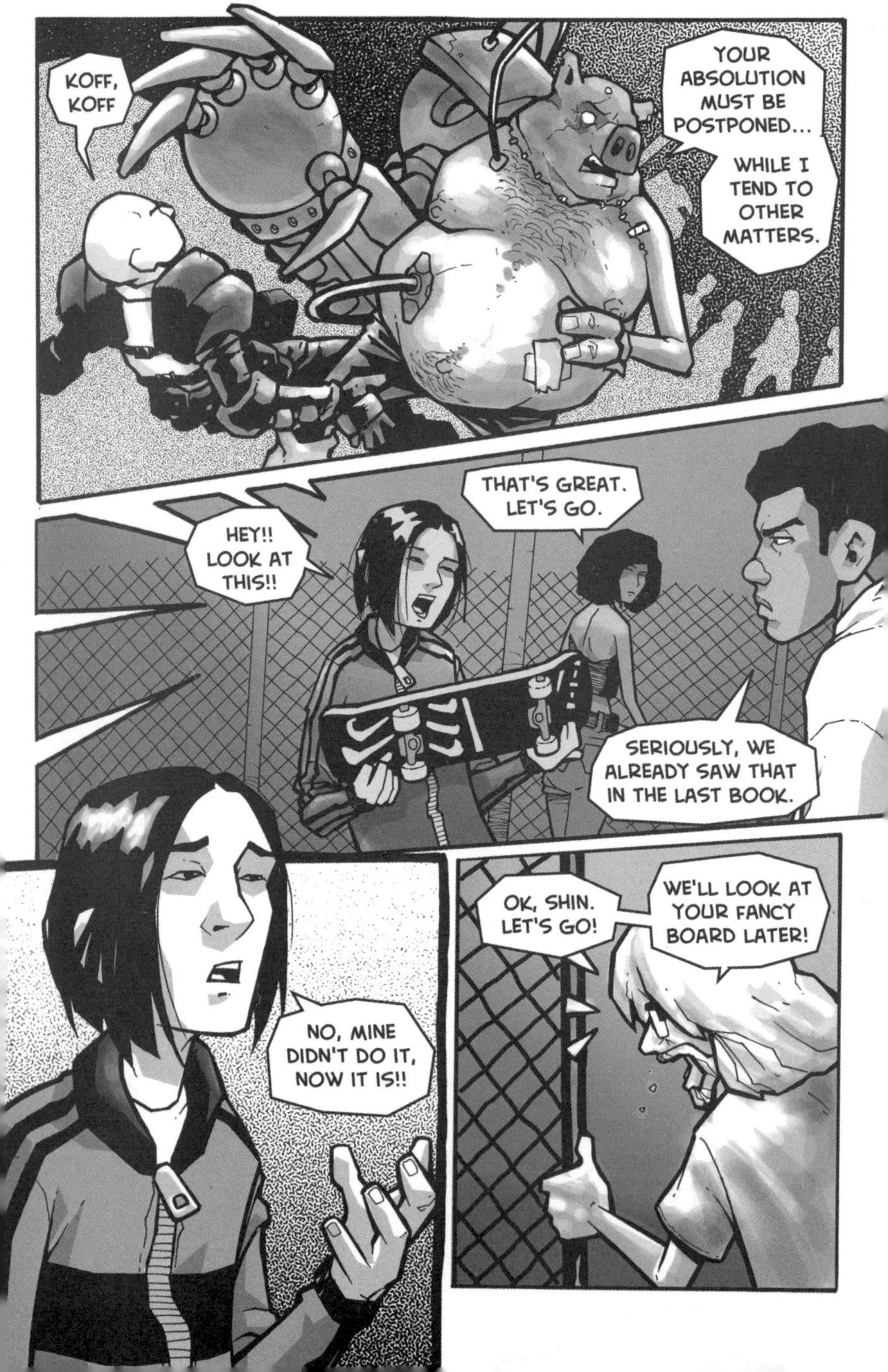
KOFF, KOFF
YOUR ABSOLUTION MUST BE POSTPONED...
WHILE I TEND TO OTHER MATTERS.
HEY!! LOOK AT THIS!!
THAT'S GREAT. LET'S GO.
SERIOUSLY, WE ALREADY SAW THAT IN THE LAST BOOK.
NO, MINE DIDN'T DO IT, NOW IT IS!!
OK, SHIN. LET'S GO!
WE'LL LOOK AT YOUR FANCY BOARD LATER!

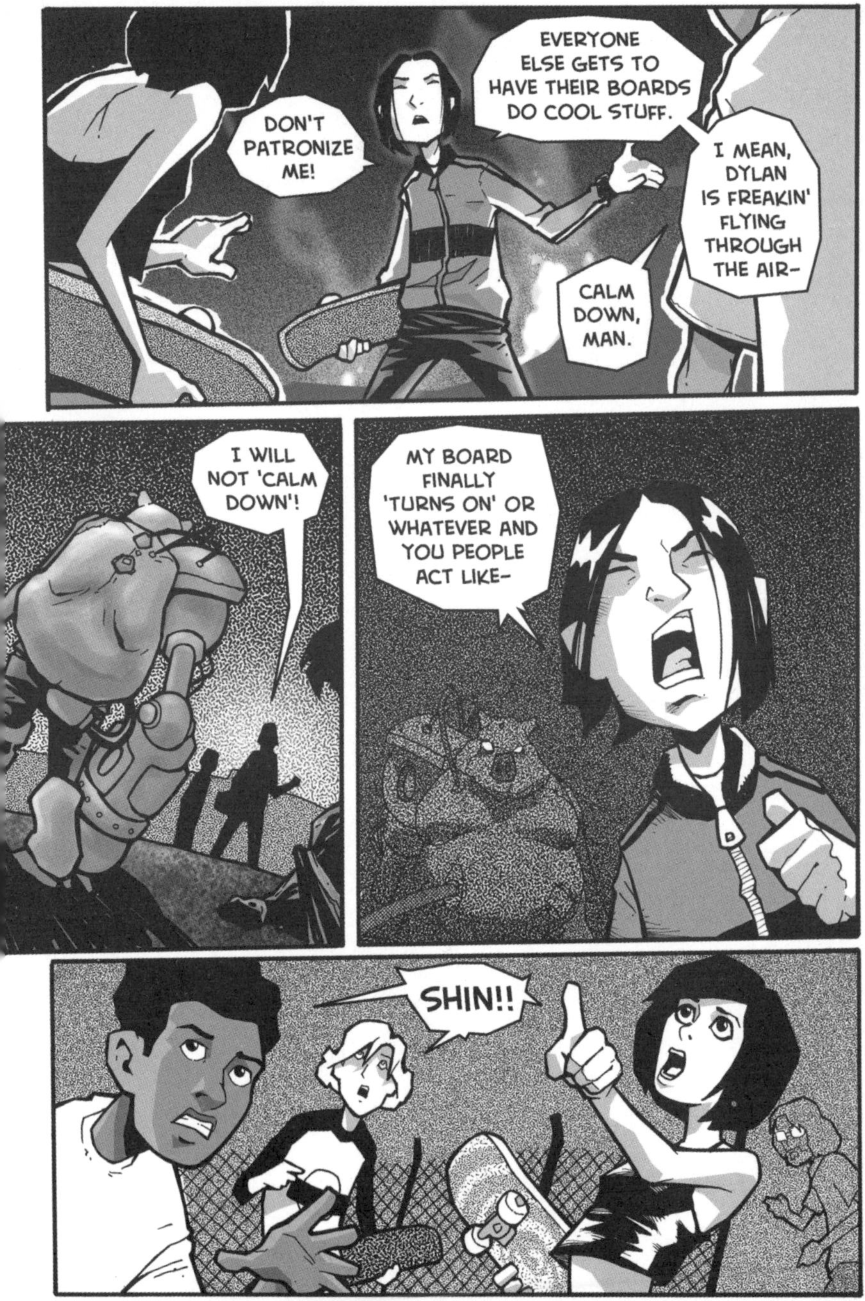
EVERYONE ELSE GETS TO HAVE THEIR BOARDS DO COOL STUFF.
DON'T PATRONIZE ME!
I MEAN, DYLAN IS FREAKIN' FLYING THROUGH THE AIR-
CALM DOWN, MAN.
I WILL NOT 'CALM DOWN'!
MY BOARD FINALLY 'TURNS ON' OR WHATEVER AND YOU PEOPLE ACT LIKE-
SHIN!!

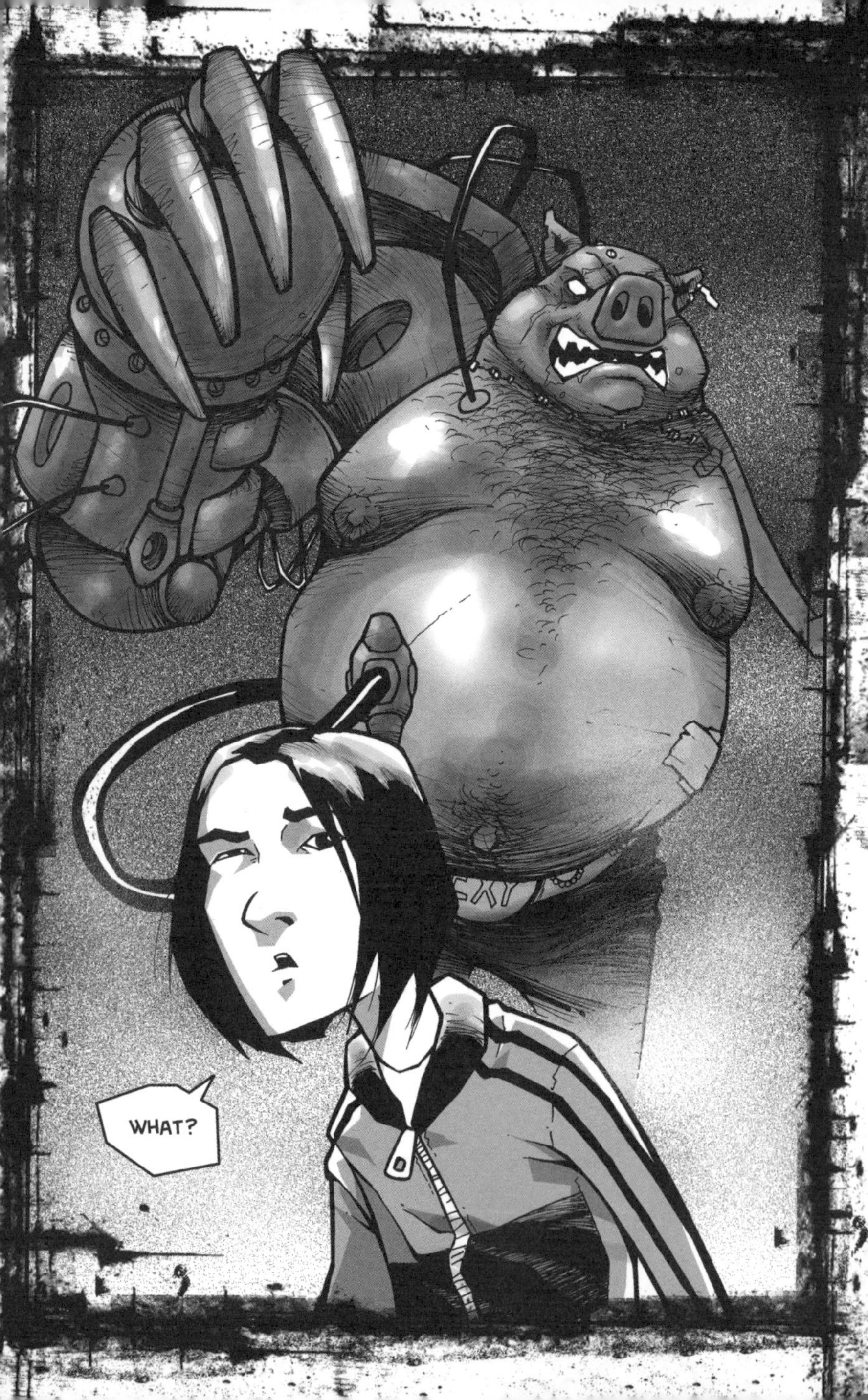
WHAT?

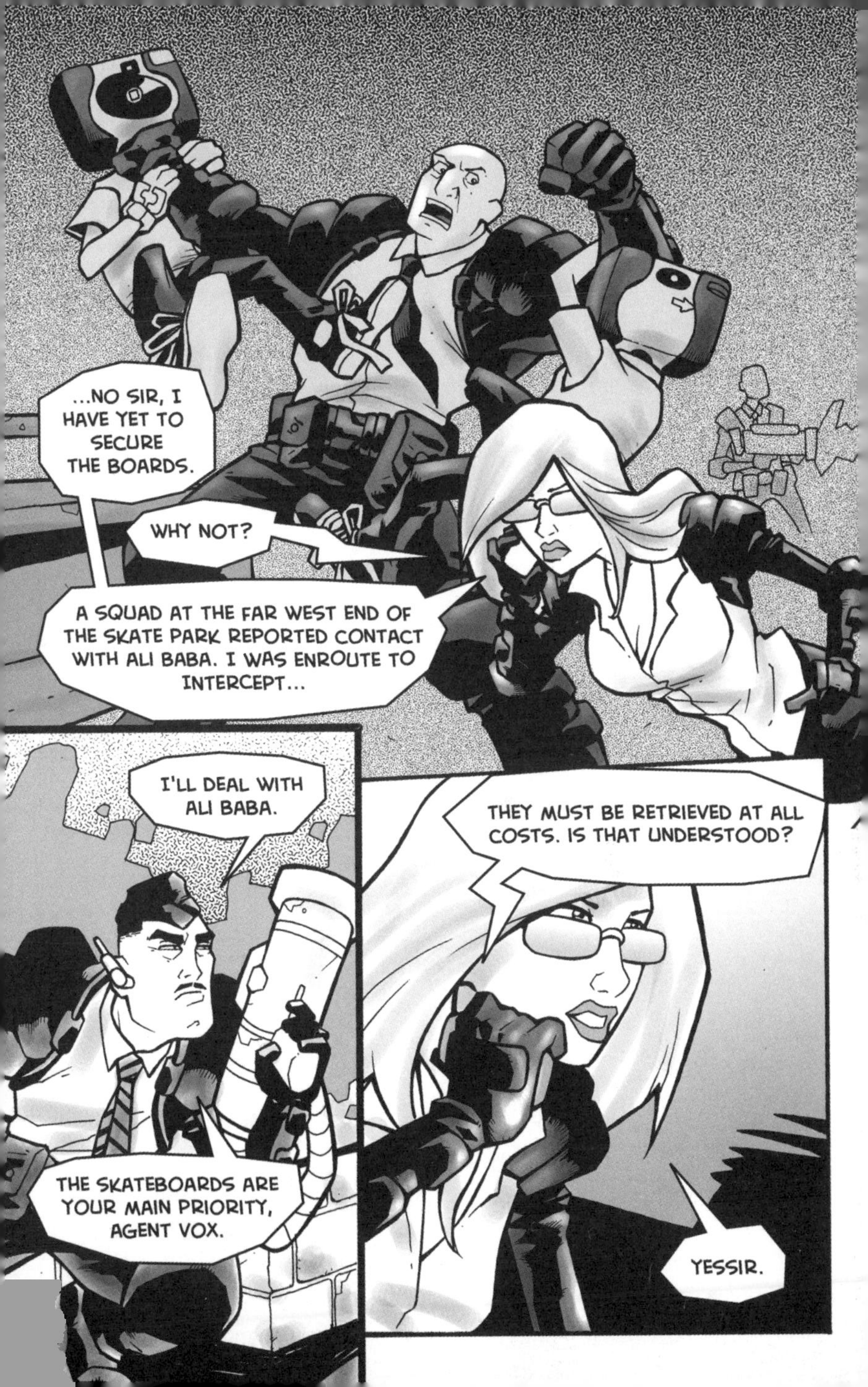
...NO SIR, I HAVE YET TO SECURE THE BOARDS.
WHY NOT?
A SQUAD AT THE FAR WEST END OF THE SKATE PARK REPORTED CONTACT WITH ALI BABA. I WAS ENROUTE TO INTERCEPT...
I'LL DEAL WITH ALI BABA.
THE SKATEBOARDS ARE YOUR MAIN PRIORITY, AGENT VOX.
THEY MUST BE RETRIEVED AT ALL COSTS. IS THAT UNDERSTOOD?
YESSIR.

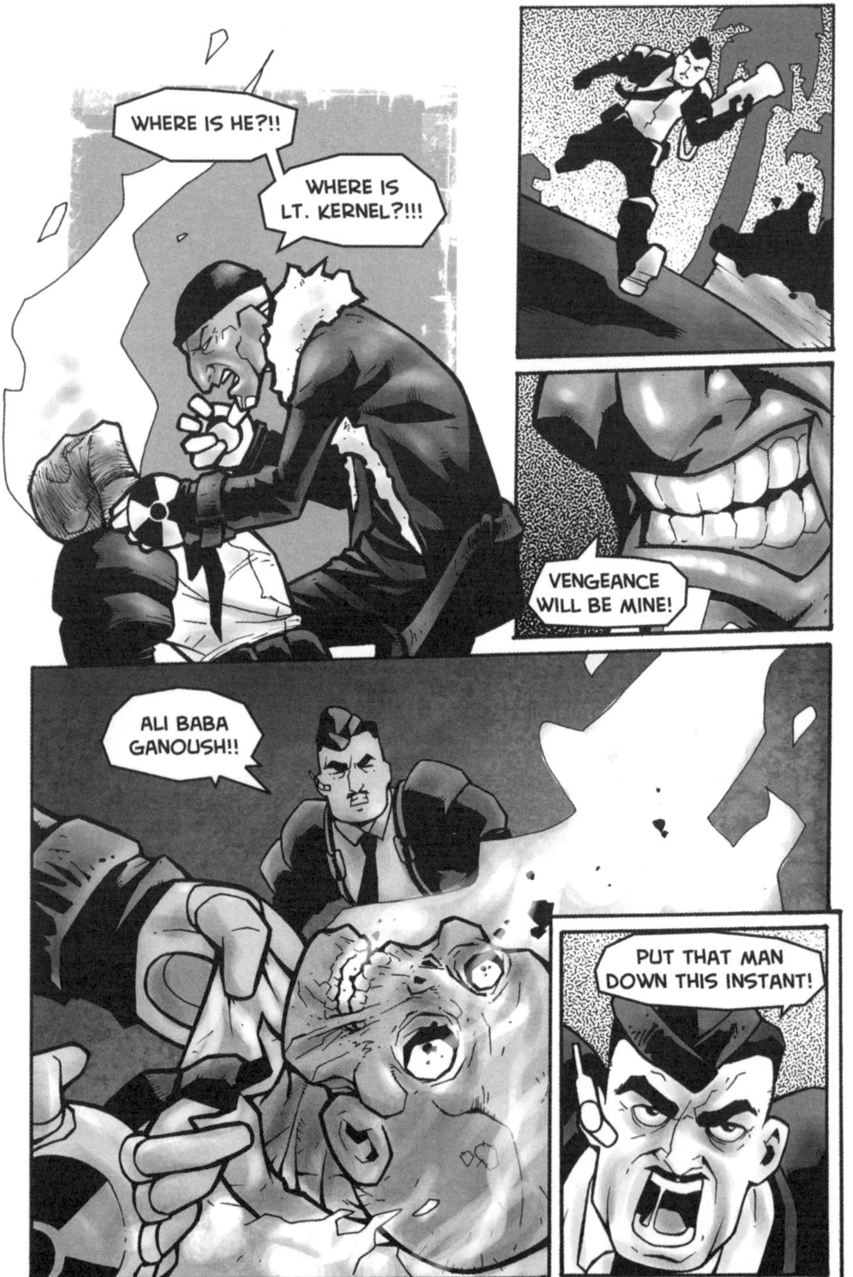
WHERE IS HE?!!
WHERE IS LT. KERNEL?!!!
VENGEANCE WILL BE MINE!
ALI BABA GANOUSH!!
PUT THAT MAN DOWN THIS INSTANT!

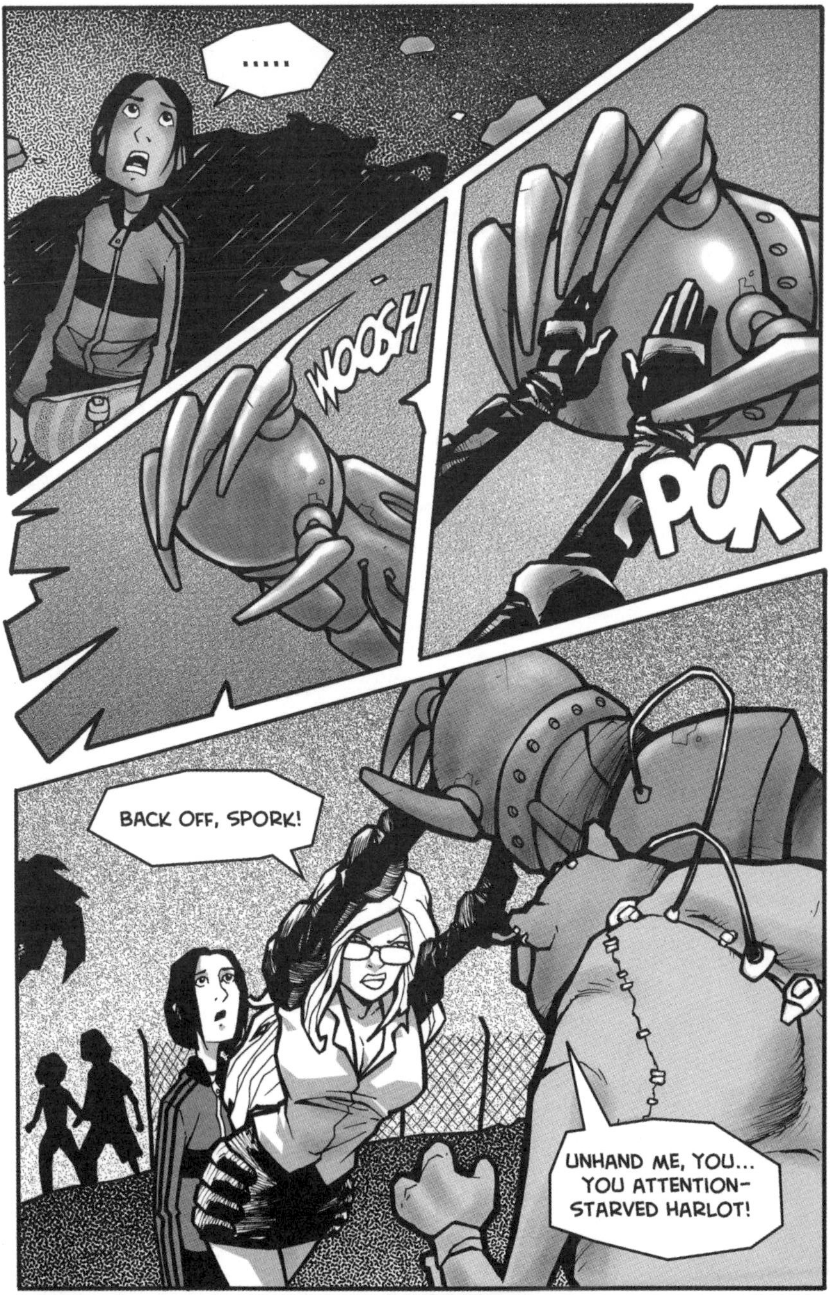
......
WOOSH
POK
BACK OFF, SPORK!
UNHAND ME, YOU...
YOU ATTENTION-
STARVED HARLOT!

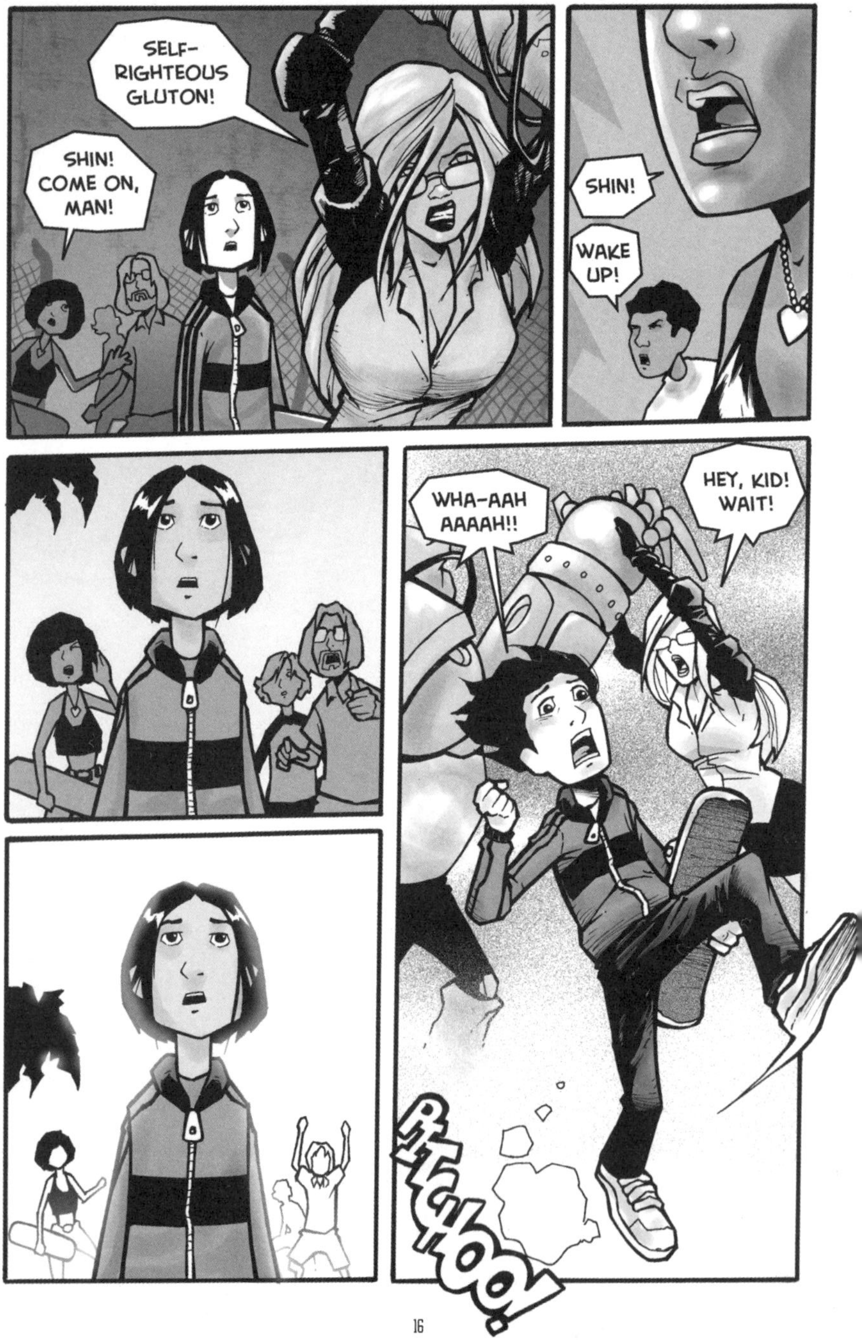
SELF-RIGHTEOUS GLUTON!
SHIN! COME ON, MAN!
SHIN!
WAKE UP!
WHA-AAH AAAAH!!
HEY, KID! WAIT!
PITCHOO!

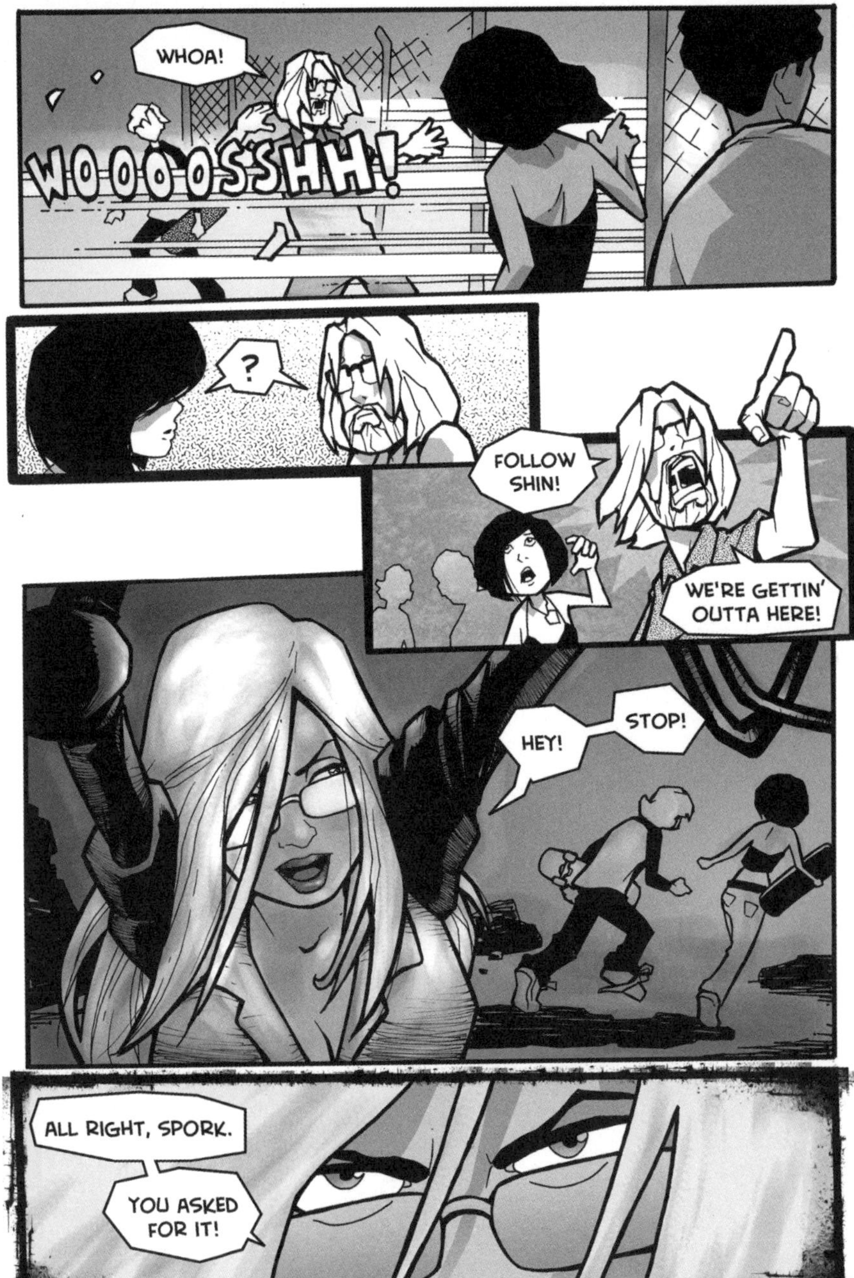
WHOA!
WOOOOSSHH!
?
FOLLOW SHIN!
WE'RE GETTIN' OUTTA HERE!
HEY!
STOP!
ALL RIGHT, SPORK.
YOU ASKED FOR IT!

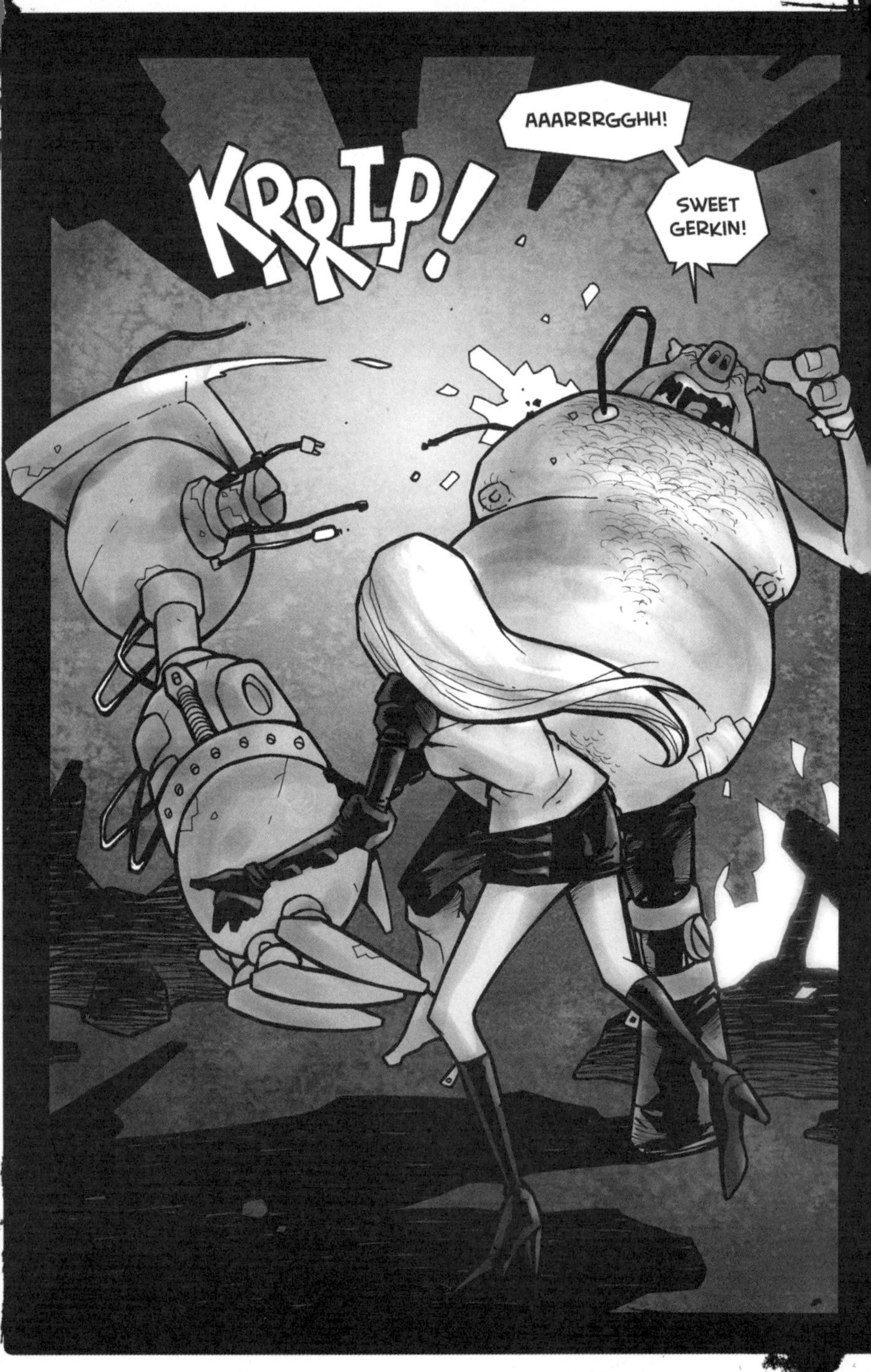
KRRRIP!
AAARRRGGHH!
SWEET GERKIN!

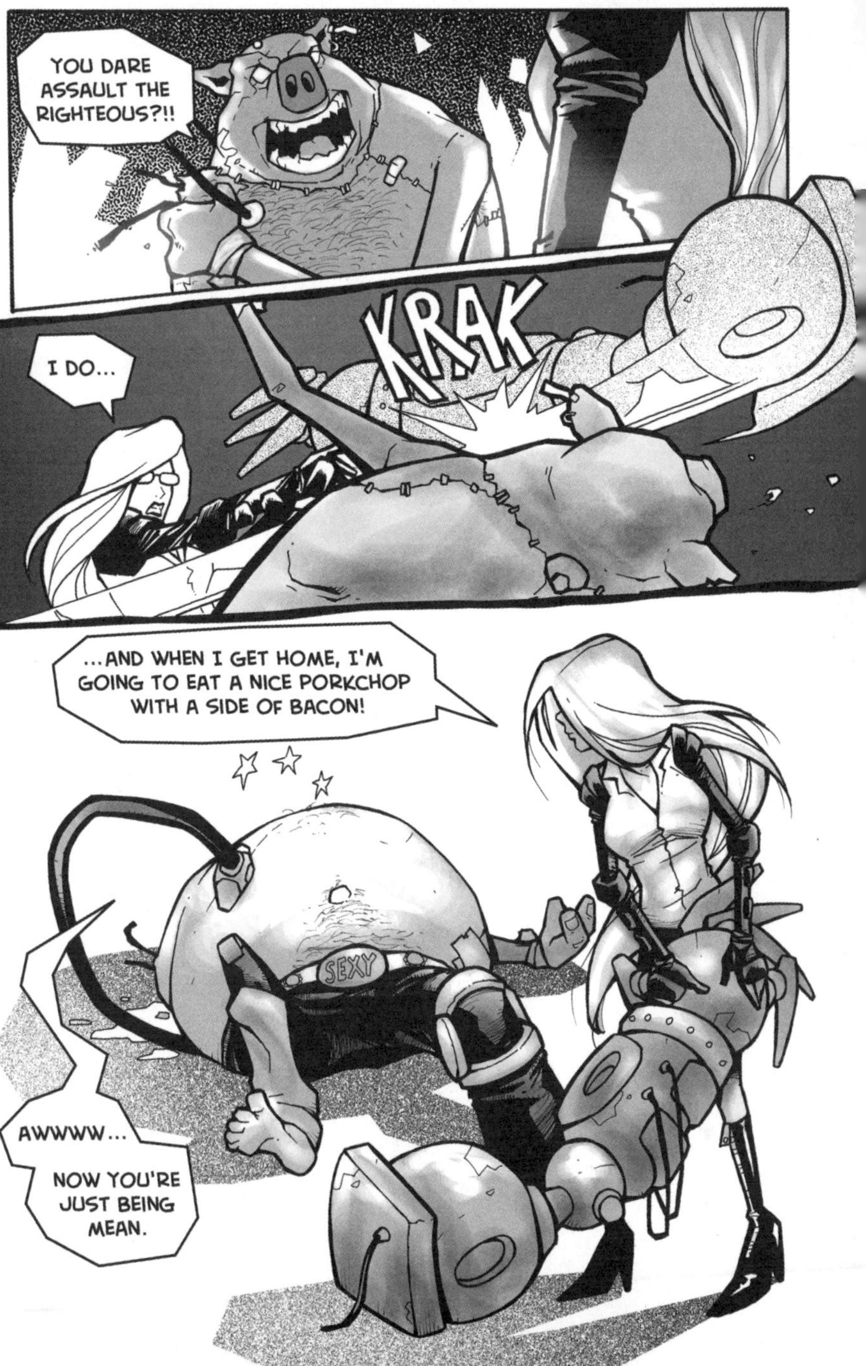
YOU DARE ASSAULT THE RIGHTEOUS?!!
KRAK
I DO...
...AND WHEN I GET HOME, I'M GOING TO EAT A NICE PORKCHOP WITH A SIDE OF BACON!
SEXY
AWWWW...
NOW YOU'RE JUST BEING MEAN.

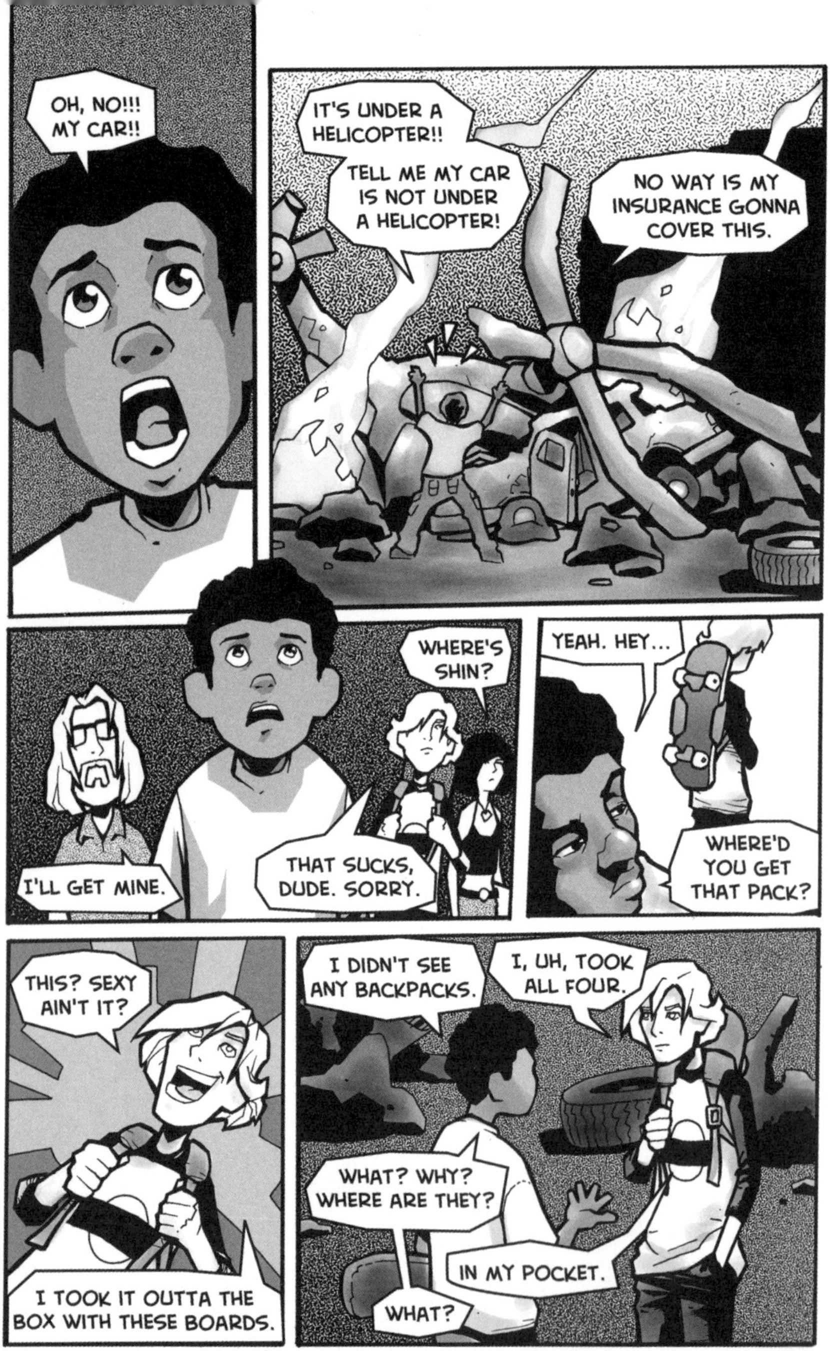
OH, NO!!! MY CAR!!
IT'S UNDER A HELICOPTER!!
TELL ME MY CAR IS NOT UNDER A HELICOPTER!
NO WAY IS MY INSURANCE GONNA COVER THIS.
WHERE'S SHIN?
I'LL GET MINE.
THAT SUCKS, DUDE. SORRY.
YEAH. HEY...
WHERE'D YOU GET THAT PACK?
THIS? SEXY AIN'T IT?
I TOOK IT OUTTA THE BOX WITH THESE BOARDS.
I DIDN'T SEE ANY BACKPACKS.
I, UH, TOOK ALL FOUR.
WHAT? WHY? WHERE ARE THEY?
IN MY POCKET.
WHAT?

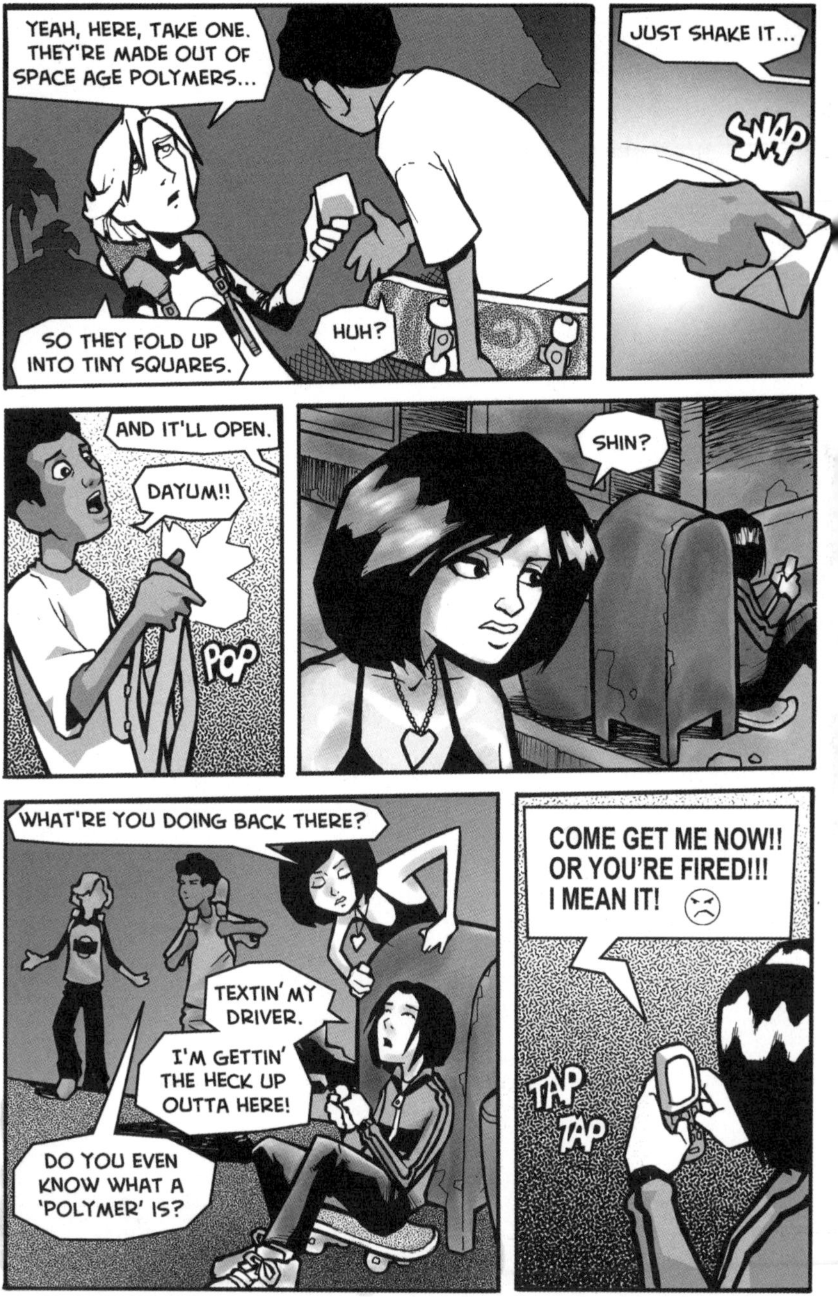
YEAH, HERE, TAKE ONE. THEY'RE MADE OUT OF SPACE AGE POLYMERS...
SO THEY FOLD UP INTO TINY SQUARES.
HUH?
JUST SHAKE IT...
SNAP
AND IT'LL OPEN.
DAYUM!!
POP
SHIN?
WHAT'RE YOU DOING BACK THERE?
TEXTIN' MY DRIVER.
I'M GETTIN' THE HECK UP OUTTA HERE!
DO YOU EVEN KNOW WHAT A 'POLYMER' IS?
COME GET ME NOW!! OR YOU'RE FIRED!!! I MEAN IT!
TAP
TAP

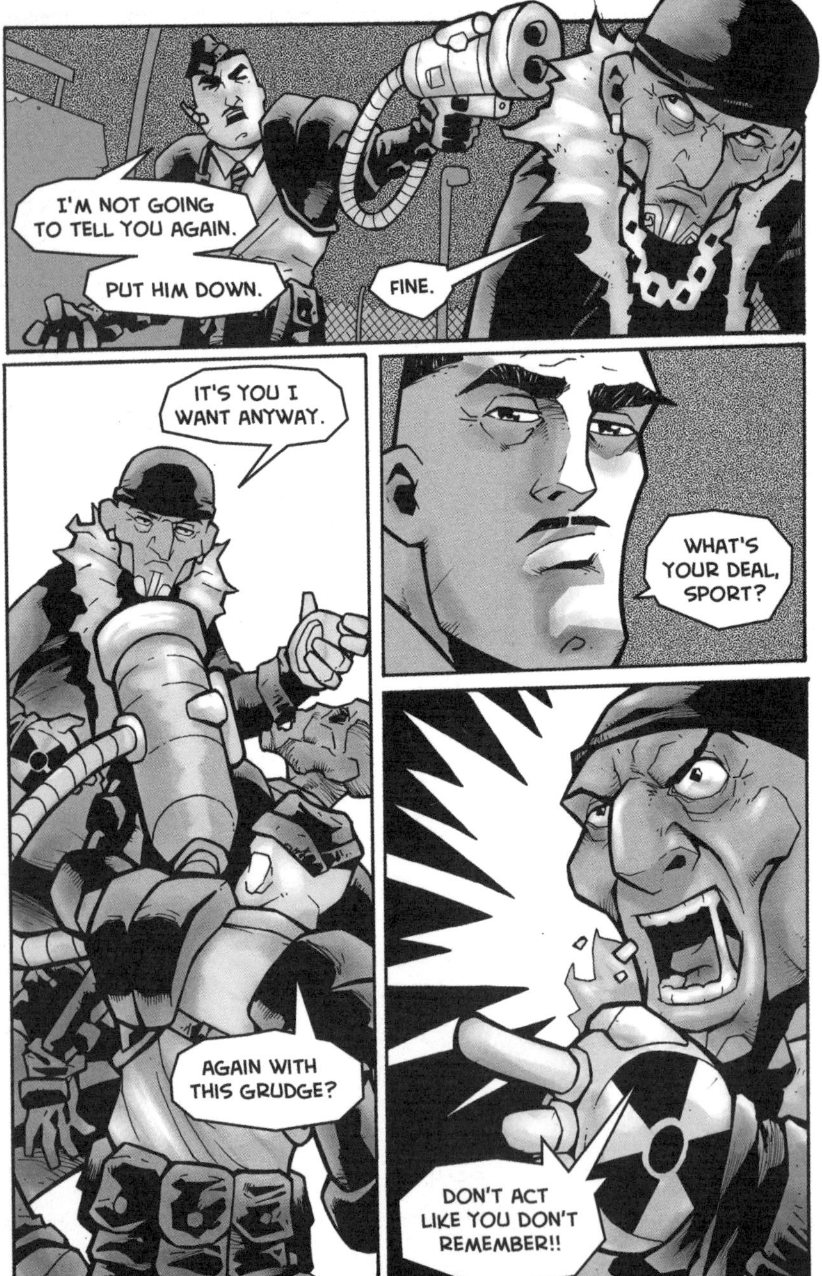
I'M NOT GOING TO TELL YOU AGAIN.
PUT HIM DOWN.
FINE.
IT'S YOU I WANT ANYWAY.
WHAT'S YOUR DEAL, SPORT?
AGAIN WITH THIS GRUDGE?
DON'T ACT LIKE YOU DON'T REMEMBER!!

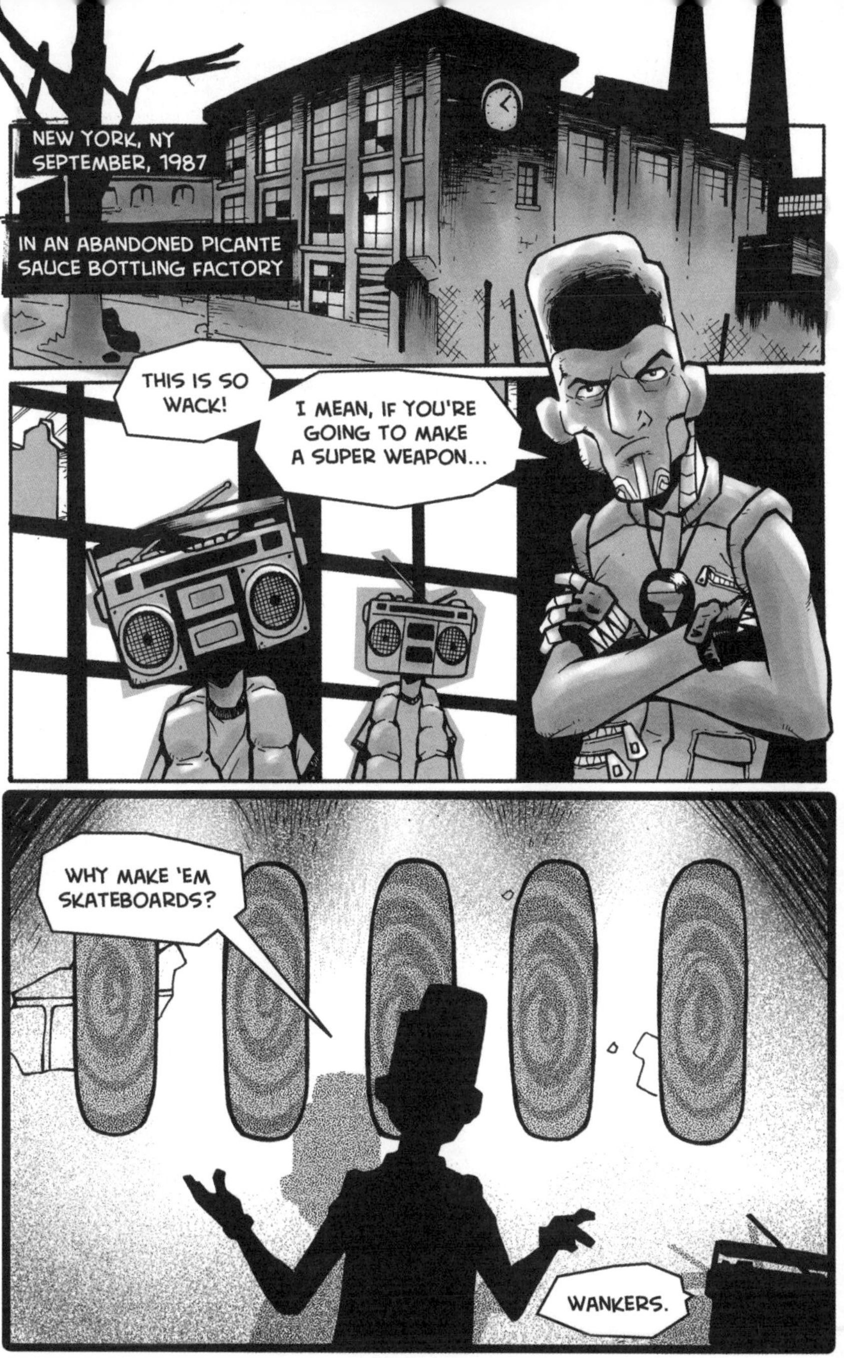
NEW YORK, NY
SEPTEMBER, 1987
IN AN ABANDONED PICANTE SAUCE BOTTLING FACTORY
THIS IS SO WACK!
I MEAN, IF YOU'RE GOING TO MAKE A SUPER WEAPON...
WHY MAKE 'EM SKATEBOARDS?
WANKERS.

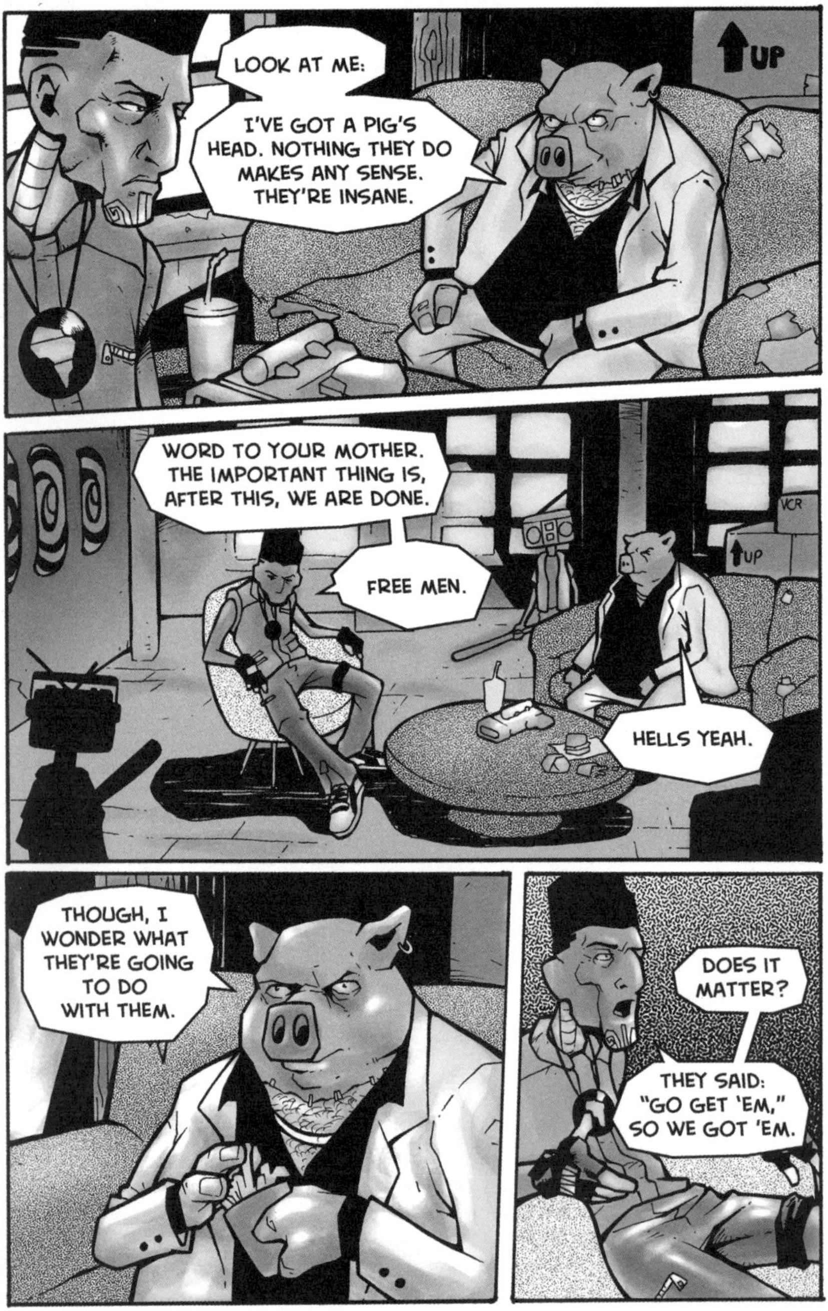
LOOK AT ME:
I'VE GOT A PIG'S HEAD. NOTHING THEY DO MAKES ANY SENSE. THEY'RE INSANE.
UP
WORD TO YOUR MOTHER. THE IMPORTANT THING IS, AFTER THIS, WE ARE DONE.
FREE MEN.
VCR
UP
HELLS YEAH.
THOUGH, I WONDER WHAT THEY'RE GOING TO DO WITH THEM.
DOES IT MATTER?
THEY SAID: "GO GET 'EM," SO WE GOT 'EM.

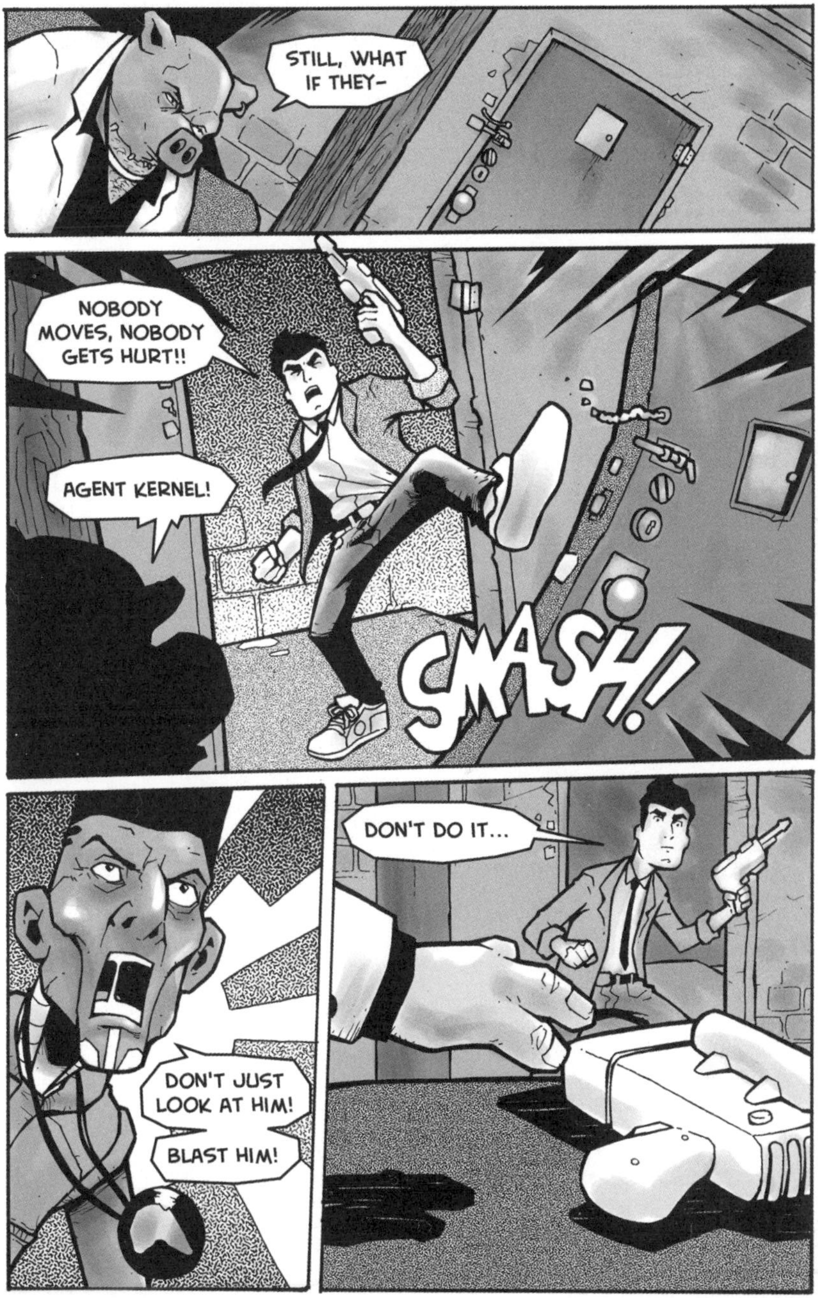
STILL, WHAT IF THEY–
NOBODY MOVES, NOBODY GETS HURT!!
AGENT KERNEL!
SMASH!
DON'T JUST LOOK AT HIM!
BLAST HIM!
DON'T DO IT...

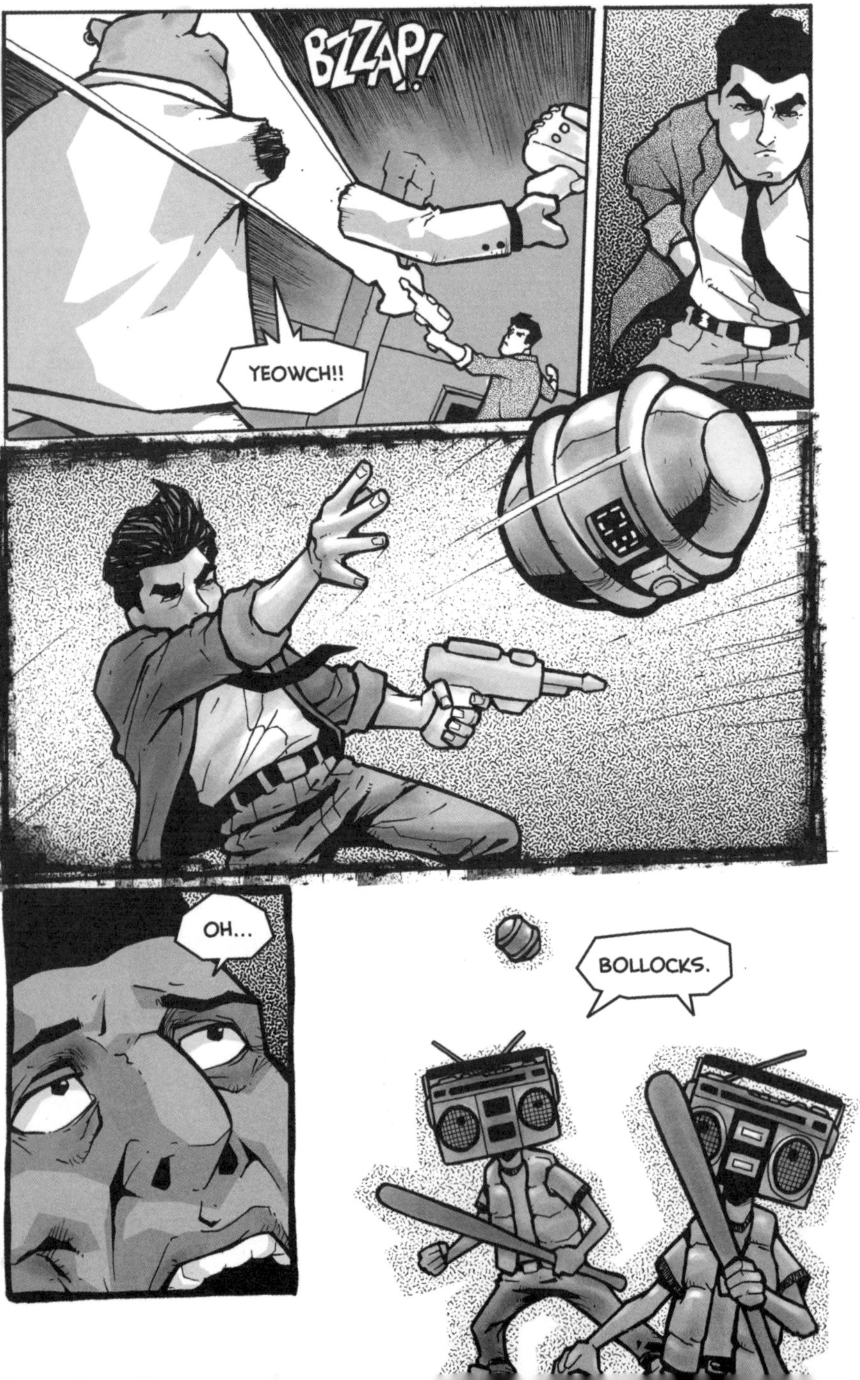
BZZAP!
YEOWCH!!
OH...
BOLLOCKS.

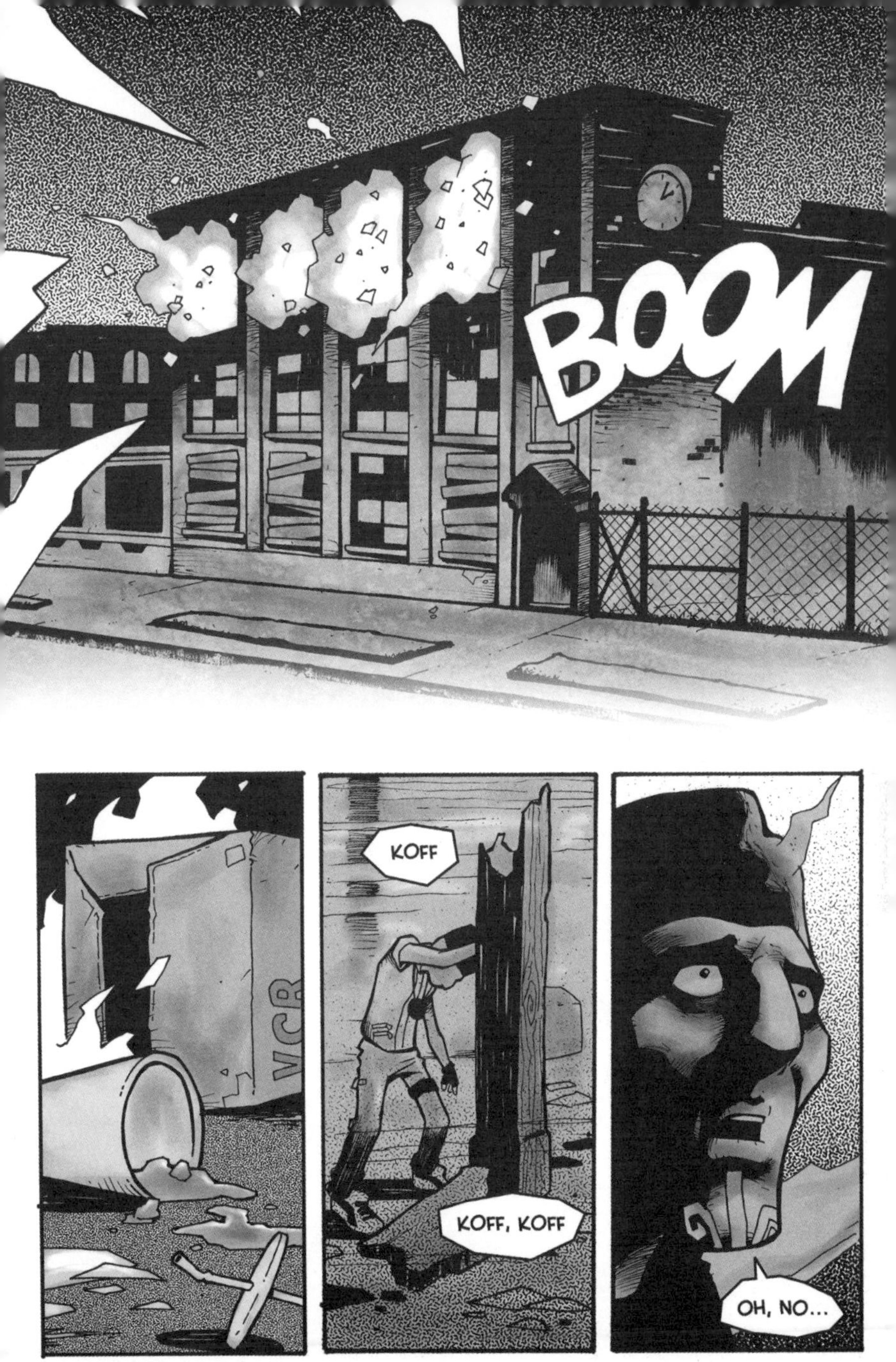
BOOM
VCR
KOFF
KOFF, KOFF
OH, NO...

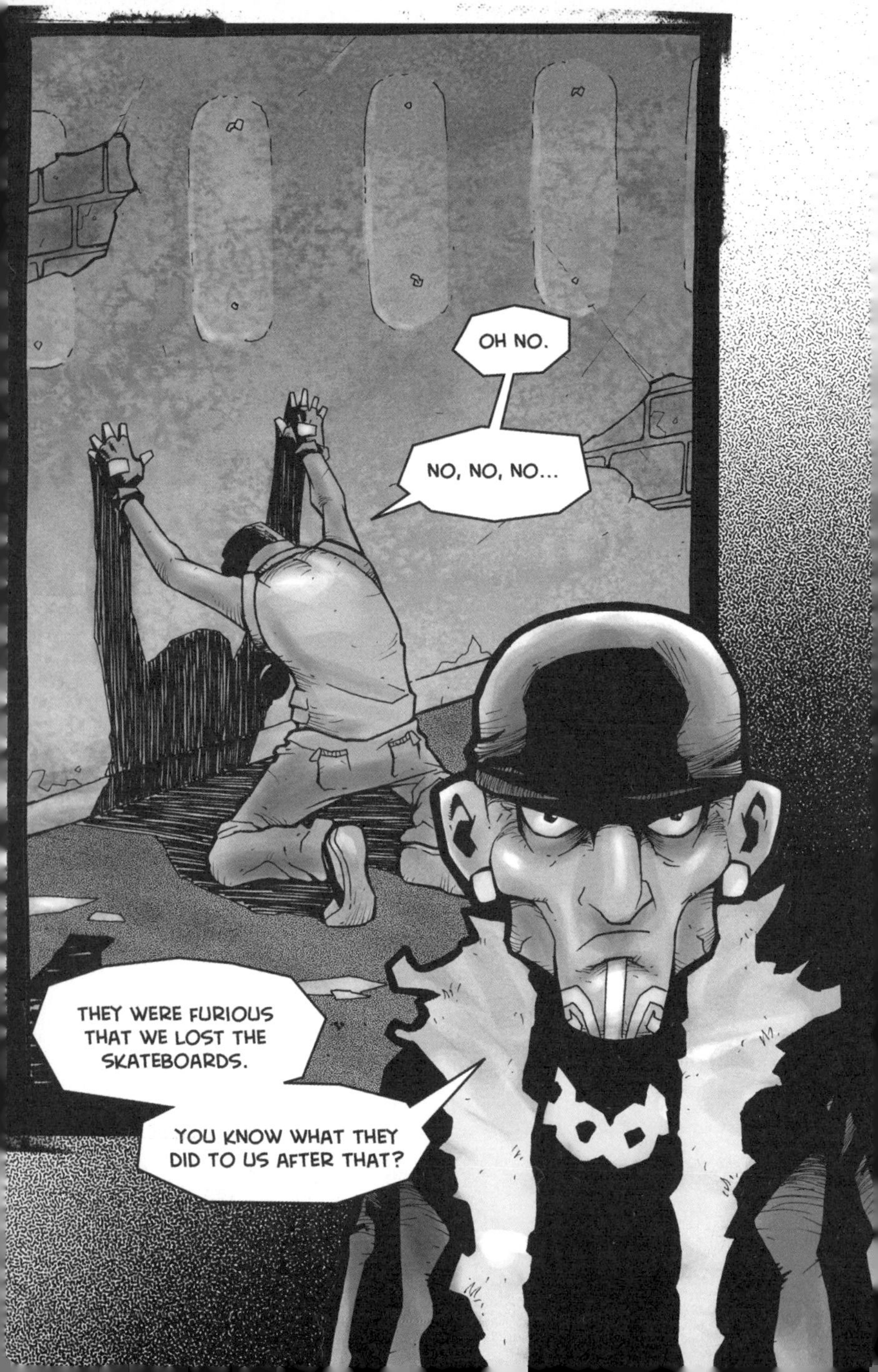
OH NO.
NO, NO, NO...
THEY WERE FURIOUS THAT WE LOST THE SKATEBOARDS.
YOU KNOW WHAT THEY DID TO US AFTER THAT?

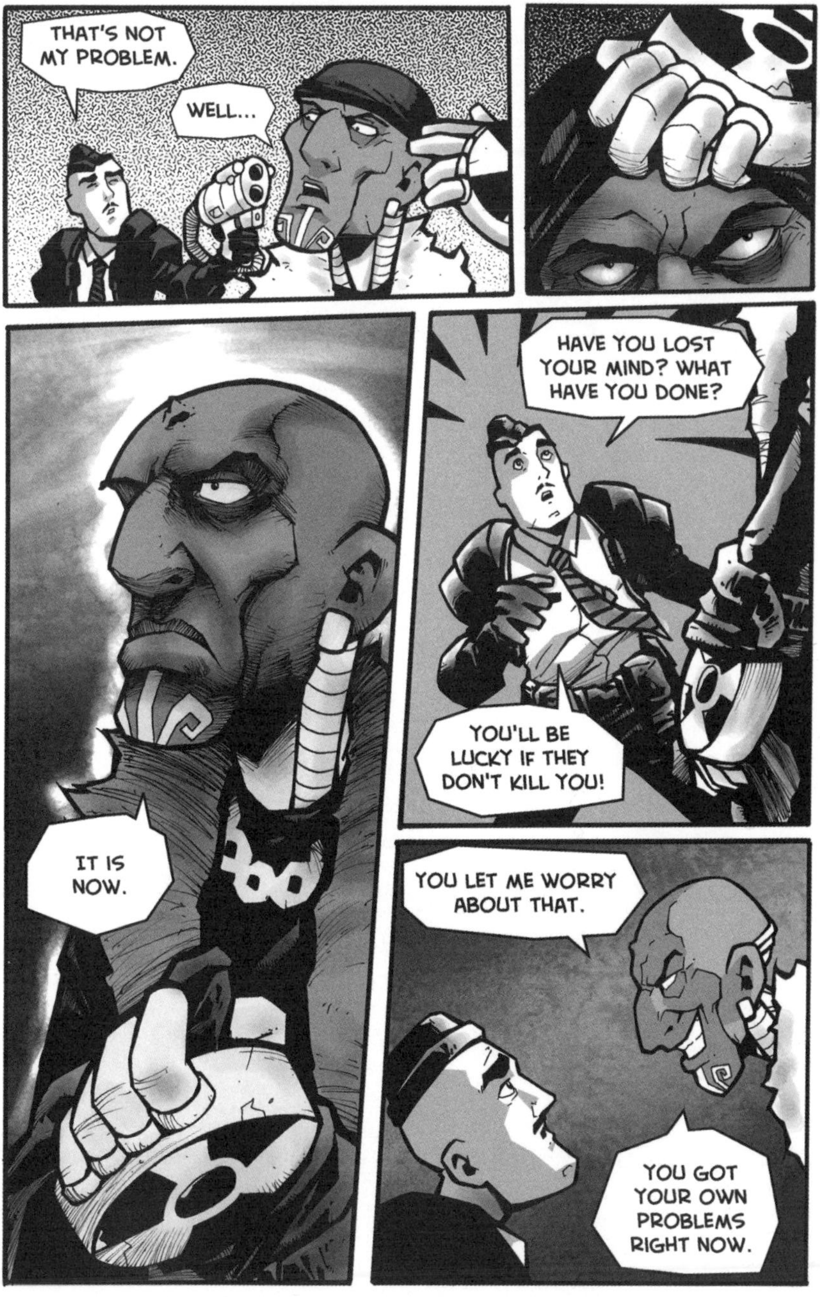
THAT'S NOT MY PROBLEM.
WELL...
IT IS NOW.
HAVE YOU LOST YOUR MIND? WHAT HAVE YOU DONE?
YOU'LL BE LUCKY IF THEY DON'T KILL YOU!
YOU LET ME WORRY ABOUT THAT.
YOU GOT YOUR OWN PROBLEMS RIGHT NOW.

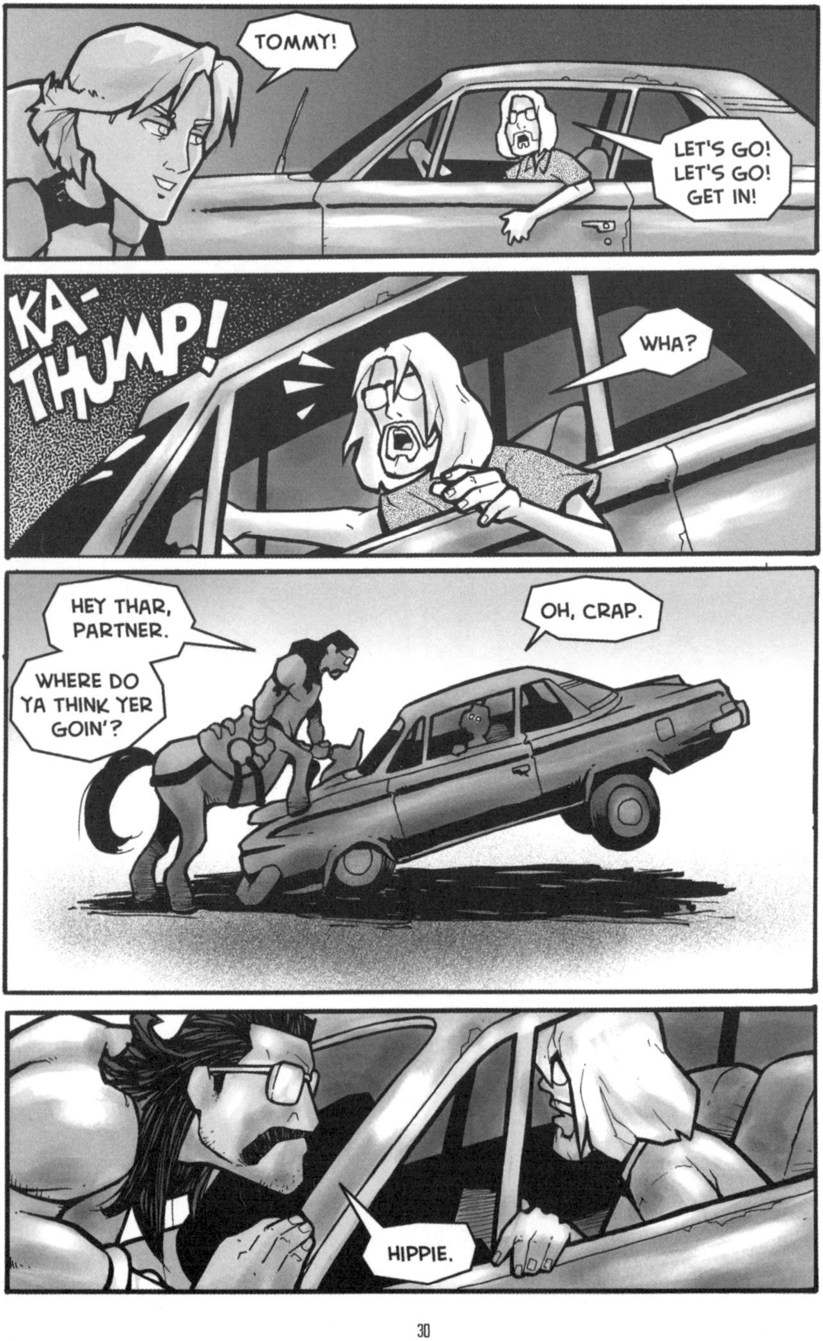
TOMMY!
LET'S GO! LET'S GO! GET IN!
KA-THUMP!
WHA?
HEY THAR, PARTNER.
WHERE DO YA THINK YER GOIN'?
OH, CRAP.
HIPPIE.

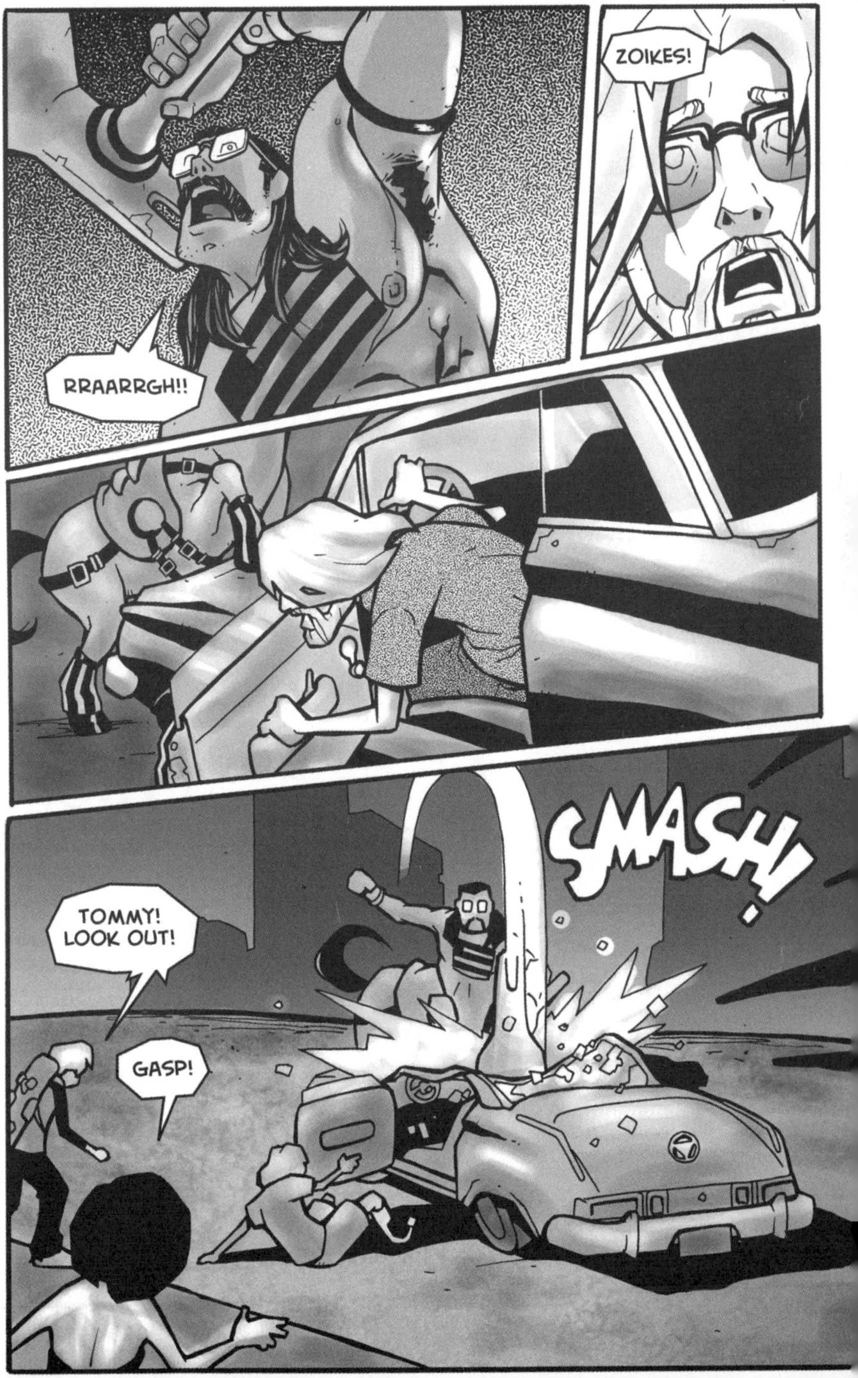
RRAARRGH!!
ZOIKES!
SMASH!
TOMMY! LOOK OUT!
GASP!

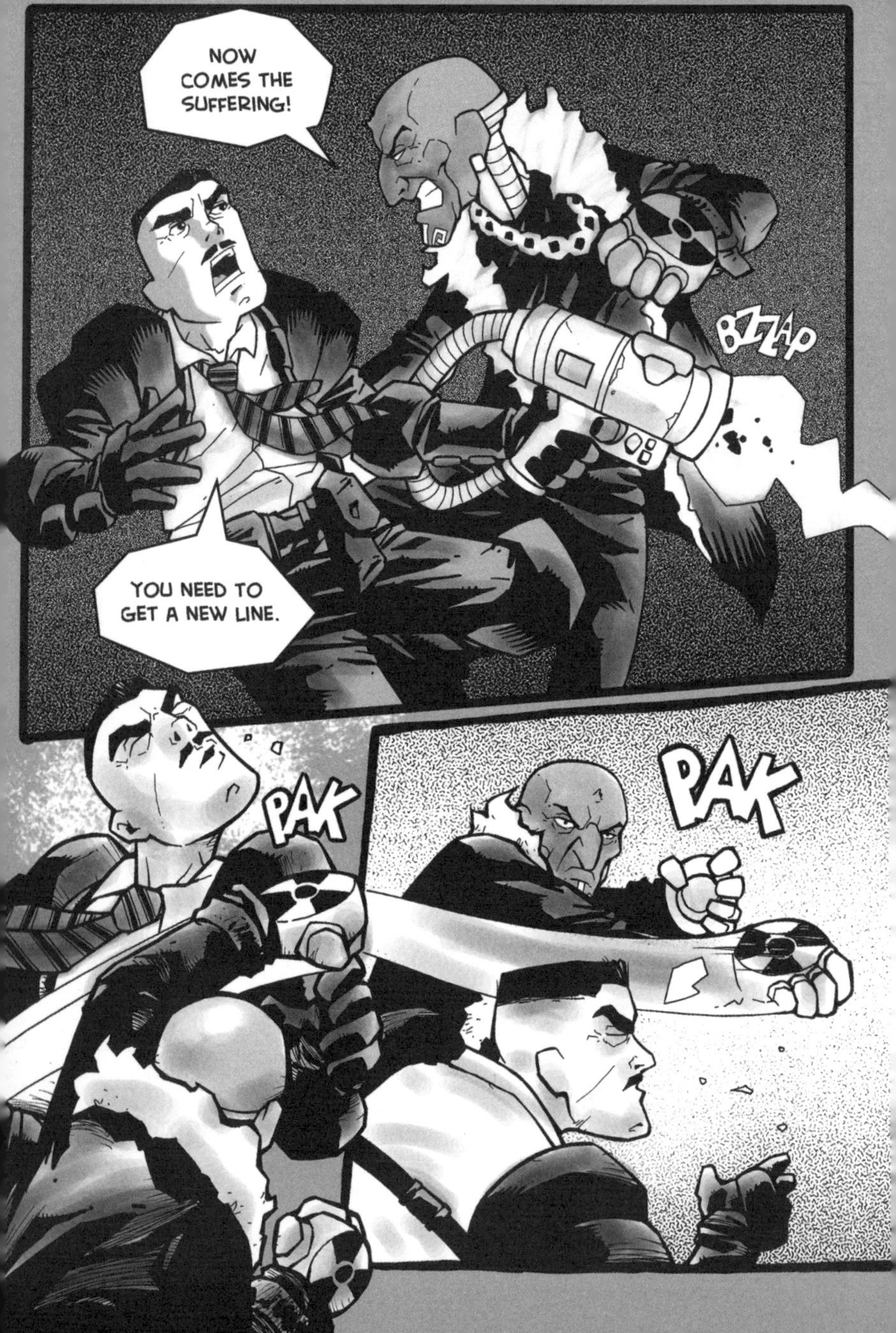
NOW COMES THE SUFFERING!
YOU NEED TO GET A NEW LINE.
BZZAP
PAK
PAK

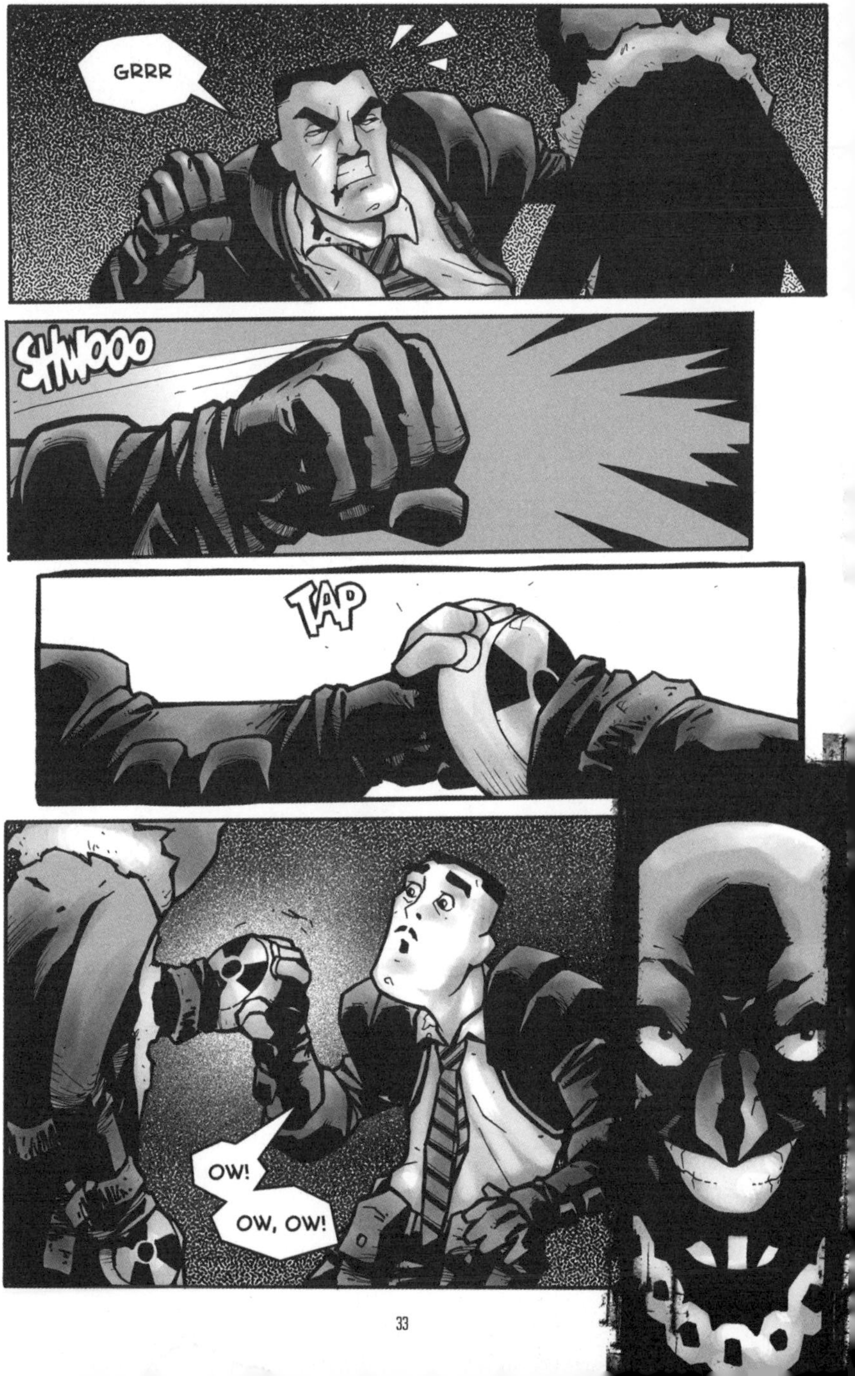
GRRR
SHWOOO
TAP
OW!
OW, OW!

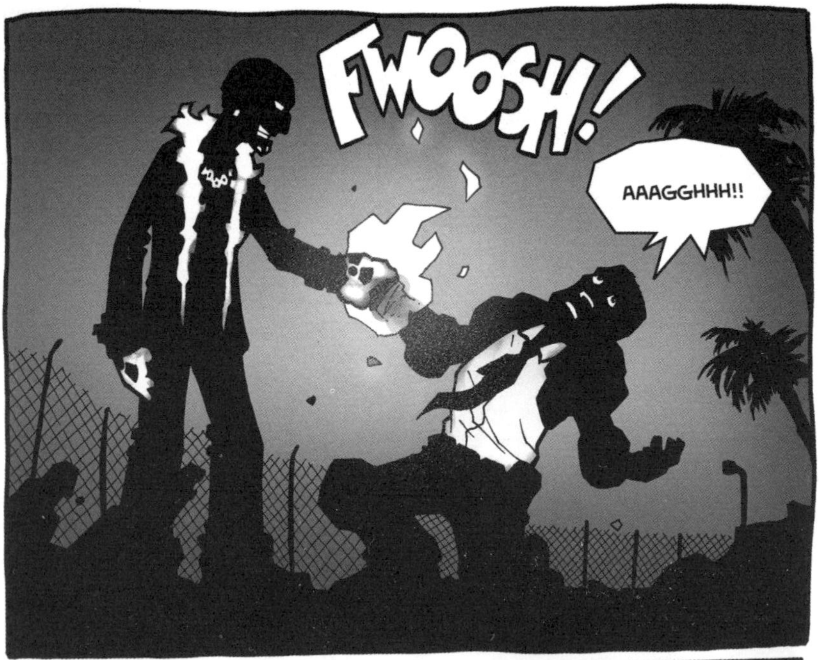
FWOOSH!
AAAGGHHH!!

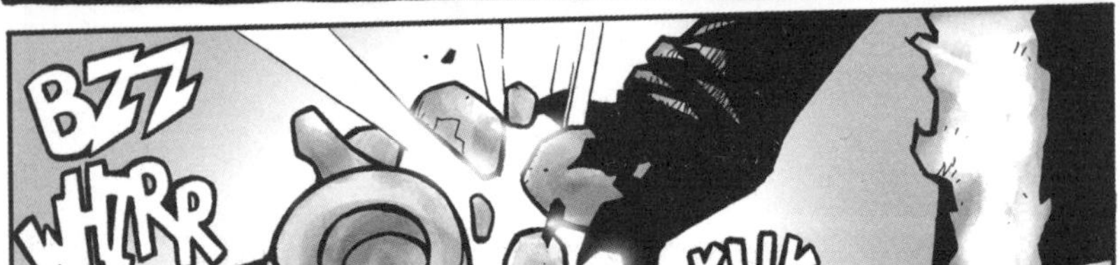
BZZ
WHIRR
KLIK

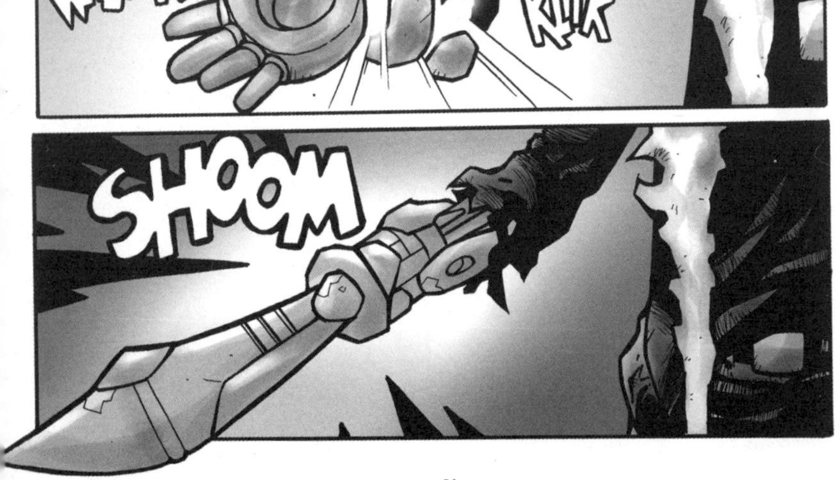
SHOOM

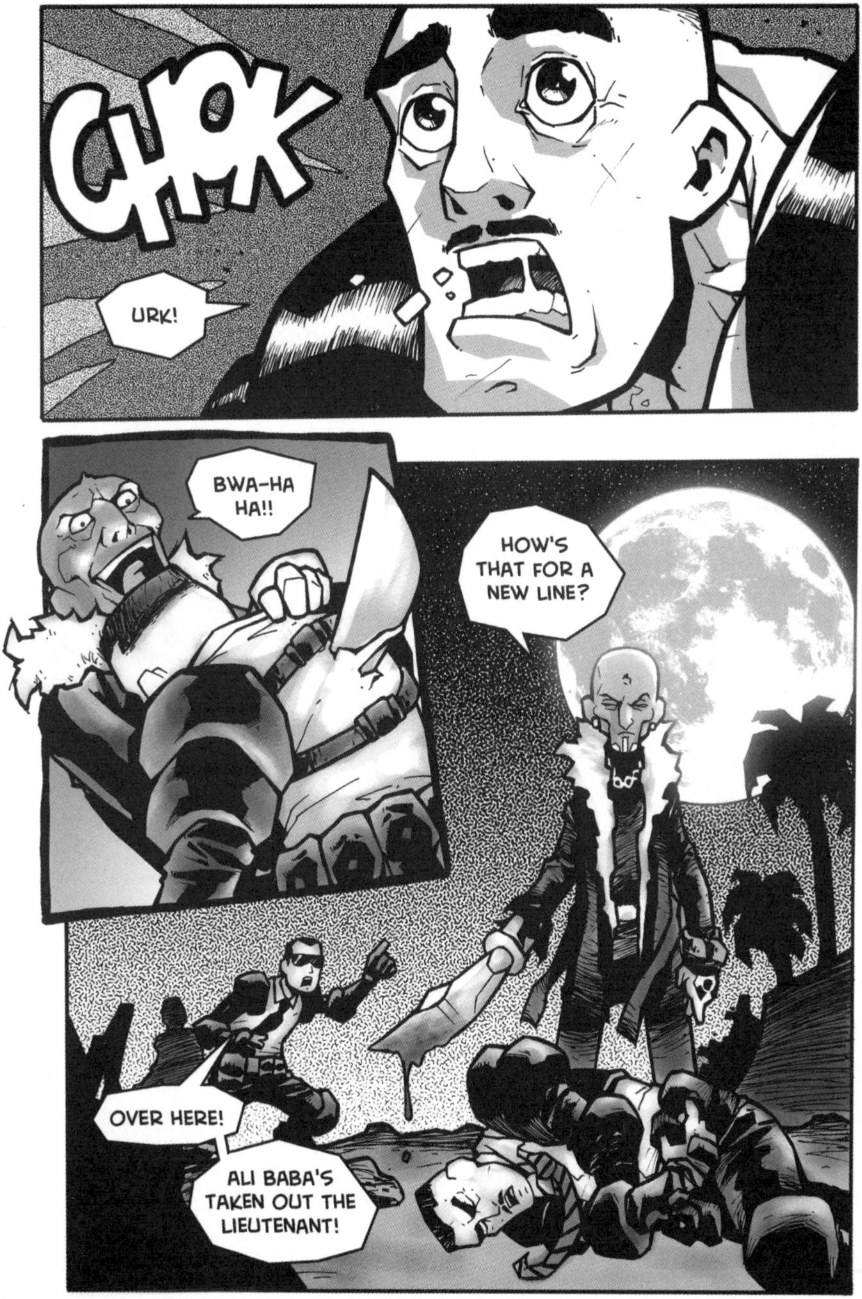
CHOK
URK!
BWA-HA HA!!
HOW'S THAT FOR A NEW LINE?
OVER HERE!
ALI BABA'S TAKEN OUT THE LIEUTENANT!

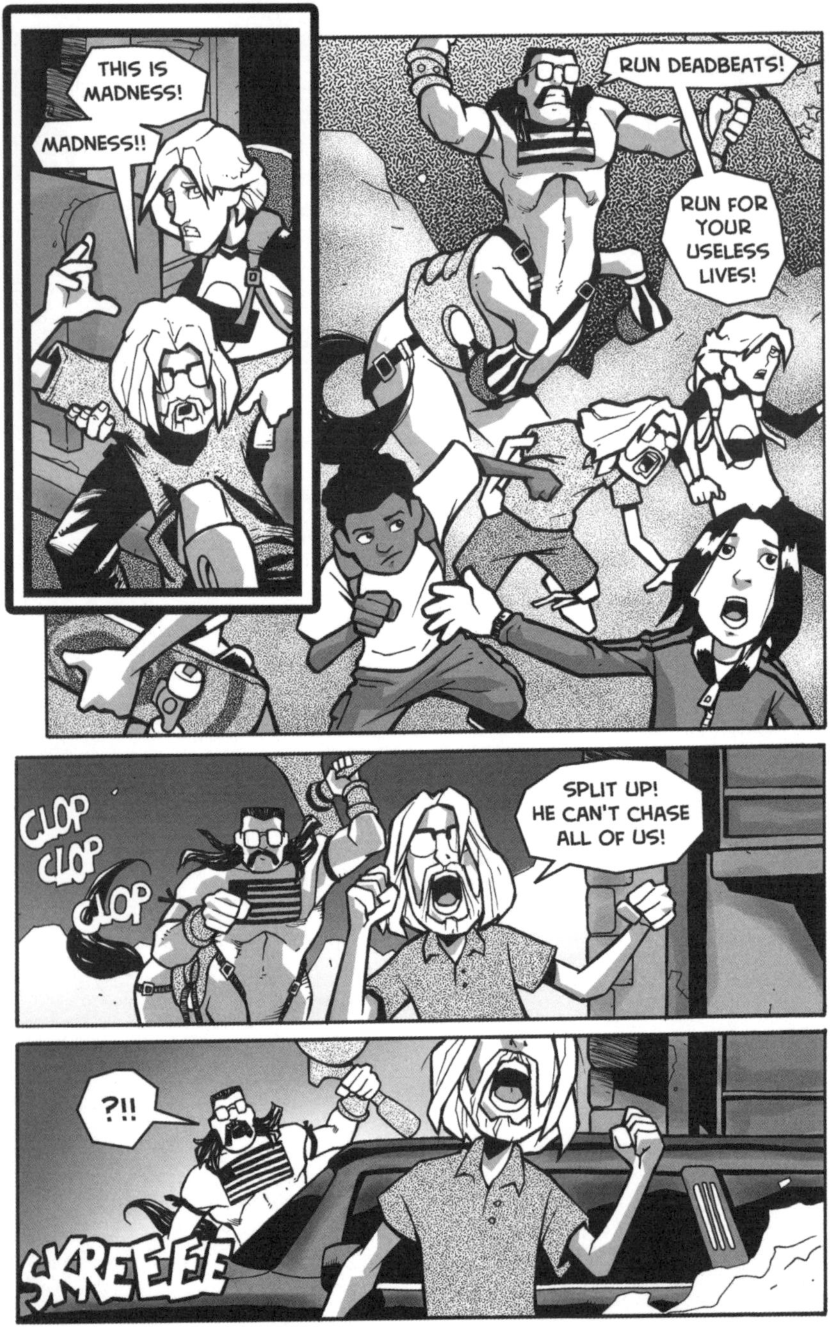
THIS IS MADNESS!
MADNESS!!
RUN DEADBEATS!
RUN FOR YOUR USELESS LIVES!
CLOP
CLOP
CLOP
SPLIT UP! HE CAN'T CHASE ALL OF US!
?!!
SKREEEE

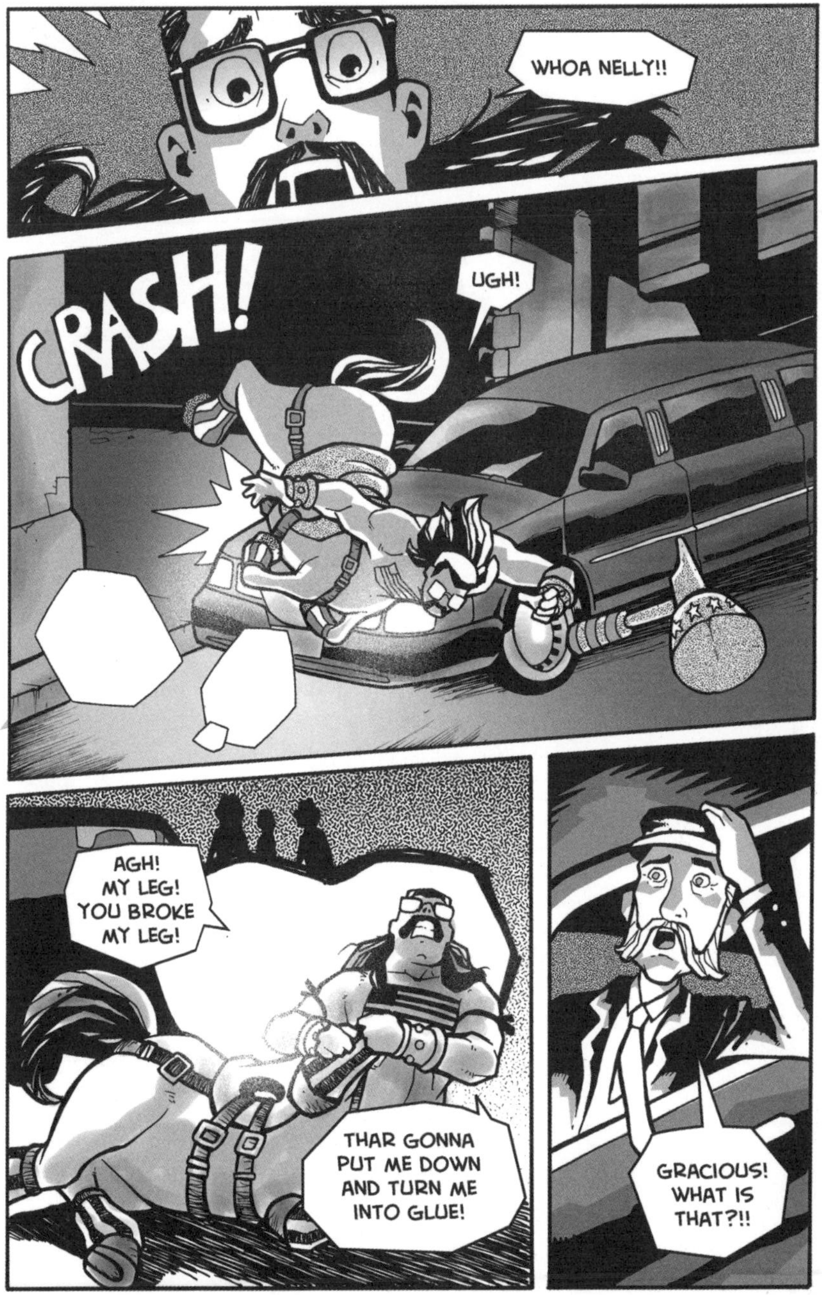
WHOA NELLY!!
CRASH!
UGH!
AGH! MY LEG! YOU BROKE MY LEG!
THAR GONNA PUT ME DOWN AND TURN ME INTO GLUE!
GRACIOUS! WHAT IS THAT?!!

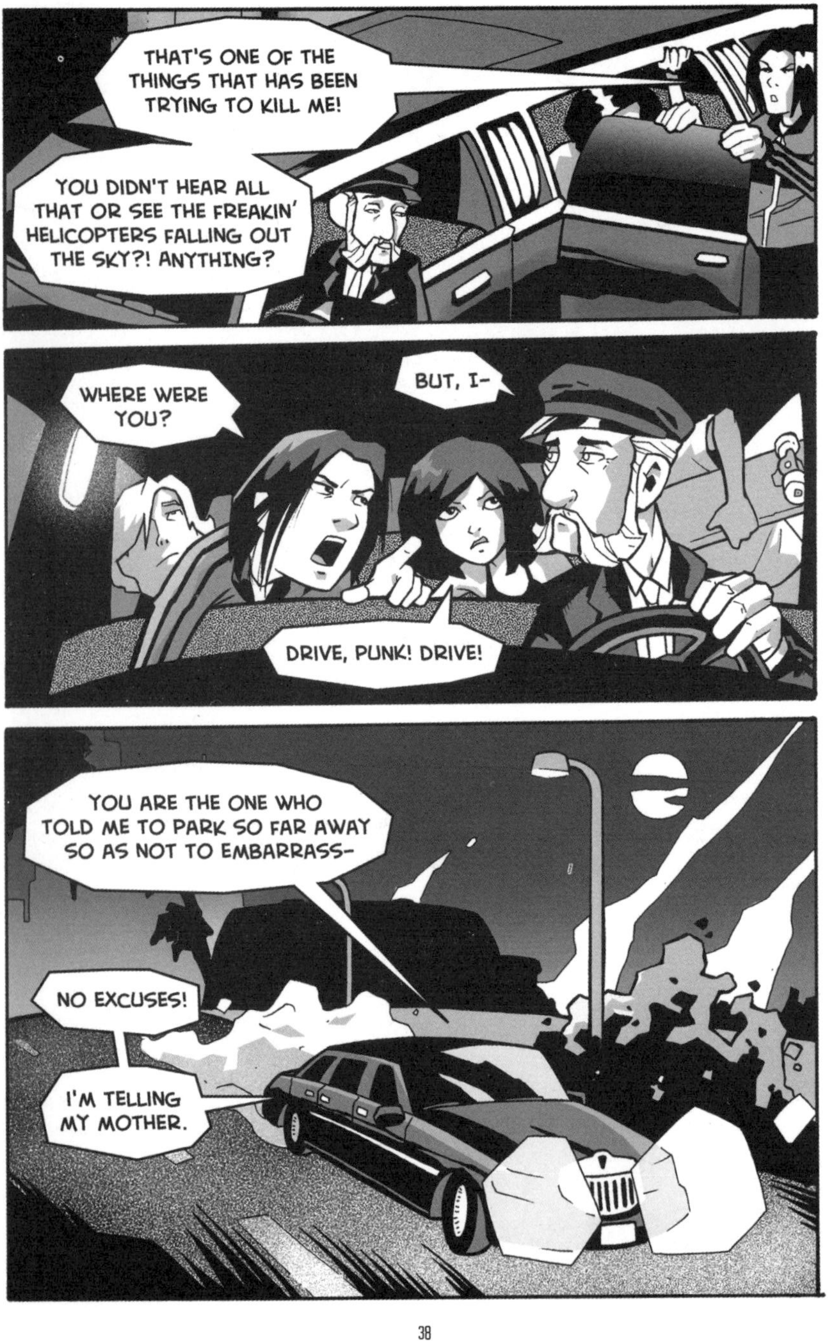
THAT'S ONE OF THE THINGS THAT HAS BEEN TRYING TO KILL ME!
YOU DIDN'T HEAR ALL THAT OR SEE THE FREAKIN' HELICOPTERS FALLING OUT THE SKY?! ANYTHING?
WHERE WERE YOU?
BUT, I-
DRIVE, PUNK! DRIVE!
YOU ARE THE ONE WHO TOLD ME TO PARK SO FAR AWAY SO AS NOT TO EMBARRASS-
NO EXCUSES!
I'M TELLING MY MOTHER.

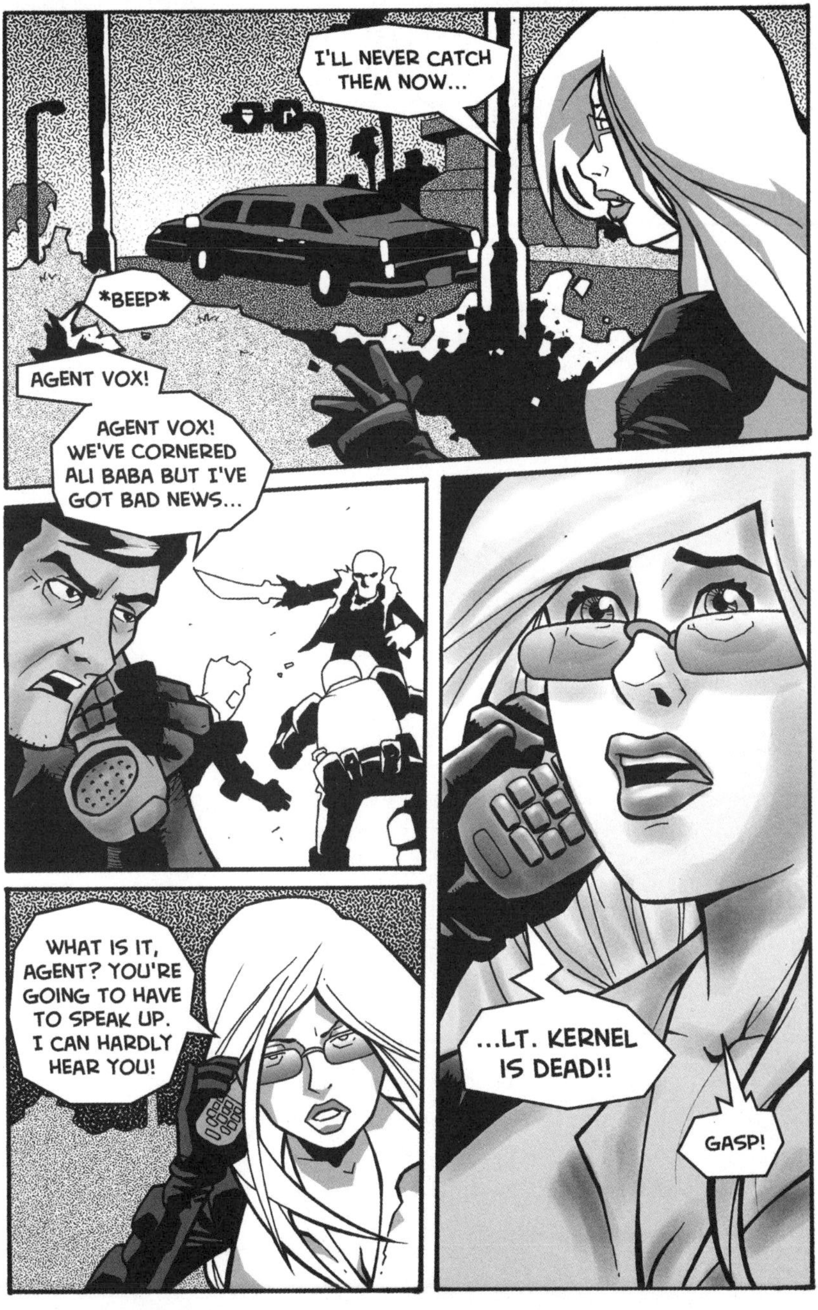

I'LL NEVER CATCH THEM NOW...
BEEP
AGENT VOX!
AGENT VOX! WE'VE CORNERED ALI BABA BUT I'VE GOT BAD NEWS...
WHAT IS IT, AGENT? YOU'RE GOING TO HAVE TO SPEAK UP. I CAN HARDLY HEAR YOU!
...LT. KERNEL IS DEAD!!
GASP!

chapter two

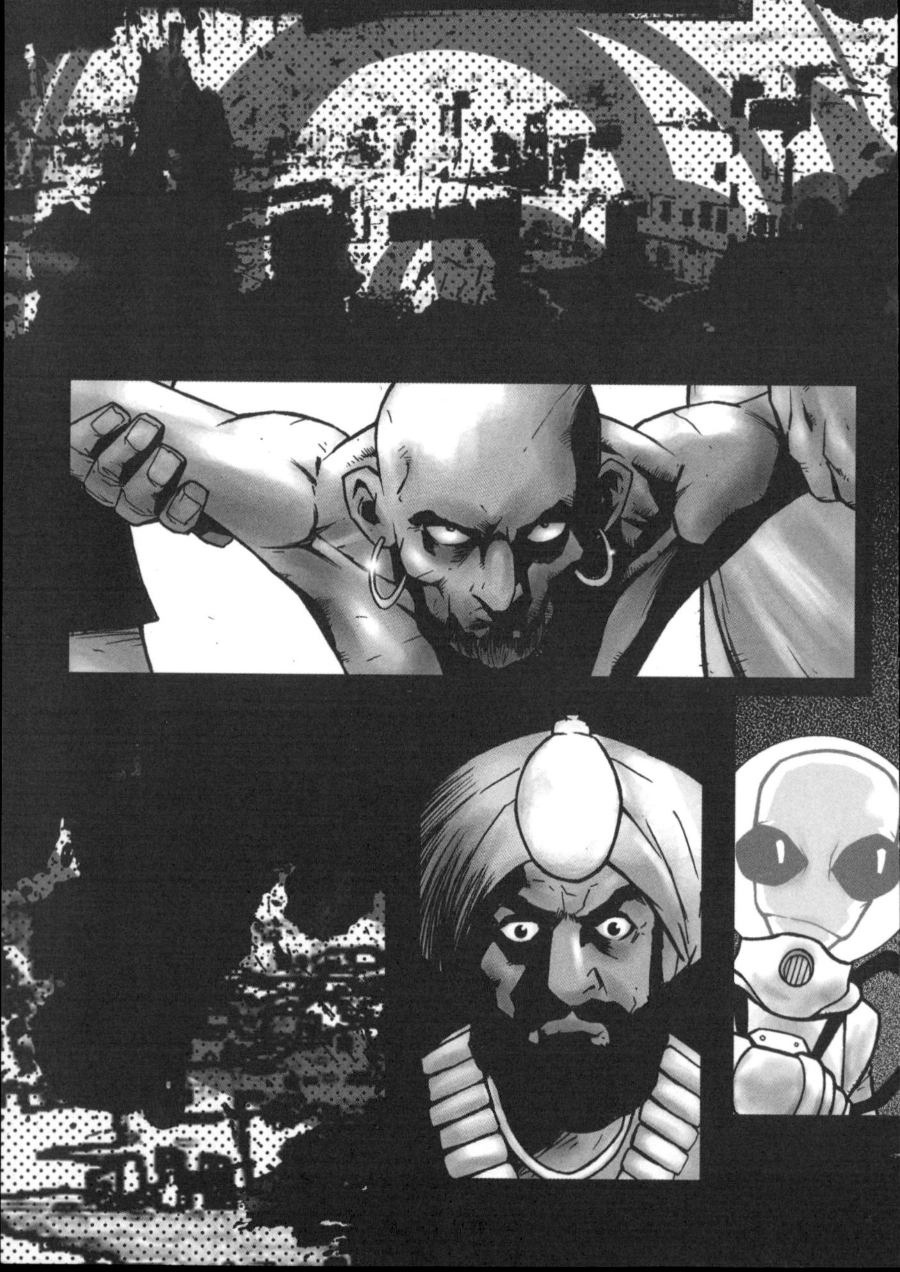

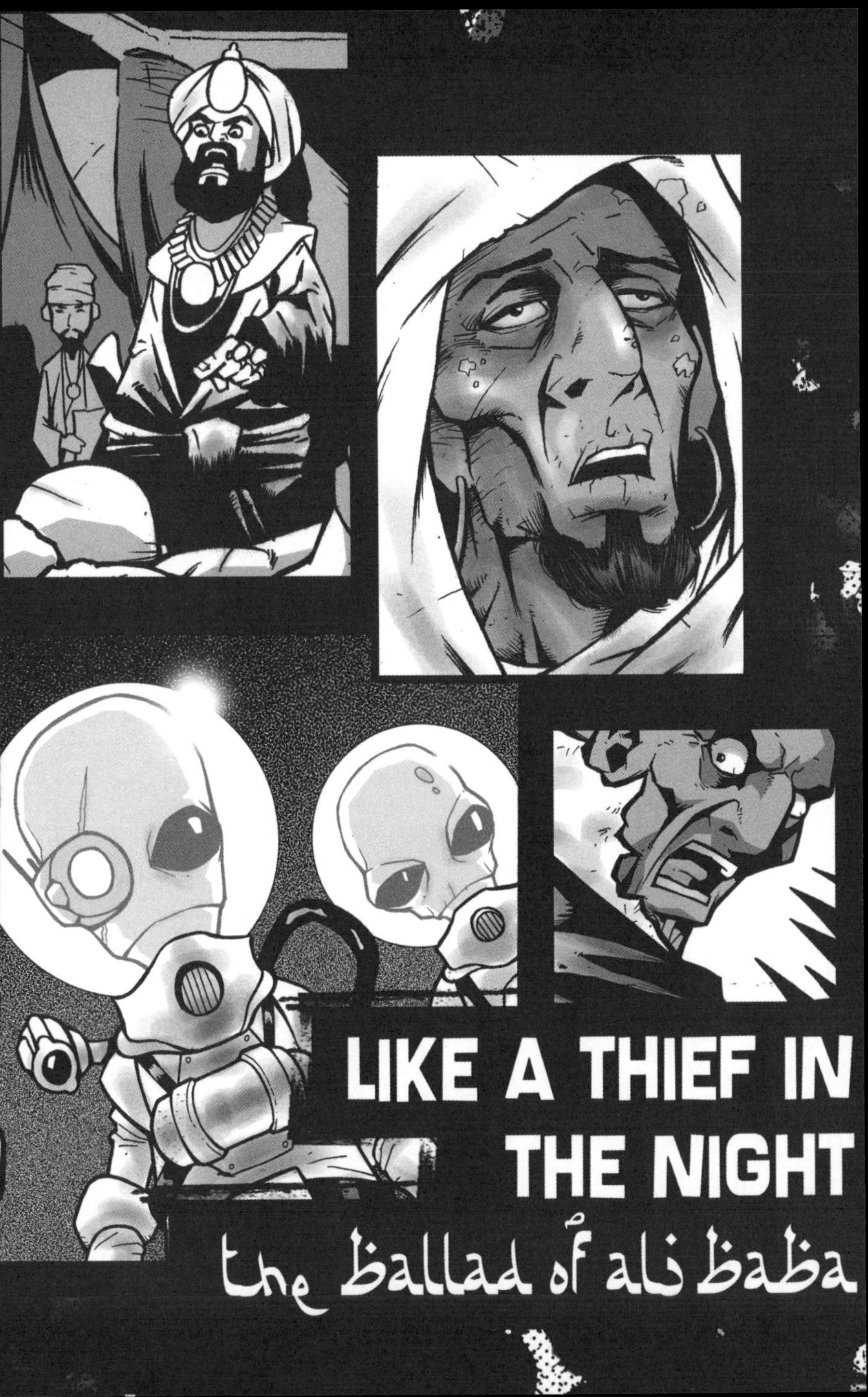
LIKE A THIEF IN THE NIGHT
the ballad of ali baba

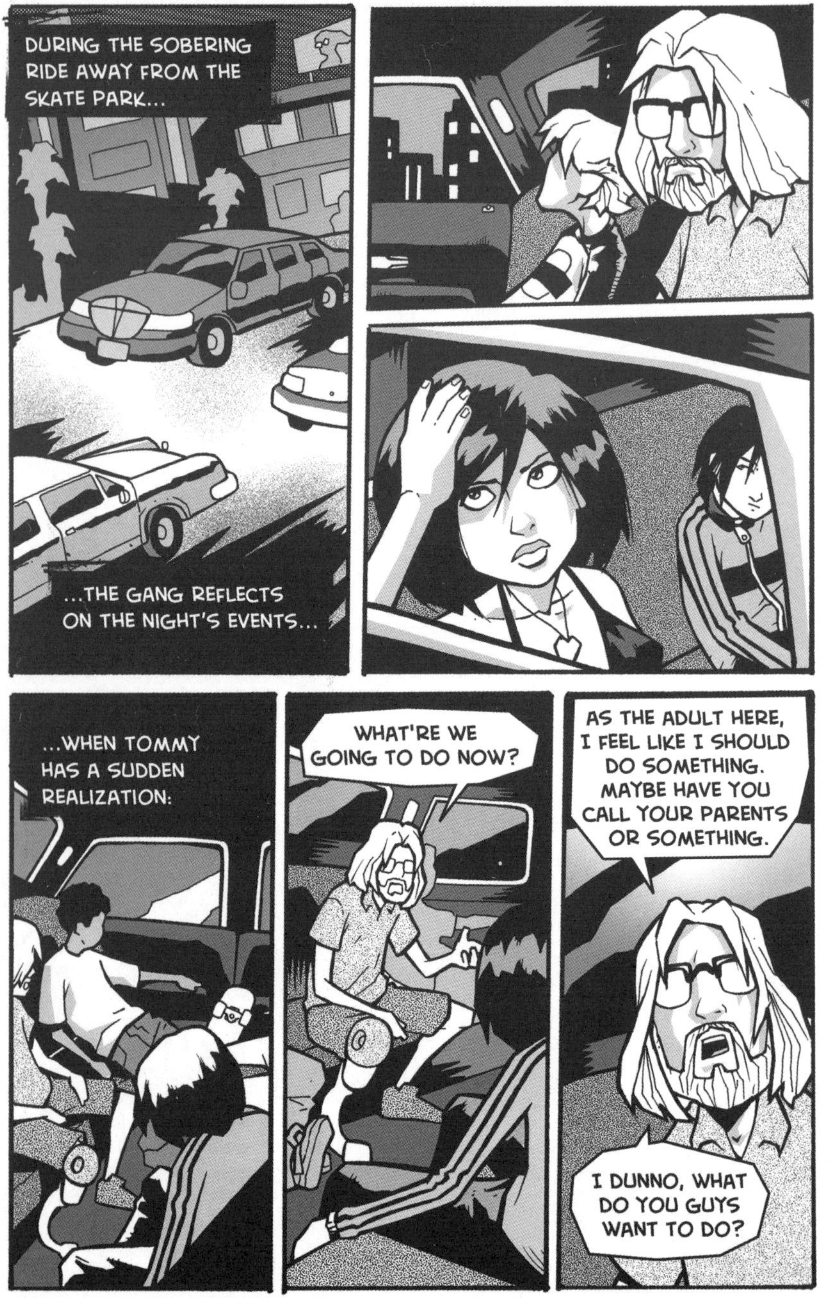
DURING THE SOBERING RIDE AWAY FROM THE SKATE PARK...
...THE GANG REFLECTS ON THE NIGHT'S EVENTS...
...WHEN TOMMY HAS A SUDDEN REALIZATION:
WHAT'RE WE GOING TO DO NOW?
AS THE ADULT HERE, I FEEL LIKE I SHOULD DO SOMETHING. MAYBE HAVE YOU CALL YOUR PARENTS OR SOMETHING.
I DUNNO, WHAT DO YOU GUYS WANT TO DO?

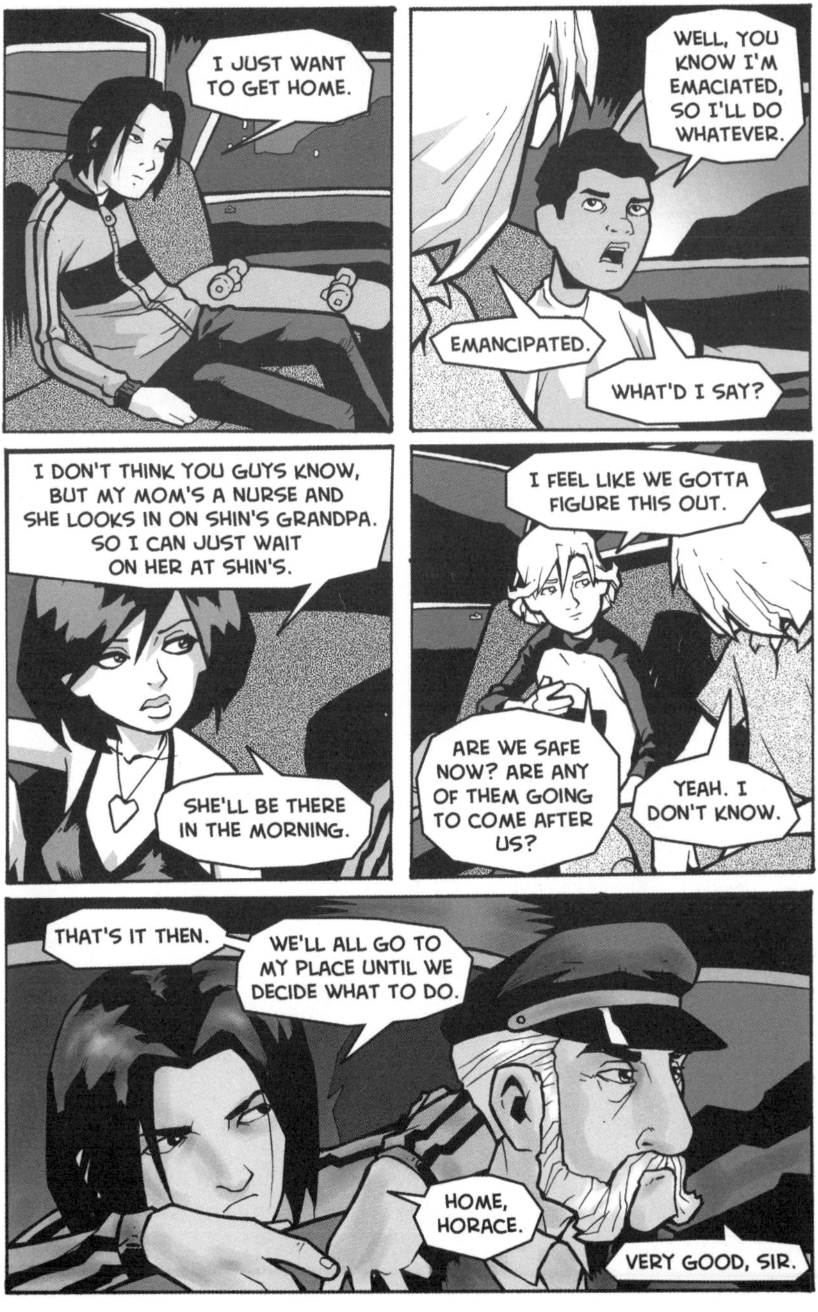
I JUST WANT TO GET HOME.
WELL, YOU KNOW I'M EMACIATED, SO I'LL DO WHATEVER.
EMANCIPATED.
WHAT'D I SAY?
I DON'T THINK YOU GUYS KNOW, BUT MY MOM'S A NURSE AND SHE LOOKS IN ON SHIN'S GRANDPA. SO I CAN JUST WAIT ON HER AT SHIN'S.
SHE'LL BE THERE IN THE MORNING.
I FEEL LIKE WE GOTTA FIGURE THIS OUT.
ARE WE SAFE NOW? ARE ANY OF THEM GOING TO COME AFTER US?
YEAH. I DON'T KNOW.
THAT'S IT THEN.
WE'LL ALL GO TO MY PLACE UNTIL WE DECIDE WHAT TO DO.
HOME, HORACE.
VERY GOOD, SIR.

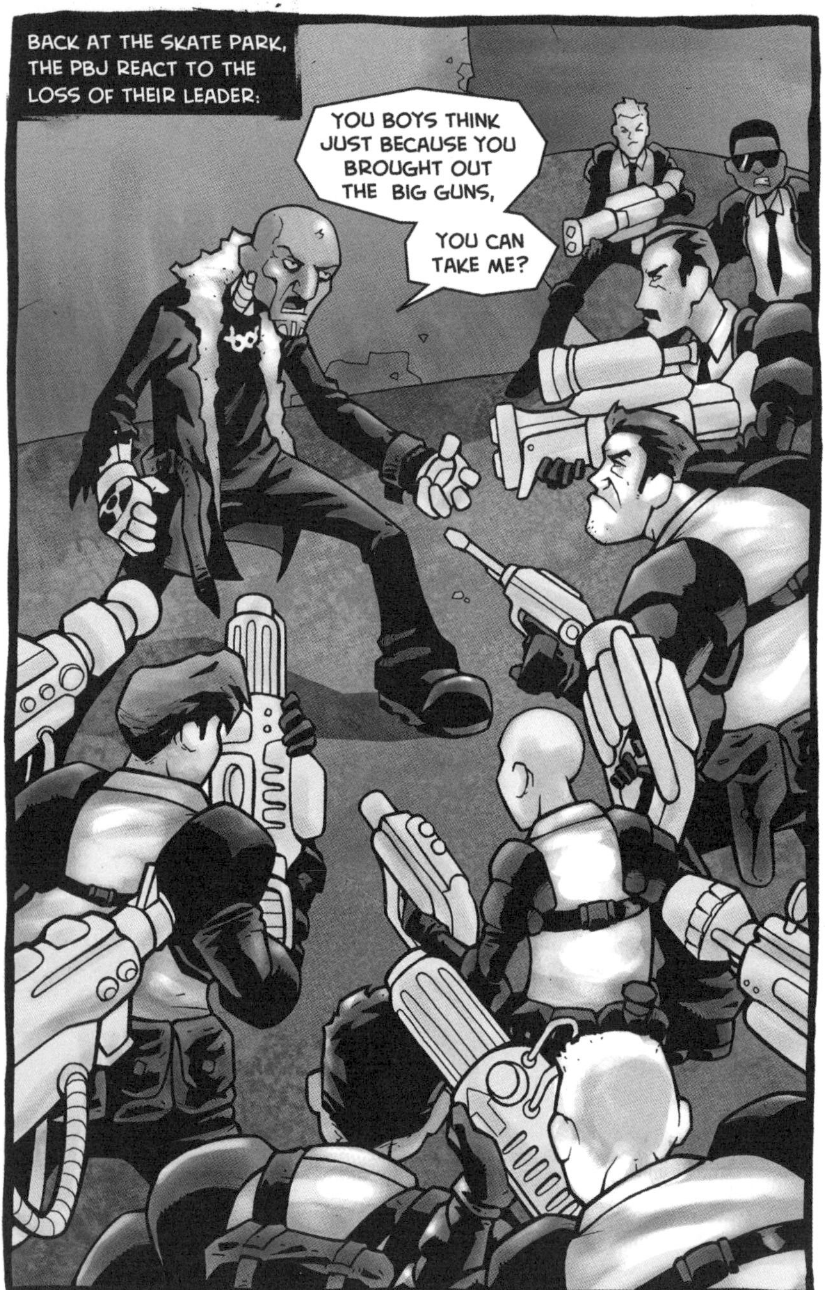
BACK AT THE SKATE PARK, THE PBJ REACT TO THE LOSS OF THEIR LEADER:
YOU BOYS THINK JUST BECAUSE YOU BROUGHT OUT THE BIG GUNS,
YOU CAN TAKE ME?

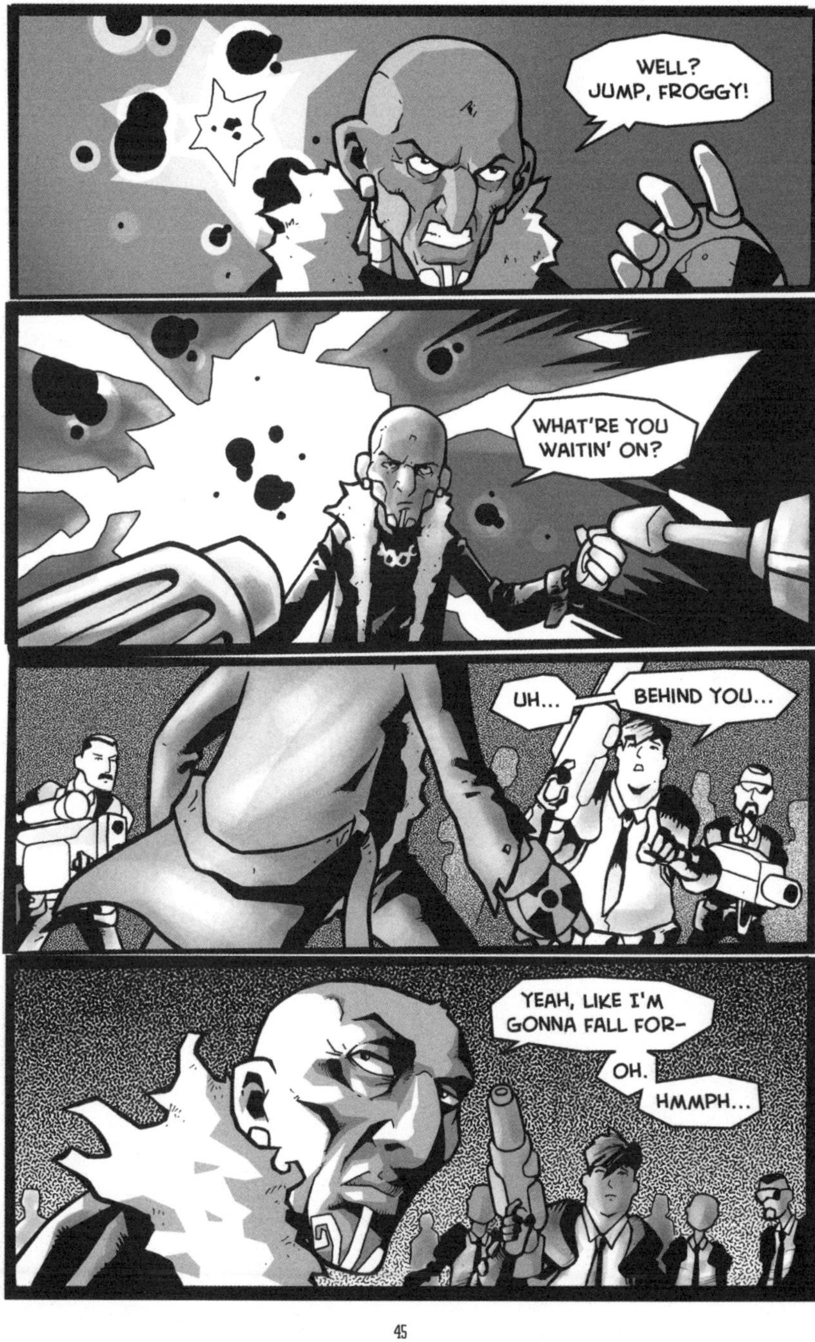
WELL? JUMP, FROGGY!
WHAT'RE YOU WAITIN' ON?
UH...
BEHIND YOU...
YEAH, LIKE I'M GONNA FALL FOR-
OH.
HMMPH...

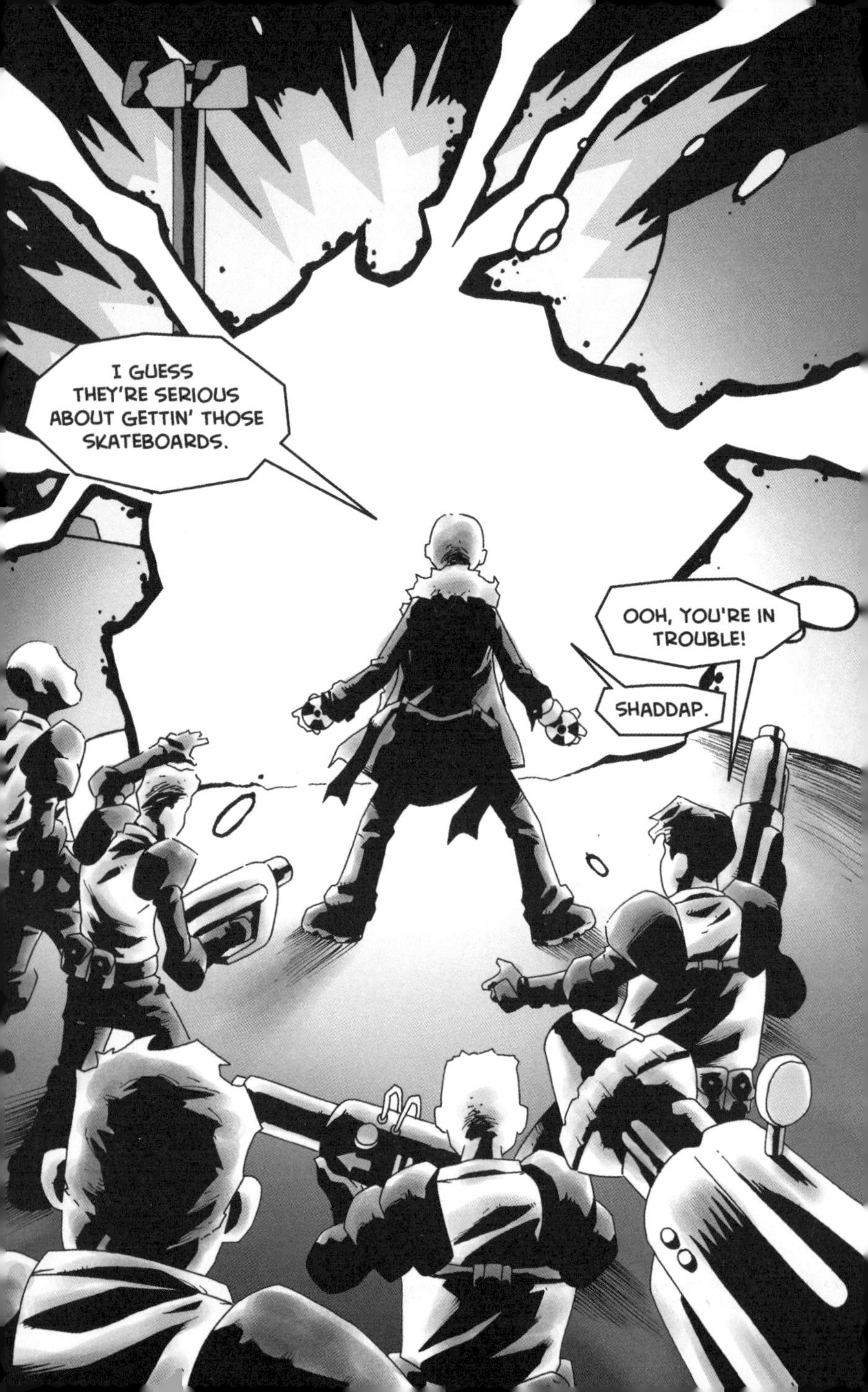
I GUESS THEY'RE SERIOUS ABOUT GETTIN' THOSE SKATEBOARDS.
OOH, YOU'RE IN TROUBLE!
SHADDAP.

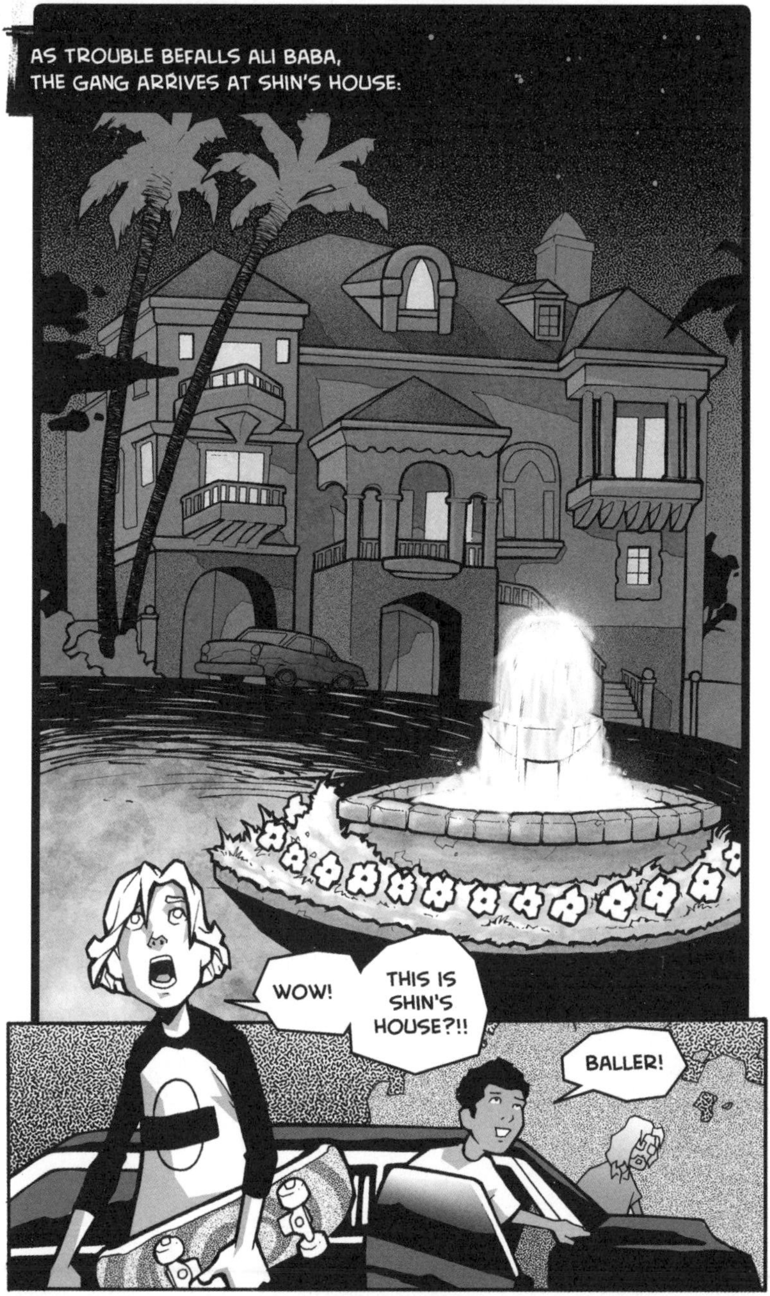
AS TROUBLE BEFALLS ALI BABA, THE GANG ARRIVES AT SHIN'S HOUSE:
WOW!
THIS IS SHIN'S HOUSE?!!
BALLER!

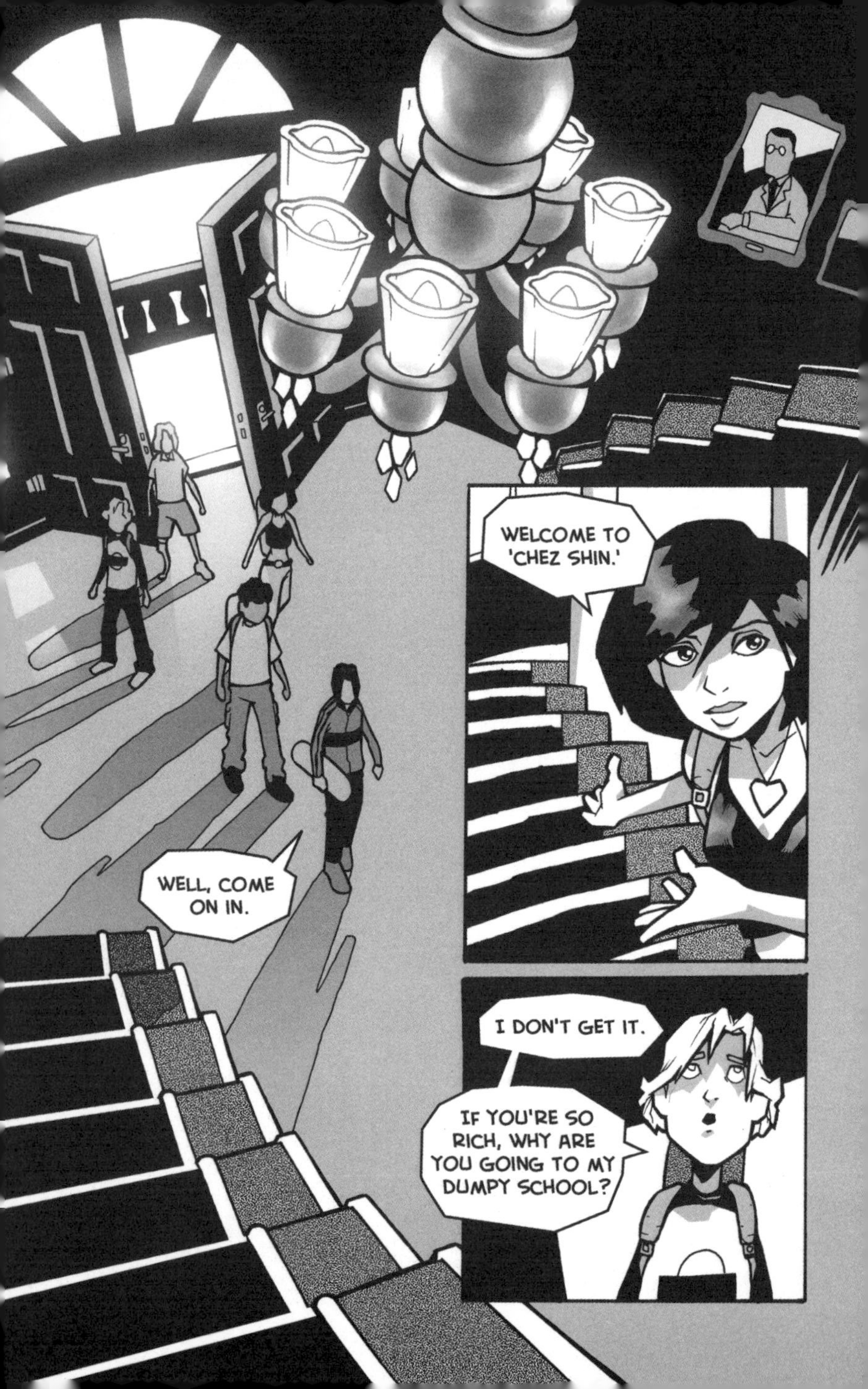

WELL, COME ON IN.
WELCOME TO 'CHEZ SHIN.'
I DON'T GET IT.
IF YOU'RE SO RICH, WHY ARE YOU GOING TO MY DUMPY SCHOOL?

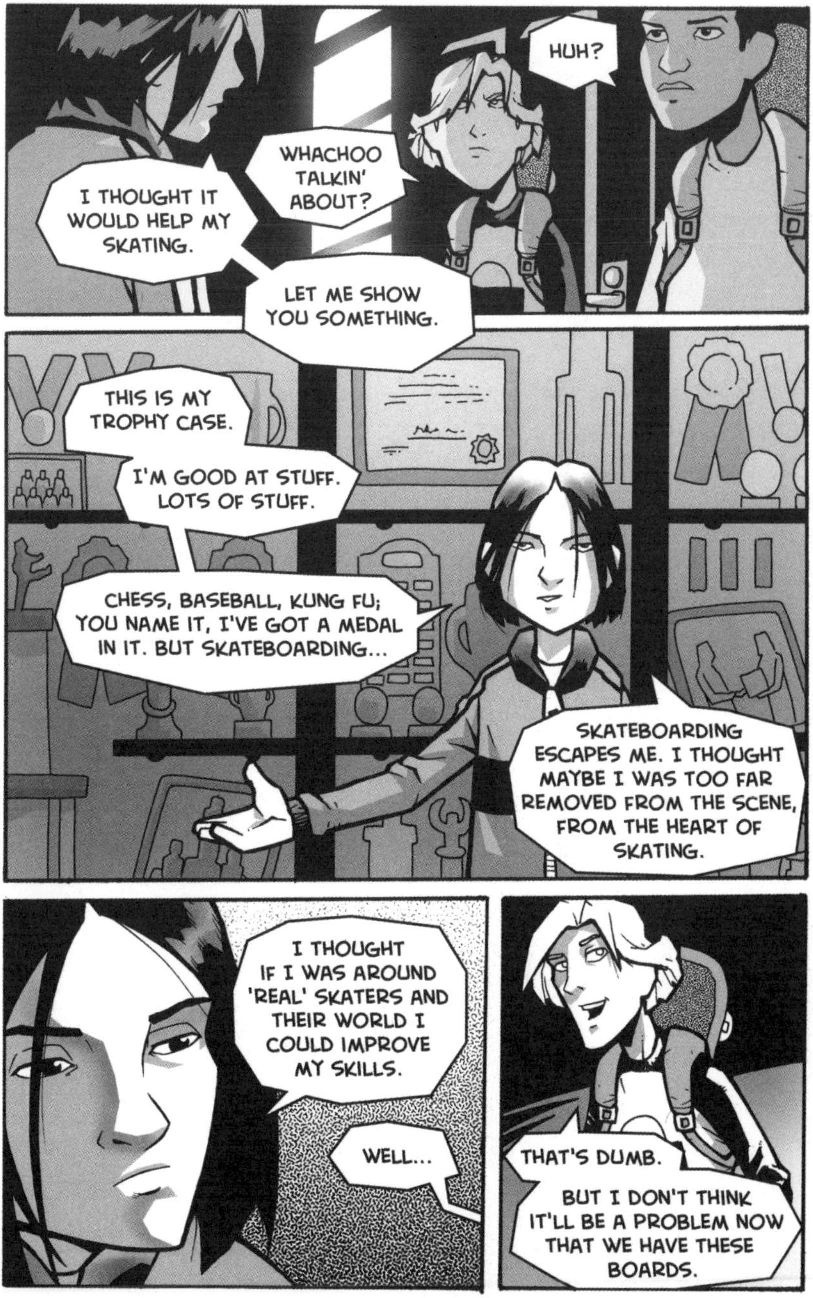
HUH?
WHACHOO TALKIN' ABOUT?
I THOUGHT IT WOULD HELP MY SKATING.
LET ME SHOW YOU SOMETHING.
THIS IS MY TROPHY CASE.
I'M GOOD AT STUFF. LOTS OF STUFF.
CHESS, BASEBALL, KUNG FU; YOU NAME IT, I'VE GOT A MEDAL IN IT. BUT SKATEBOARDING...
SKATEBOARDING ESCAPES ME. I THOUGHT MAYBE I WAS TOO FAR REMOVED FROM THE SCENE, FROM THE HEART OF SKATING.
I THOUGHT IF I WAS AROUND 'REAL' SKATERS AND THEIR WORLD I COULD IMPROVE MY SKILLS.
WELL...
THAT'S DUMB.
BUT I DON'T THINK IT'LL BE A PROBLEM NOW THAT WE HAVE THESE BOARDS.

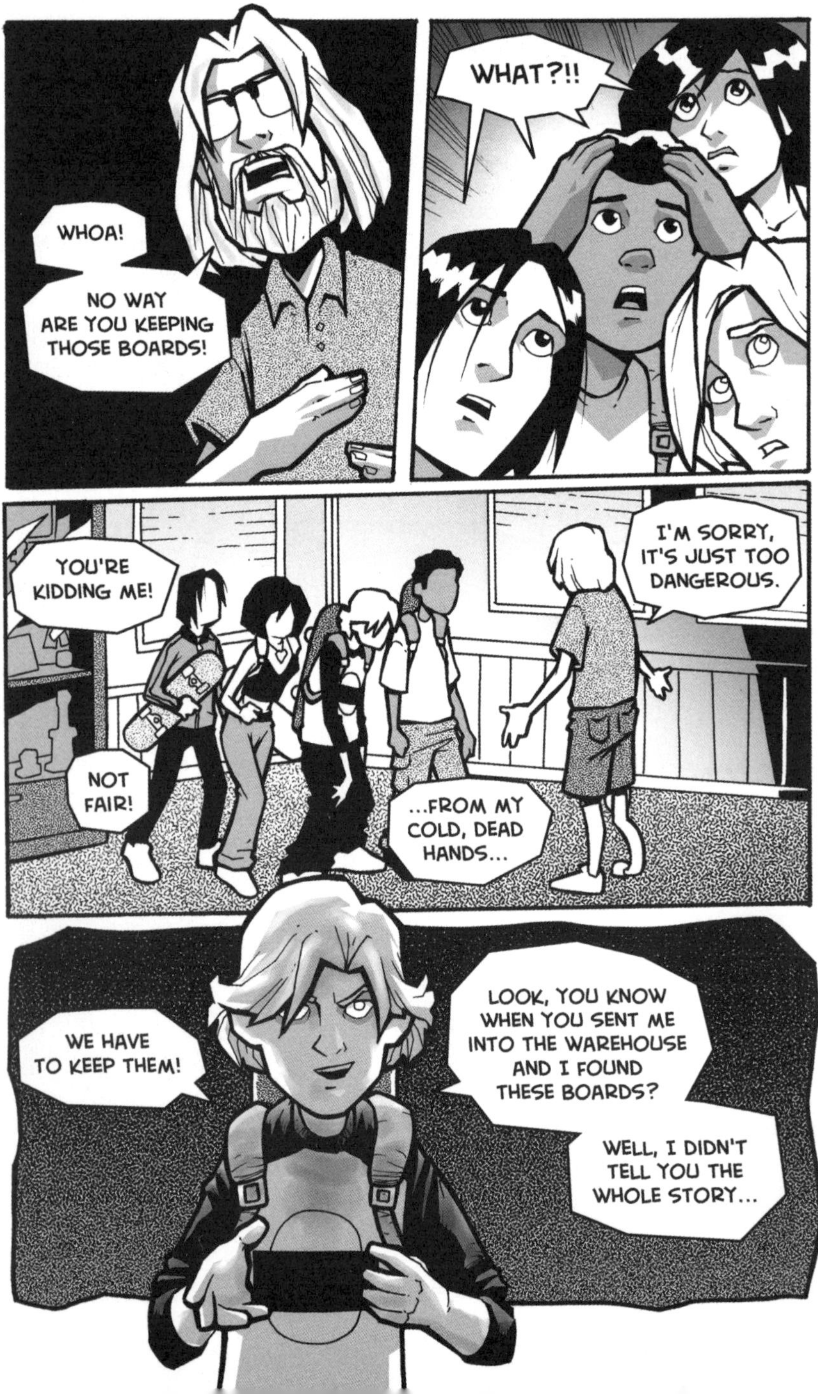
WHOA!
NO WAY ARE YOU KEEPING THOSE BOARDS!
WHAT?!!
YOU'RE KIDDING ME!
NOT FAIR!
...FROM MY COLD, DEAD HANDS...
I'M SORRY, IT'S JUST TOO DANGEROUS.
WE HAVE TO KEEP THEM!
LOOK, YOU KNOW WHEN YOU SENT ME INTO THE WAREHOUSE AND I FOUND THESE BOARDS?
WELL, I DIDN'T TELL YOU THE WHOLE STORY...

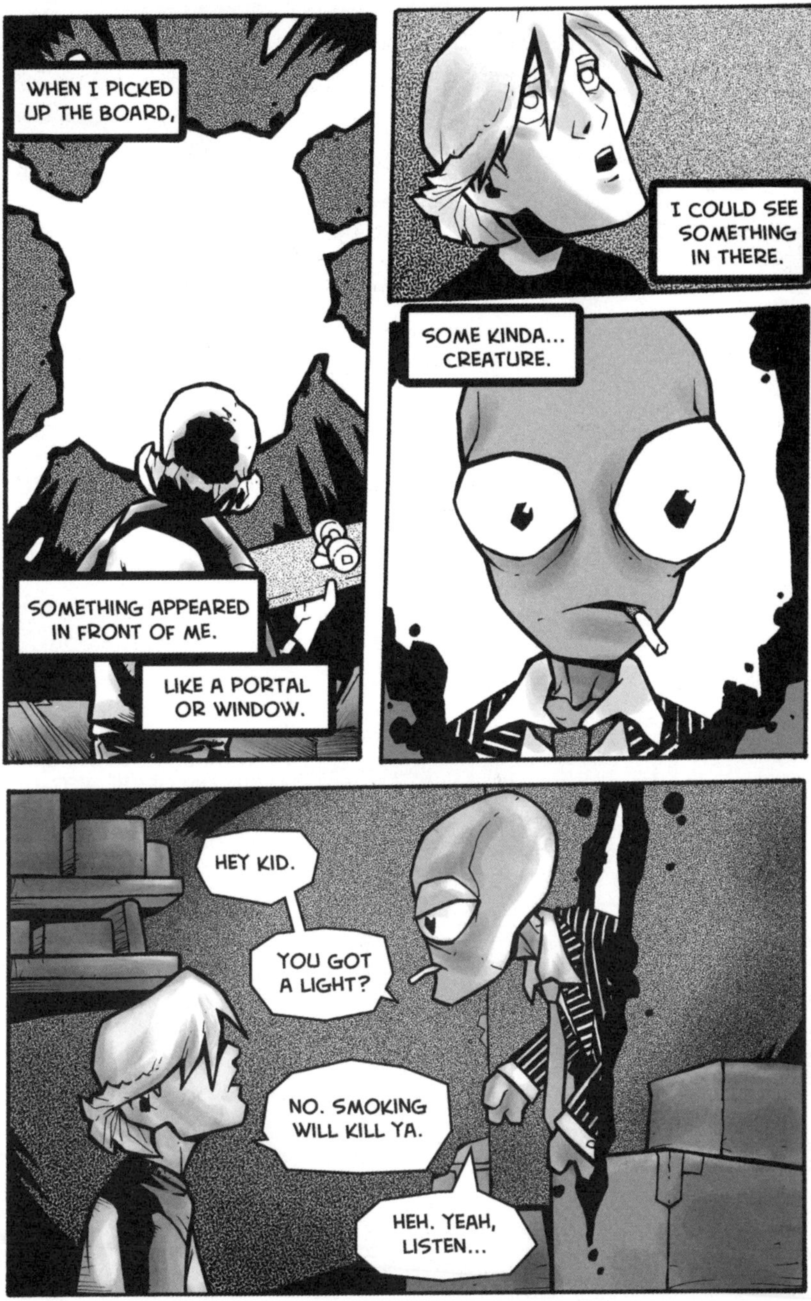
WHEN I PICKED UP THE BOARD,
SOMETHING APPEARED IN FRONT OF ME.
LIKE A PORTAL OR WINDOW.
I COULD SEE SOMETHING IN THERE.
SOME KINDA... CREATURE.
HEY KID.
YOU GOT A LIGHT?
NO. SMOKING WILL KILL YA.
HEH. YEAH, LISTEN...

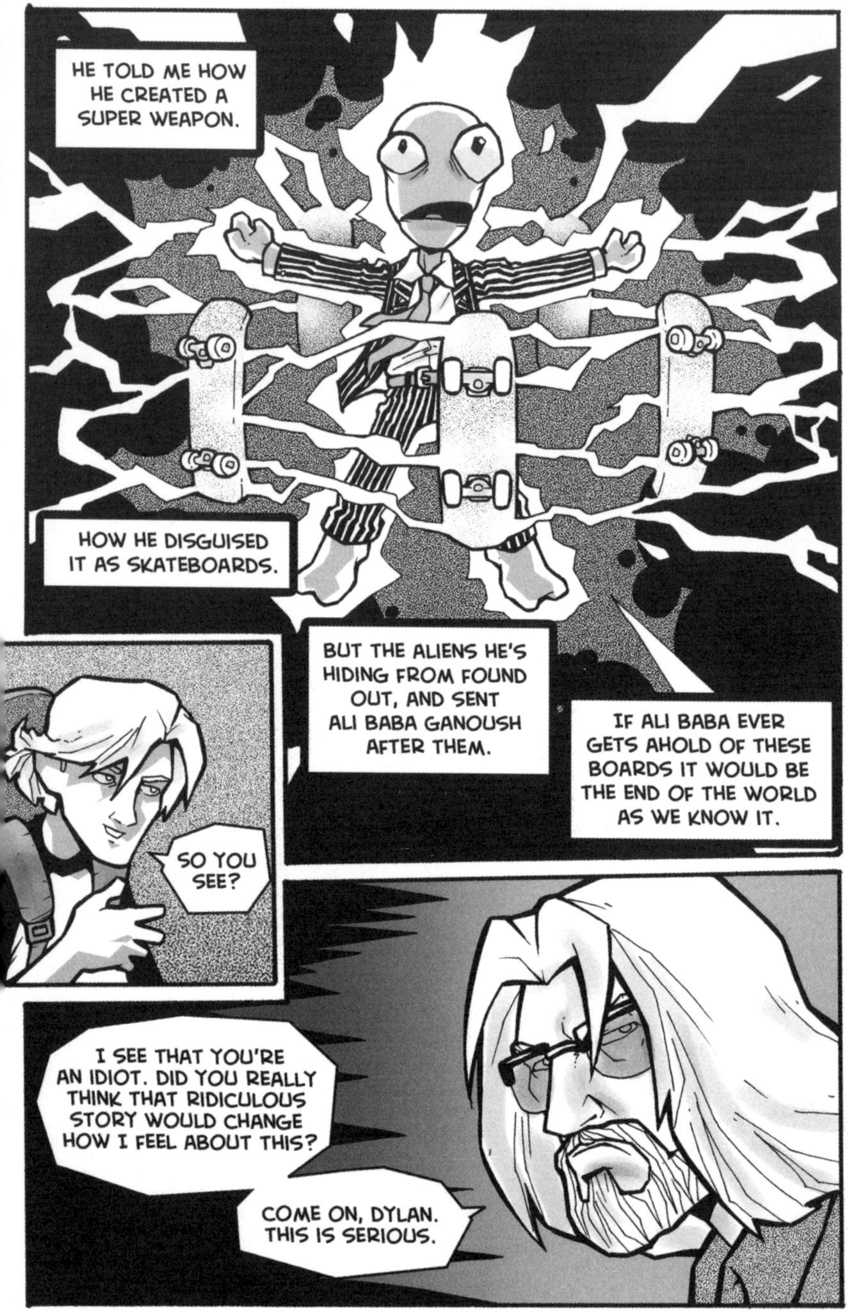
HE TOLD ME HOW HE CREATED A SUPER WEAPON.
HOW HE DISGUISED IT AS SKATEBOARDS.
BUT THE ALIENS HE'S HIDING FROM FOUND OUT, AND SENT ALI BABA GANOUSH AFTER THEM.
IF ALI BABA EVER GETS AHOLD OF THESE BOARDS IT WOULD BE THE END OF THE WORLD AS WE KNOW IT.
SO YOU SEE?
I SEE THAT YOU'RE AN IDIOT. DID YOU REALLY THINK THAT RIDICULOUS STORY WOULD CHANGE HOW I FEEL ABOUT THIS?
COME ON, DYLAN. THIS IS SERIOUS.

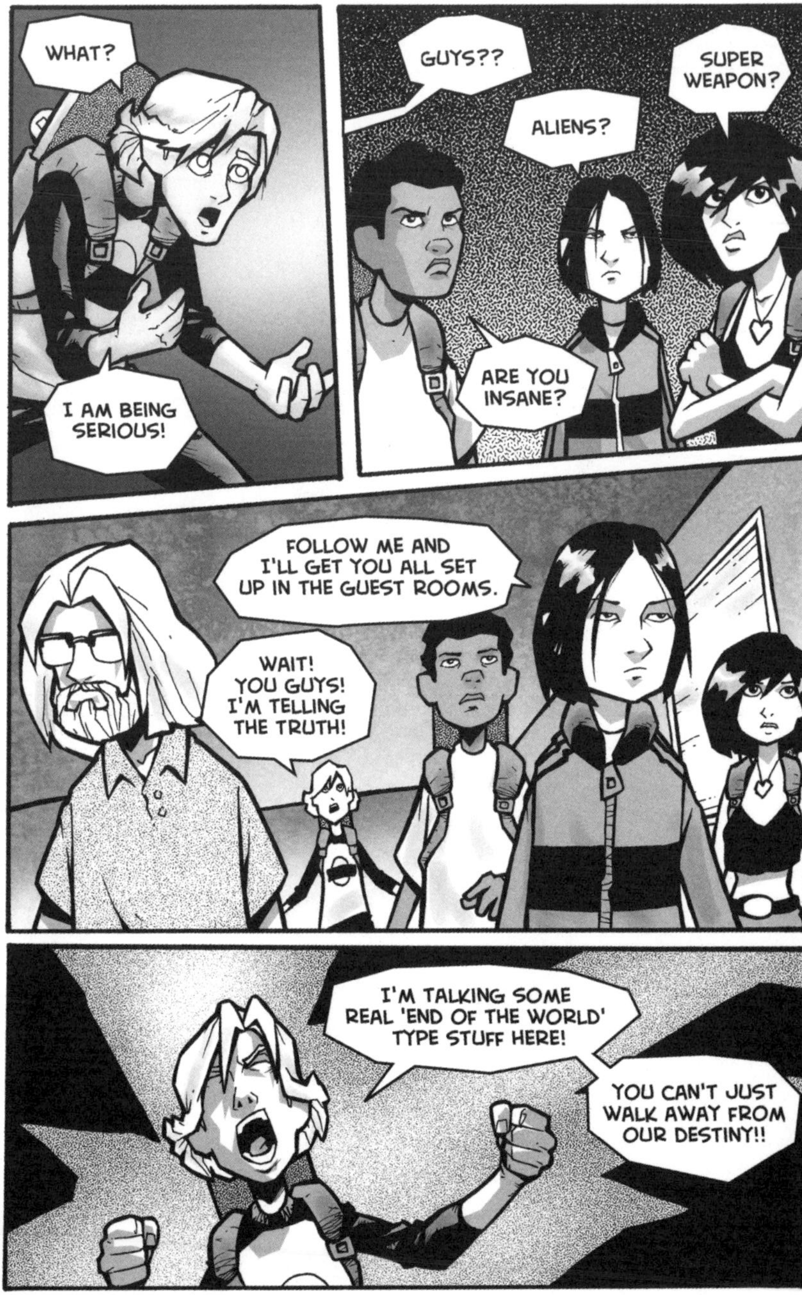
WHAT?
I AM BEING SERIOUS!
GUYS??
ALIENS?
SUPER WEAPON?
ARE YOU INSANE?
FOLLOW ME AND I'LL GET YOU ALL SET UP IN THE GUEST ROOMS.
WAIT! YOU GUYS! I'M TELLING THE TRUTH!
I'M TALKING SOME REAL 'END OF THE WORLD' TYPE STUFF HERE!
YOU CAN'T JUST WALK AWAY FROM OUR DESTINY!!

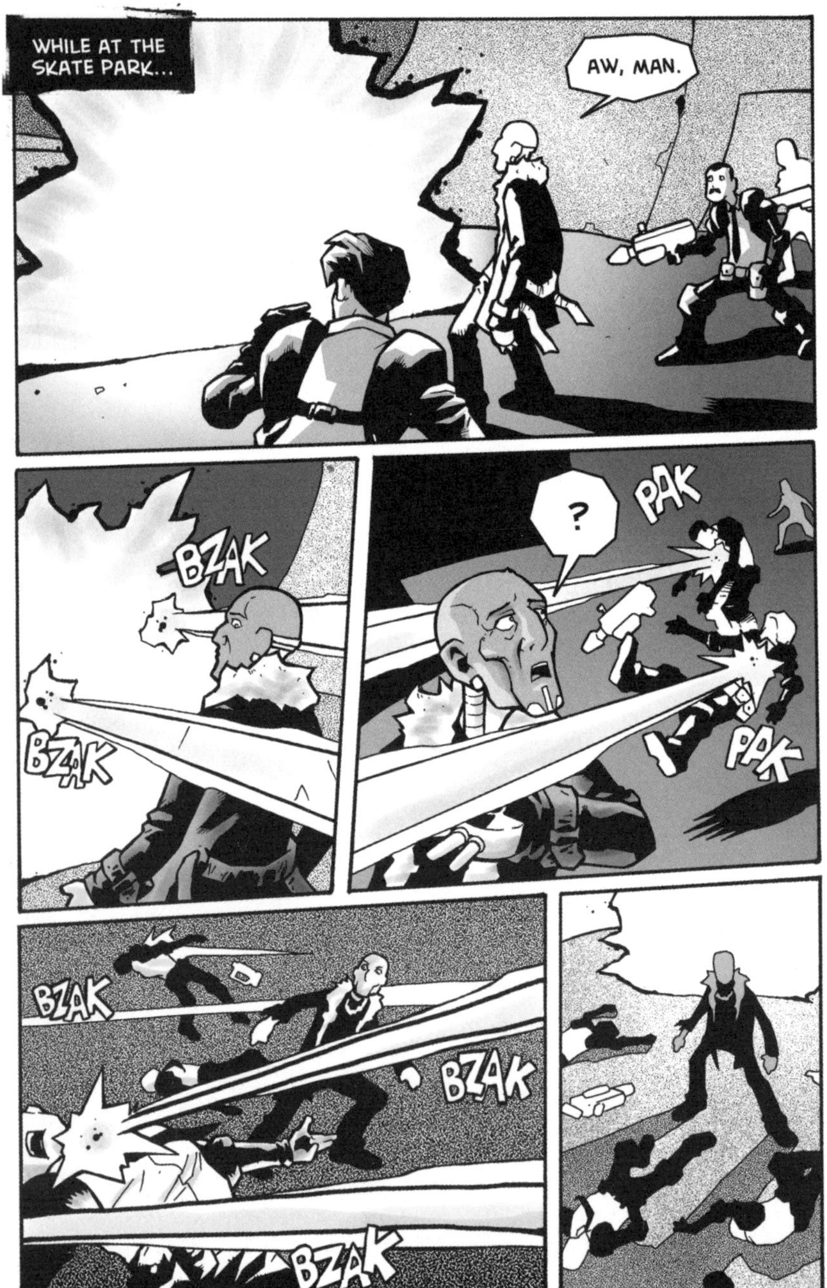
WHILE AT THE SKATE PARK...
AW, MAN.
BZAK
BZAK
?
PAK
PAK
BZAK
BZAK
BZAK

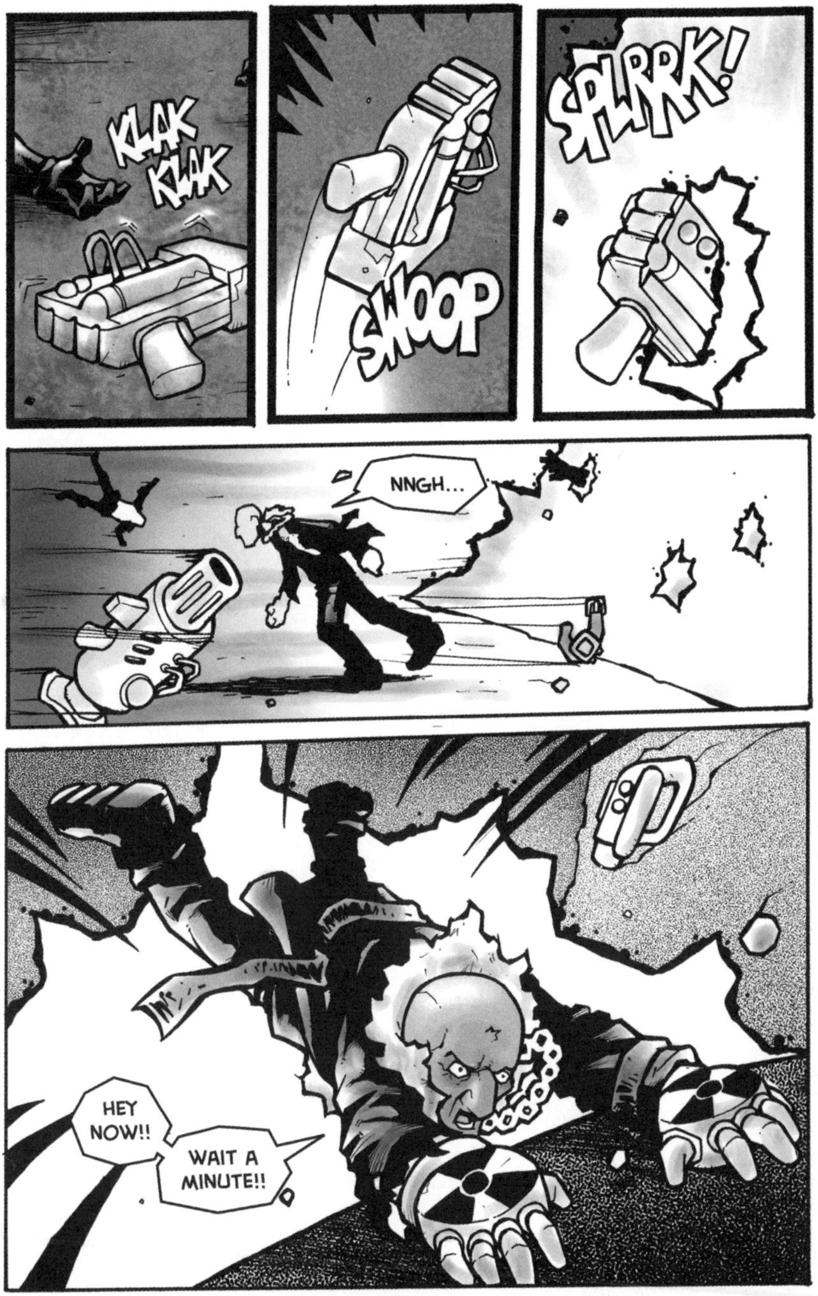
KLAK
KLAK
SWOOP
SPLRRK!
NNGH...
HEY NOW!!
WAIT A MINUTE!!

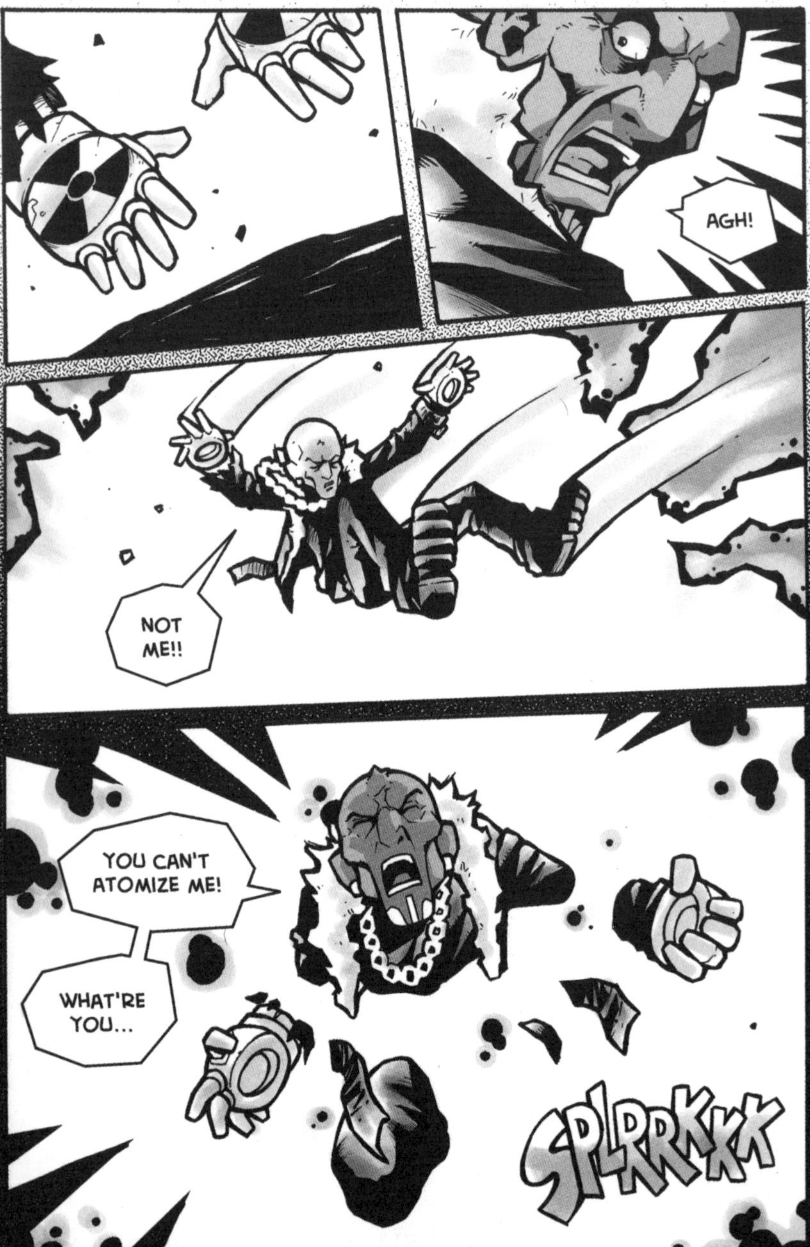
AGH!
NOT ME!!
YOU CAN'T ATOMIZE ME!
WHAT'RE YOU...
SPLRRKKK

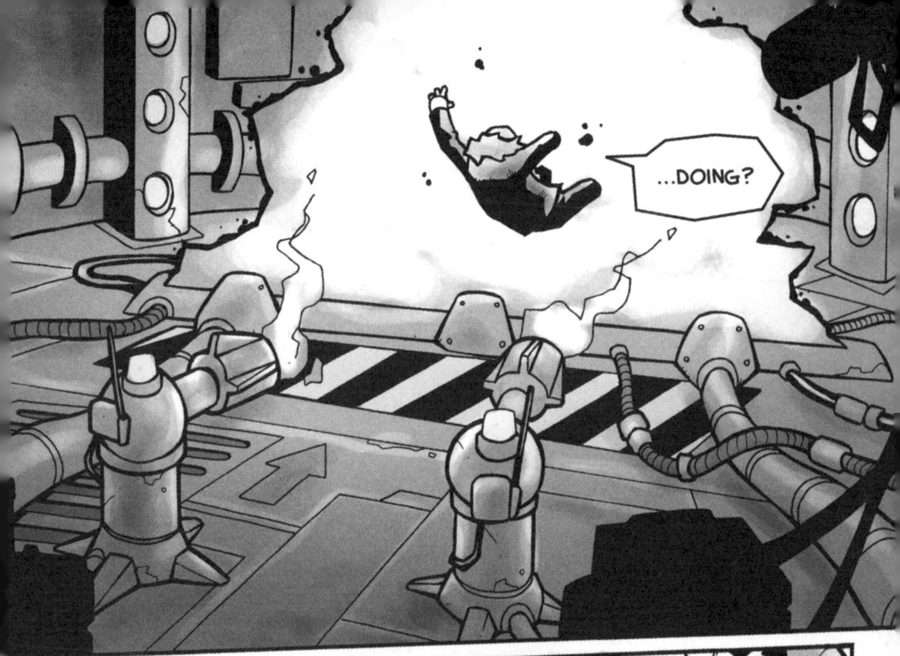
...DOING?

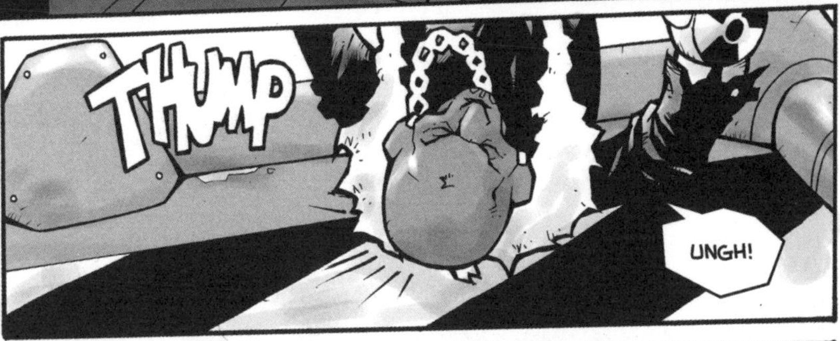
THUMP
UNGH!

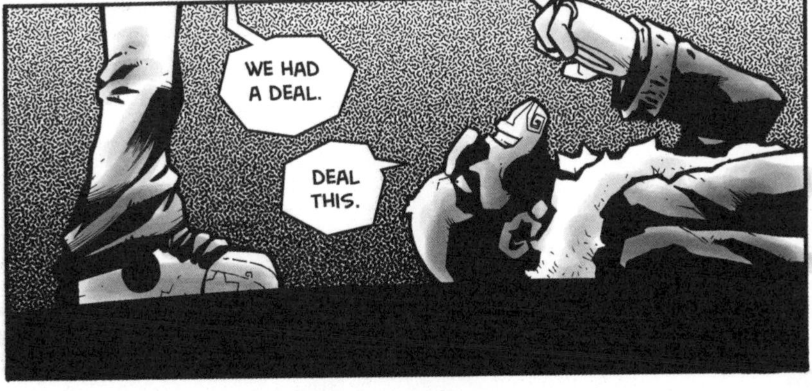
WE HAD A DEAL.
DEAL THIS.

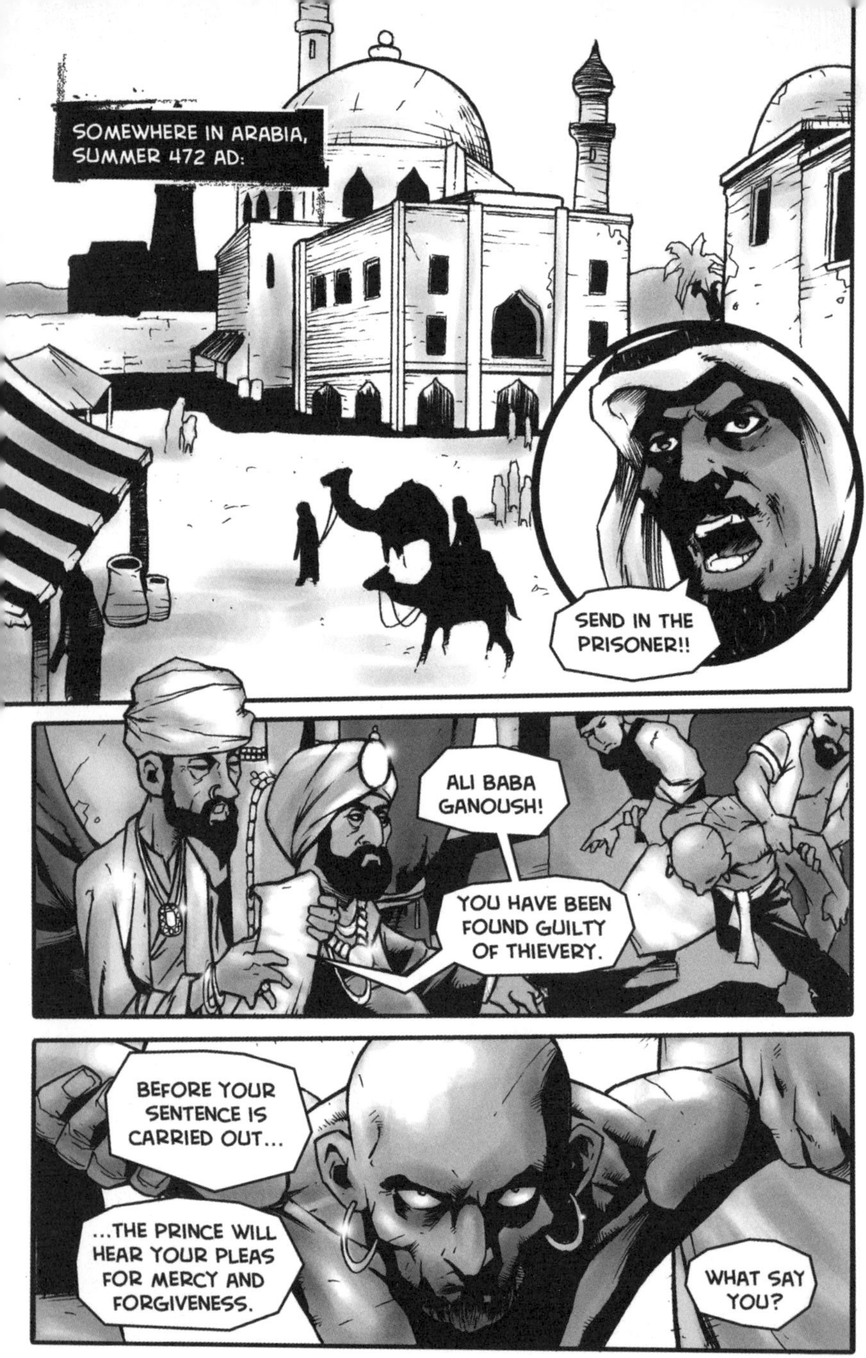
SOMEWHERE IN ARABIA, SUMMER 472 AD:
SEND IN THE PRISONER!!
ALI BABA GANOUSH!
YOU HAVE BEEN FOUND GUILTY OF THIEVERY.
BEFORE YOUR SENTENCE IS CARRIED OUT...
...THE PRINCE WILL HEAR YOUR PLEAS FOR MERCY AND FORGIVENESS.
WHAT SAY YOU?

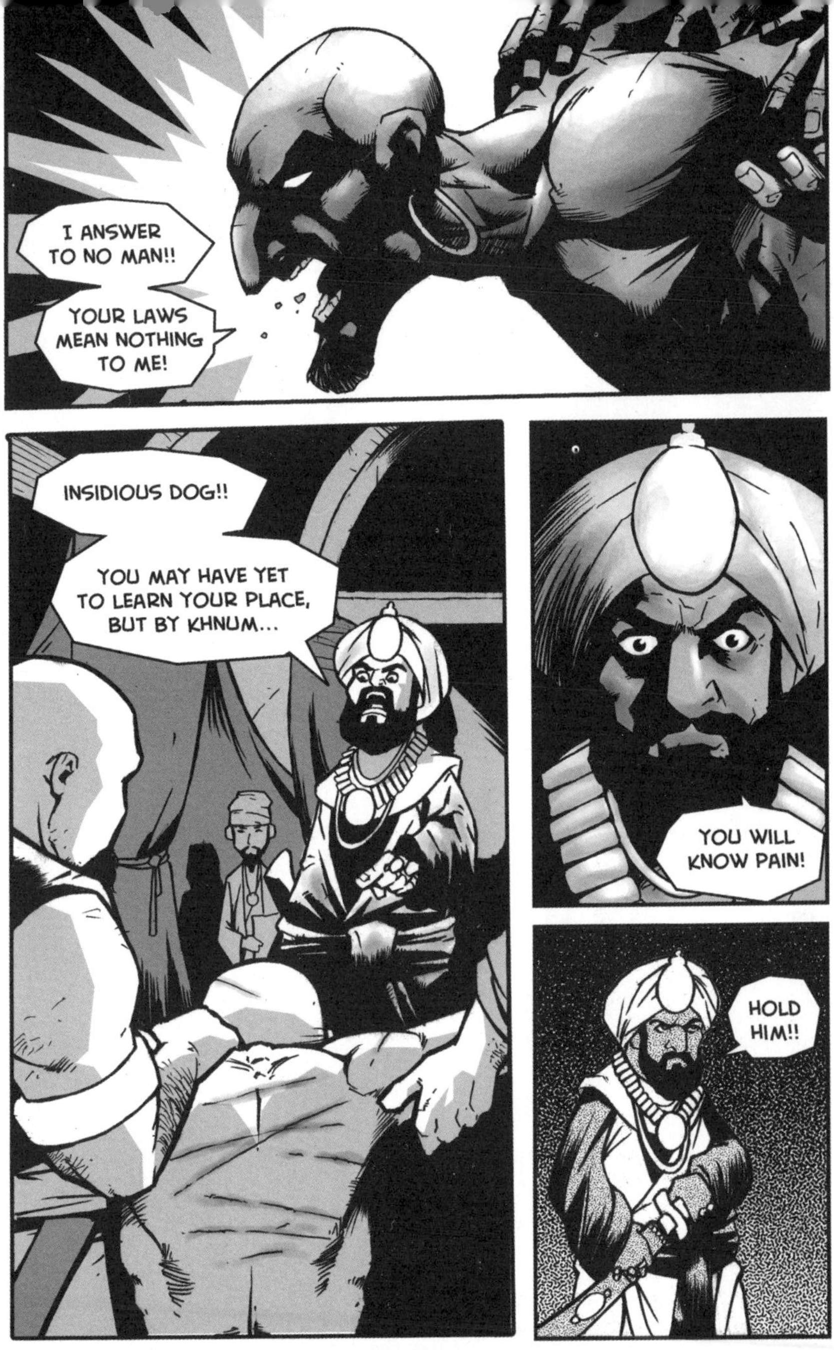
I ANSWER TO NO MAN!!
YOUR LAWS MEAN NOTHING TO ME!
INSIDIOUS DOG!!
YOU MAY HAVE YET TO LEARN YOUR PLACE, BUT BY KHNUM...
YOU WILL KNOW PAIN!
HOLD HIM!!

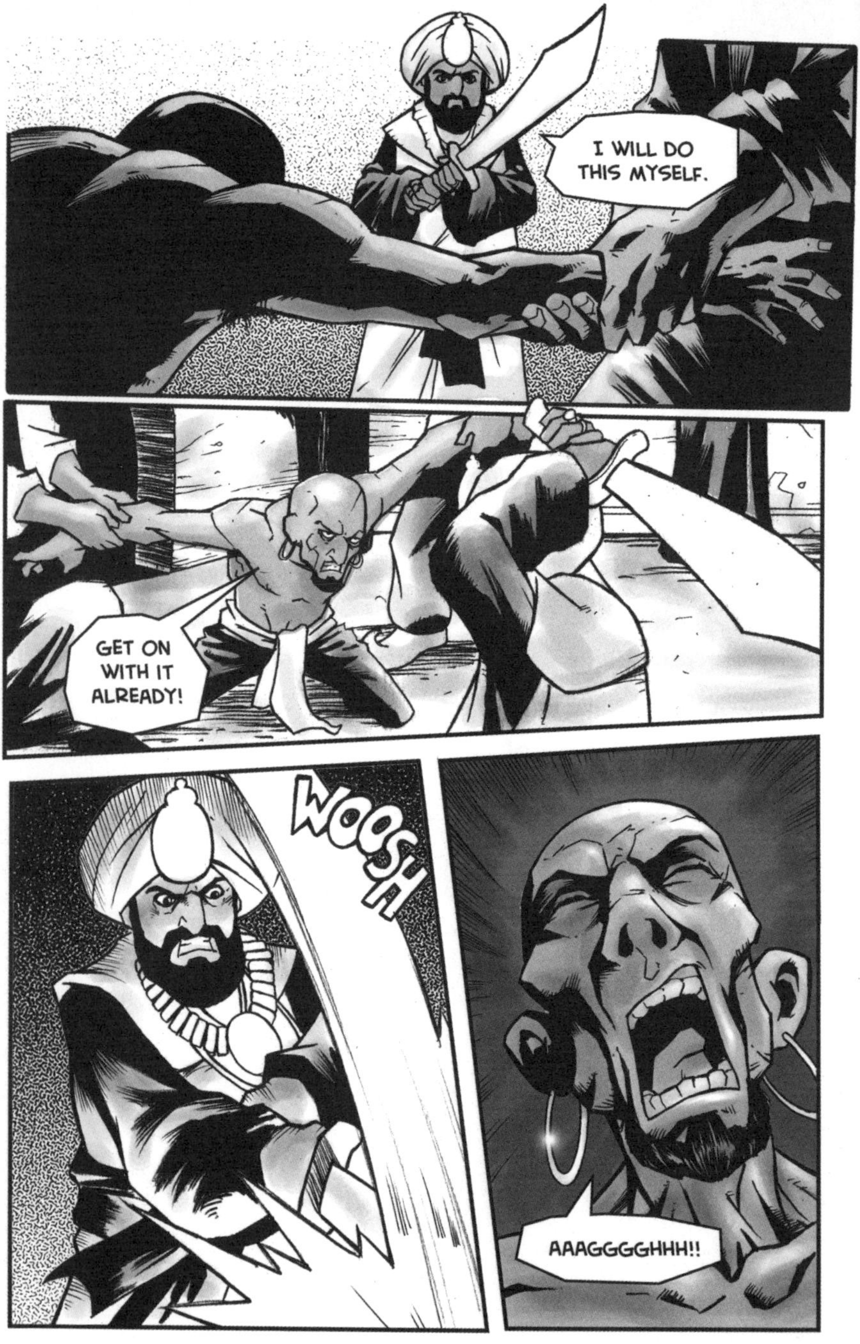
I WILL DO THIS MYSELF.
GET ON WITH IT ALREADY!
WOOSH
AAAGGGGHHH!!

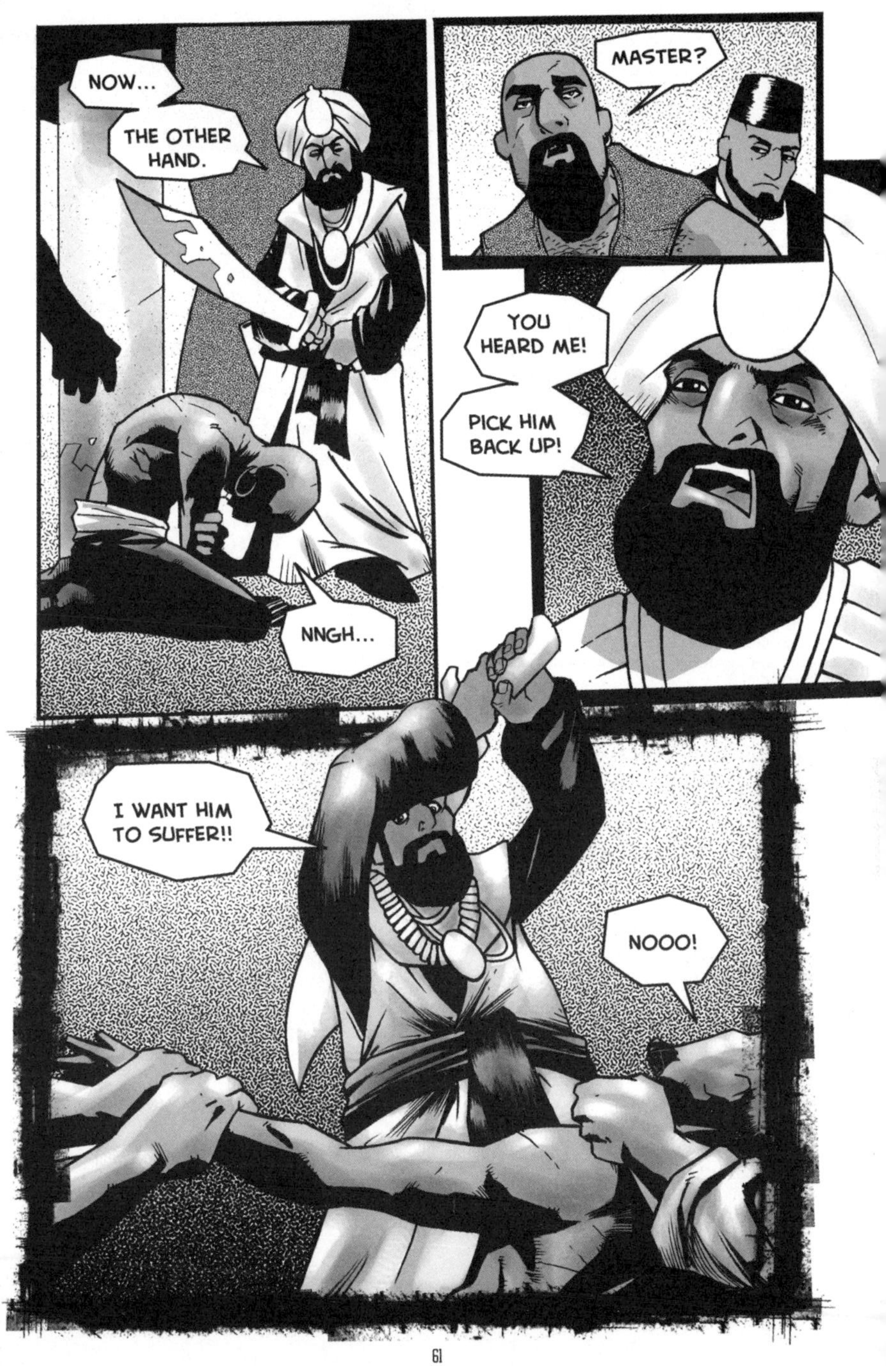
NOW...
THE OTHER HAND.
NNGH...
MASTER?
YOU HEARD ME!
PICK HIM BACK UP!
I WANT HIM TO SUFFER!!
NOOO!

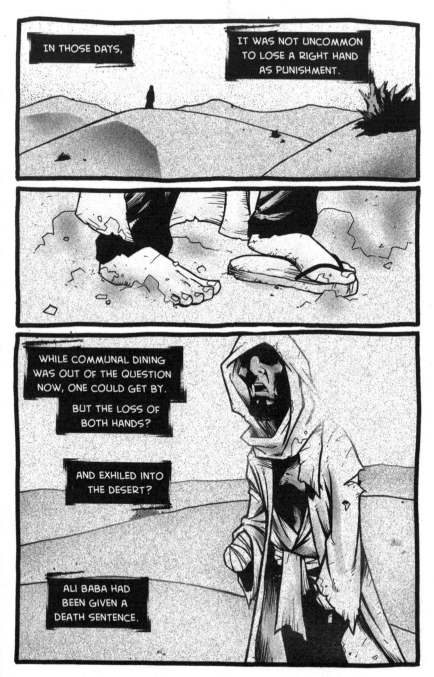

IN THOSE DAYS,

IT WAS NOT UNCOMMON TO LOSE A RIGHT HAND AS PUNISHMENT.

WHILE COMMUNAL DINING WAS OUT OF THE QUESTION NOW, ONE COULD GET BY.

BUT THE LOSS OF BOTH HANDS?

AND EXHILED INTO THE DESERT?

ALI BABA HAD BEEN GIVEN A DEATH SENTENCE.

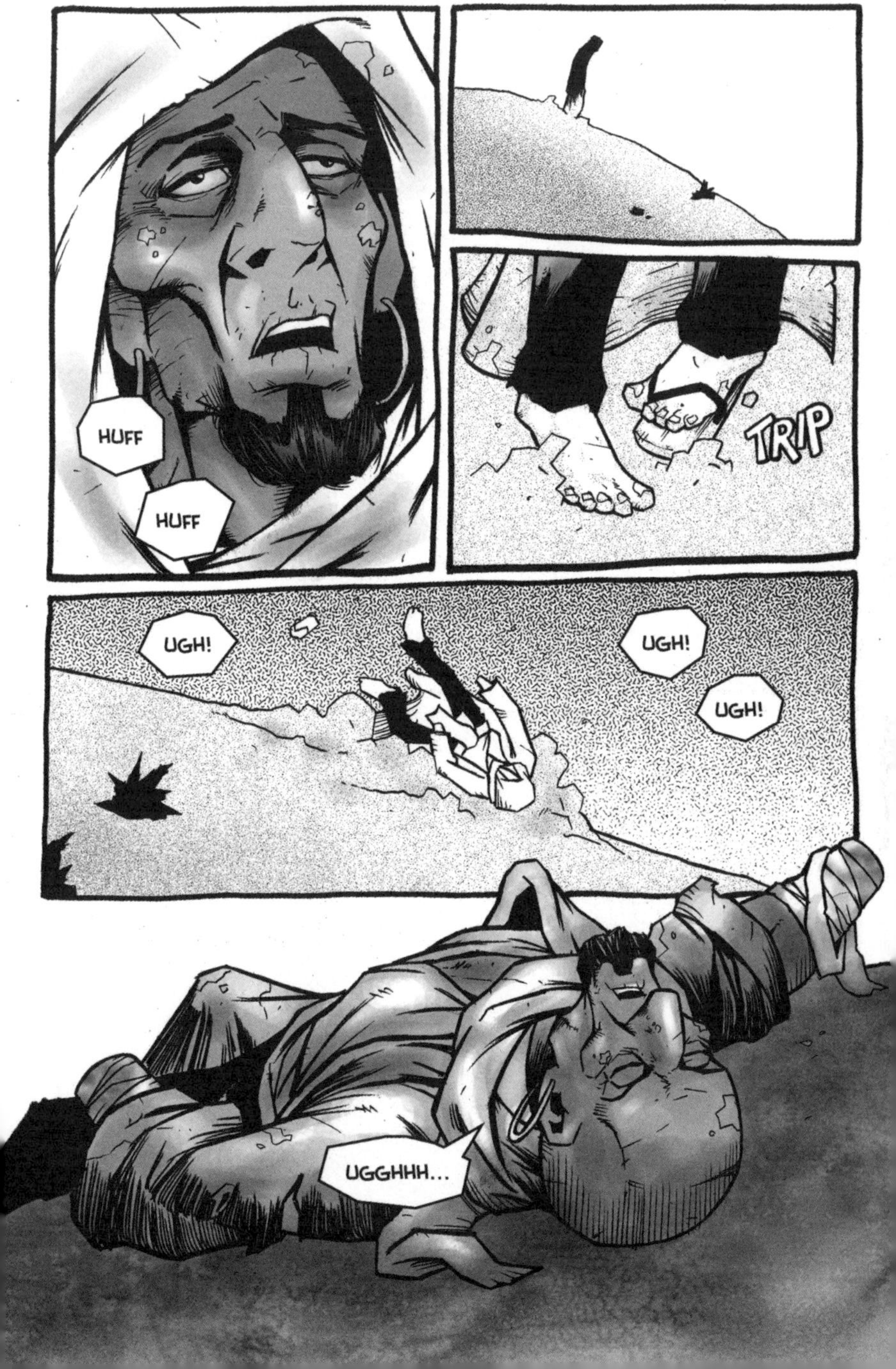
HUFF
HUFF
TRIP
UGH!
UGH!
UGH!
UGGHHH...

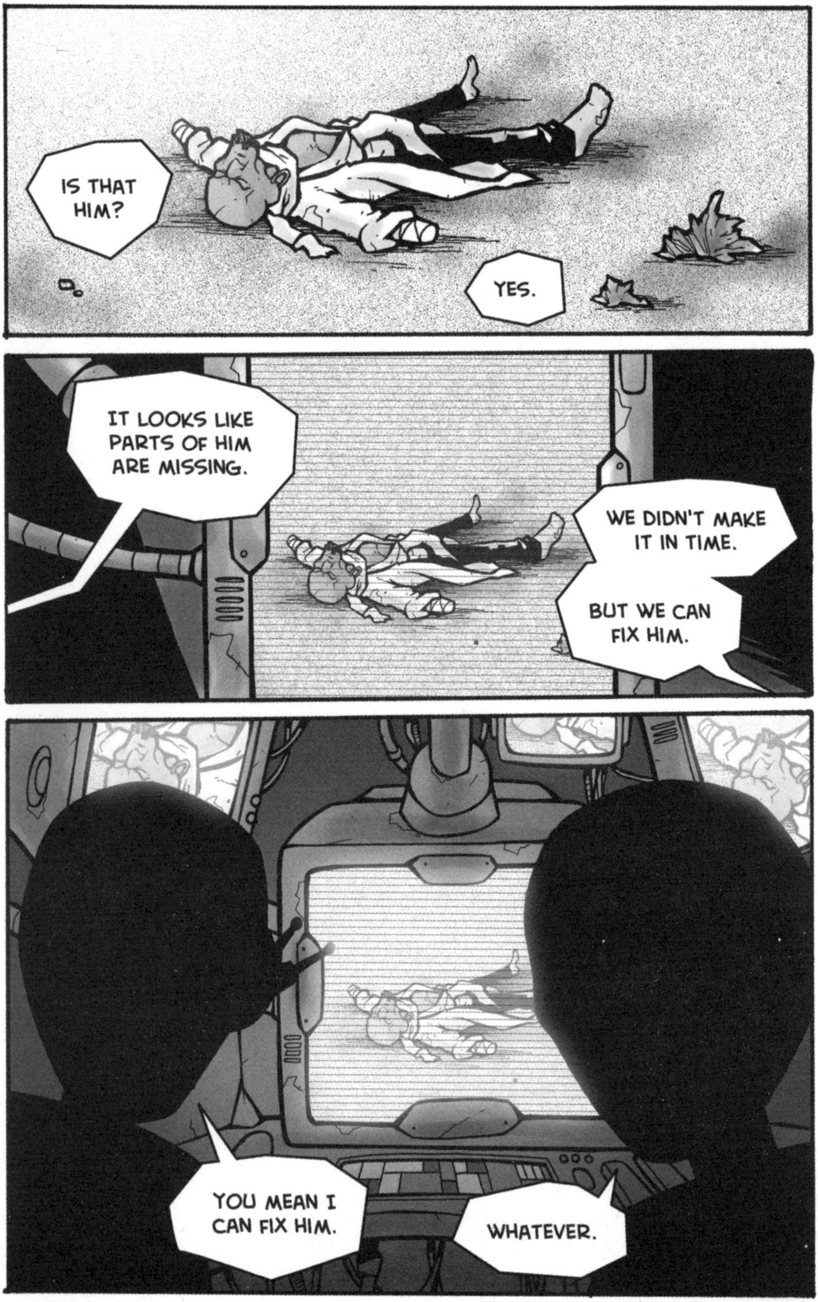
IS THAT HIM?
YES.
IT LOOKS LIKE PARTS OF HIM ARE MISSING.
WE DIDN'T MAKE IT IN TIME.
BUT WE CAN FIX HIM.
YOU MEAN I CAN FIX HIM.
WHATEVER.

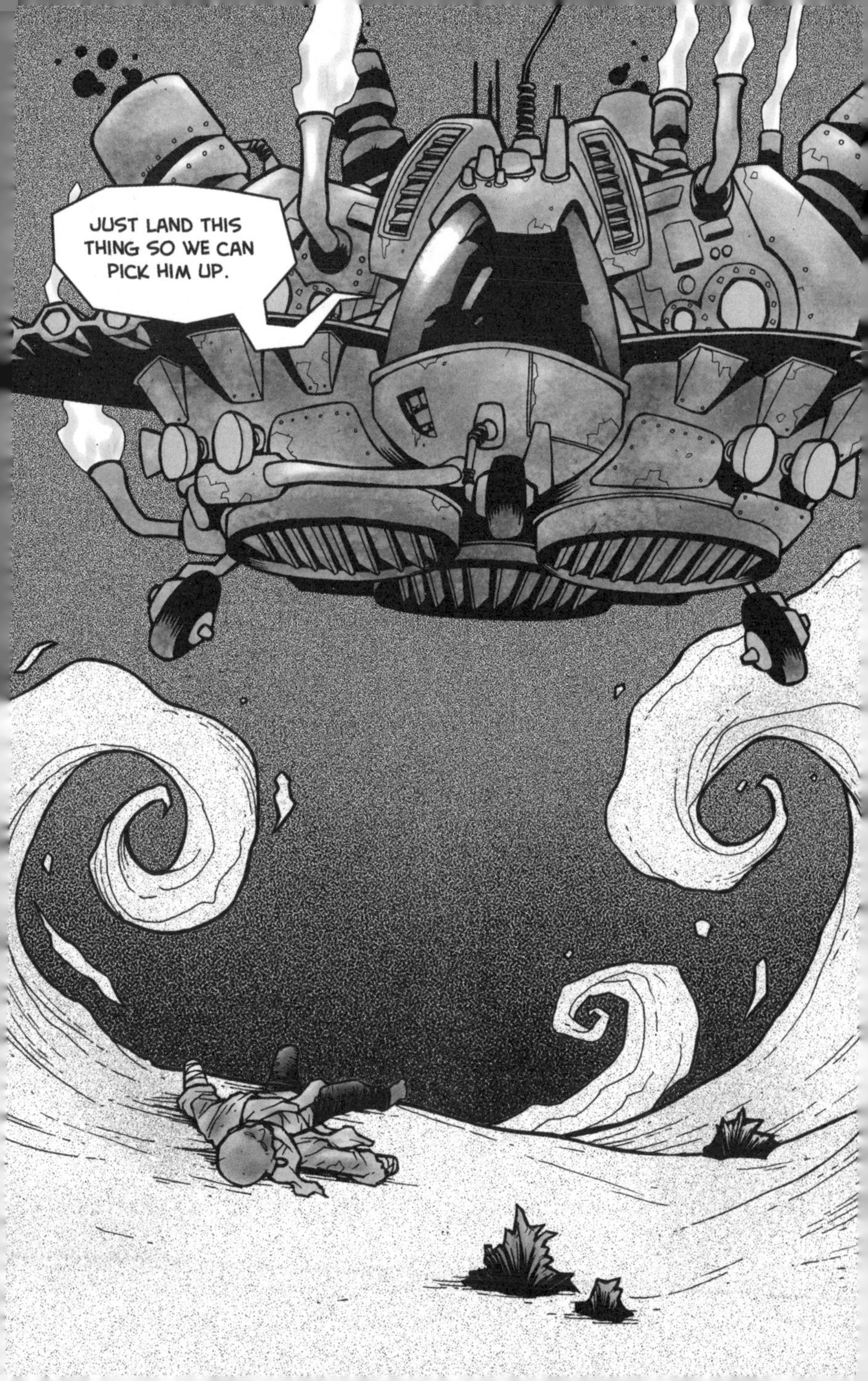
JUST LAND THIS THING SO WE CAN PICK HIM UP.

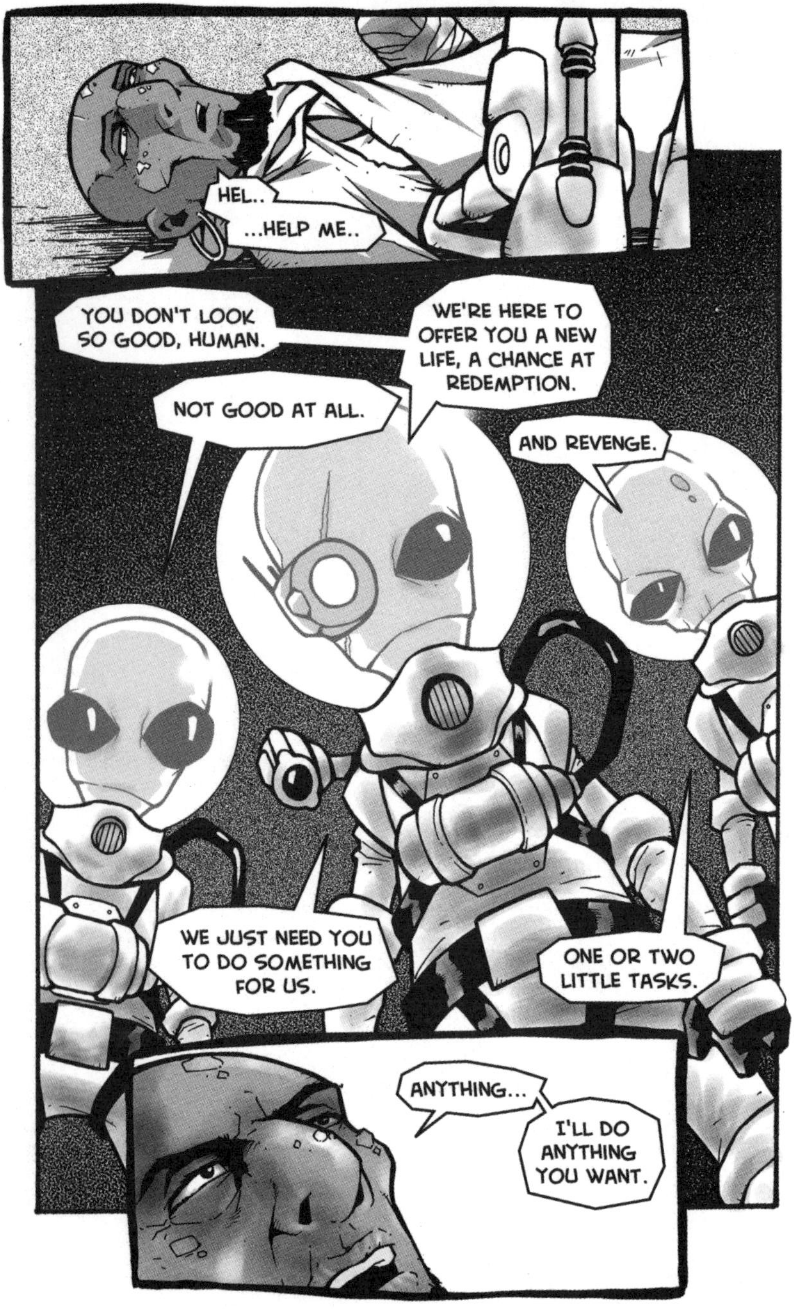
HEL..
...HELP ME..
YOU DON'T LOOK SO GOOD, HUMAN.
NOT GOOD AT ALL.
WE'RE HERE TO OFFER YOU A NEW LIFE, A CHANCE AT REDEMPTION.
AND REVENGE.
WE JUST NEED YOU TO DO SOMETHING FOR US.
ONE OR TWO LITTLE TASKS.
ANYTHING...
I'LL DO ANYTHING YOU WANT.

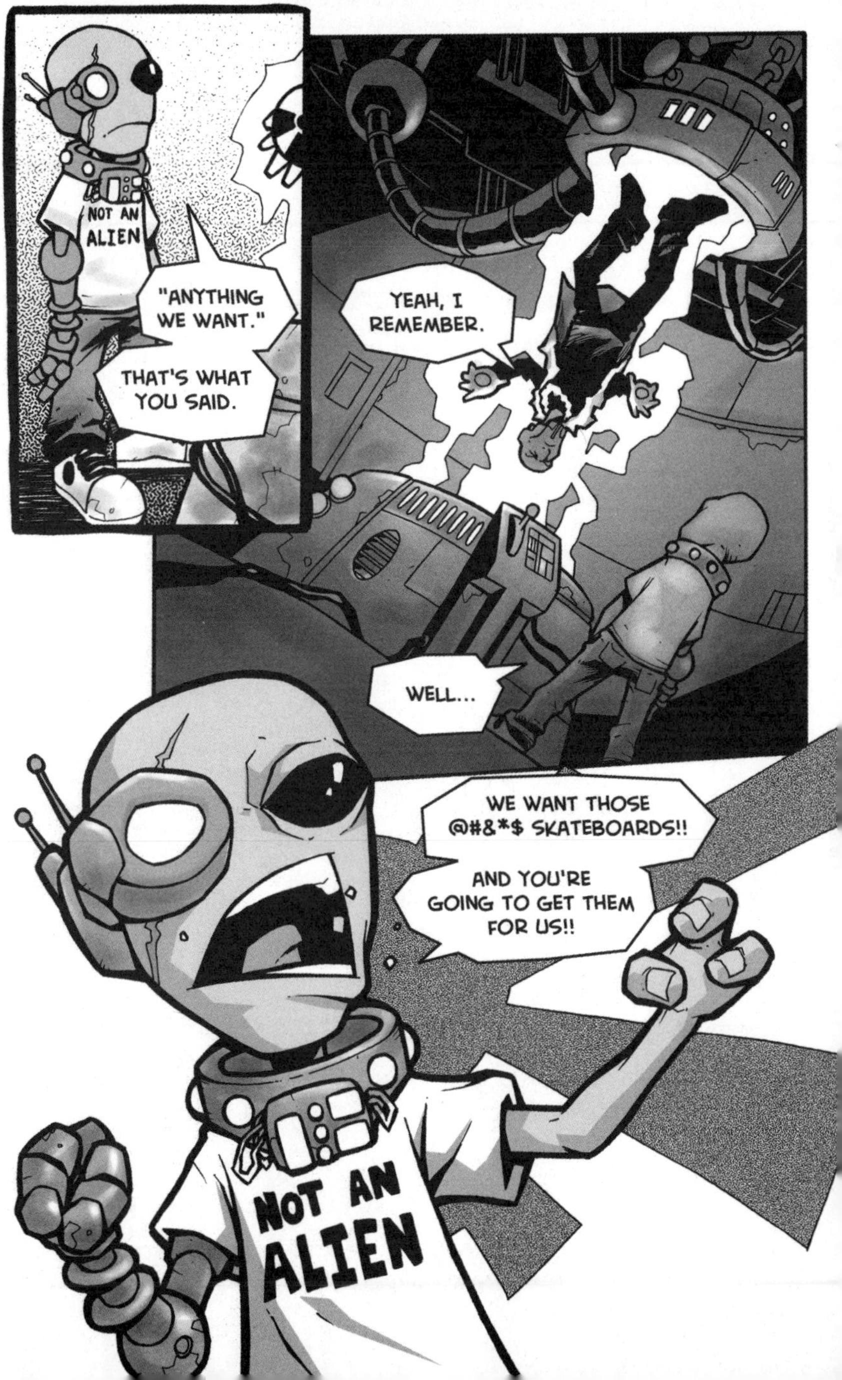
NOT AN ALIEN
"ANYTHING WE WANT."
THAT'S WHAT YOU SAID.
YEAH, I REMEMBER.
WELL...
WE WANT THOSE @#&*$ SKATEBOARDS!!
AND YOU'RE GOING TO GET THEM FOR US!!
NOT AN ALIEN

chapter three

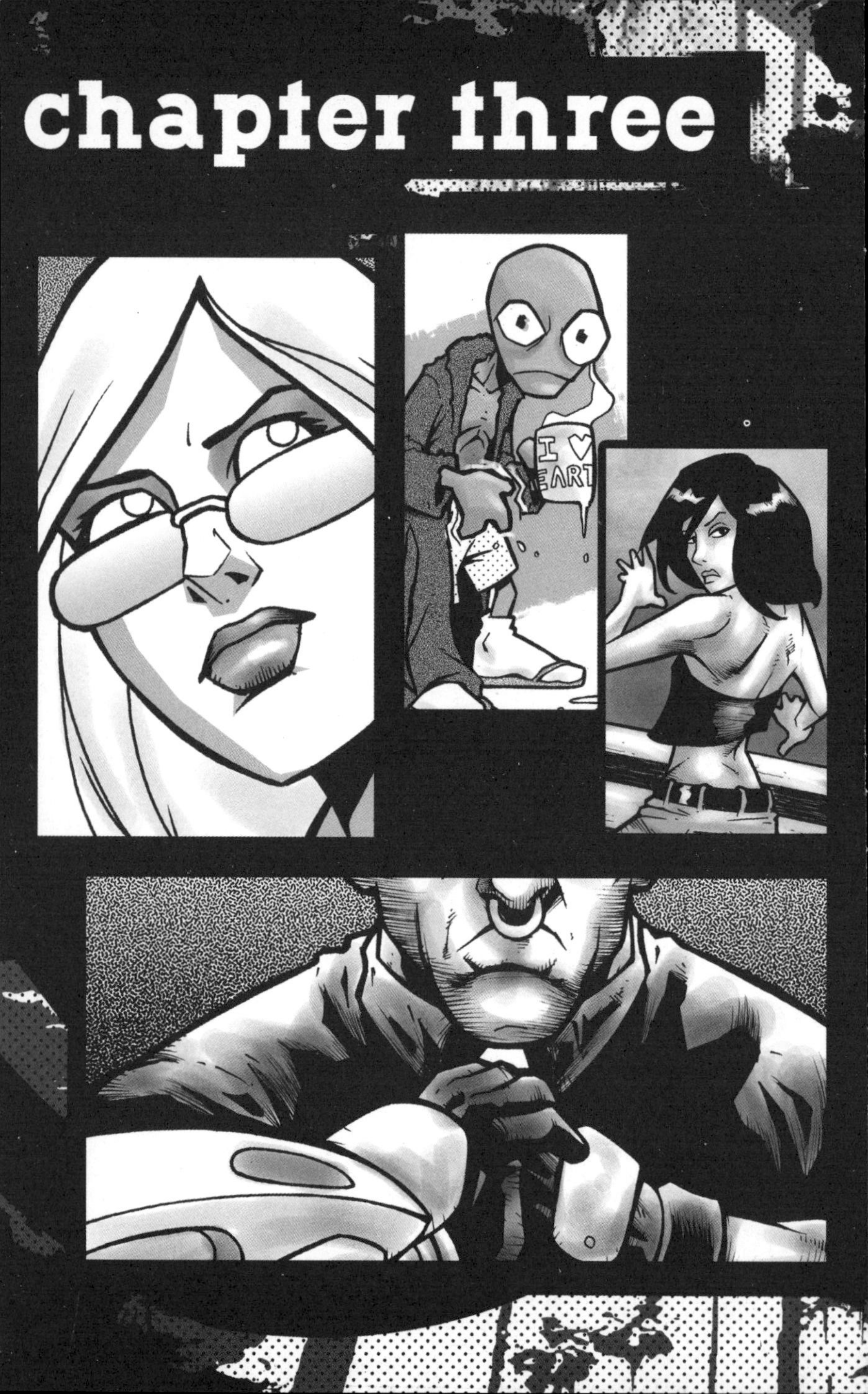

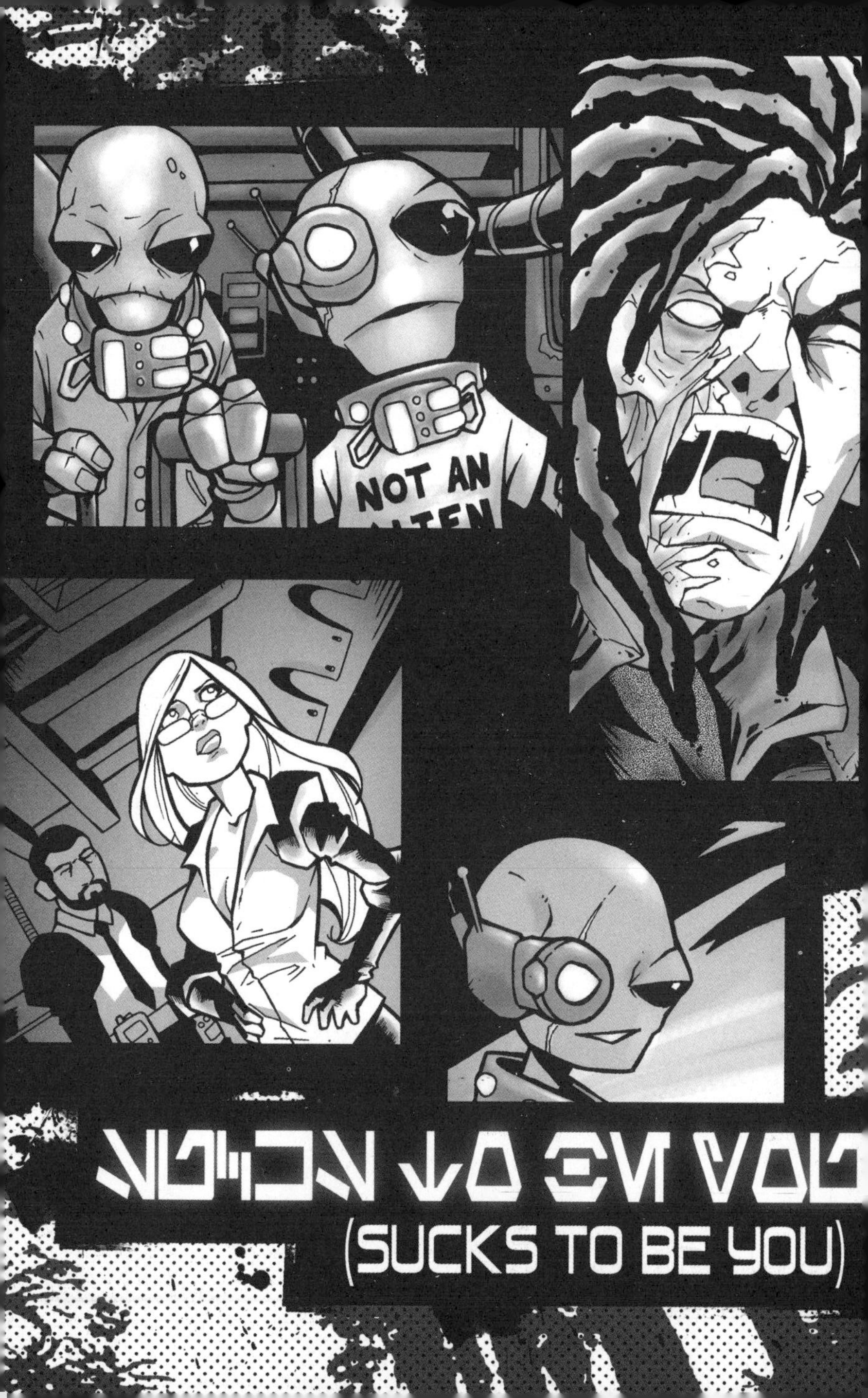
NOT AN
(SUCKS TO BE YOU)

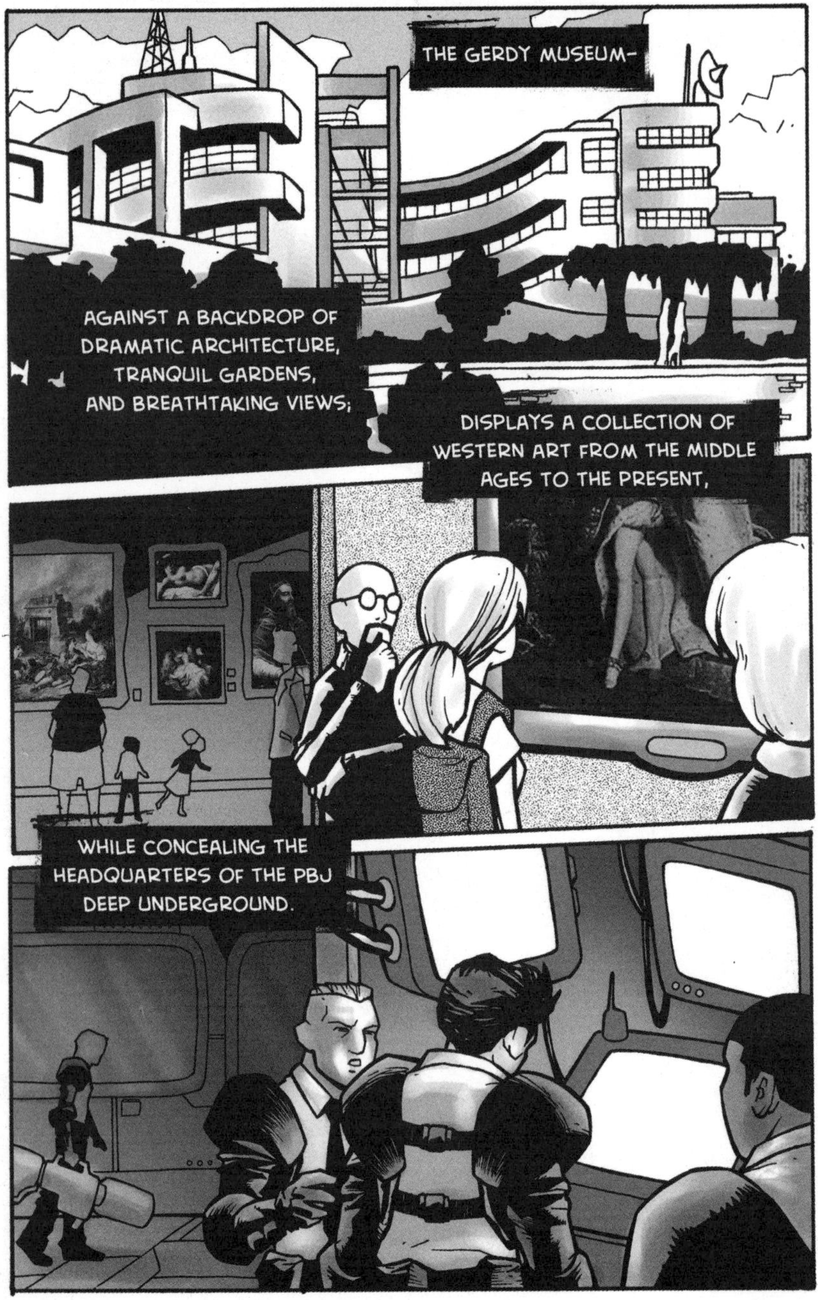
THE GERDY MUSEUM-
AGAINST A BACKDROP OF DRAMATIC ARCHITECTURE, TRANQUIL GARDENS, AND BREATHTAKING VIEWS;
DISPLAYS A COLLECTION OF WESTERN ART FROM THE MIDDLE AGES TO THE PRESENT,
WHILE CONCEALING THE HEADQUARTERS OF THE PBJ DEEP UNDERGROUND.

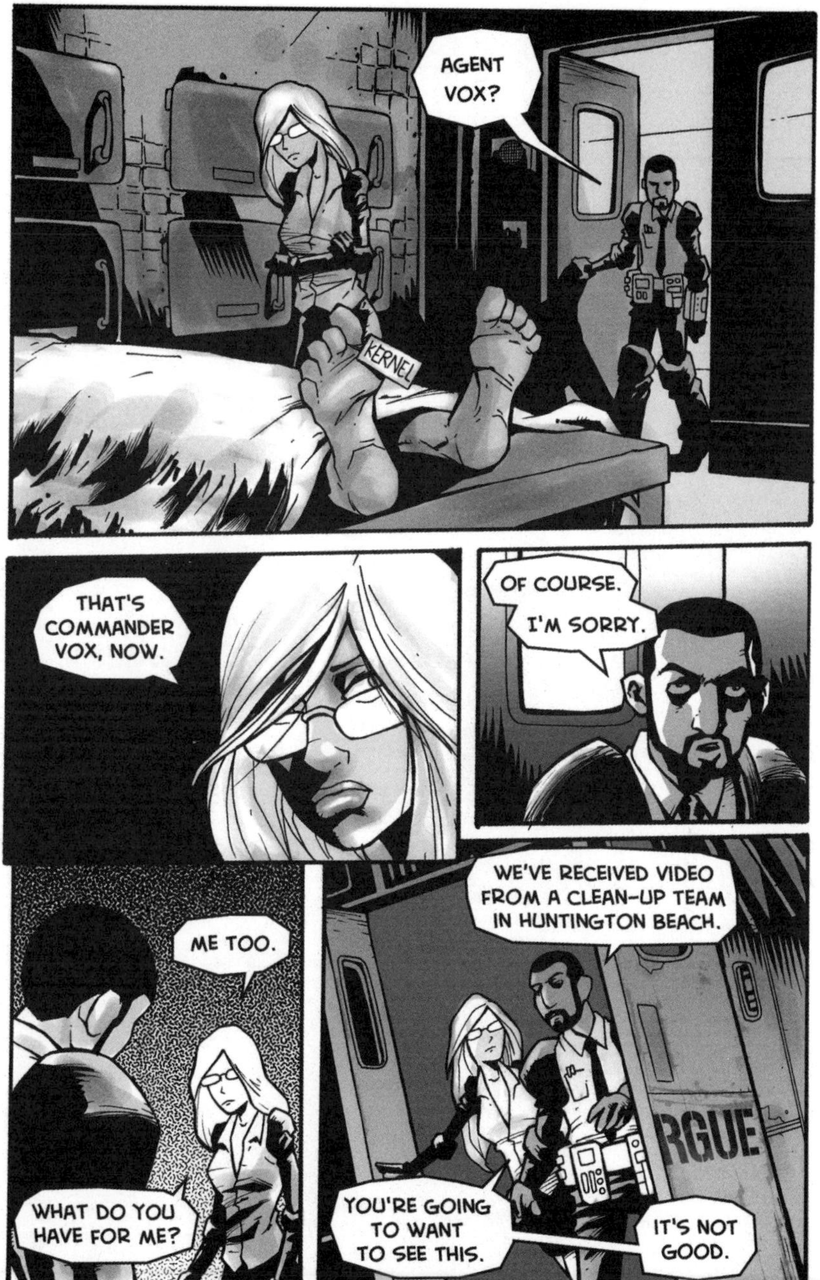
AGENT VOX?
KERNEL
THAT'S COMMANDER VOX, NOW.
OF COURSE.
I'M SORRY.
ME TOO.
WHAT DO YOU HAVE FOR ME?
WE'VE RECEIVED VIDEO FROM A CLEAN-UP TEAM IN HUNTINGTON BEACH.
RGUE
YOU'RE GOING TO WANT TO SEE THIS.
IT'S NOT GOOD.

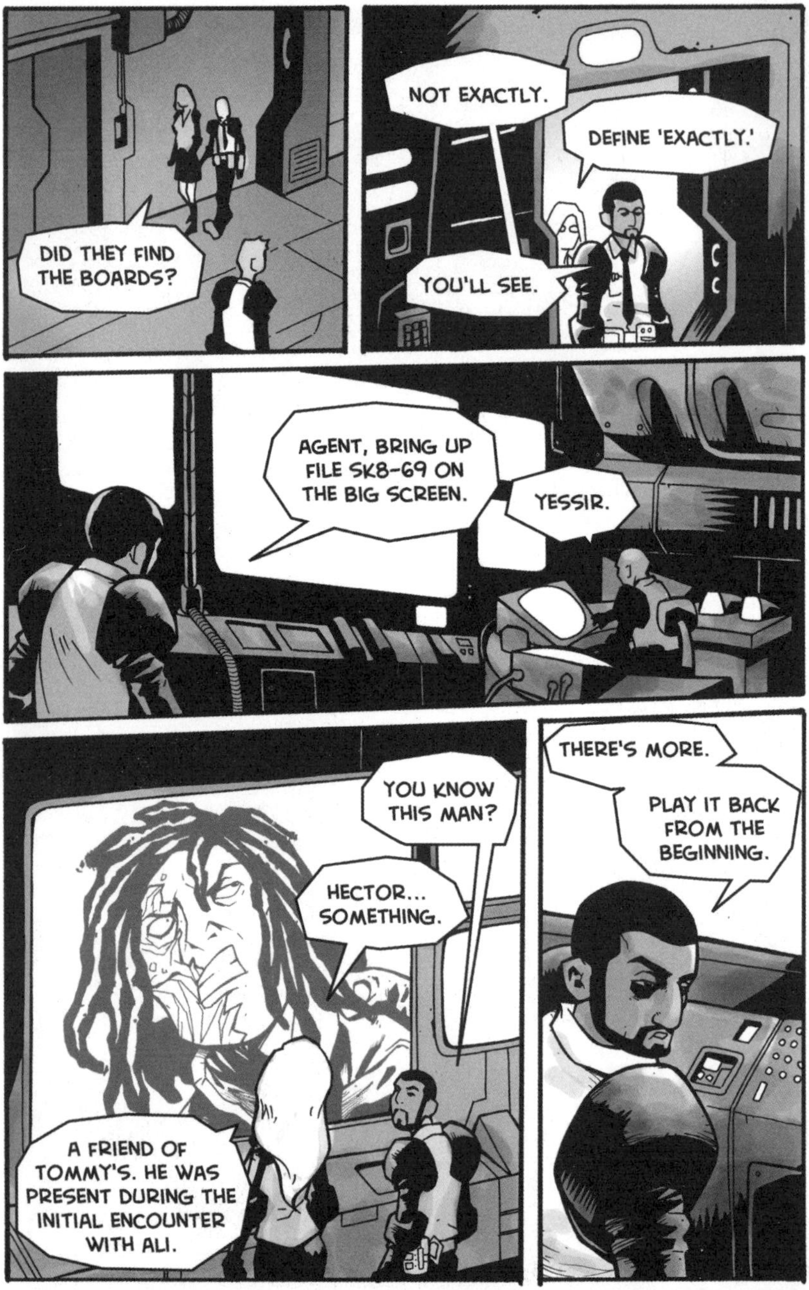
DID THEY FIND THE BOARDS?
NOT EXACTLY.
DEFINE 'EXACTLY.'
YOU'LL SEE.
AGENT, BRING UP FILE SK8-69 ON THE BIG SCREEN.
YESSIR.
YOU KNOW THIS MAN?
HECTOR... SOMETHING.
A FRIEND OF TOMMY'S. HE WAS PRESENT DURING THE INITIAL ENCOUNTER WITH ALI.
THERE'S MORE.
PLAY IT BACK FROM THE BEGINNING.

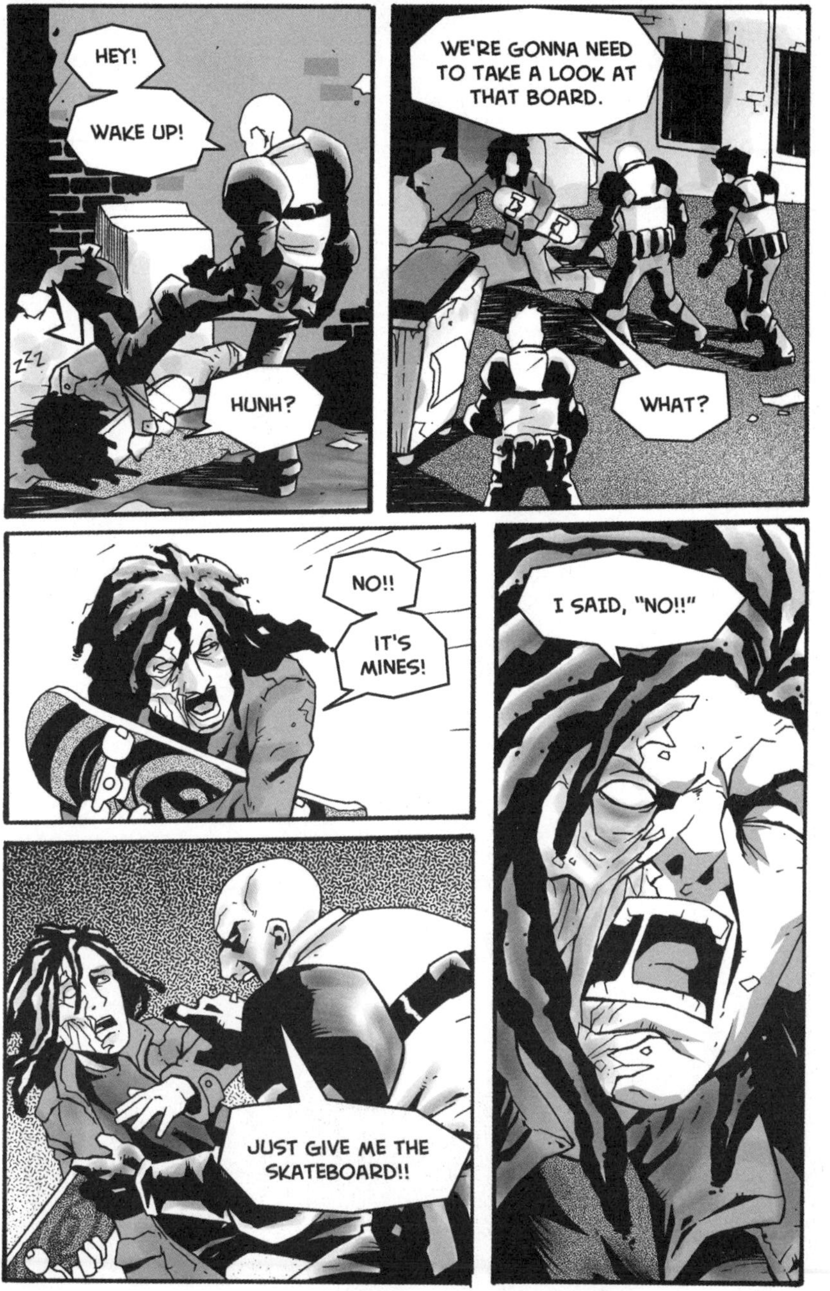
HEY!
WAKE UP!
ZZZ
HUNH?
WE'RE GONNA NEED TO TAKE A LOOK AT THAT BOARD.
WHAT?
NO!!
IT'S MINES!
I SAID, "NO!!"
JUST GIVE ME THE SKATEBOARD!!

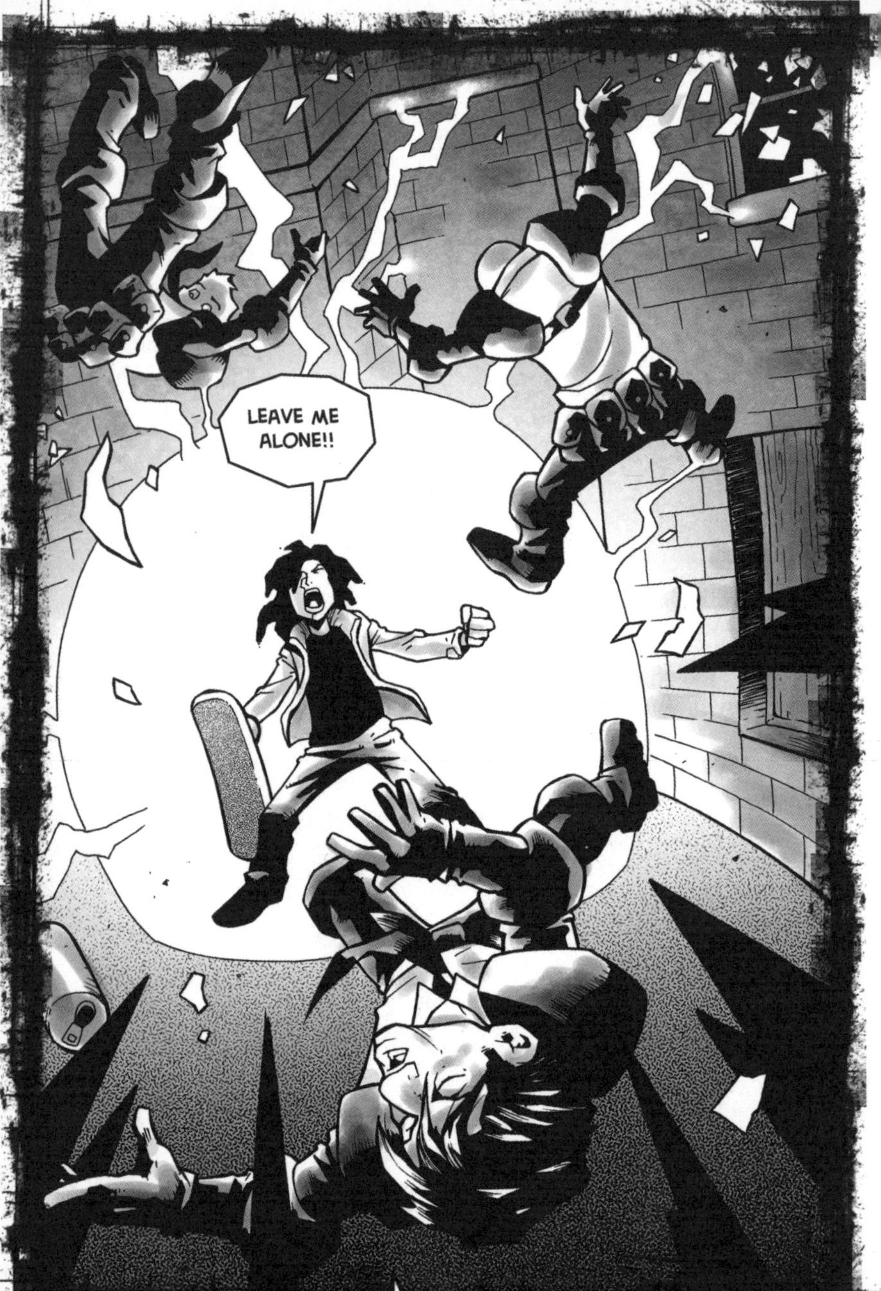
LEAVE ME ALONE!!

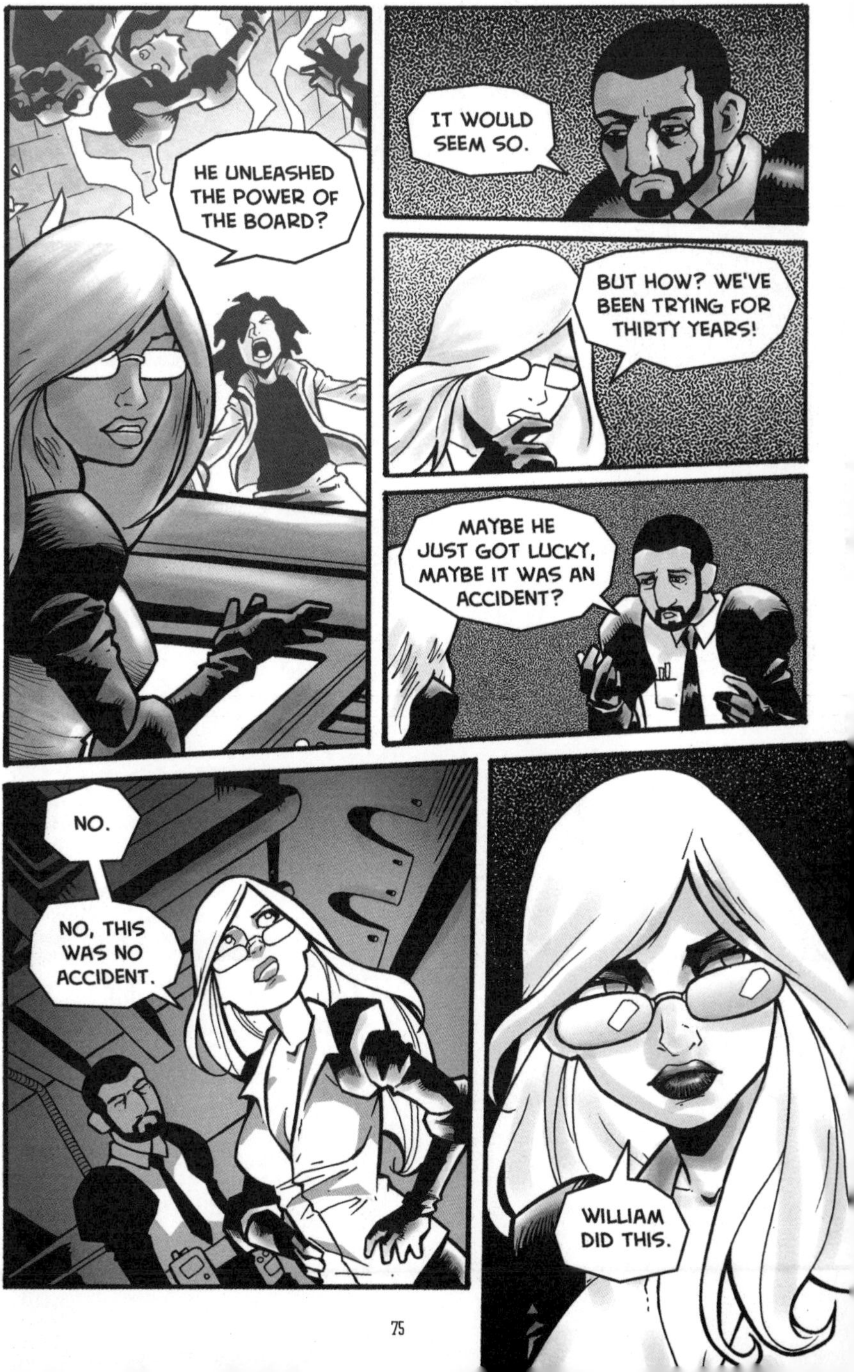

HE UNLEASHED THE POWER OF THE BOARD?
IT WOULD SEEM SO.
BUT HOW? WE'VE BEEN TRYING FOR THIRTY YEARS!
MAYBE HE JUST GOT LUCKY, MAYBE IT WAS AN ACCIDENT?
NO.
NO, THIS WAS NO ACCIDENT.
WILLIAM DID THIS.

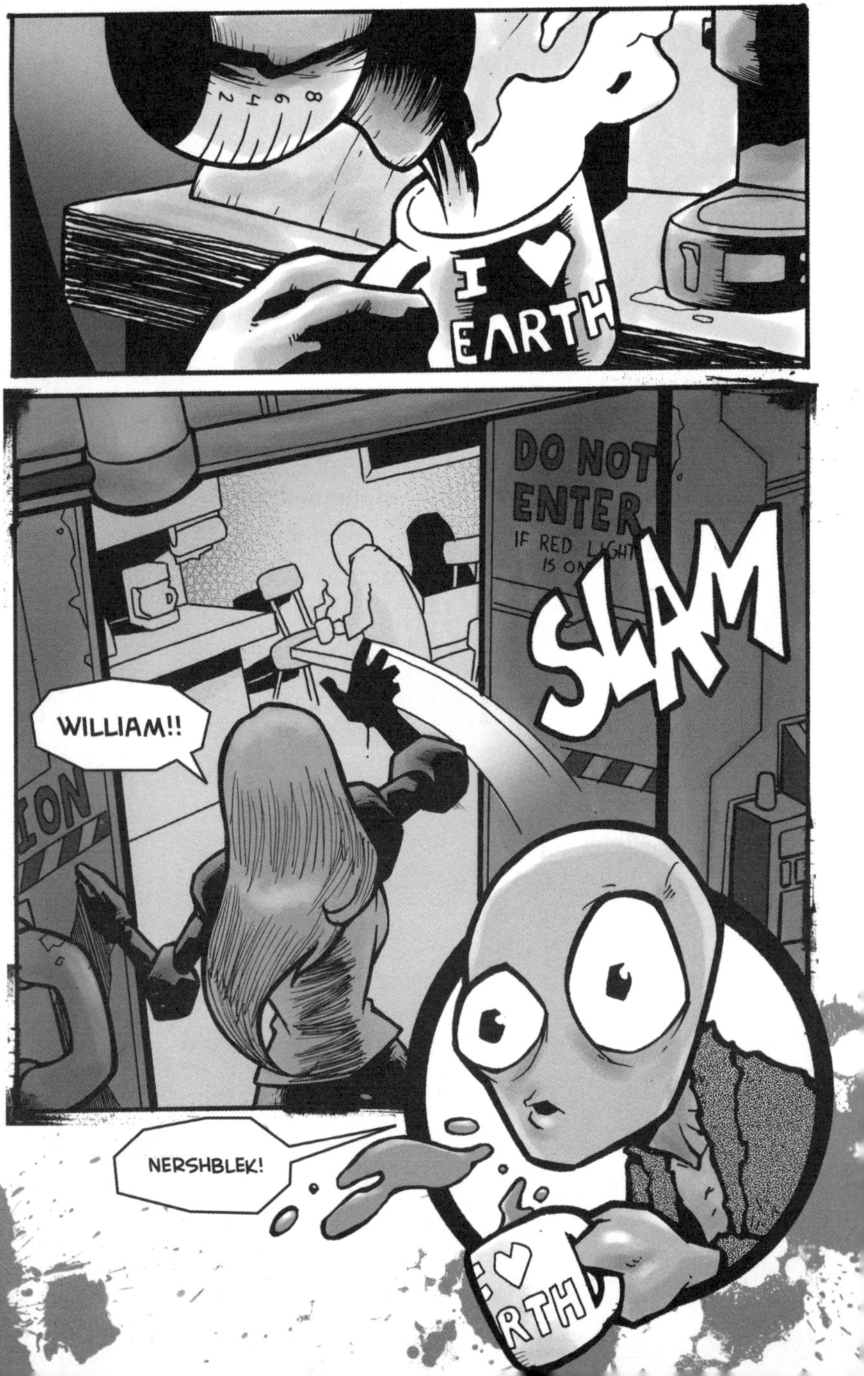

8
9
4
2
I ♥
EARTH
DO NOT
ENTER
IF RED LIGHT
IS ON
SLAM
WILLIAM!!
NERSHBLEK!
♥
RTH

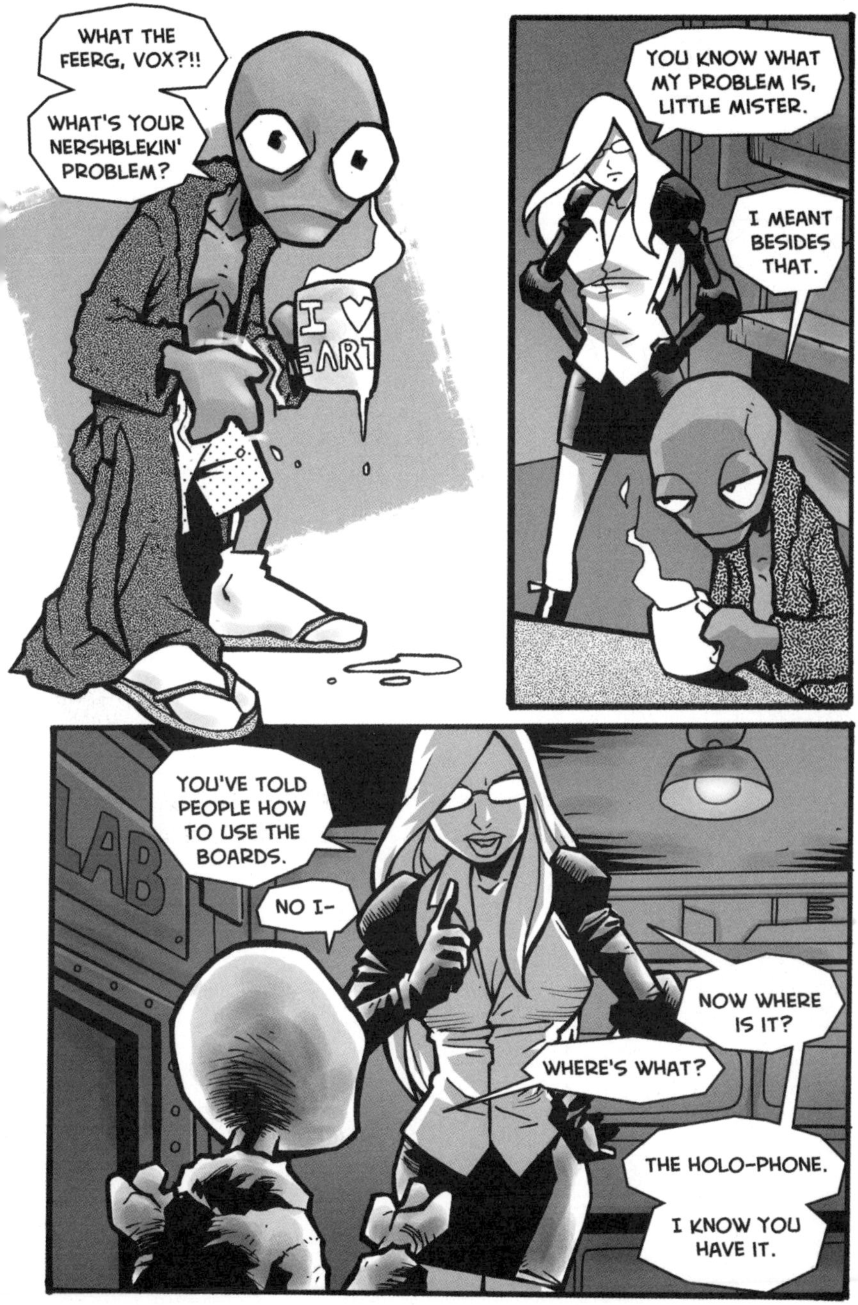
WHAT THE FEERG, VOX?!!
WHAT'S YOUR NERSHBLEKIN' PROBLEM?
I ♥ EART
YOU KNOW WHAT MY PROBLEM IS, LITTLE MISTER.
I MEANT BESIDES THAT.
LAB
YOU'VE TOLD PEOPLE HOW TO USE THE BOARDS.
NO I-
NOW WHERE IS IT?
WHERE'S WHAT?
THE HOLO-PHONE.
I KNOW YOU HAVE IT.

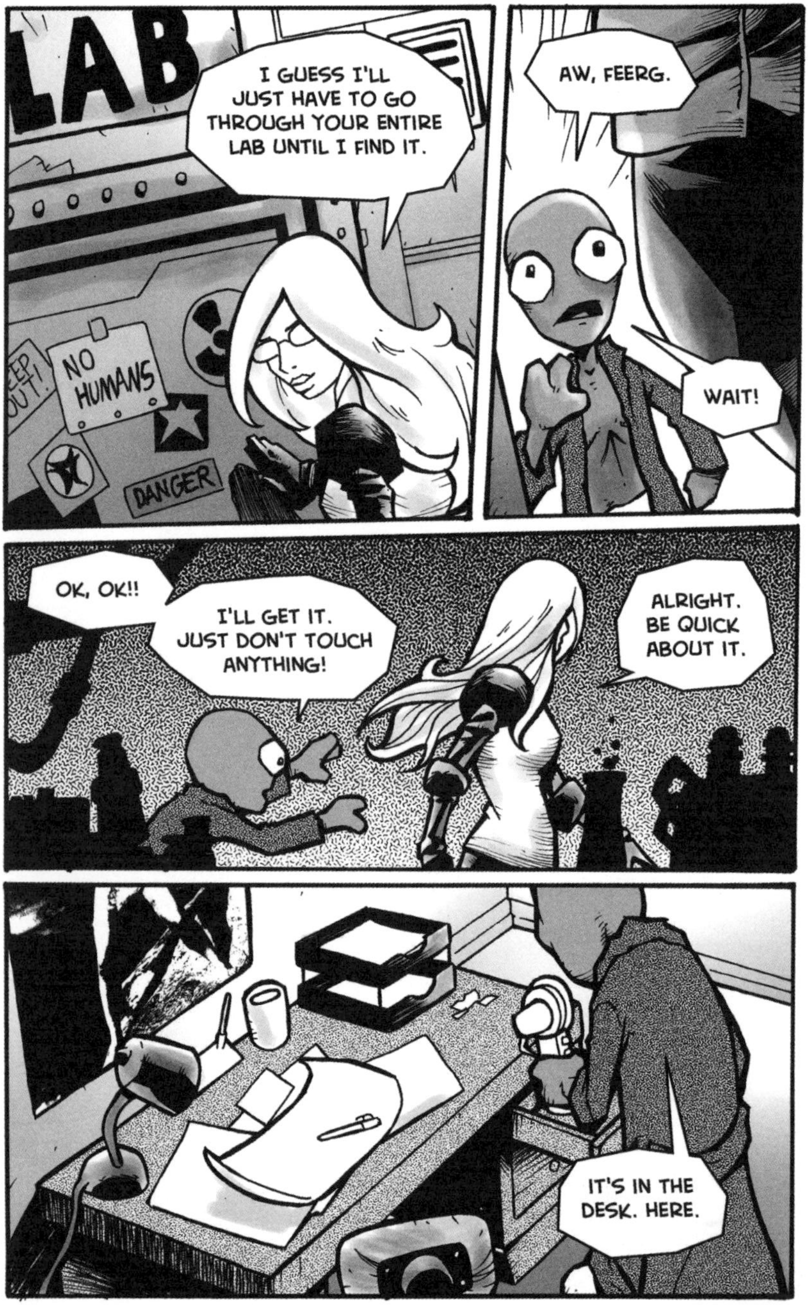
LAB
I GUESS I'LL JUST HAVE TO GO THROUGH YOUR ENTIRE LAB UNTIL I FIND IT.
NO HUMANS
DANGER
AW, FEERG.
WAIT!
OK, OK!!
I'LL GET IT. JUST DON'T TOUCH ANYTHING!
ALRIGHT. BE QUICK ABOUT IT.
IT'S IN THE DESK. HERE.

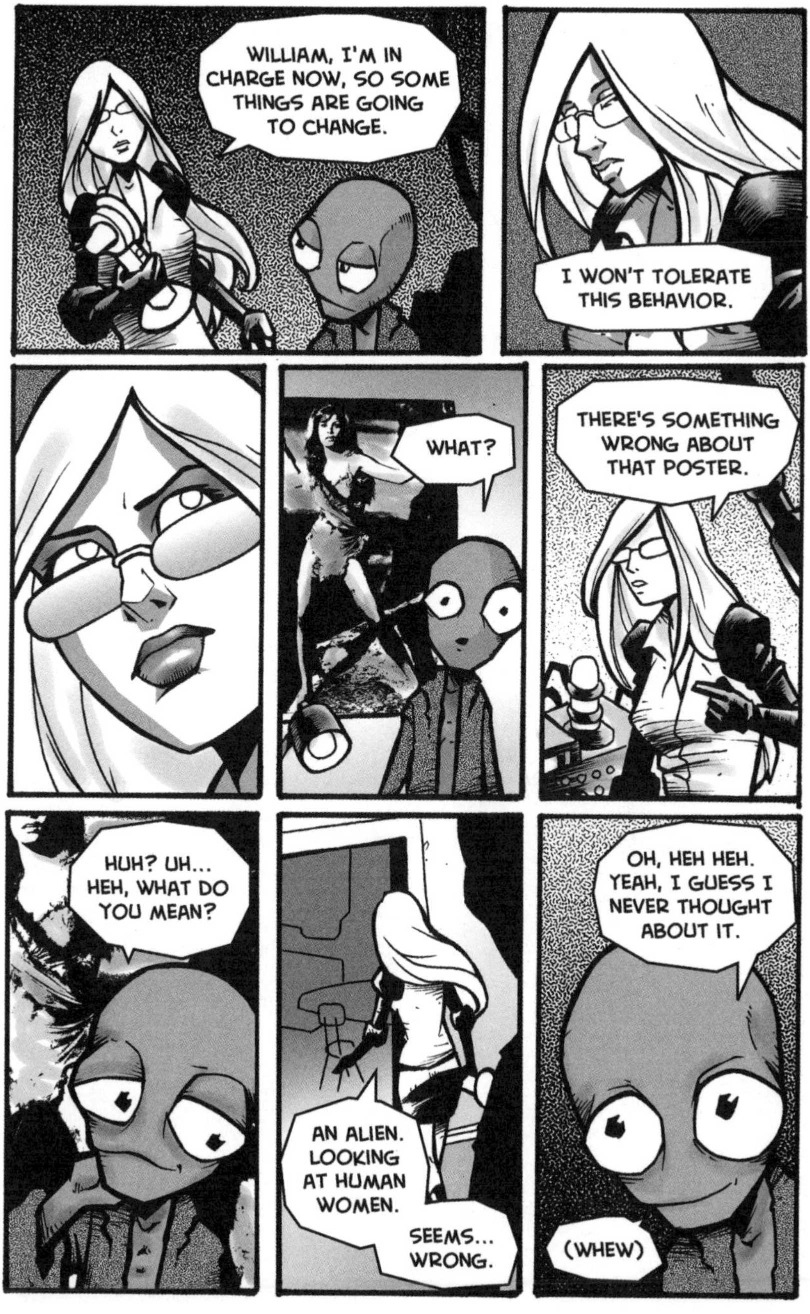
WILLIAM, I'M IN CHARGE NOW, SO SOME THINGS ARE GOING TO CHANGE.
I WON'T TOLERATE THIS BEHAVIOR.
WHAT?
THERE'S SOMETHING WRONG ABOUT THAT POSTER.
HUH? UH... HEH, WHAT DO YOU MEAN?
AN ALIEN. LOOKING AT HUMAN WOMEN.
SEEMS... WRONG.
OH, HEH HEH. YEAH, I GUESS I NEVER THOUGHT ABOUT IT.
(WHEW)

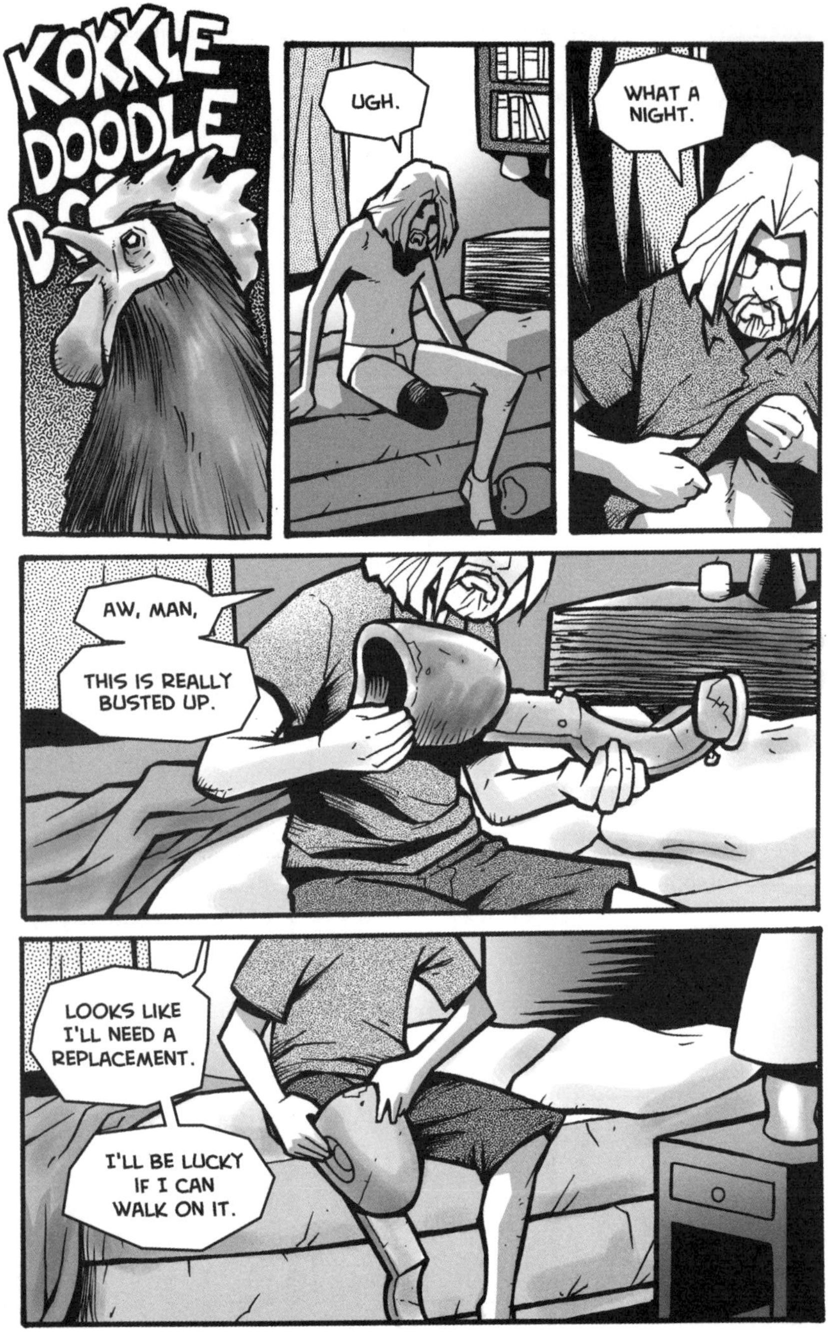
KOKKLE DOODLE D
UGH.
WHAT A NIGHT.
AW, MAN,
THIS IS REALLY BUSTED UP.
LOOKS LIKE I'LL NEED A REPLACEMENT.
I'LL BE LUCKY IF I CAN WALK ON IT.

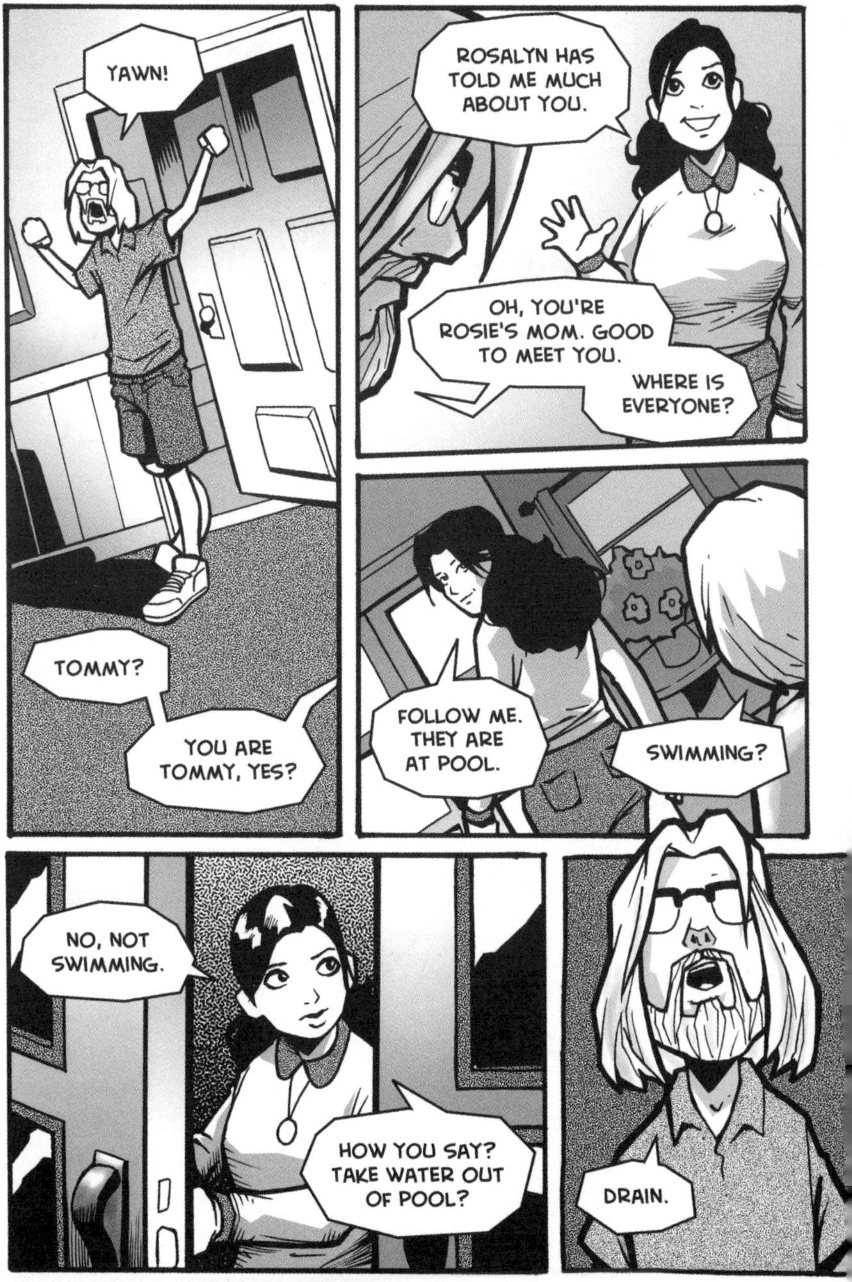
YAWN!
TOMMY?
YOU ARE TOMMY, YES?
ROSALYN HAS TOLD ME MUCH ABOUT YOU.
OH, YOU'RE ROSIE'S MOM. GOOD TO MEET YOU.
WHERE IS EVERYONE?
FOLLOW ME. THEY ARE AT POOL.
SWIMMING?
NO, NOT SWIMMING.
HOW YOU SAY? TAKE WATER OUT OF POOL?
DRAIN.

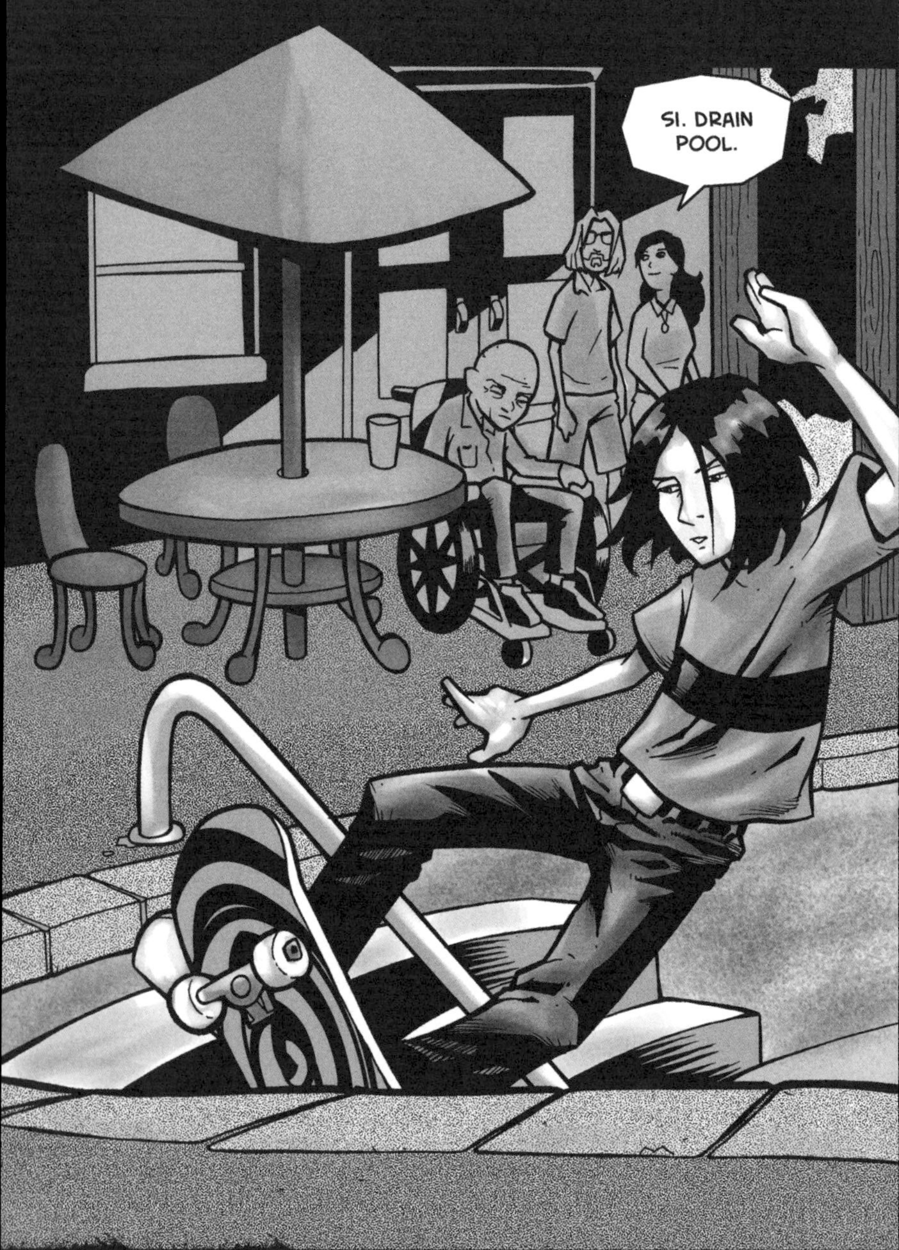
SI. DRAIN POOL.

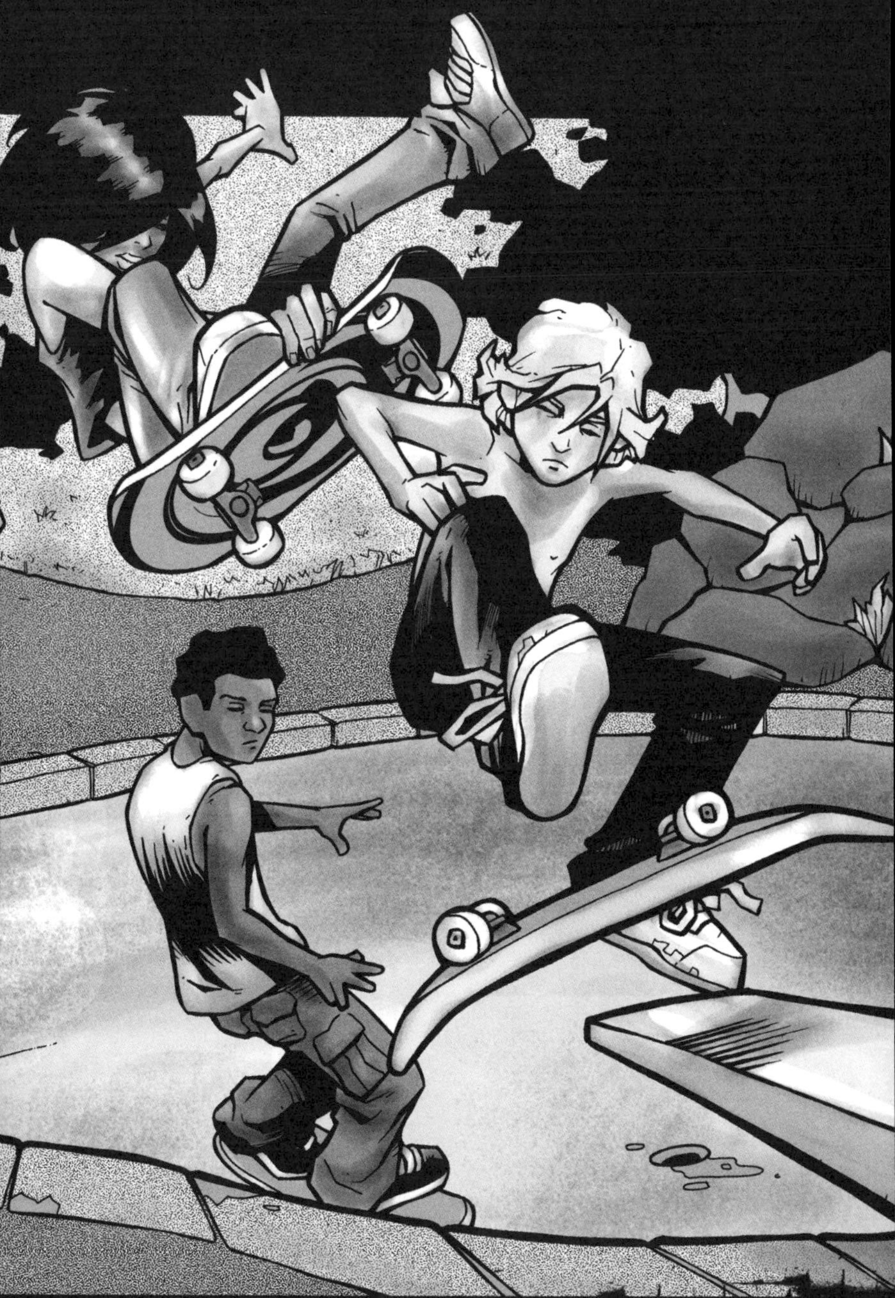

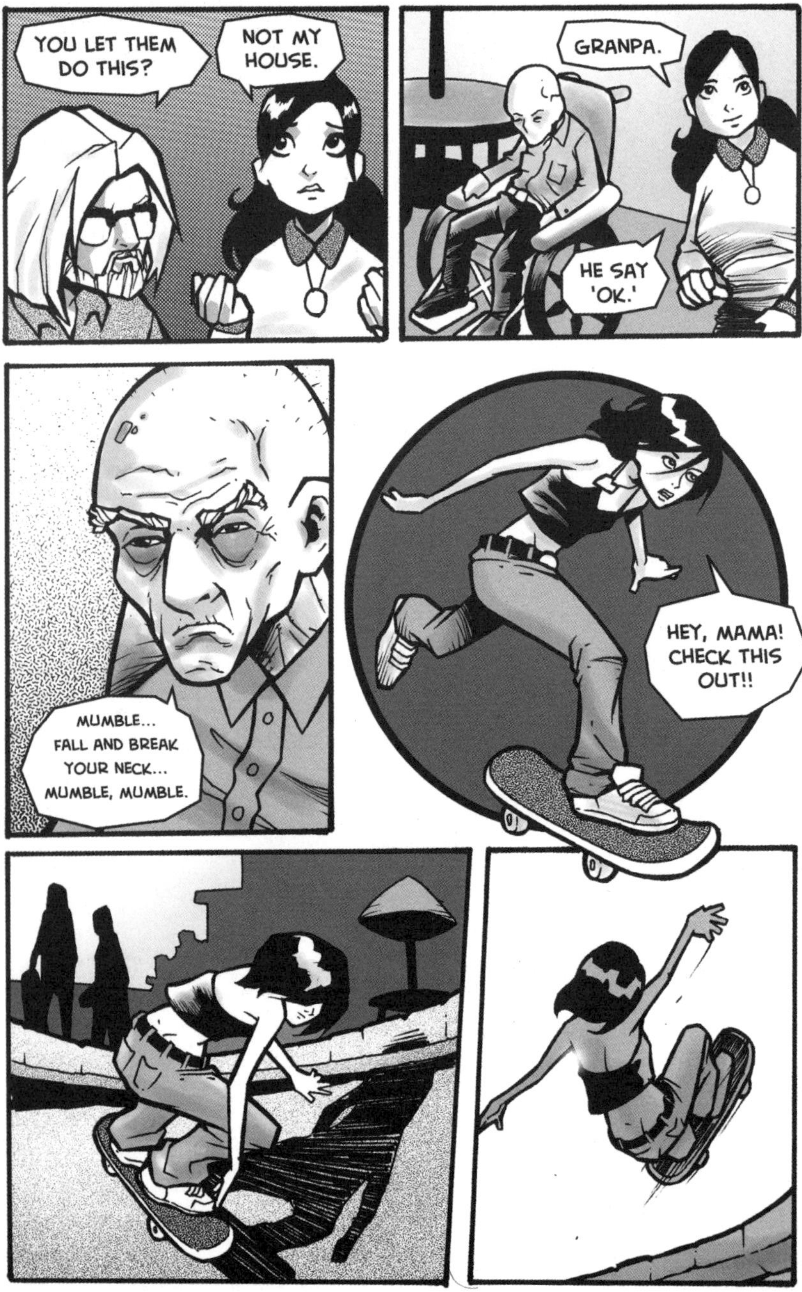
YOU LET THEM DO THIS?
NOT MY HOUSE.
GRANPA.
HE SAY 'OK.'
MUMBLE... FALL AND BREAK YOUR NECK... MUMBLE, MUMBLE.
HEY, MAMA! CHECK THIS OUT!!

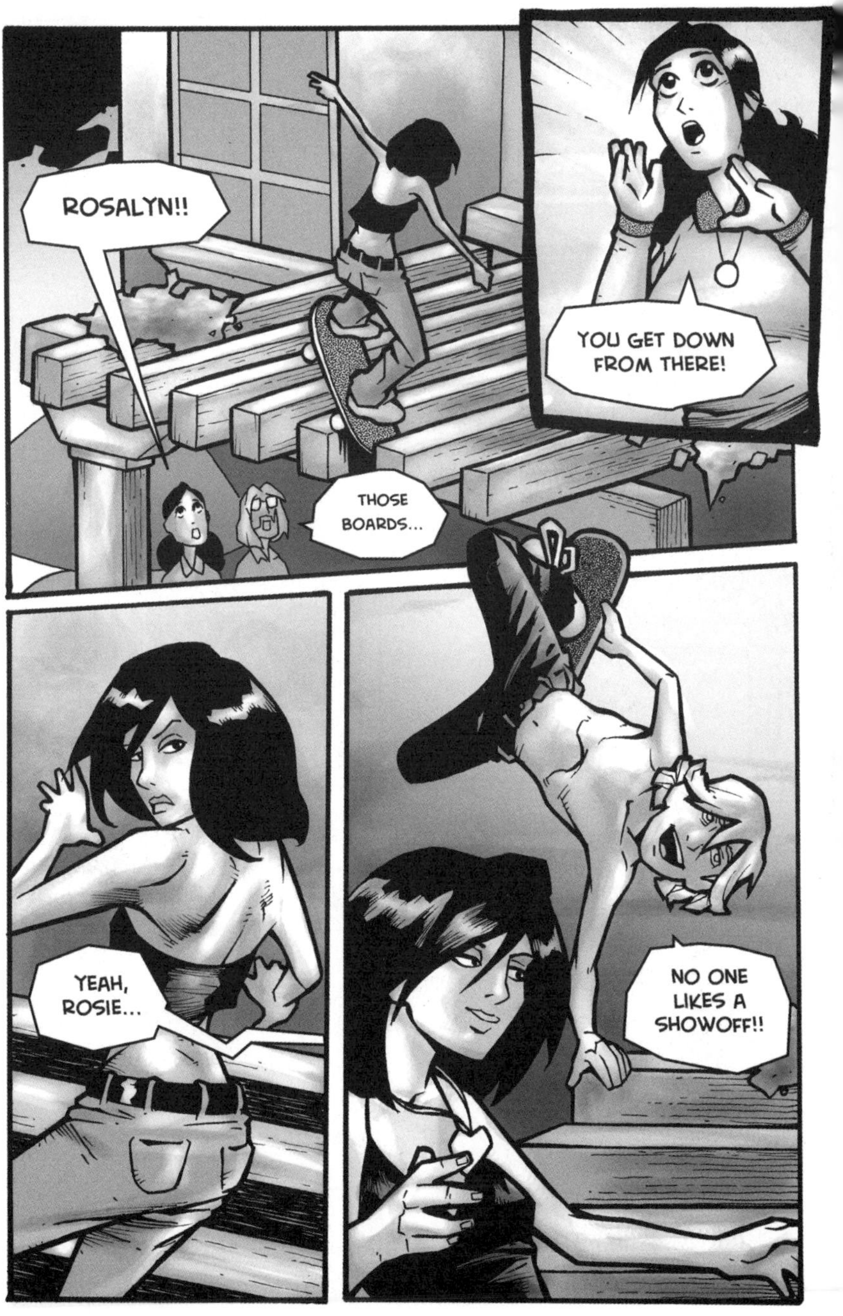

ROSALYN!!
YOU GET DOWN FROM THERE!
THOSE BOARDS...
YEAH, ROSIE...
NO ONE LIKES A SHOWOFF!!

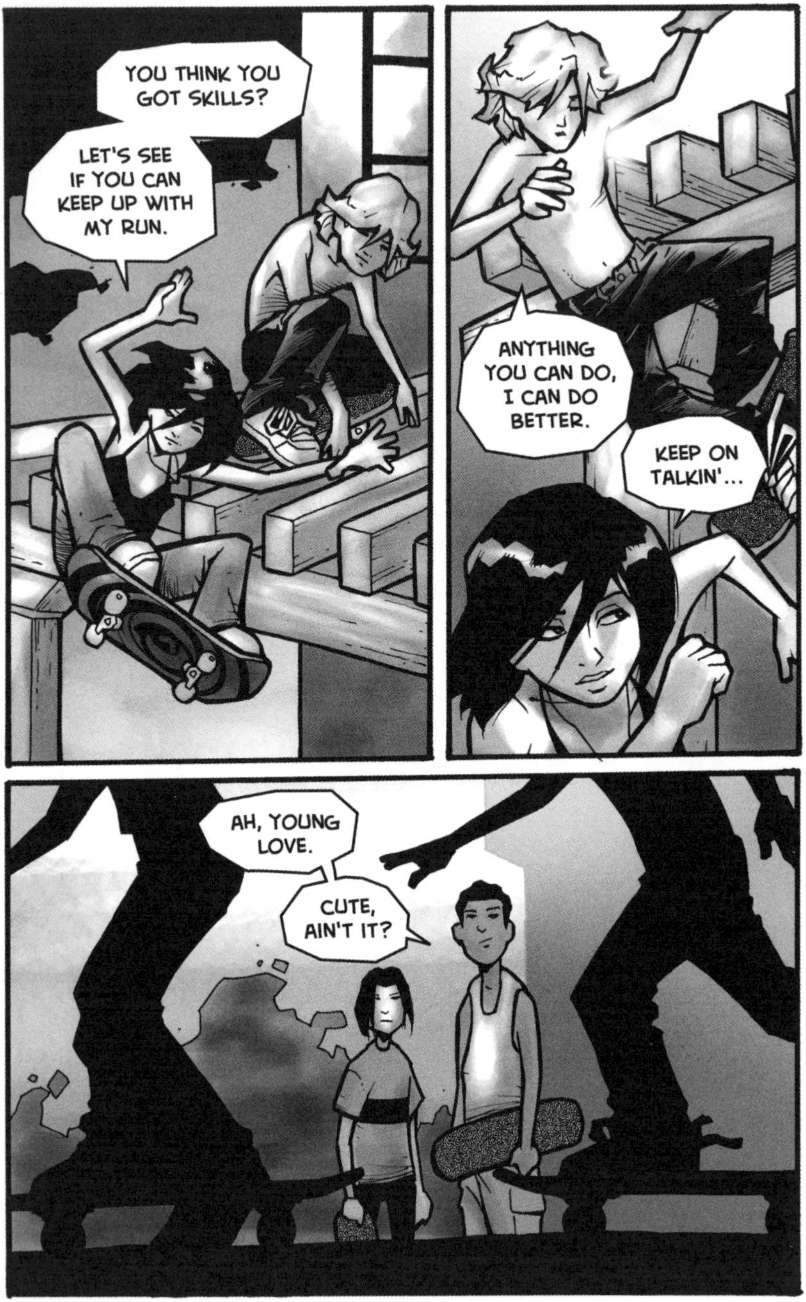
YOU THINK YOU GOT SKILLS?
LET'S SEE IF YOU CAN KEEP UP WITH MY RUN.
ANYTHING YOU CAN DO, I CAN DO BETTER.
KEEP ON TALKIN'...
AH, YOUNG LOVE.
CUTE, AIN'T IT?

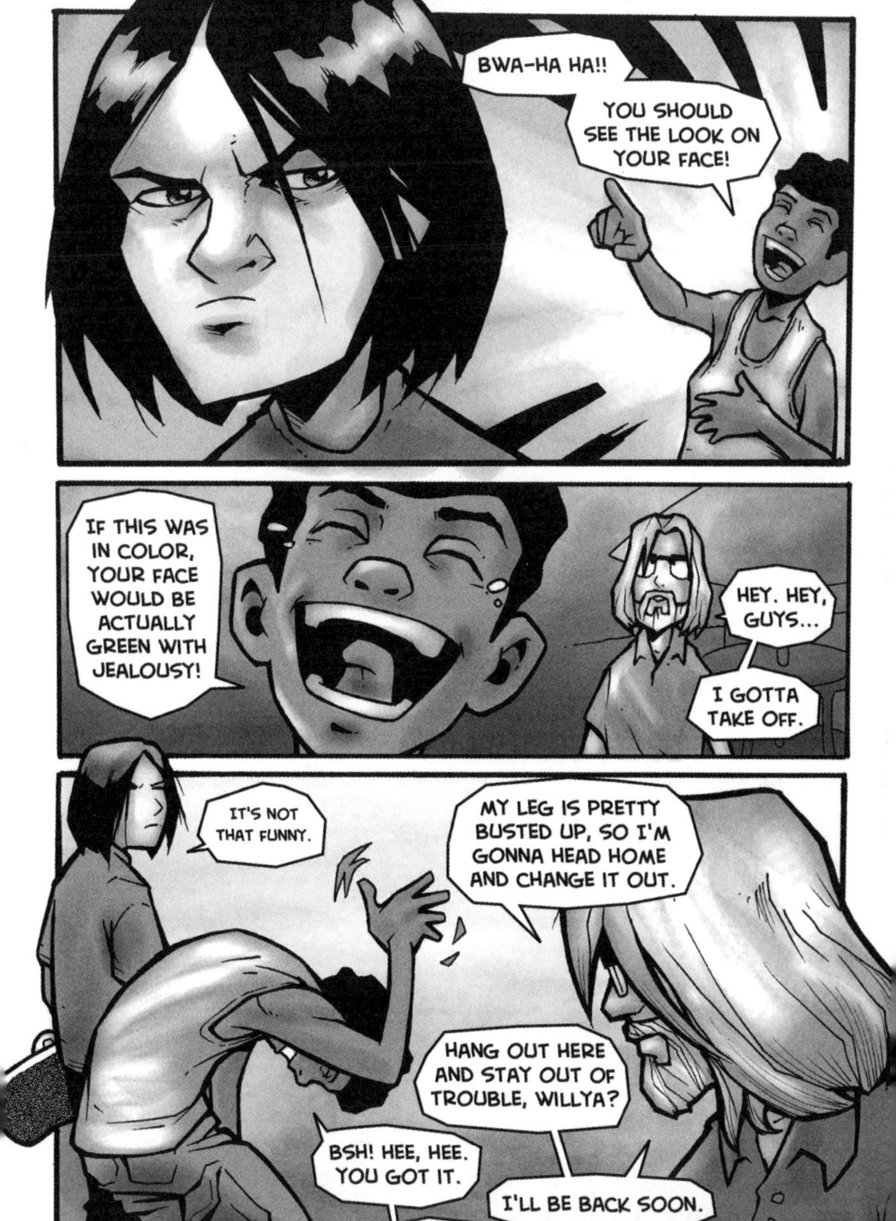
BWA-HA HA!!
YOU SHOULD SEE THE LOOK ON YOUR FACE!
IF THIS WAS IN COLOR, YOUR FACE WOULD BE ACTUALLY GREEN WITH JEALOUSY!
HEY. HEY, GUYS...
I GOTTA TAKE OFF.
IT'S NOT THAT FUNNY.
MY LEG IS PRETTY BUSTED UP, SO I'M GONNA HEAD HOME AND CHANGE IT OUT.
HANG OUT HERE AND STAY OUT OF TROUBLE, WILLYA?
BSH! HEE, HEE. YOU GOT IT.
HA HA HA LATER.
I'LL BE BACK SOON.

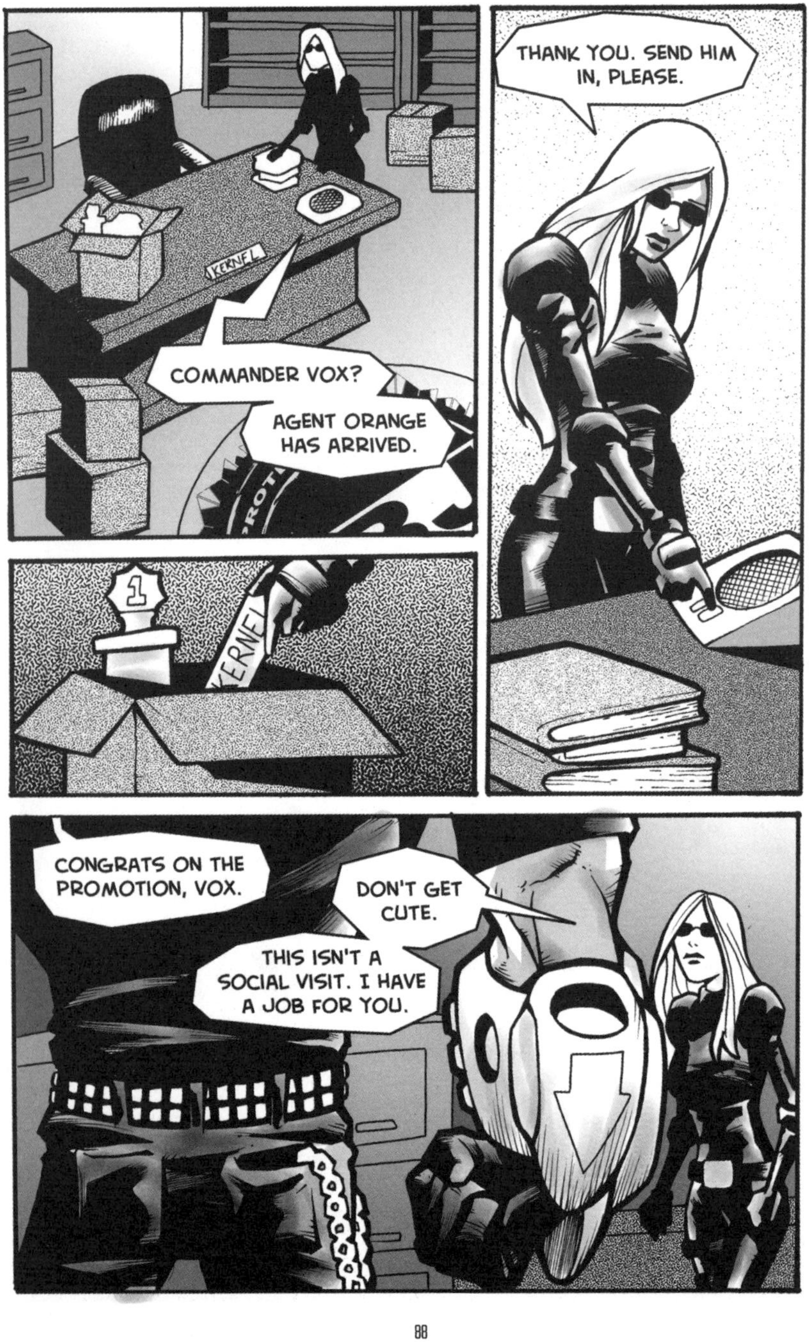
KERNEL
COMMANDER VOX?
AGENT ORANGE HAS ARRIVED.
THANK YOU. SEND HIM IN, PLEASE.
1
KERNEL
CONGRATS ON THE PROMOTION, VOX.
DON'T GET CUTE.
THIS ISN'T A SOCIAL VISIT. I HAVE A JOB FOR YOU.

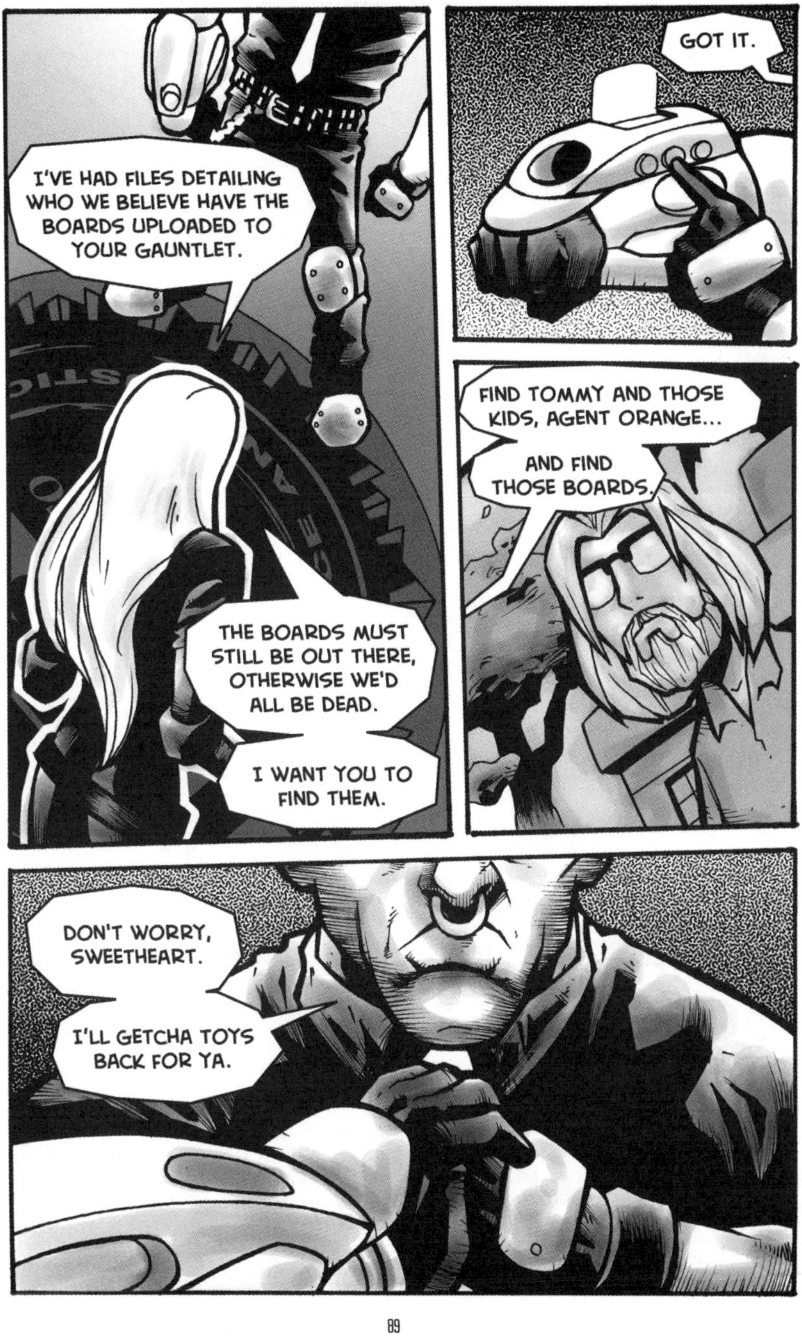
I'VE HAD FILES DETAILING WHO WE BELIEVE HAVE THE BOARDS UPLOADED TO YOUR GAUNTLET.
GOT IT.
THE BOARDS MUST STILL BE OUT THERE, OTHERWISE WE'D ALL BE DEAD.
I WANT YOU TO FIND THEM.
FIND TOMMY AND THOSE KIDS, AGENT ORANGE...
AND FIND THOSE BOARDS.
DON'T WORRY, SWEETHEART.
I'LL GETCHA TOYS BACK FOR YA.

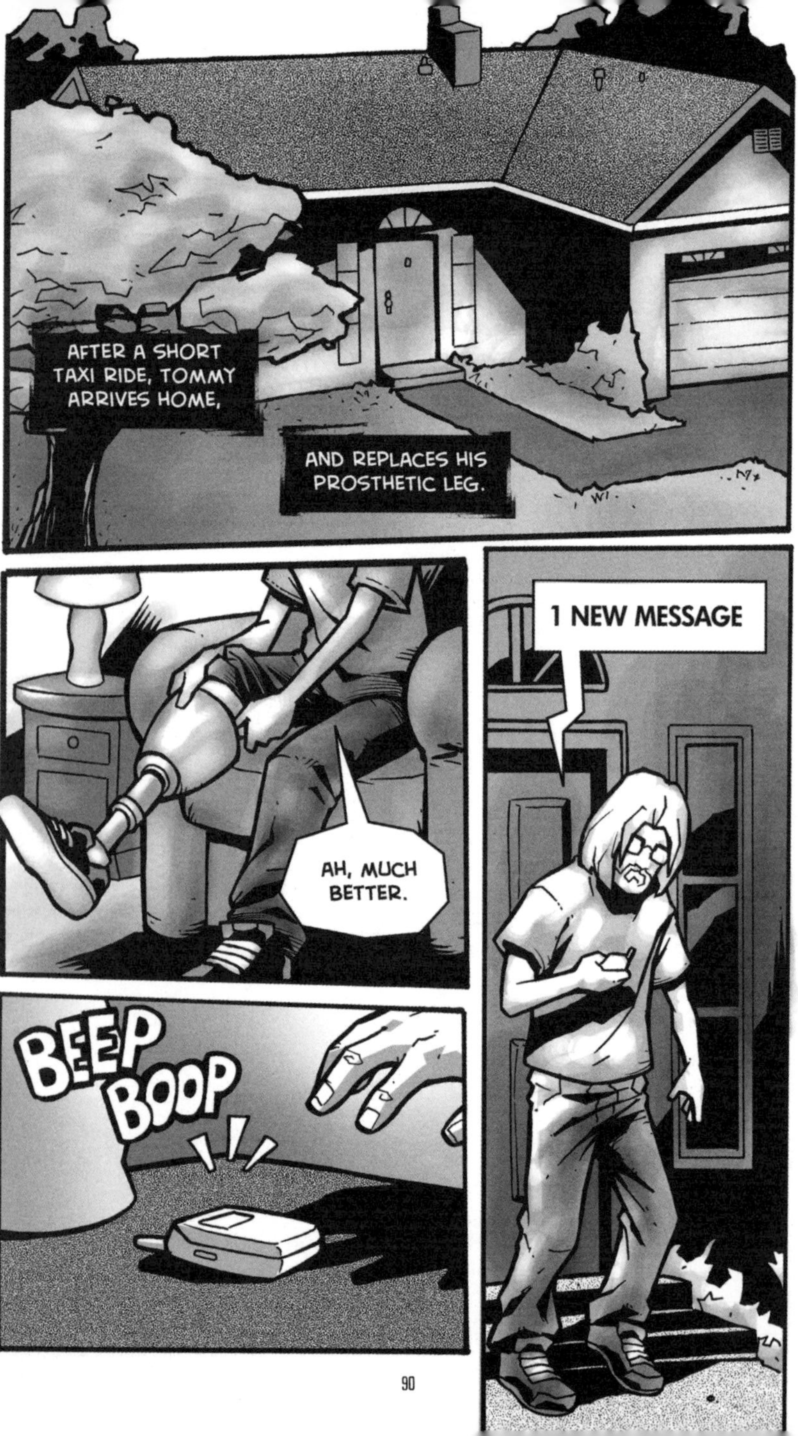
AFTER A SHORT TAXI RIDE, TOMMY ARRIVES HOME,
AND REPLACES HIS PROSTHETIC LEG.
AH, MUCH BETTER.
BEEP BOOP
1 NEW MESSAGE

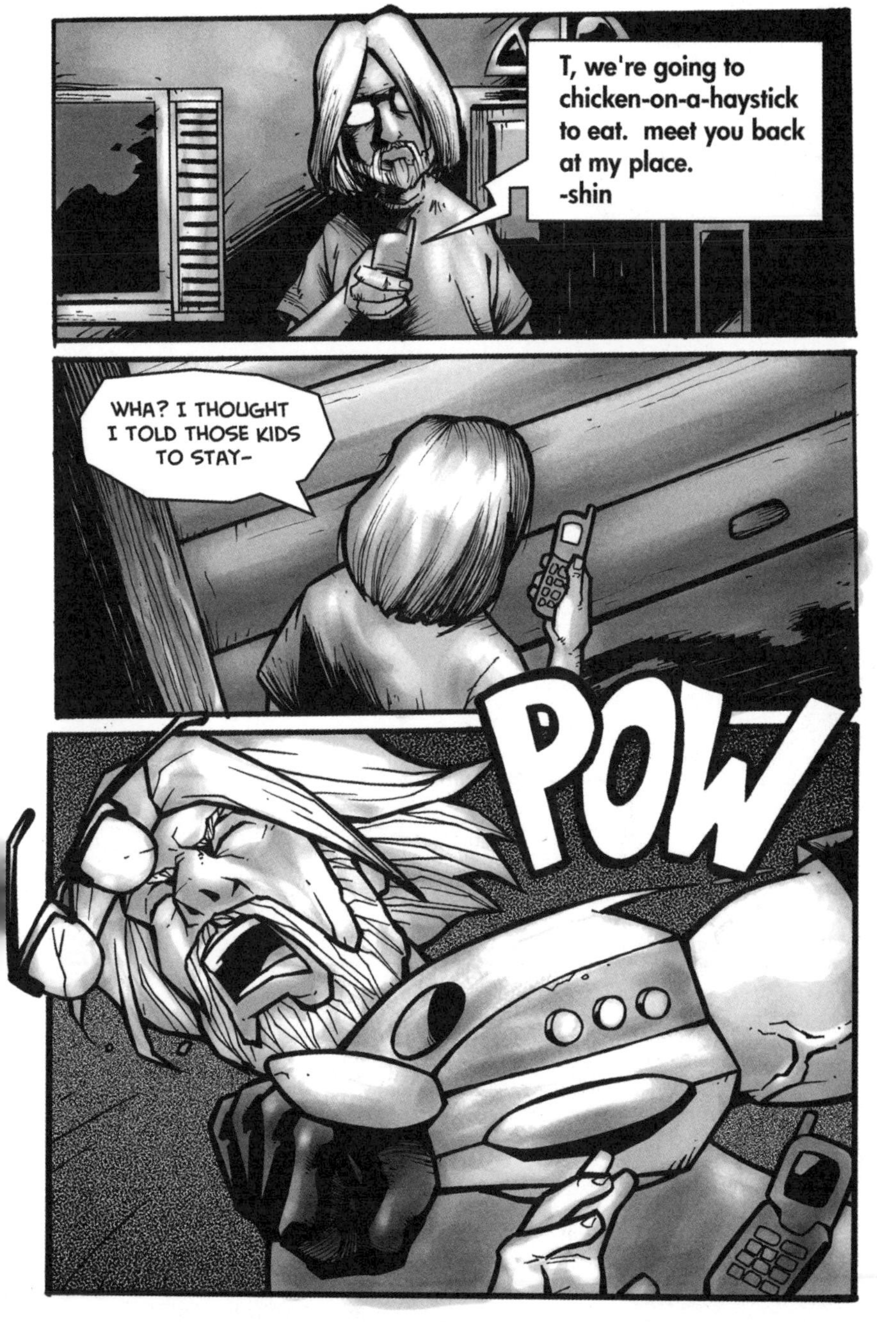
T, we're going to chicken-on-a-haystick to eat. meet you back at my place.
-shin
WHA? I THOUGHT I TOLD THOSE KIDS TO STAY-
POW

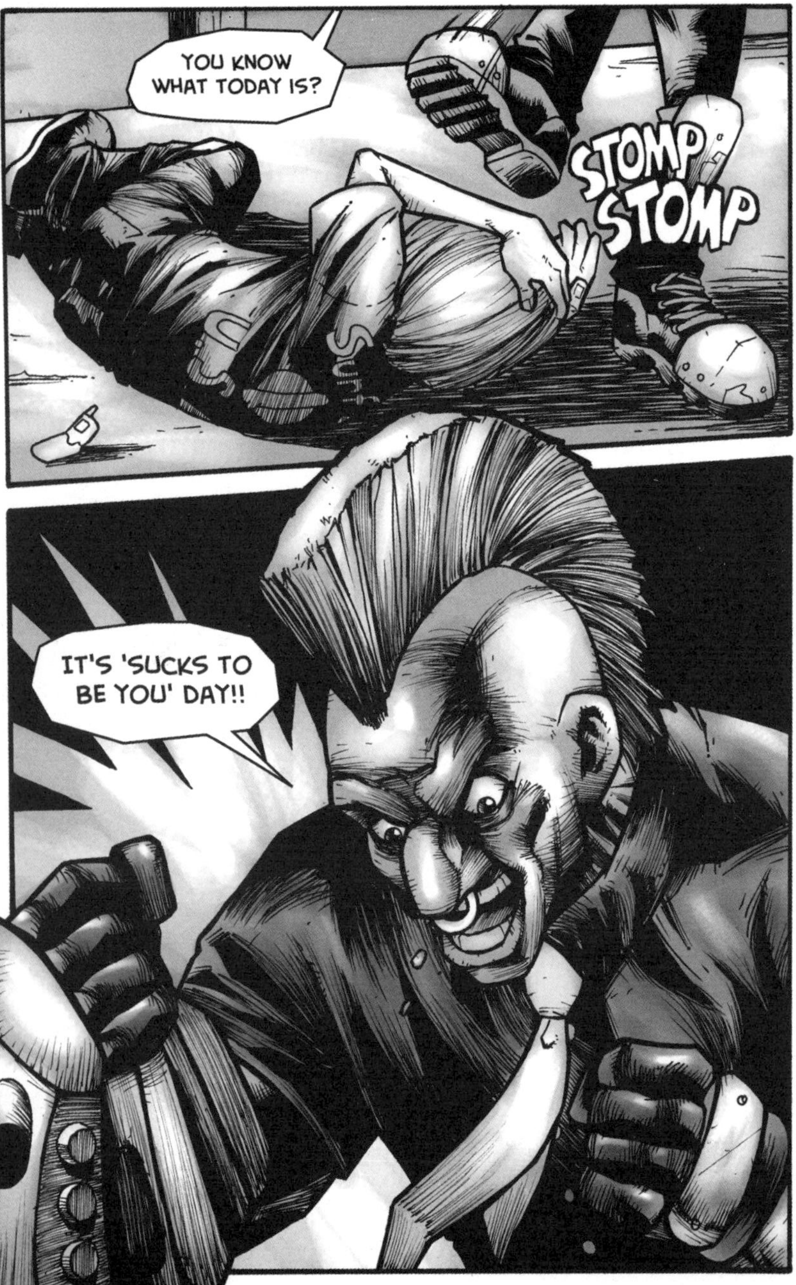
YOU KNOW WHAT TODAY IS?
STOMP STOMP
IT'S 'SUCKS TO BE YOU' DAY!!

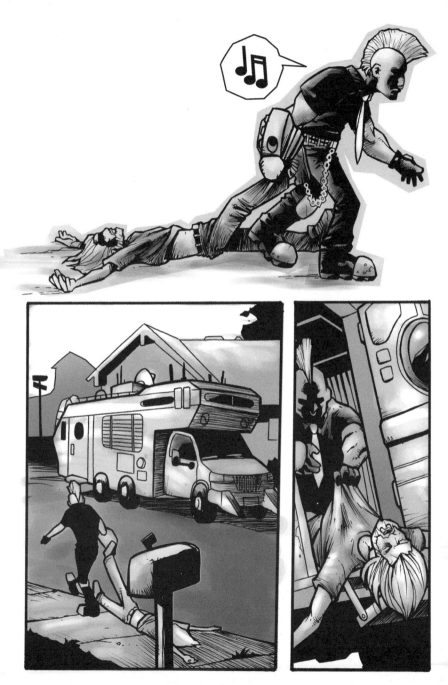

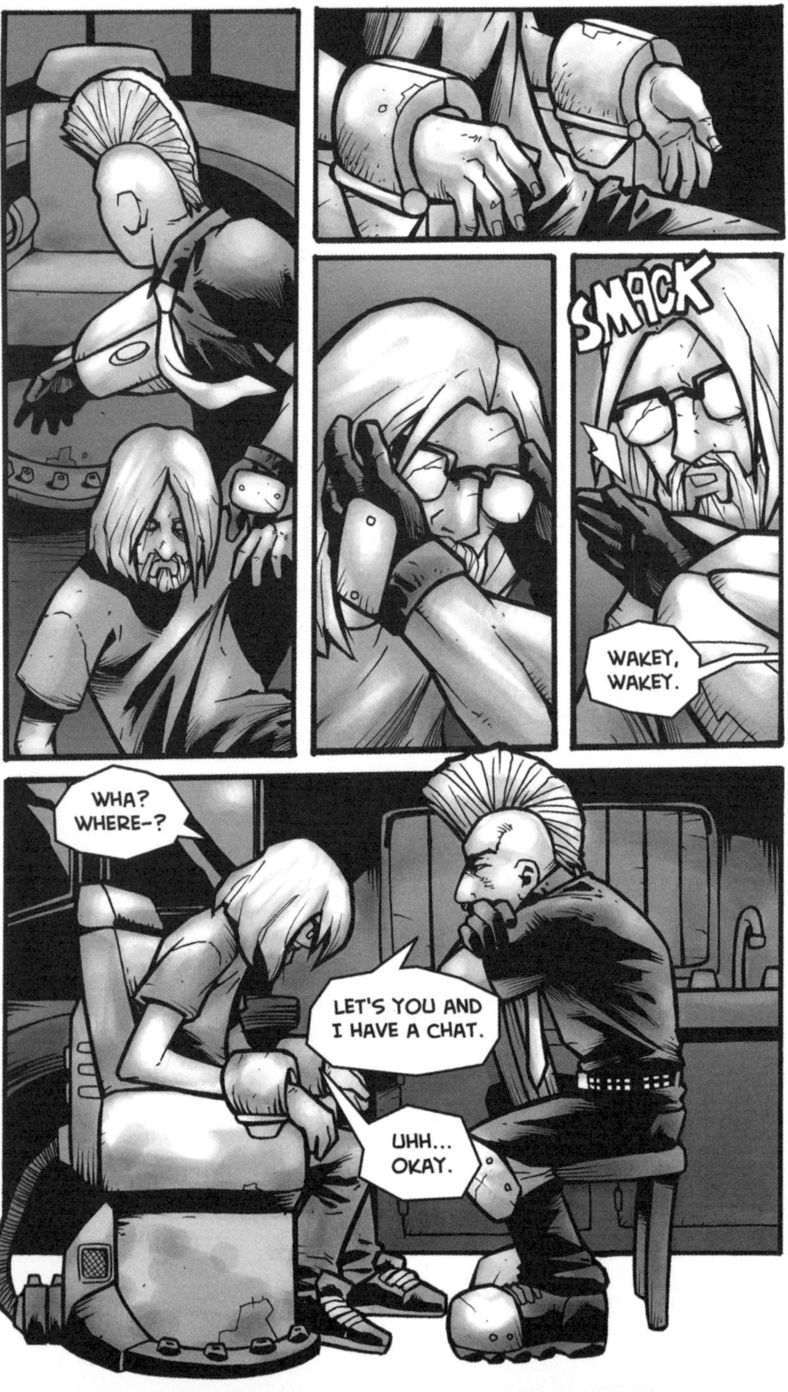
SMACK
WAKEY, WAKEY.
WHA? WHERE-?
LET'S YOU AND I HAVE A CHAT.
UHH... OKAY.

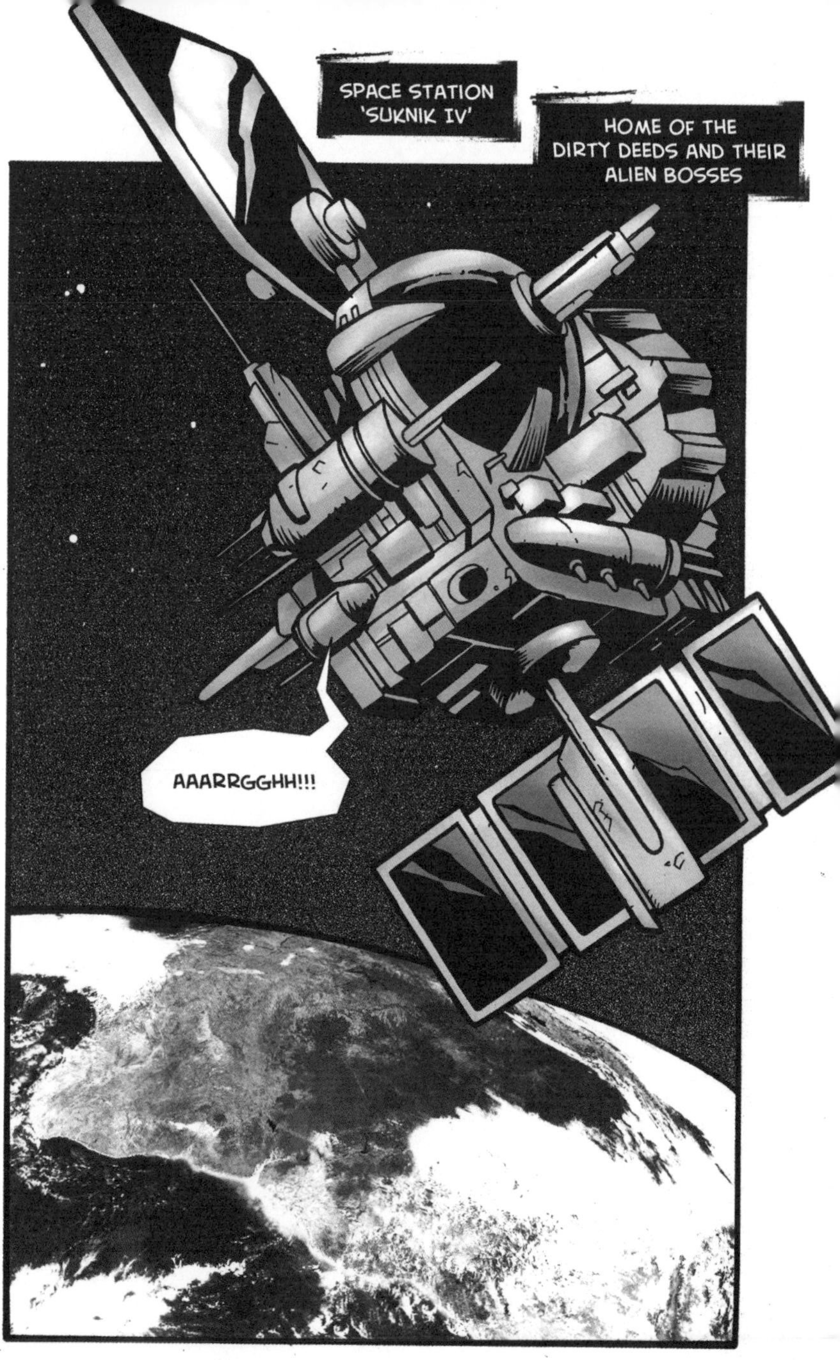
SPACE STATION 'SUKNIK IV'
HOME OF THE DIRTY DEEDS AND THEIR ALIEN BOSSES
AAARRGGHH!!!

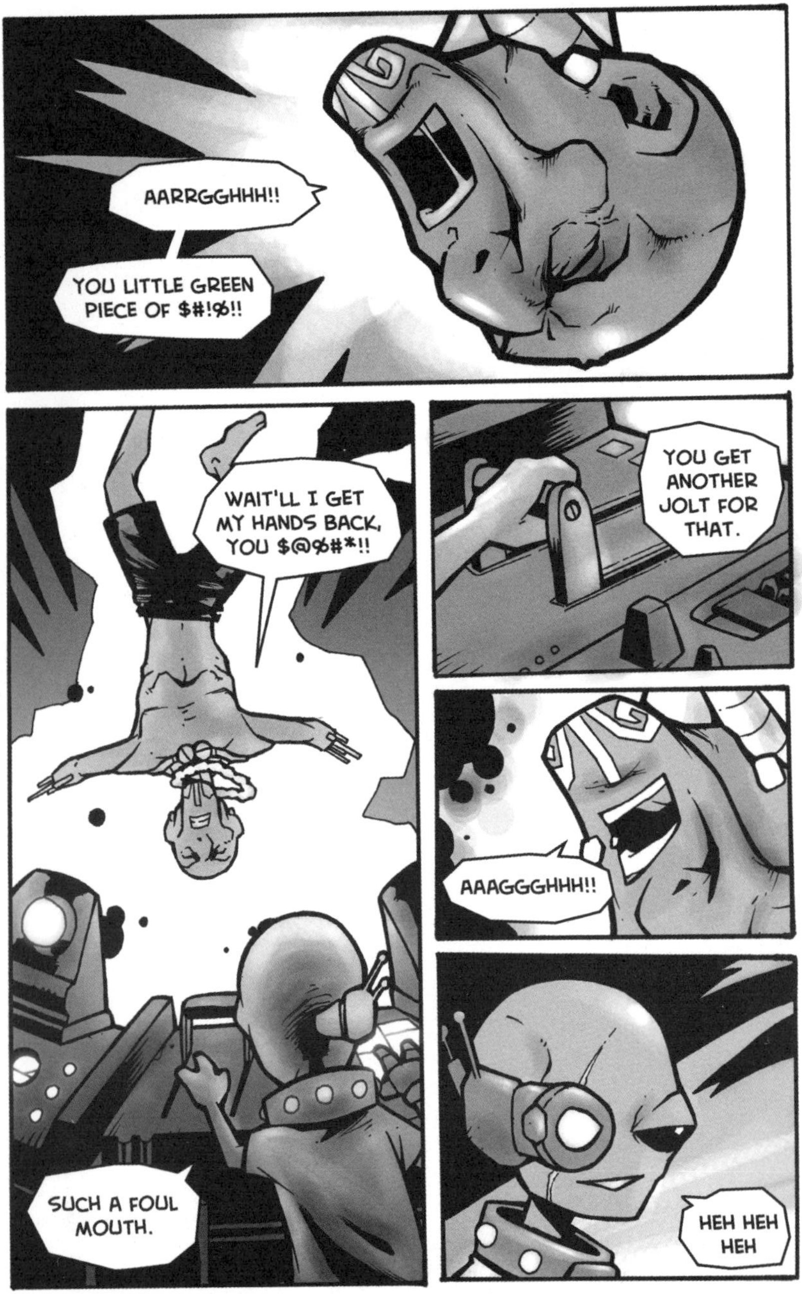
AARRGGHHH!!
YOU LITTLE GREEN PIECE OF $#!%!!
WAIT'LL I GET MY HANDS BACK, YOU $@%#*!!
YOU GET ANOTHER JOLT FOR THAT.
AAAGGGHHH!!
SUCH A FOUL MOUTH.
HEH HEH HEH

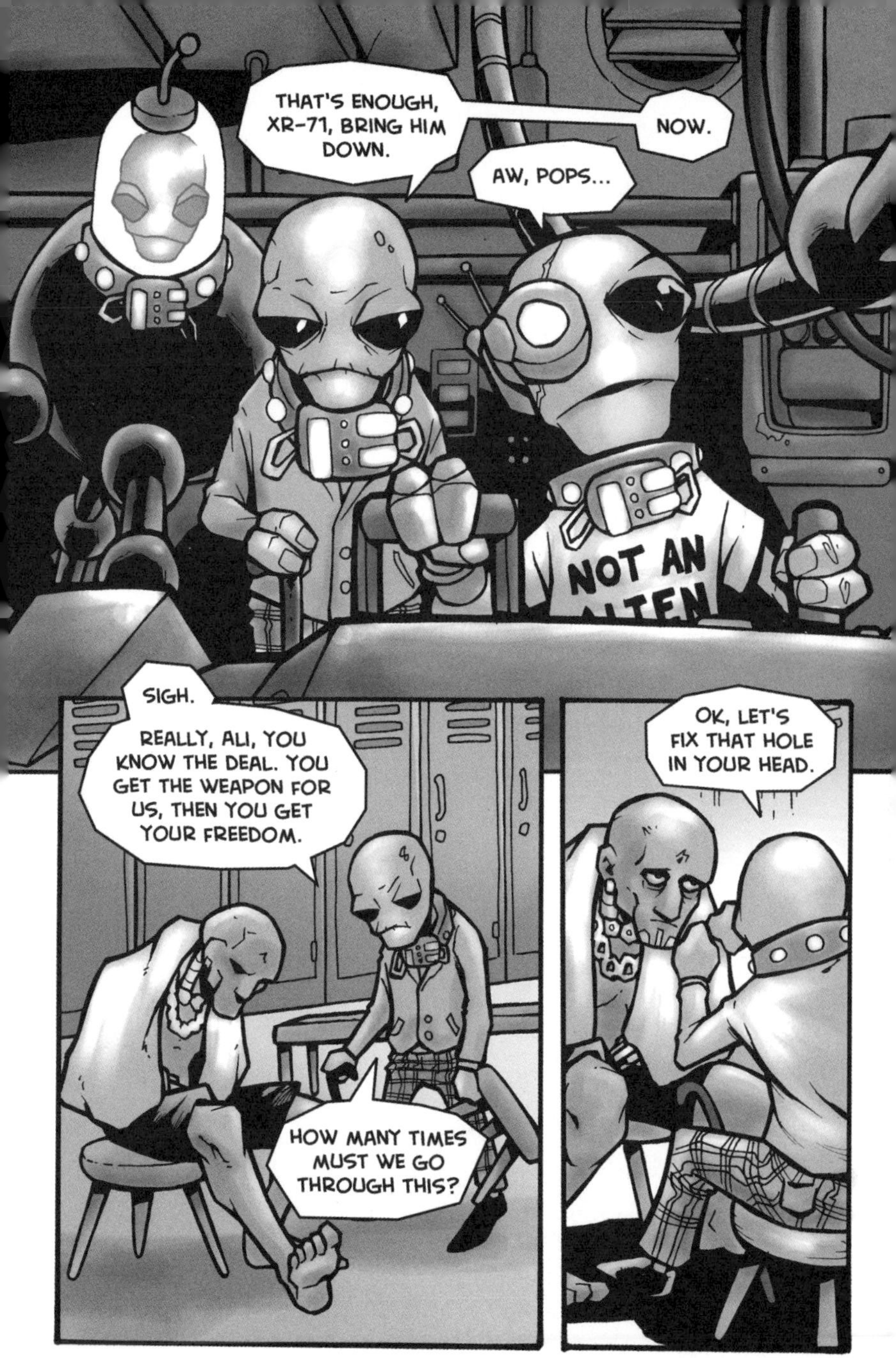
THAT'S ENOUGH, XR-71, BRING HIM DOWN.
NOW.
AW, POPS...
NOT AN
SIGH.
REALLY, ALI, YOU KNOW THE DEAL. YOU GET THE WEAPON FOR US, THEN YOU GET YOUR FREEDOM.
HOW MANY TIMES MUST WE GO THROUGH THIS?
OK, LET'S FIX THAT HOLE IN YOUR HEAD.

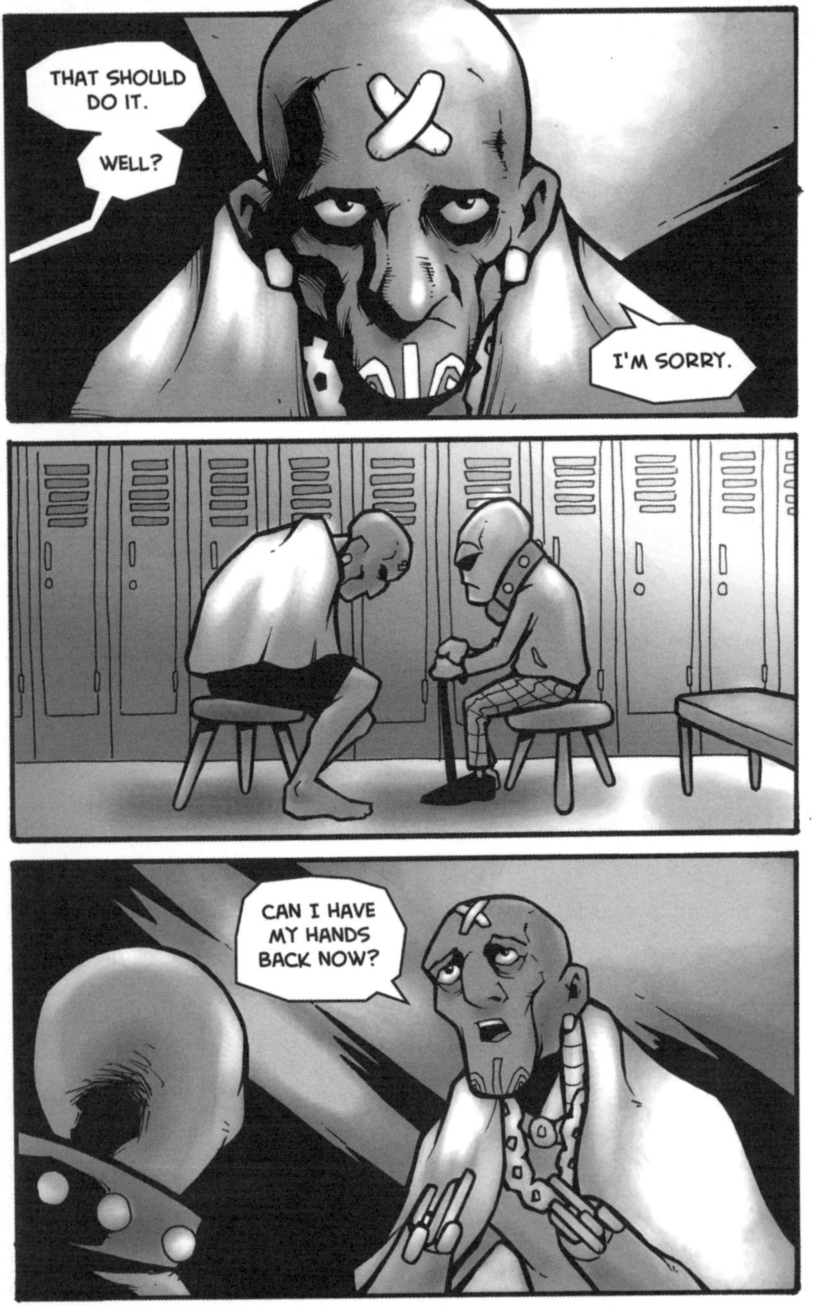
THAT SHOULD DO IT.
WELL?
I'M SORRY.
CAN I HAVE MY HANDS BACK NOW?

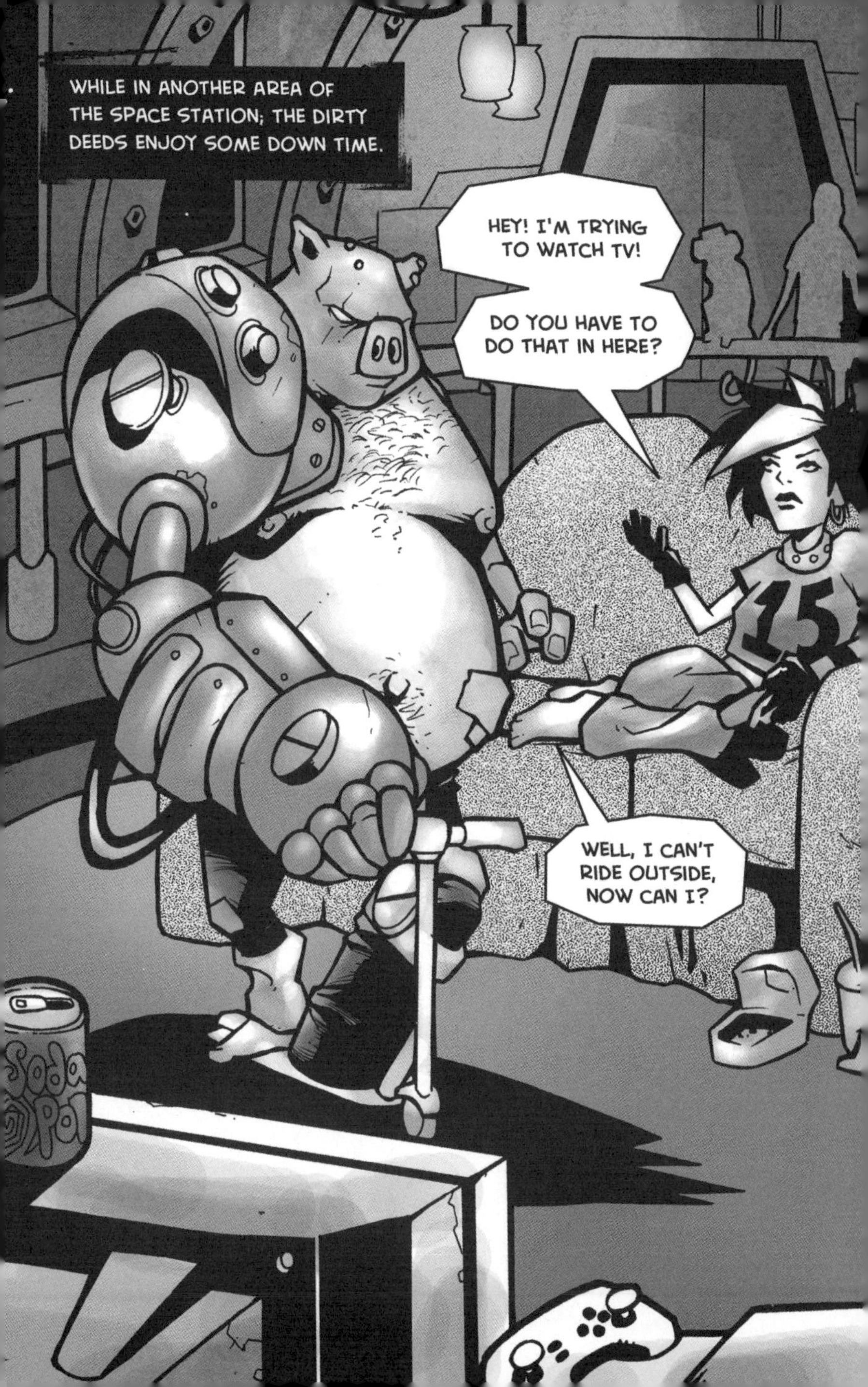
WHILE IN ANOTHER AREA OF THE SPACE STATION; THE DIRTY DEEDS ENJOY SOME DOWN TIME.
HEY! I'M TRYING TO WATCH TV!
DO YOU HAVE TO DO THAT IN HERE?
WELL, I CAN'T RIDE OUTSIDE, NOW CAN I?
Soda Pop

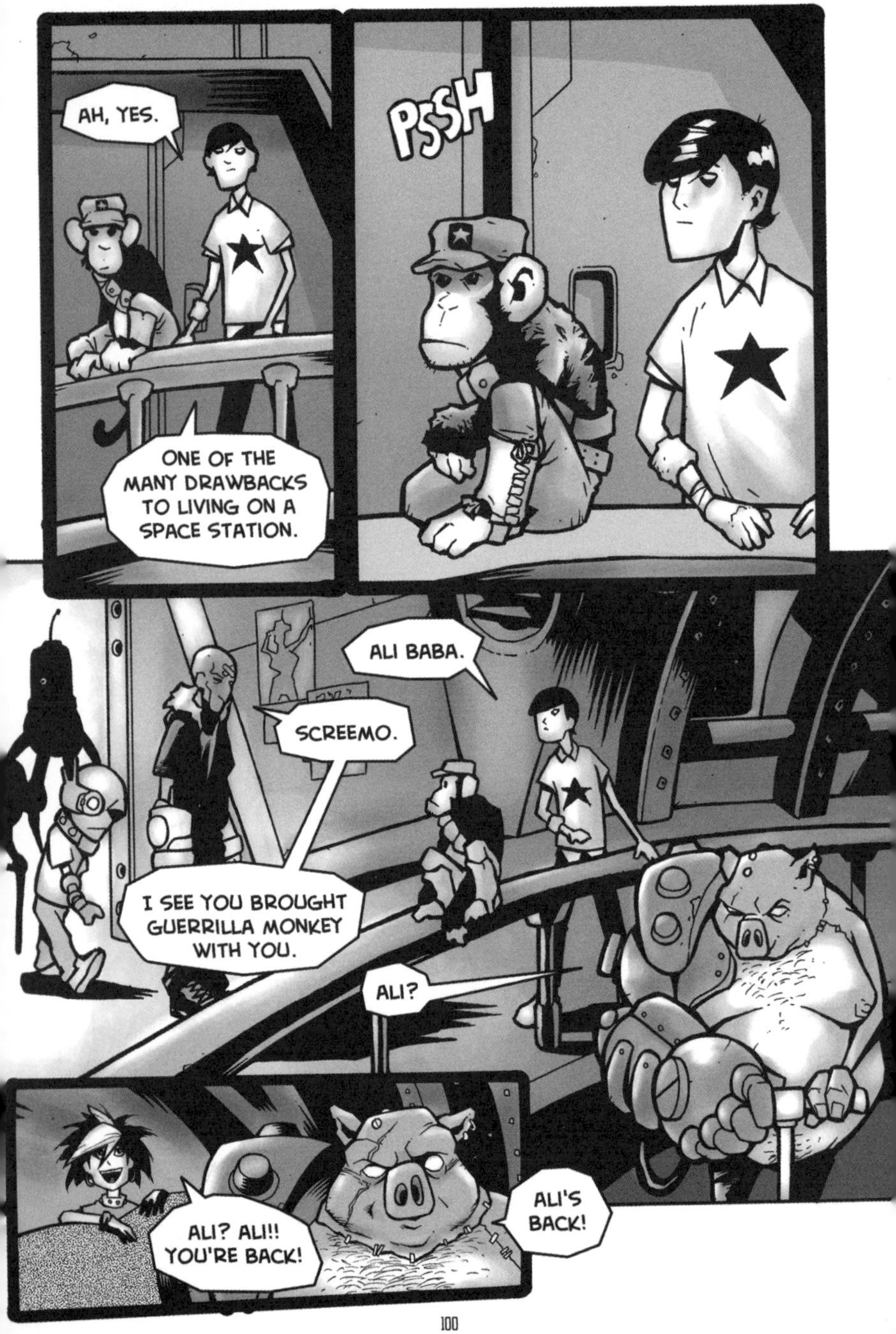
AH, YES.
ONE OF THE MANY DRAWBACKS TO LIVING ON A SPACE STATION.
PSSH
ALI BABA.
SCREEMO.
I SEE YOU BROUGHT GUERRILLA MONKEY WITH YOU.
ALI?
ALI? ALI!! YOU'RE BACK!
ALI'S BACK!

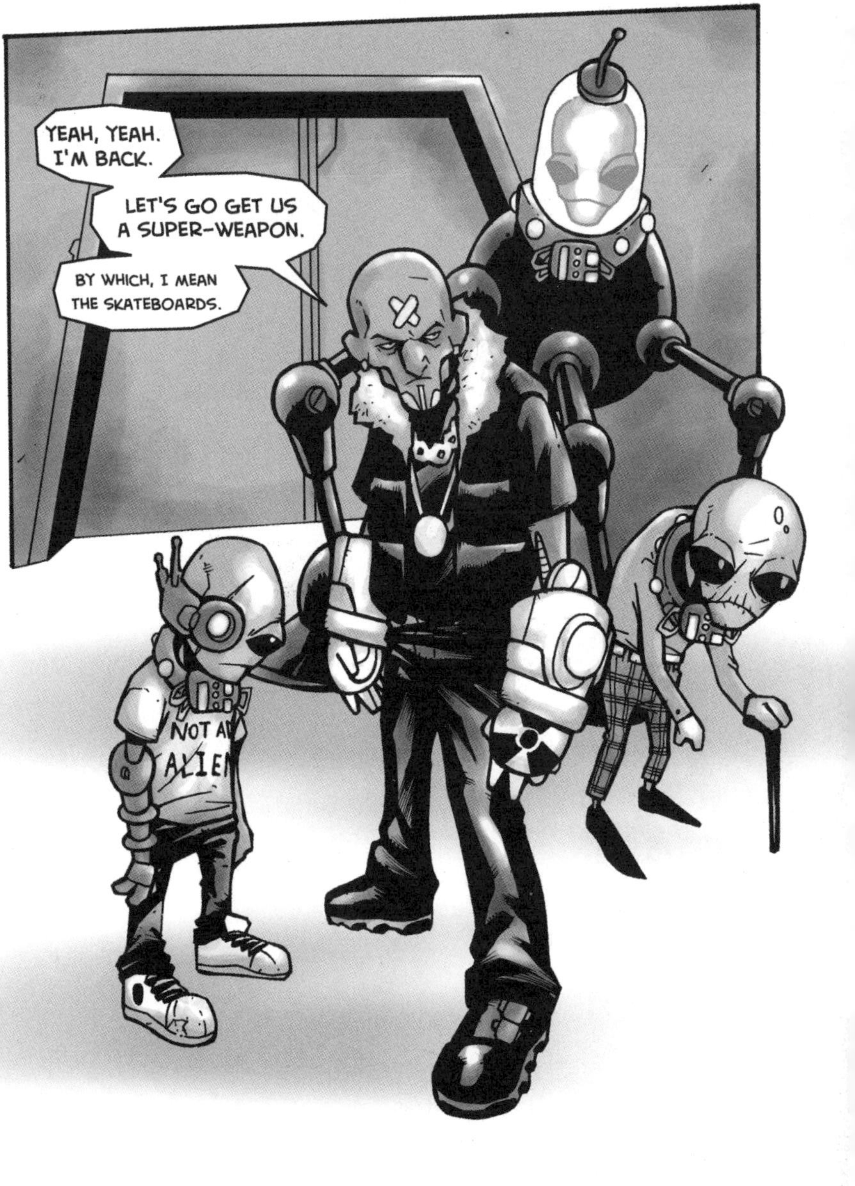
YEAH, YEAH. I'M BACK.
LET'S GO GET US A SUPER-WEAPON.
BY WHICH, I MEAN THE SKATEBOARDS.
NOT AN ALIEN

chapter four

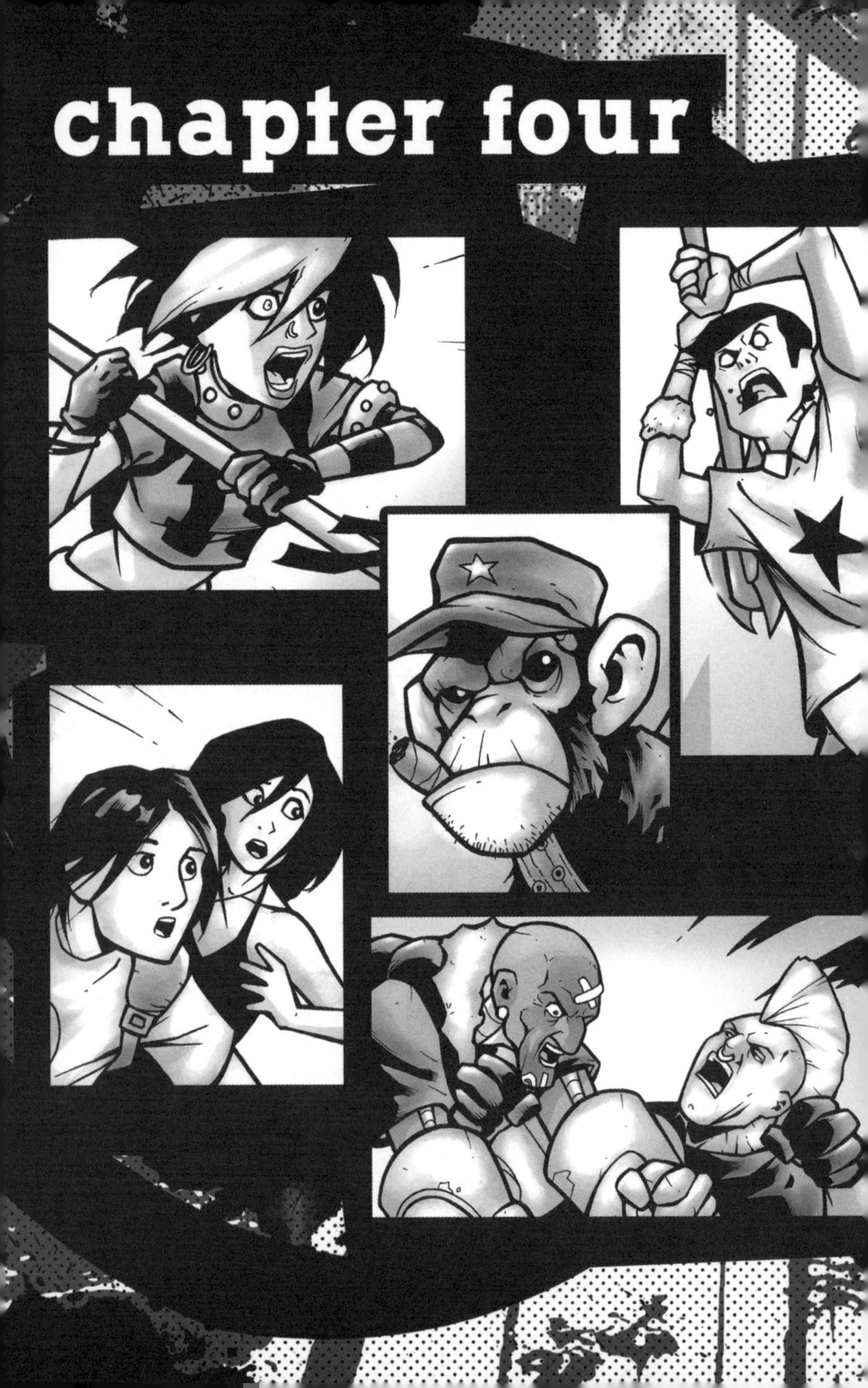

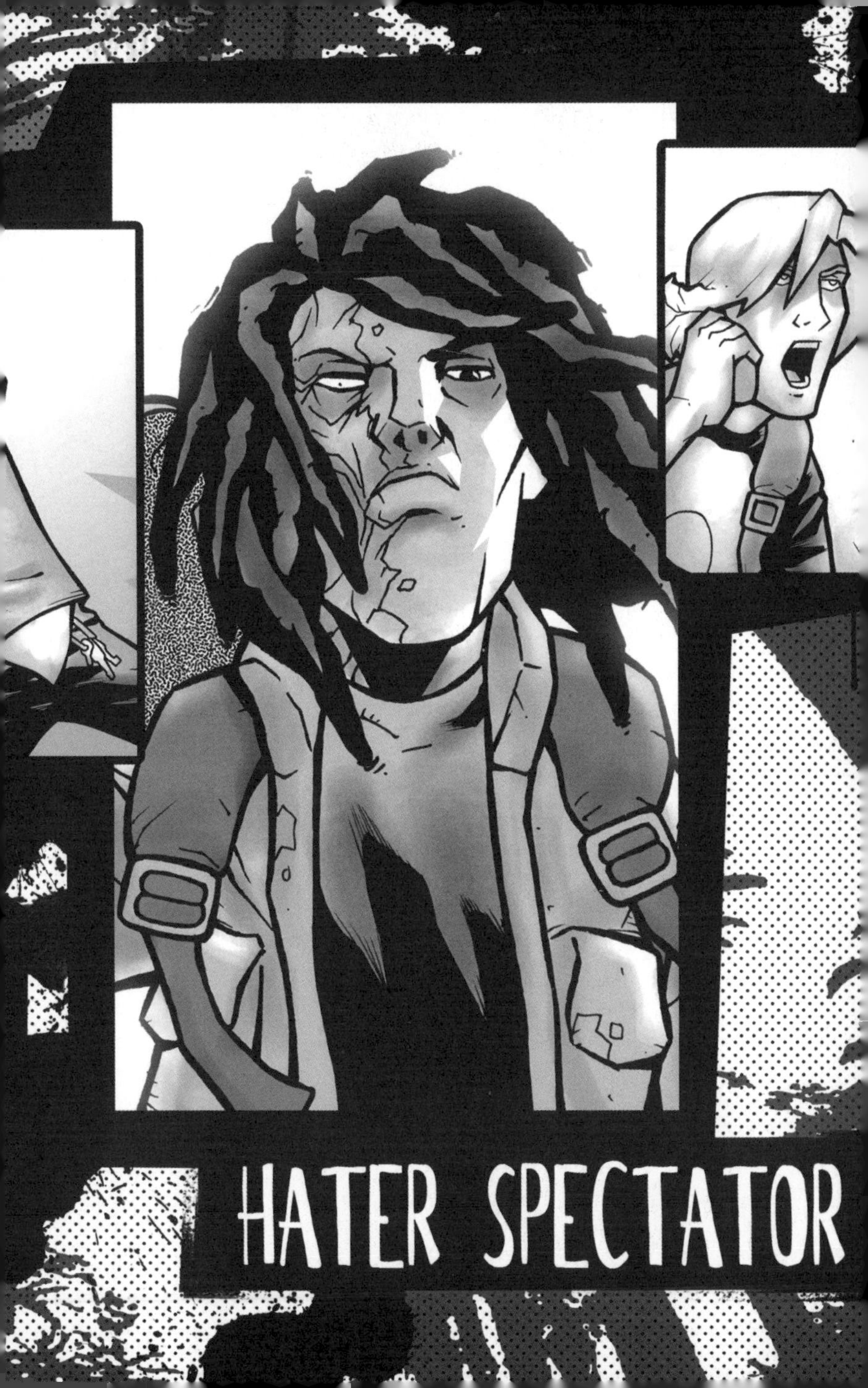
HATER SPECTATOR

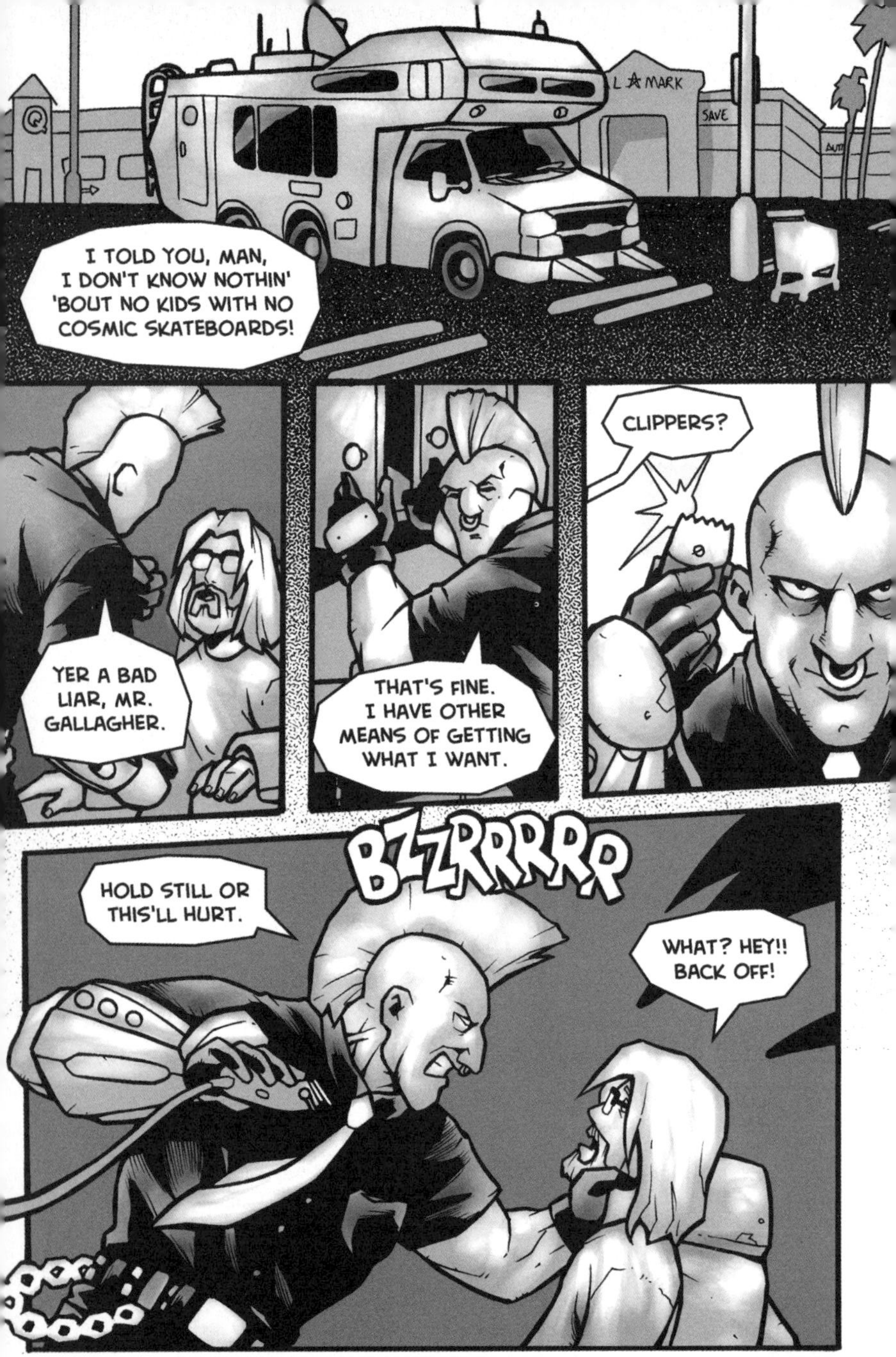
I TOLD YOU, MAN, I DON'T KNOW NOTHIN' 'BOUT NO KIDS WITH NO COSMIC SKATEBOARDS!
YER A BAD LIAR, MR. GALLAGHER.
THAT'S FINE. I HAVE OTHER MEANS OF GETTING WHAT I WANT.
CLIPPERS?
BZZRRRRRP
HOLD STILL OR THIS'LL HURT.
WHAT? HEY!! BACK OFF!

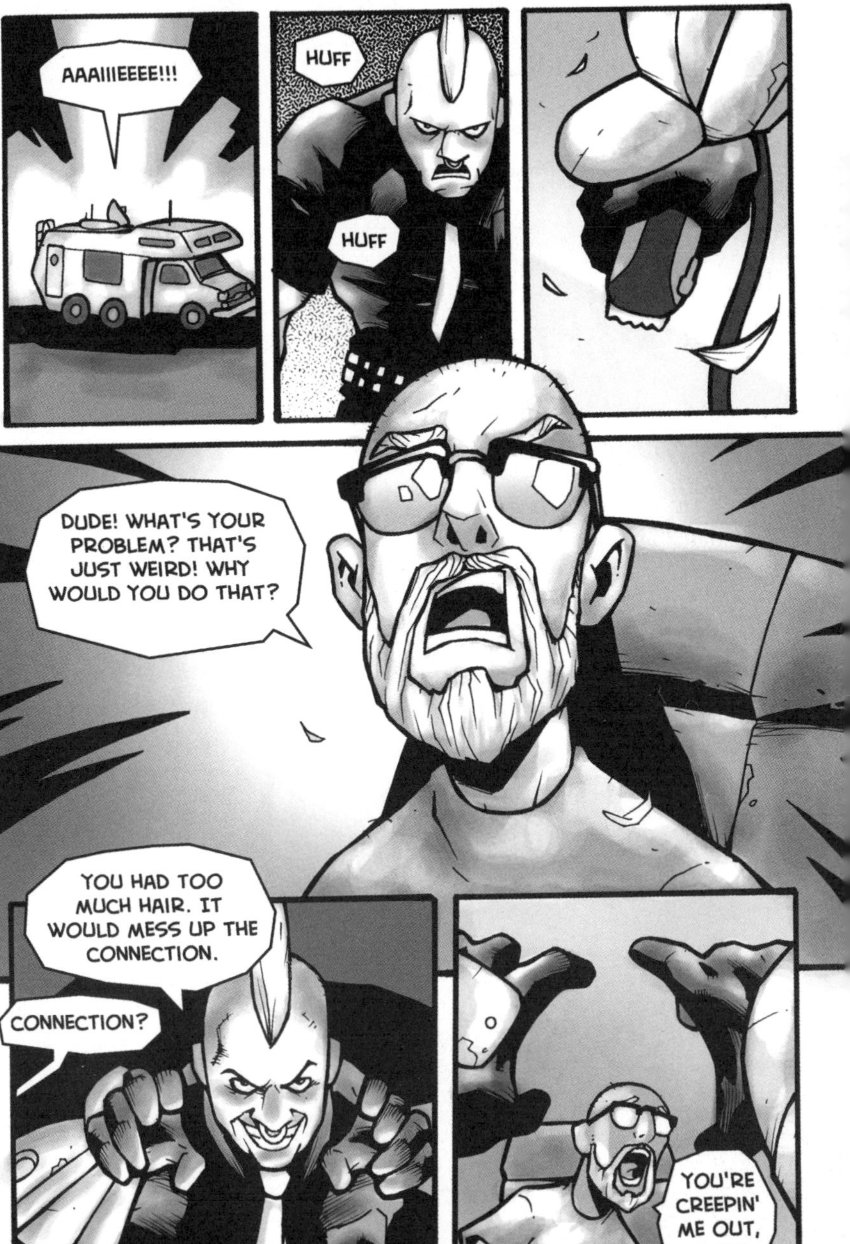
AAAIIIEEEE!!!
HUFF
HUFF
DUDE! WHAT'S YOUR PROBLEM? THAT'S JUST WEIRD! WHY WOULD YOU DO THAT?
YOU HAD TOO MUCH HAIR. IT WOULD MESS UP THE CONNECTION.
CONNECTION?
YOU'RE CREEPIN' ME OUT, MAN!

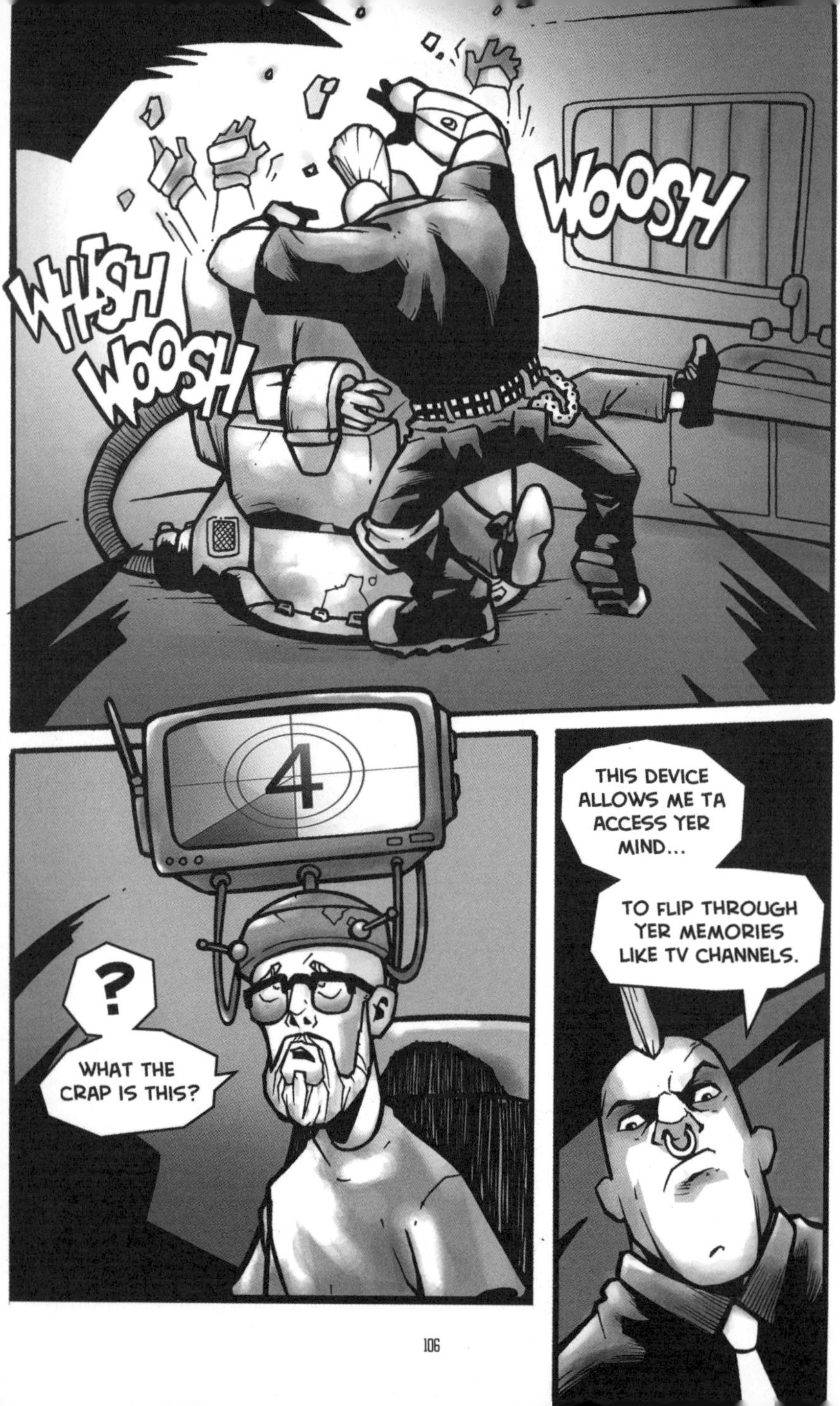
WOOSH
WHISH
WOOSH
?
WHAT THE CRAP IS THIS?
THIS DEVICE ALLOWS ME TA ACCESS YER MIND...
TO FLIP THROUGH YER MEMORIES LIKE TV CHANNELS.

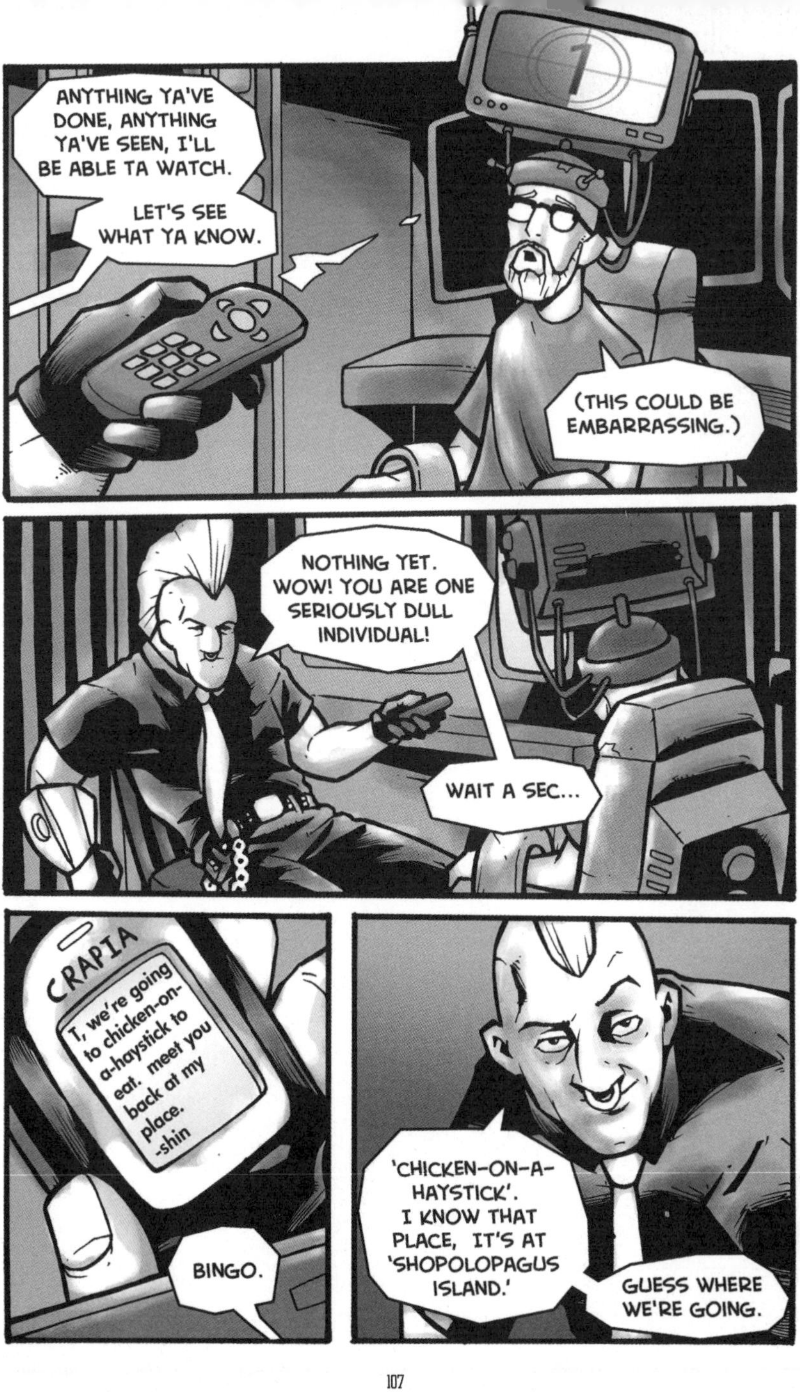
ANYTHING YA'VE DONE, ANYTHING YA'VE SEEN, I'LL BE ABLE TA WATCH.
LET'S SEE WHAT YA KNOW.
(THIS COULD BE EMBARRASSING.)
NOTHING YET. WOW! YOU ARE ONE SERIOUSLY DULL INDIVIDUAL!
WAIT A SEC...
CRAPIA
T, we're going to chicken-on-a-haystick to eat. meet you back at my place. -shin
BINGO.
'CHICKEN-ON-A-HAYSTICK'. I KNOW THAT PLACE, IT'S AT 'SHOPOLOPAGUS ISLAND.'
GUESS WHERE WE'RE GOING.

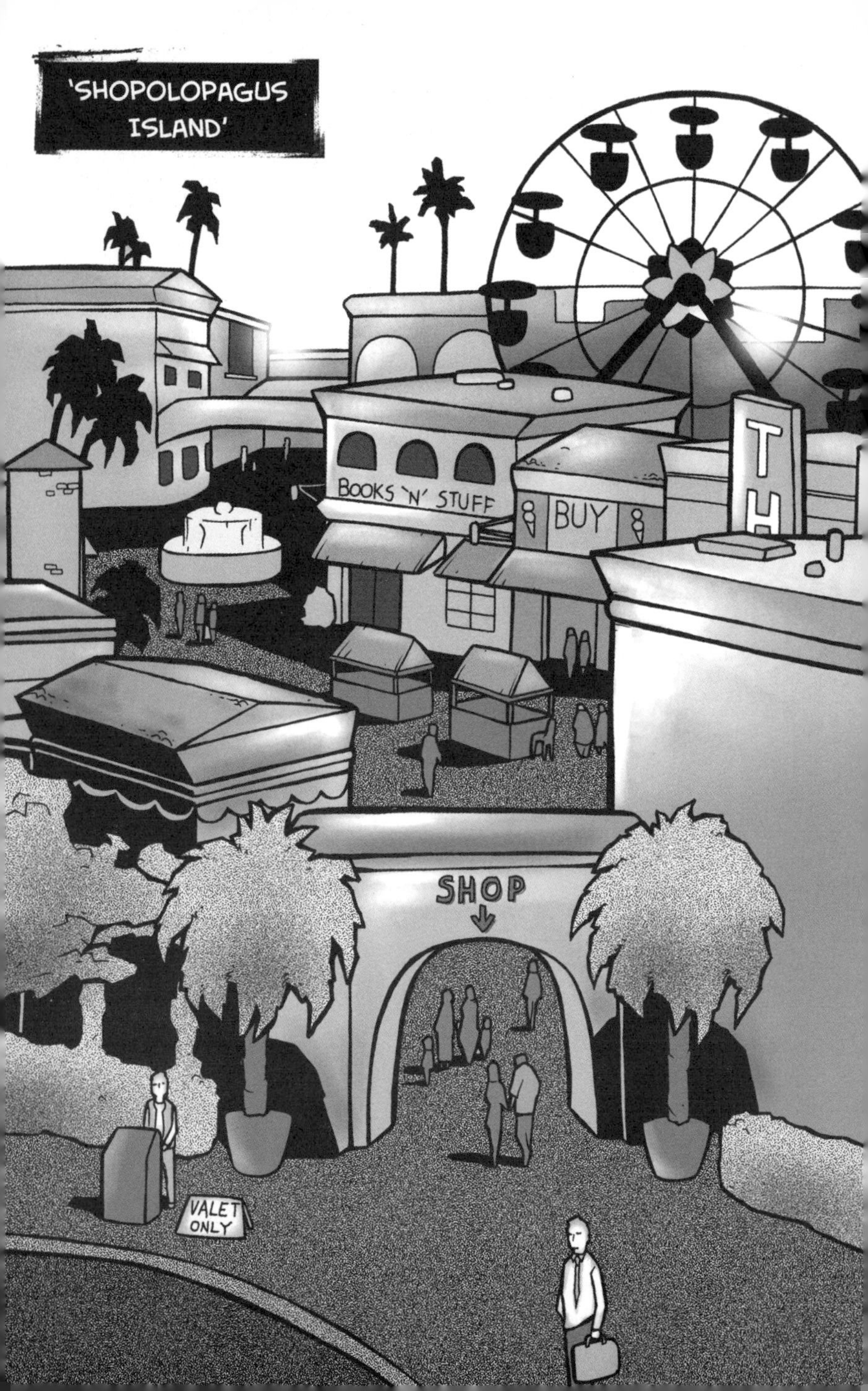
'SHOPOLOPAGUS ISLAND'
BOOKS 'N' STUFF
BUY
TH
SHOP
VALET ONLY

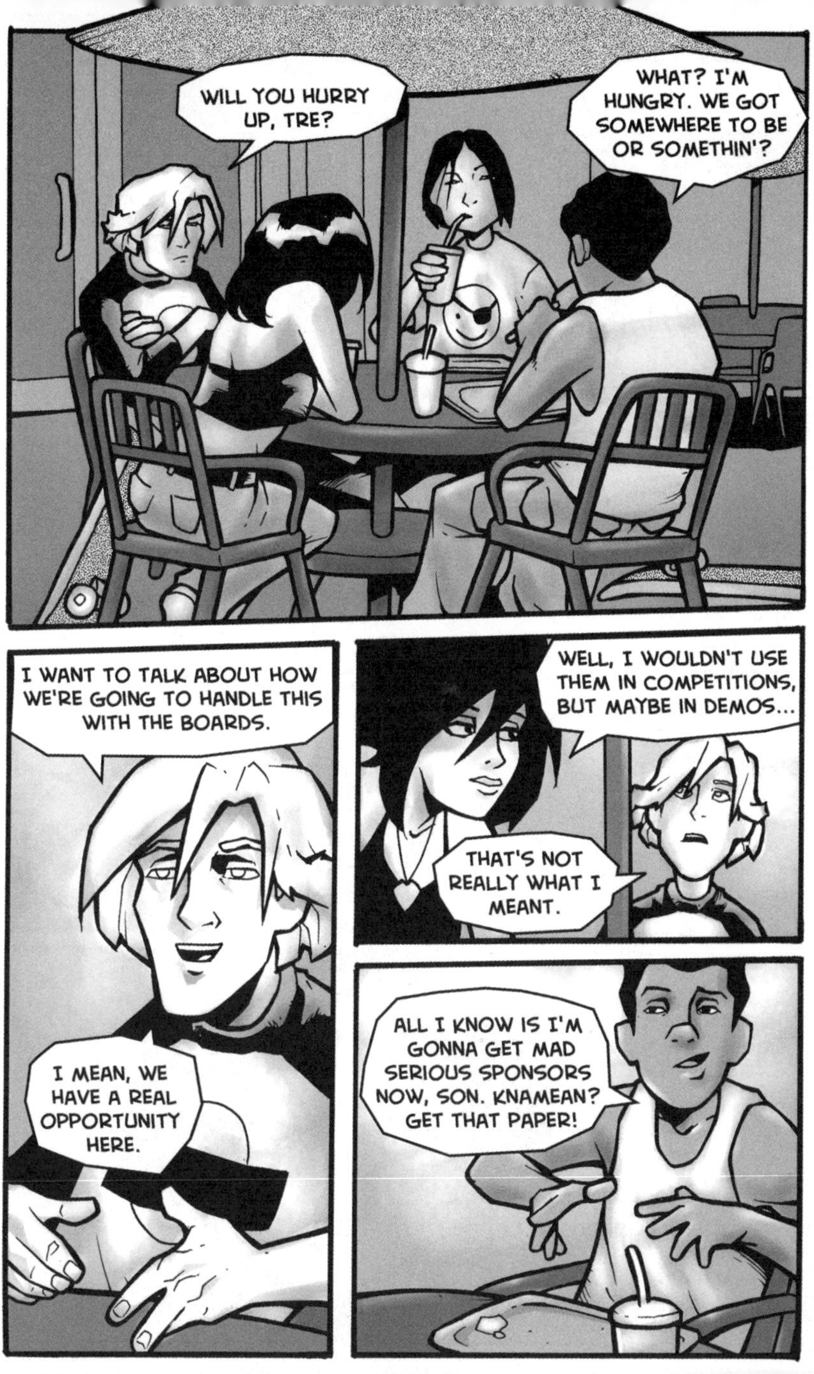
WILL YOU HURRY UP, TRE?
WHAT? I'M HUNGRY. WE GOT SOMEWHERE TO BE OR SOMETHIN'?
I WANT TO TALK ABOUT HOW WE'RE GOING TO HANDLE THIS WITH THE BOARDS.
I MEAN, WE HAVE A REAL OPPORTUNITY HERE.
WELL, I WOULDN'T USE THEM IN COMPETITIONS, BUT MAYBE IN DEMOS...
THAT'S NOT REALLY WHAT I MEANT.
ALL I KNOW IS I'M GONNA GET MAD SERIOUS SPONSORS NOW, SON. KNAMEAN? GET THAT PAPER!

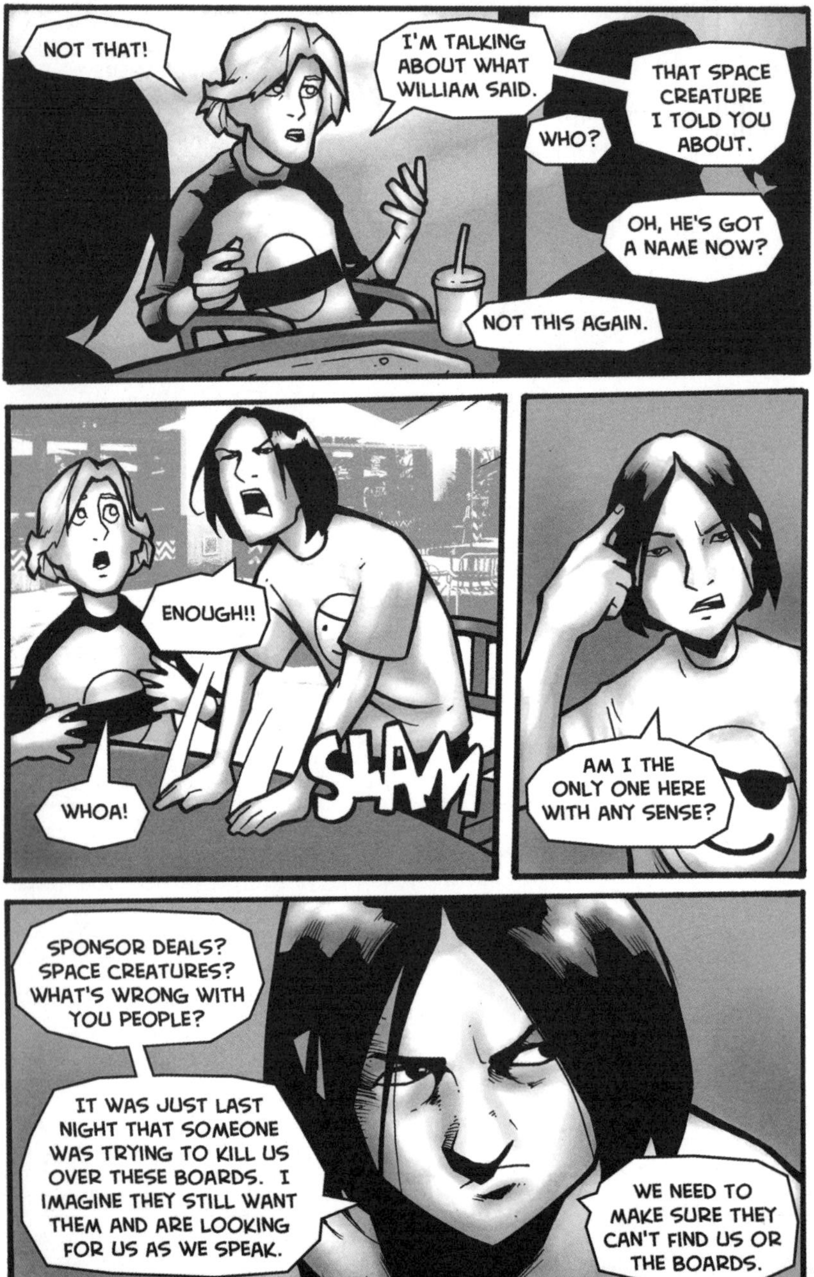
NOT THAT!
I'M TALKING ABOUT WHAT WILLIAM SAID.
WHO?
THAT SPACE CREATURE I TOLD YOU ABOUT.
OH, HE'S GOT A NAME NOW?
NOT THIS AGAIN.
ENOUGH!!
WHOA!
SLAM
AM I THE ONLY ONE HERE WITH ANY SENSE?
SPONSOR DEALS? SPACE CREATURES? WHAT'S WRONG WITH YOU PEOPLE?
IT WAS JUST LAST NIGHT THAT SOMEONE WAS TRYING TO KILL US OVER THESE BOARDS. I IMAGINE THEY STILL WANT THEM AND ARE LOOKING FOR US AS WE SPEAK.
WE NEED TO MAKE SURE THEY CAN'T FIND US OR THE BOARDS.

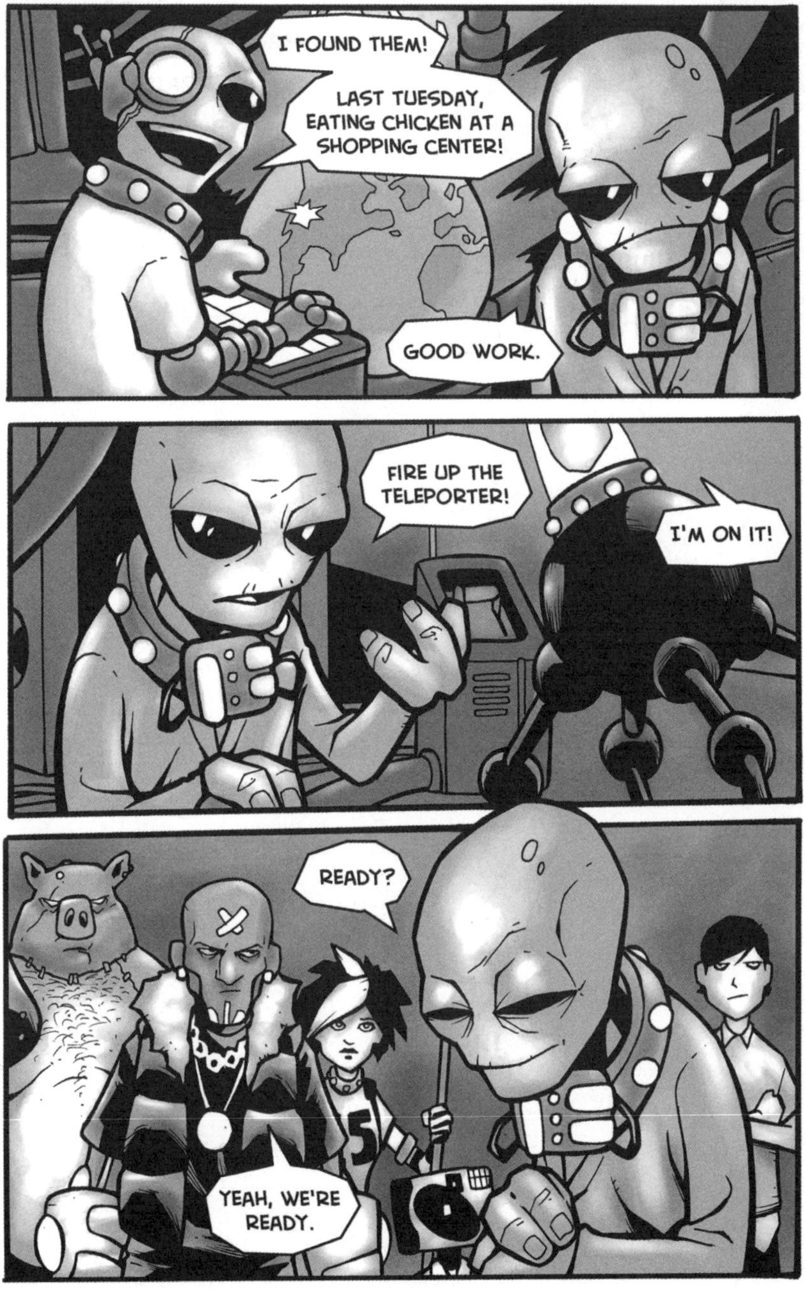
I FOUND THEM!
LAST TUESDAY, EATING CHICKEN AT A SHOPPING CENTER!
GOOD WORK.
FIRE UP THE TELEPORTER!
I'M ON IT!
READY?
YEAH, WE'RE READY.

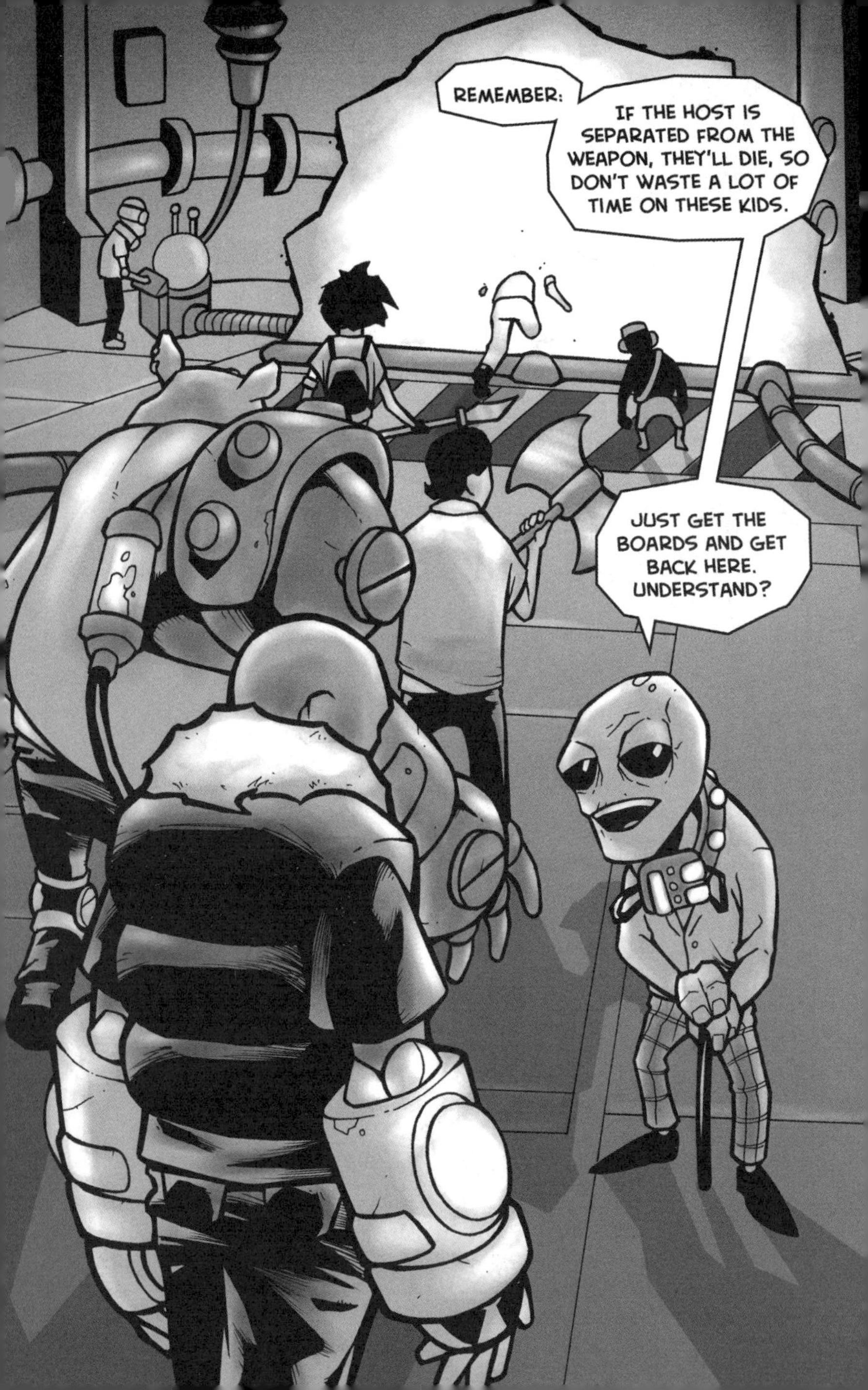
REMEMBER:
IF THE HOST IS SEPARATED FROM THE WEAPON, THEY'LL DIE, SO DON'T WASTE A LOT OF TIME ON THESE KIDS.
JUST GET THE BOARDS AND GET BACK HERE. UNDERSTAND?

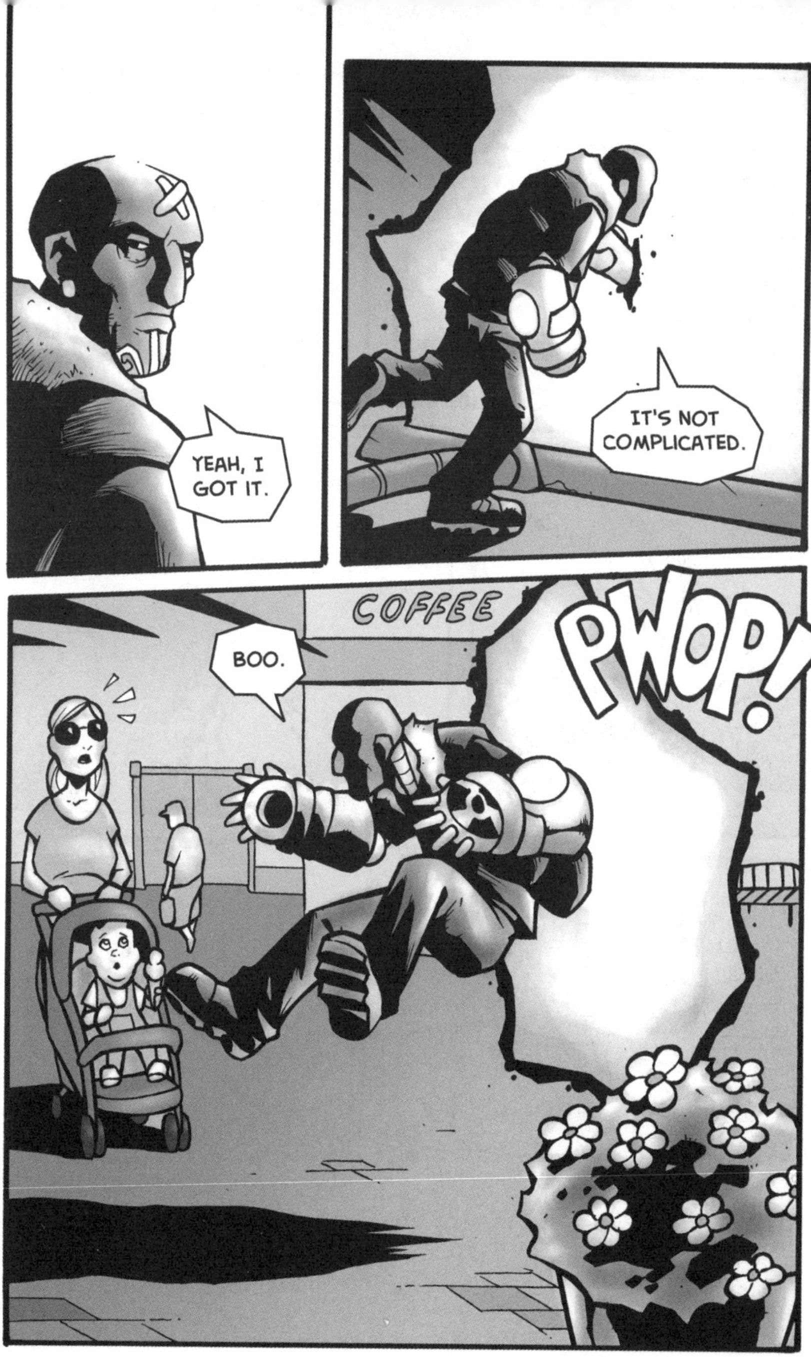
YEAH, I GOT IT.
IT'S NOT COMPLICATED.
COFFEE
BOO.
PWOP!

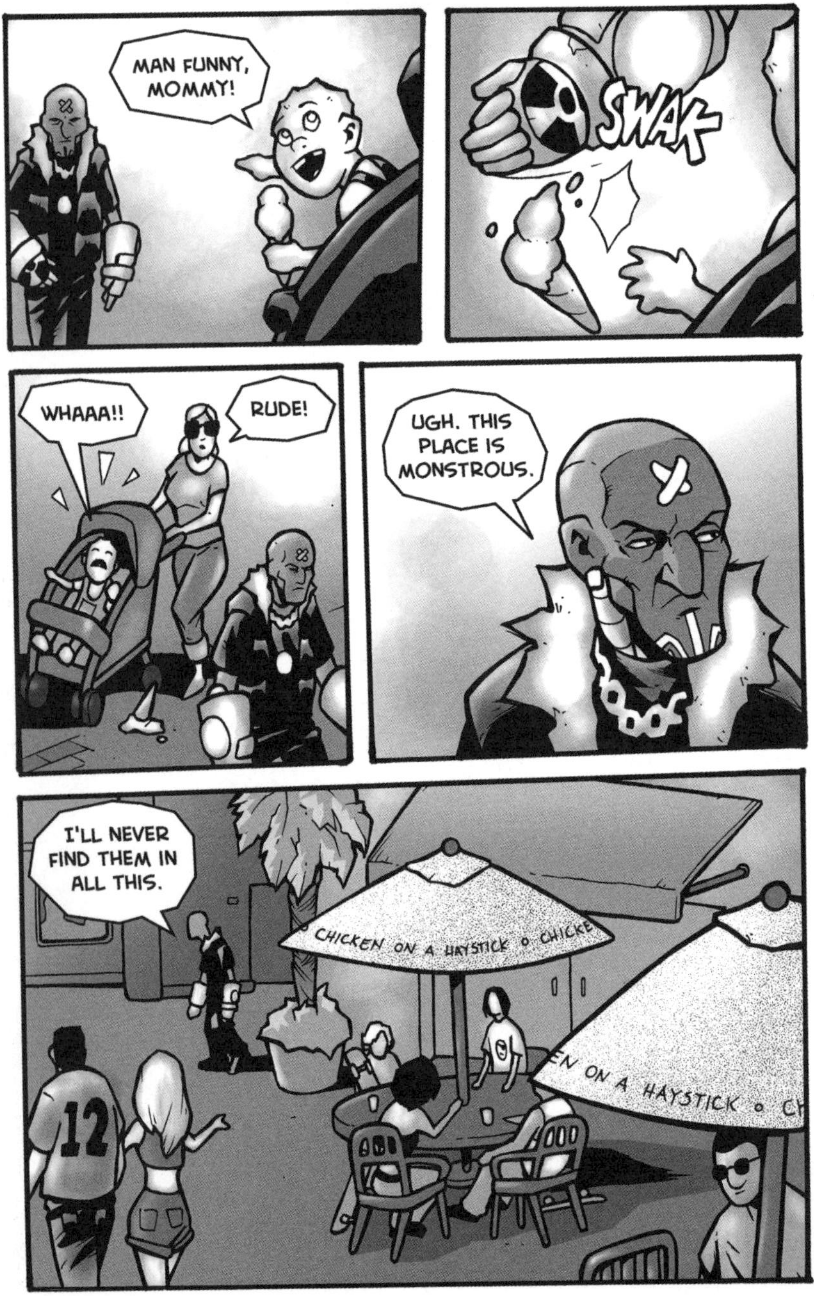
MAN FUNNY, MOMMY!
SWAK
WHAAA!!
RUDE!
UGH. THIS PLACE IS MONSTROUS.
I'LL NEVER FIND THEM IN ALL THIS.
CHICKEN ON A HAYSTICK
12

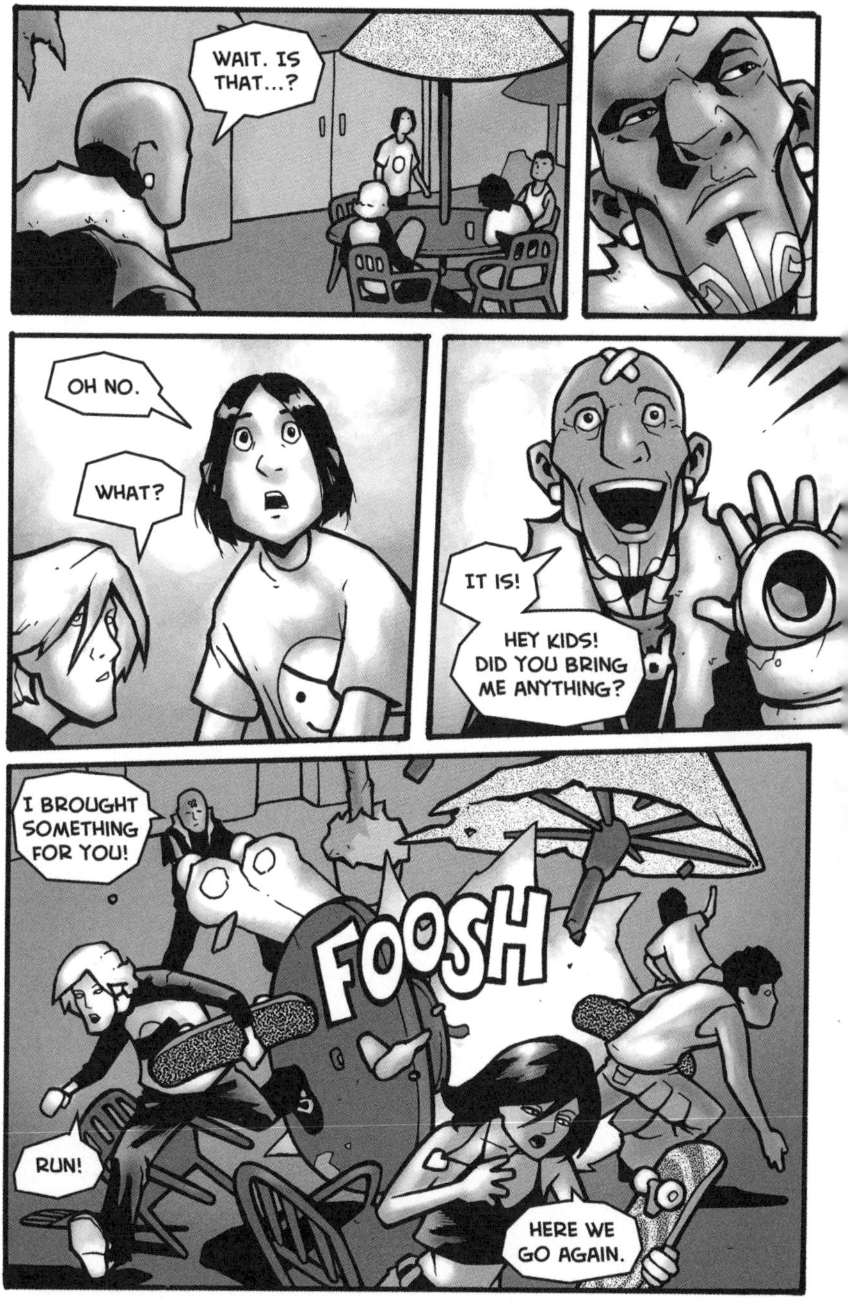
WAIT. IS THAT...?
OH NO.
WHAT?
IT IS!
HEY KIDS! DID YOU BRING ME ANYTHING?
I BROUGHT SOMETHING FOR YOU!
FOOSH
RUN!
HERE WE GO AGAIN.

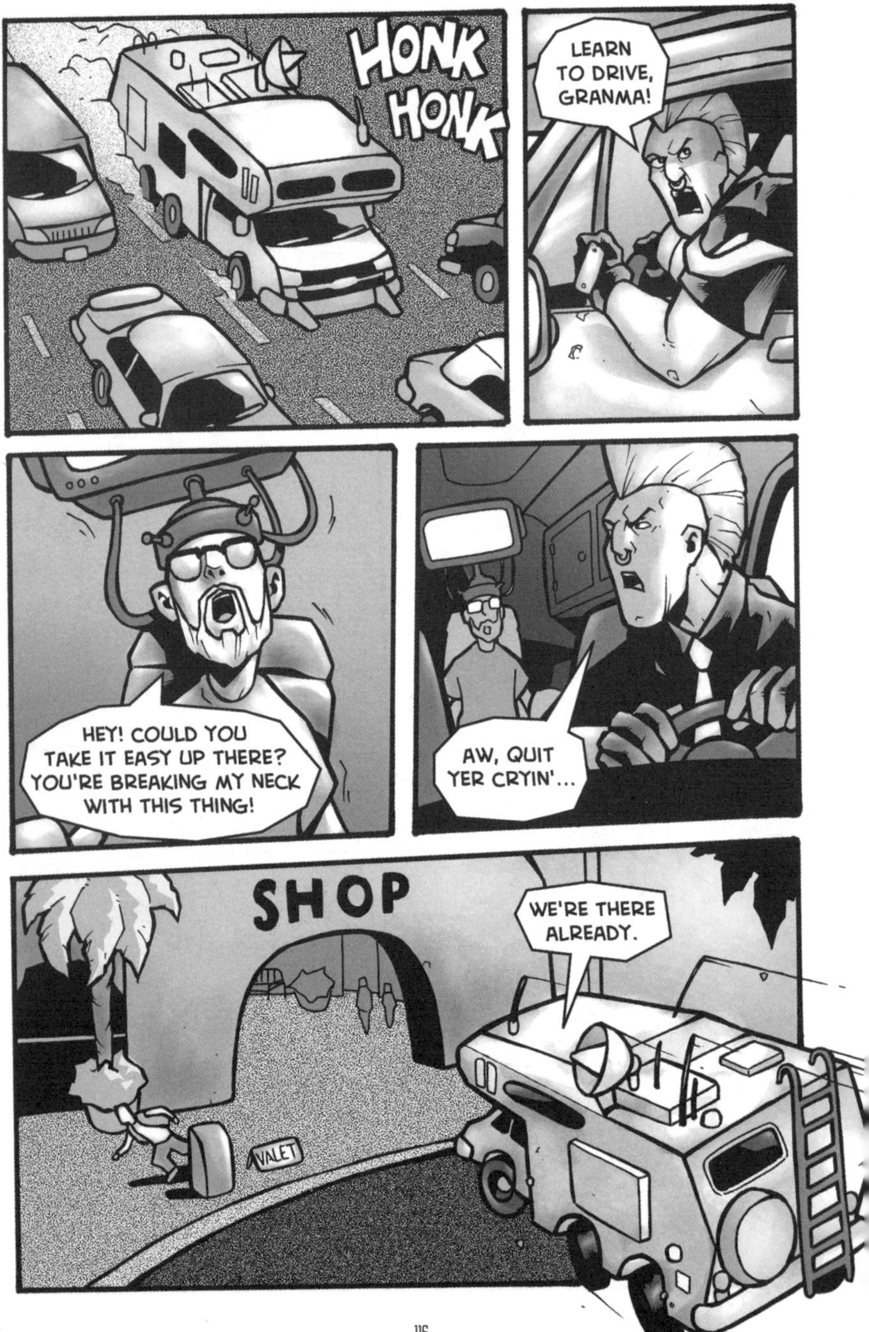
HONK
HONK
LEARN TO DRIVE, GRANMA!
HEY! COULD YOU TAKE IT EASY UP THERE? YOU'RE BREAKING MY NECK WITH THIS THING!
AW, QUIT YER CRYIN'...
SHOP
WE'RE THERE ALREADY.
VALET

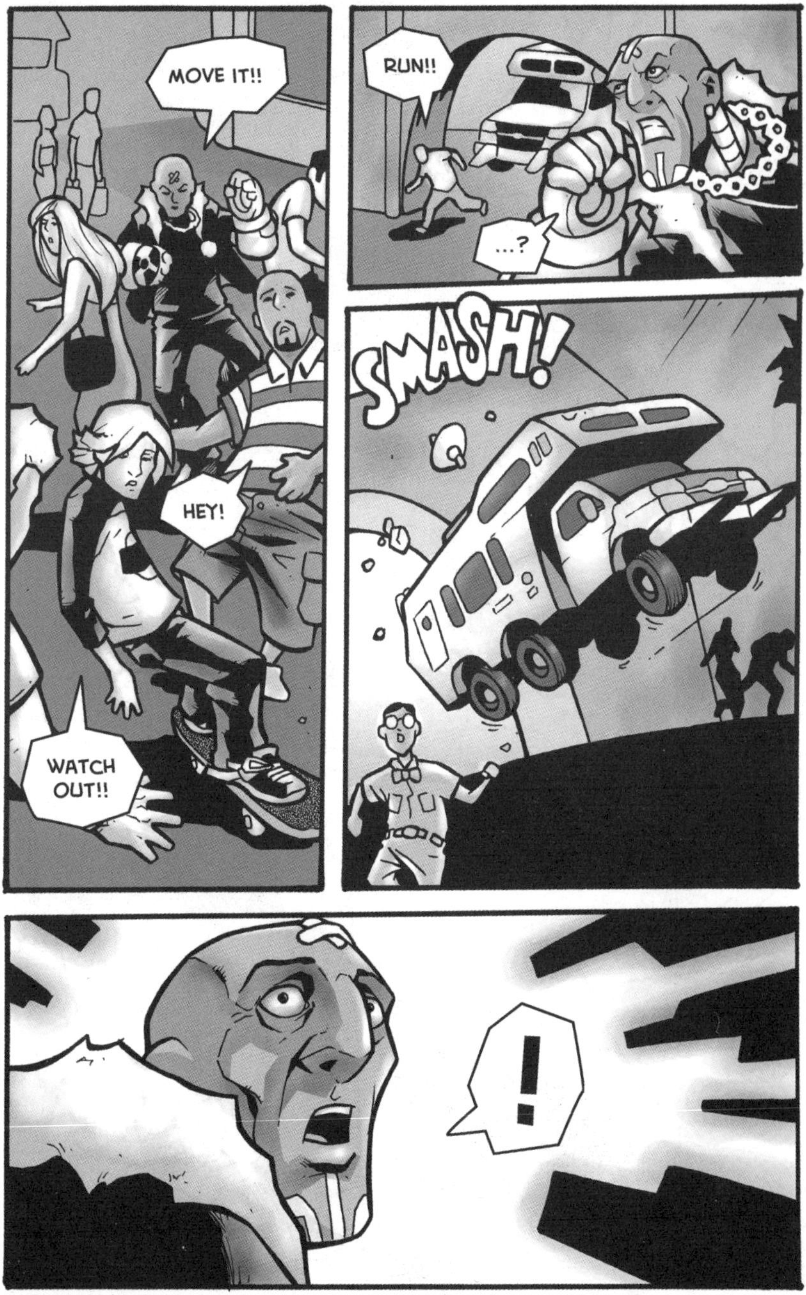
MOVE IT!!
HEY!
WATCH OUT!!
RUN!!
...?
SMASH!
!

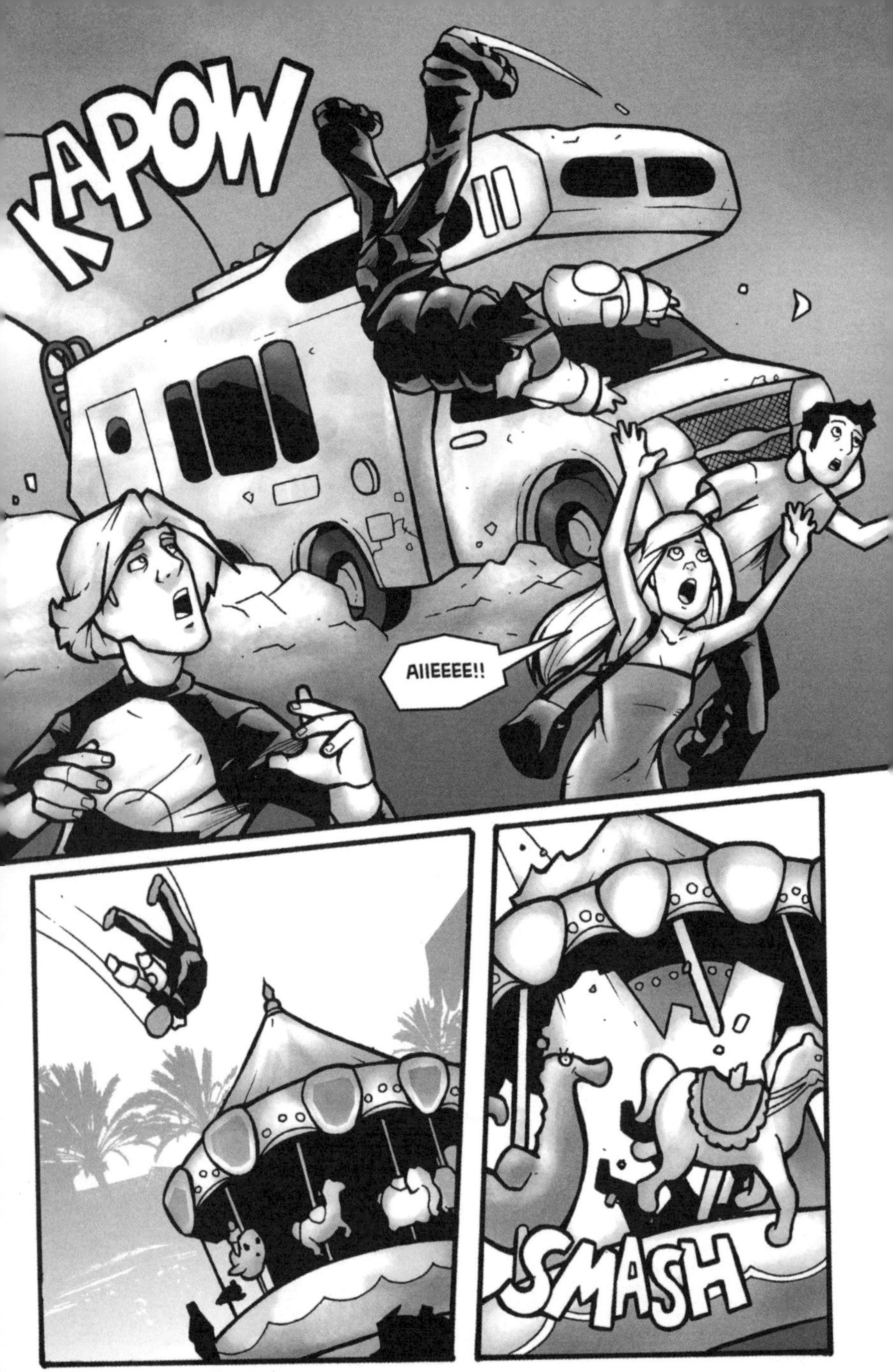
KAPOW
AIIEEEE!!
SMASH

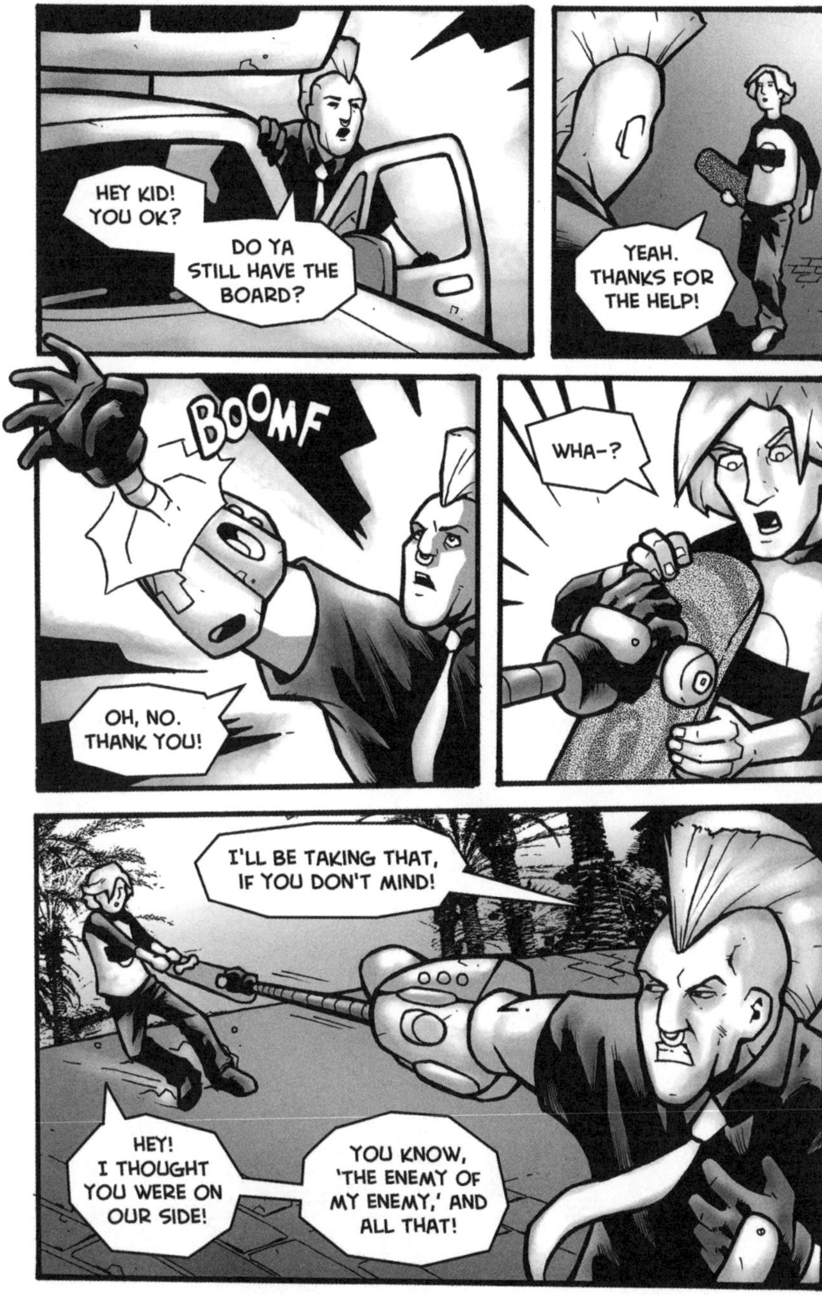
HEY KID!
YOU OK?
DO YA
STILL HAVE THE
BOARD?
YEAH.
THANKS FOR
THE HELP!
BOOMF
OH, NO.
THANK YOU!
WHA-?
I'LL BE TAKING THAT,
IF YOU DON'T MIND!
HEY!
I THOUGHT
YOU WERE ON
OUR SIDE!
YOU KNOW,
'THE ENEMY OF
MY ENEMY,' AND
ALL THAT!

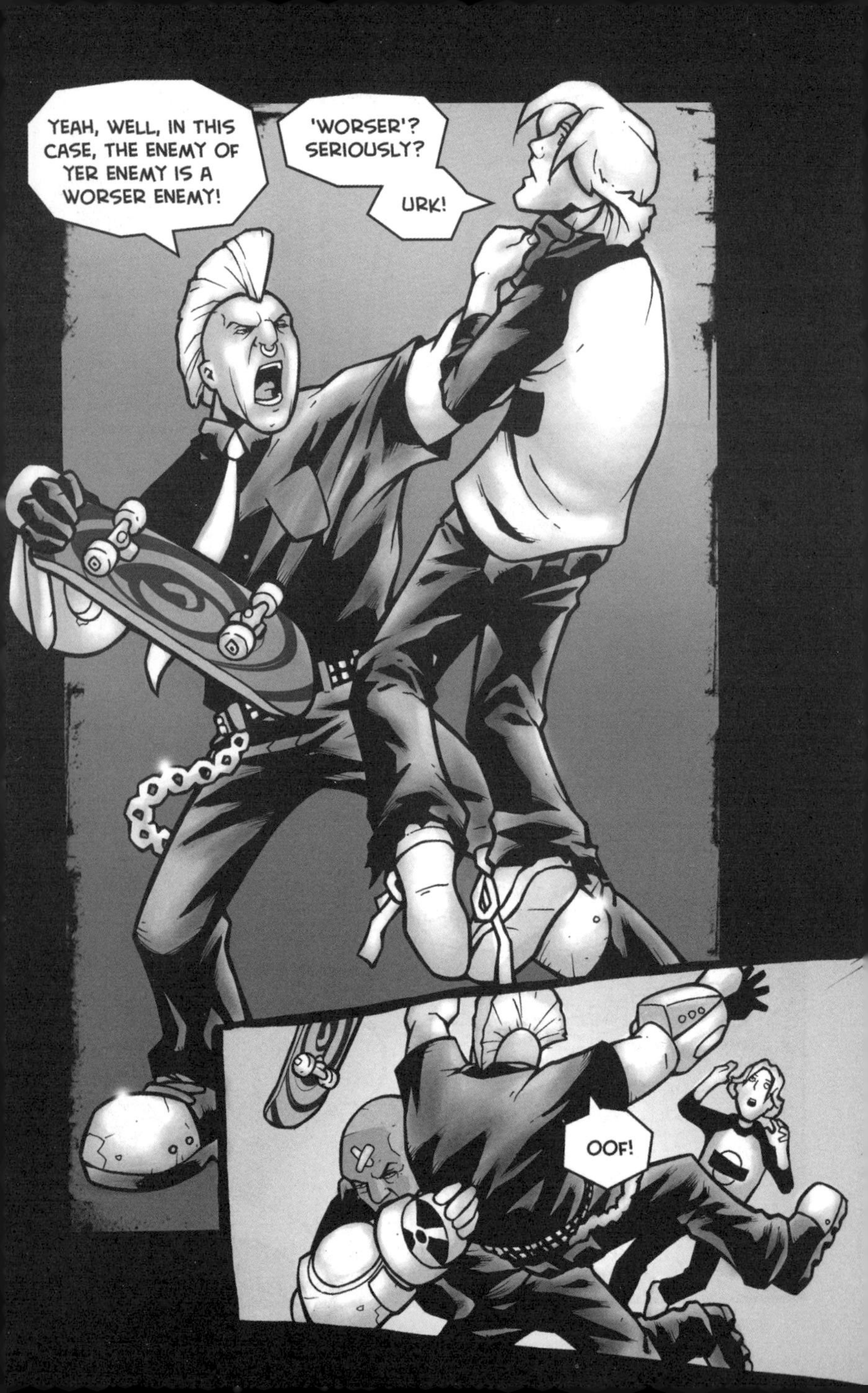
YEAH, WELL, IN THIS CASE, THE ENEMY OF YER ENEMY IS A WORSER ENEMY!
'WORSER'? SERIOUSLY?
URK!
OOF!

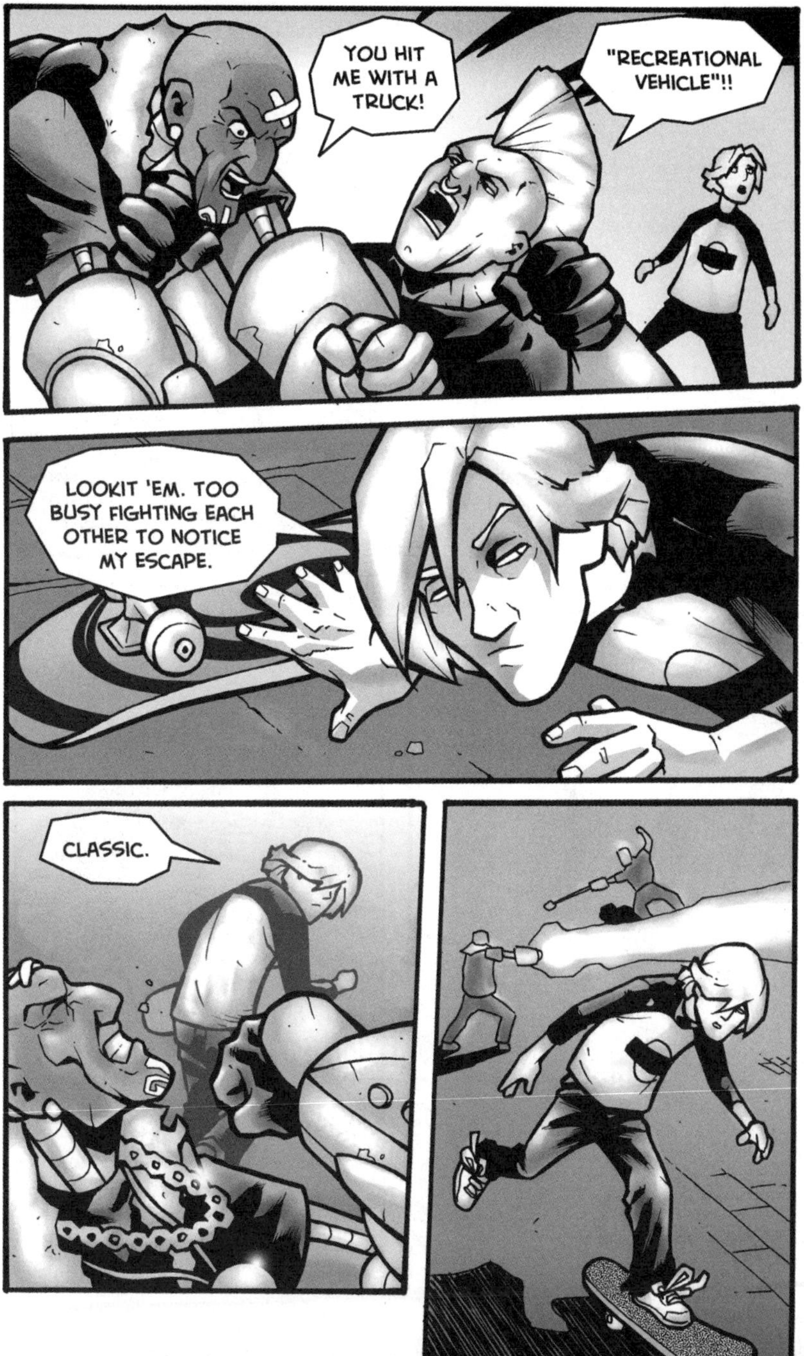
YOU HIT ME WITH A TRUCK!
"RECREATIONAL VEHICLE"!!
LOOKIT 'EM. TOO BUSY FIGHTING EACH OTHER TO NOTICE MY ESCAPE.
CLASSIC.

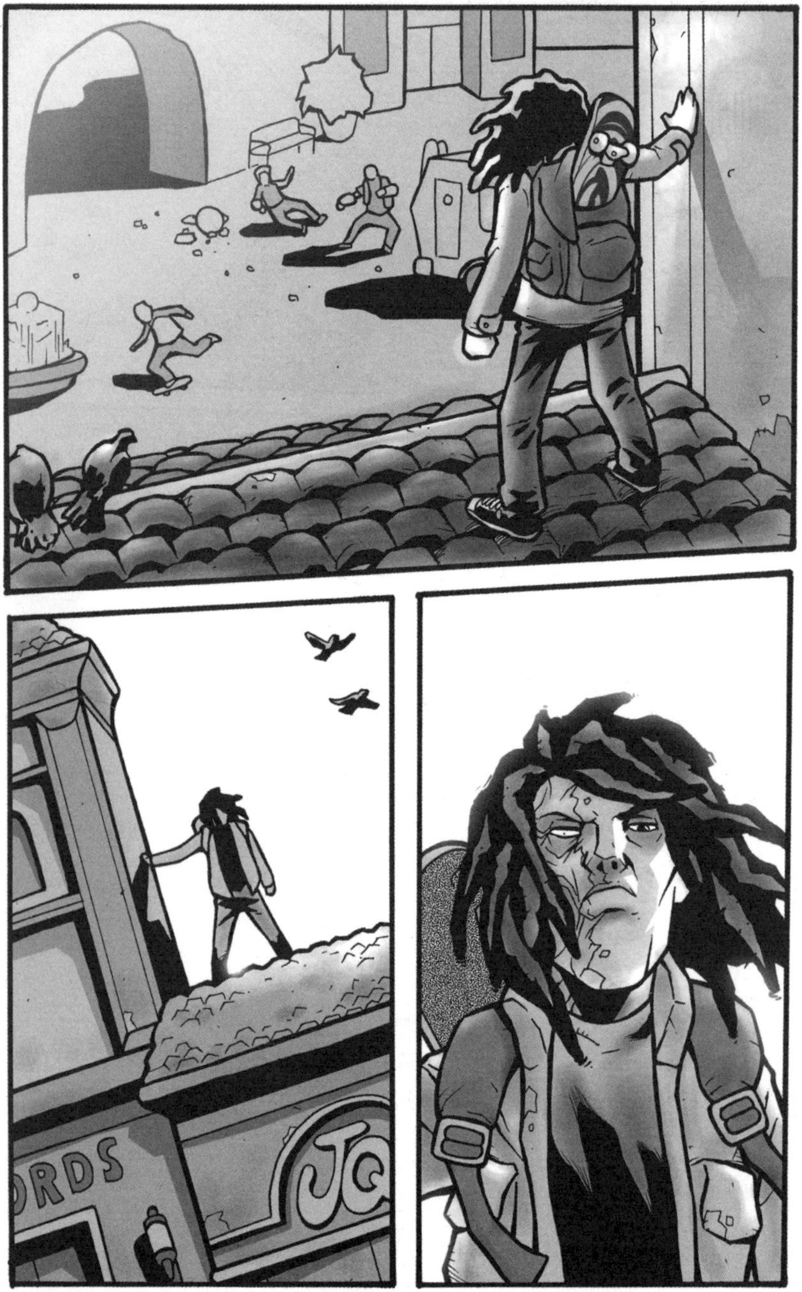
ORDS

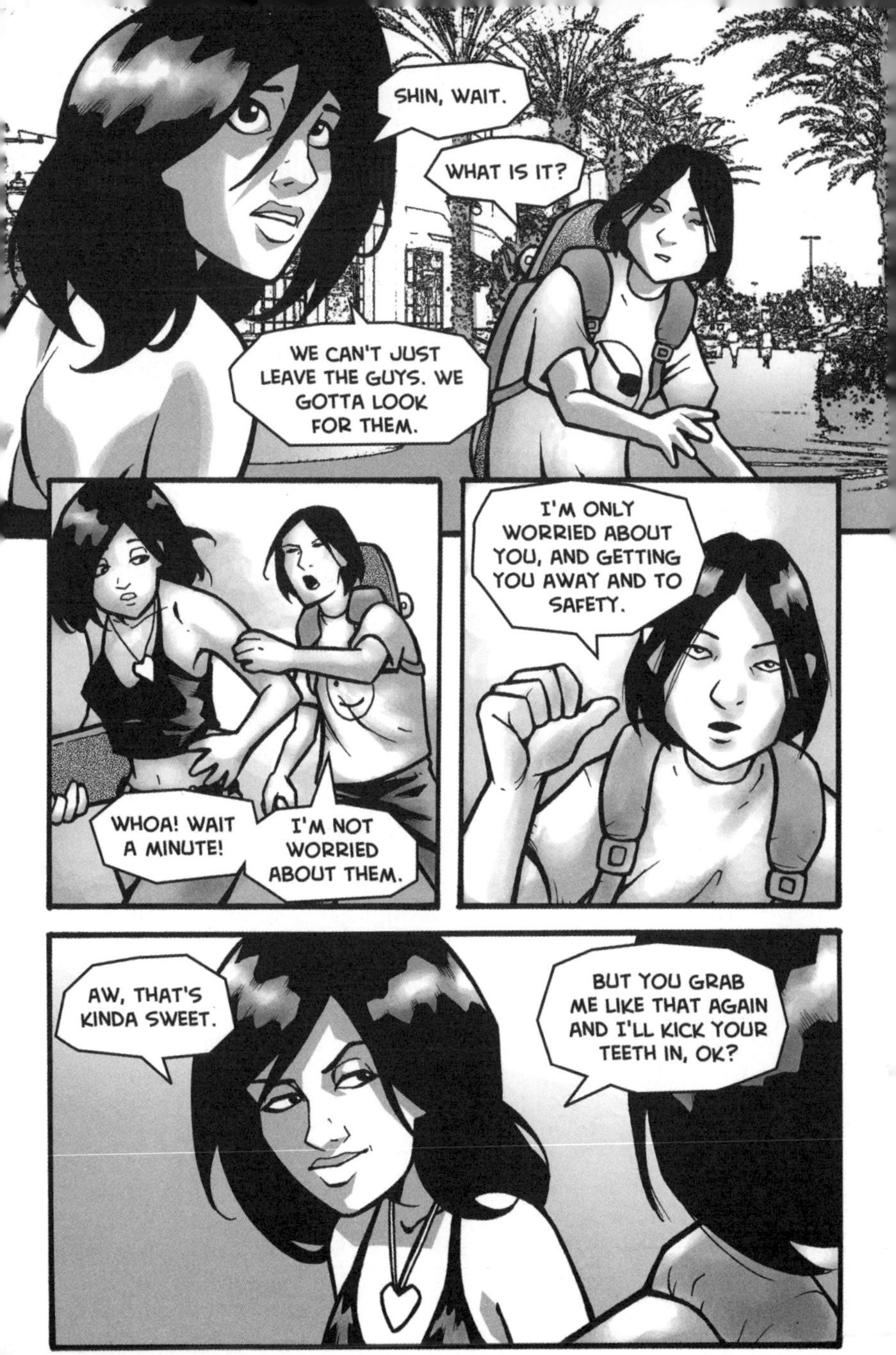

SHIN, WAIT.
WHAT IS IT?
WE CAN'T JUST LEAVE THE GUYS. WE GOTTA LOOK FOR THEM.
WHOA! WAIT A MINUTE!
I'M NOT WORRIED ABOUT THEM.
I'M ONLY WORRIED ABOUT YOU, AND GETTING YOU AWAY AND TO SAFETY.
AW, THAT'S KINDA SWEET.
BUT YOU GRAB ME LIKE THAT AGAIN AND I'LL KICK YOUR TEETH IN, OK?

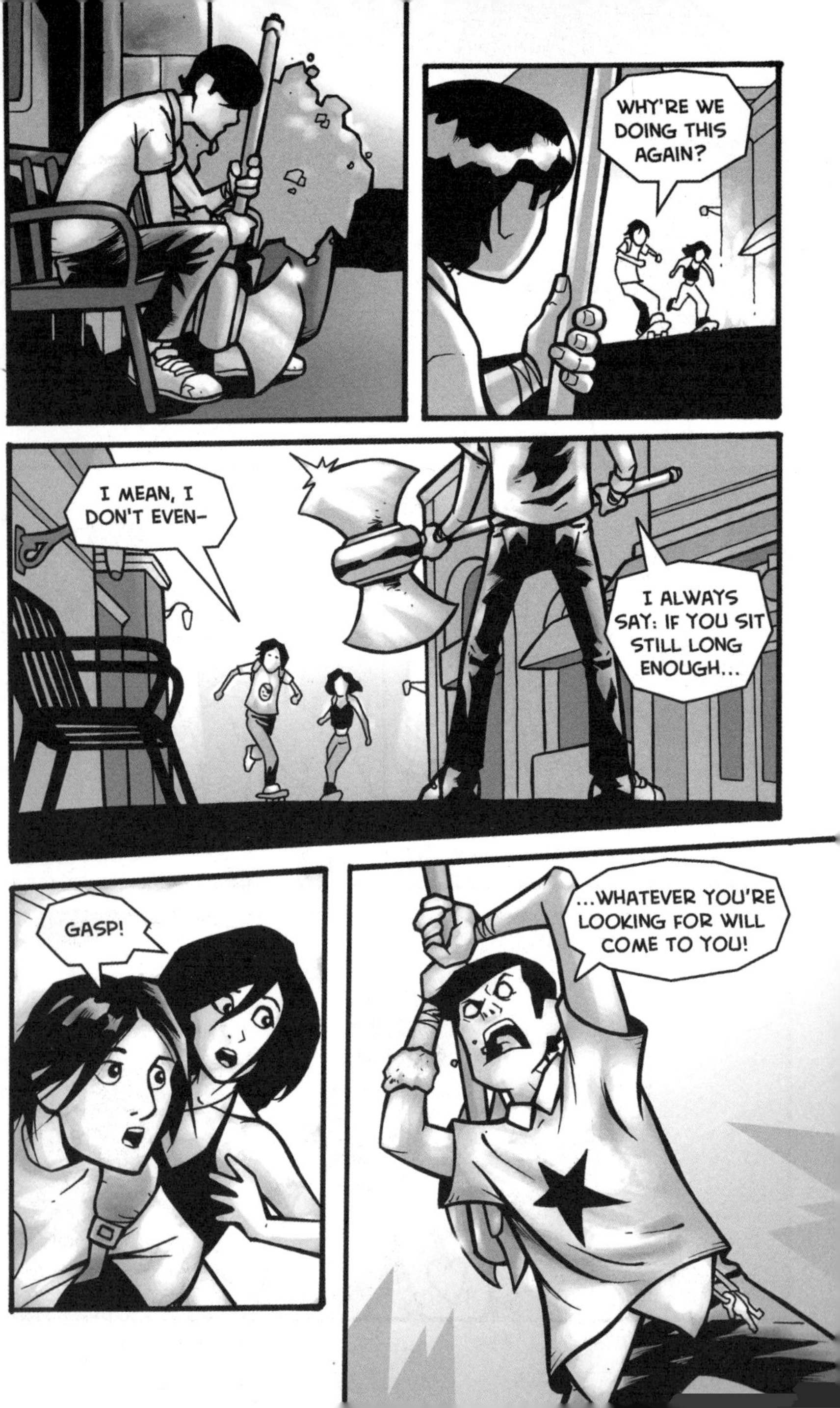
WHY'RE WE DOING THIS AGAIN?
I MEAN, I DON'T EVEN-
I ALWAYS SAY: IF YOU SIT STILL LONG ENOUGH...
GASP!
...WHATEVER YOU'RE LOOKING FOR WILL COME TO YOU!

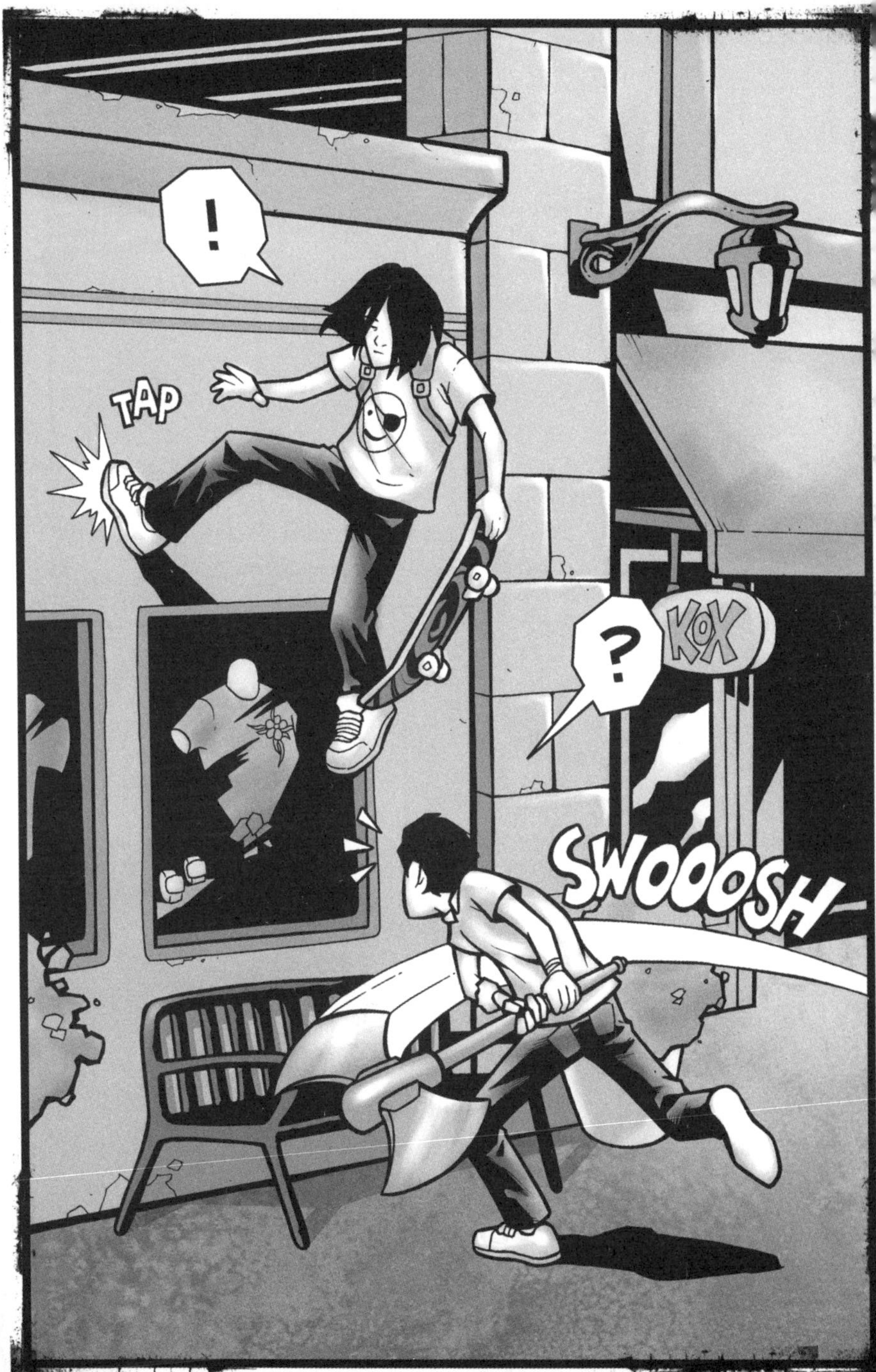
!
TAP
?
KOX
SWOOOSH

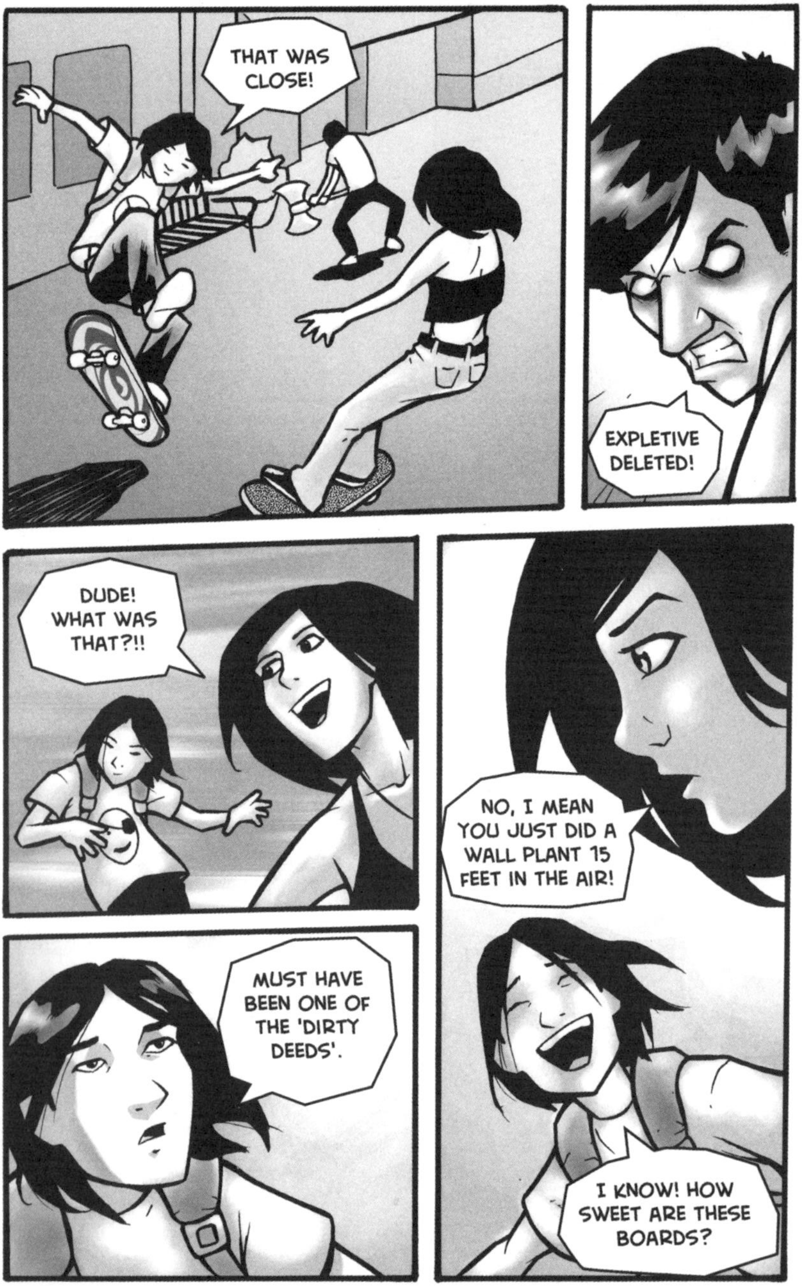
THAT WAS CLOSE!
EXPLETIVE DELETED!
DUDE! WHAT WAS THAT?!!
NO, I MEAN YOU JUST DID A WALL PLANT 15 FEET IN THE AIR!
MUST HAVE BEEN ONE OF THE 'DIRTY DEEDS'.
I KNOW! HOW SWEET ARE THESE BOARDS?

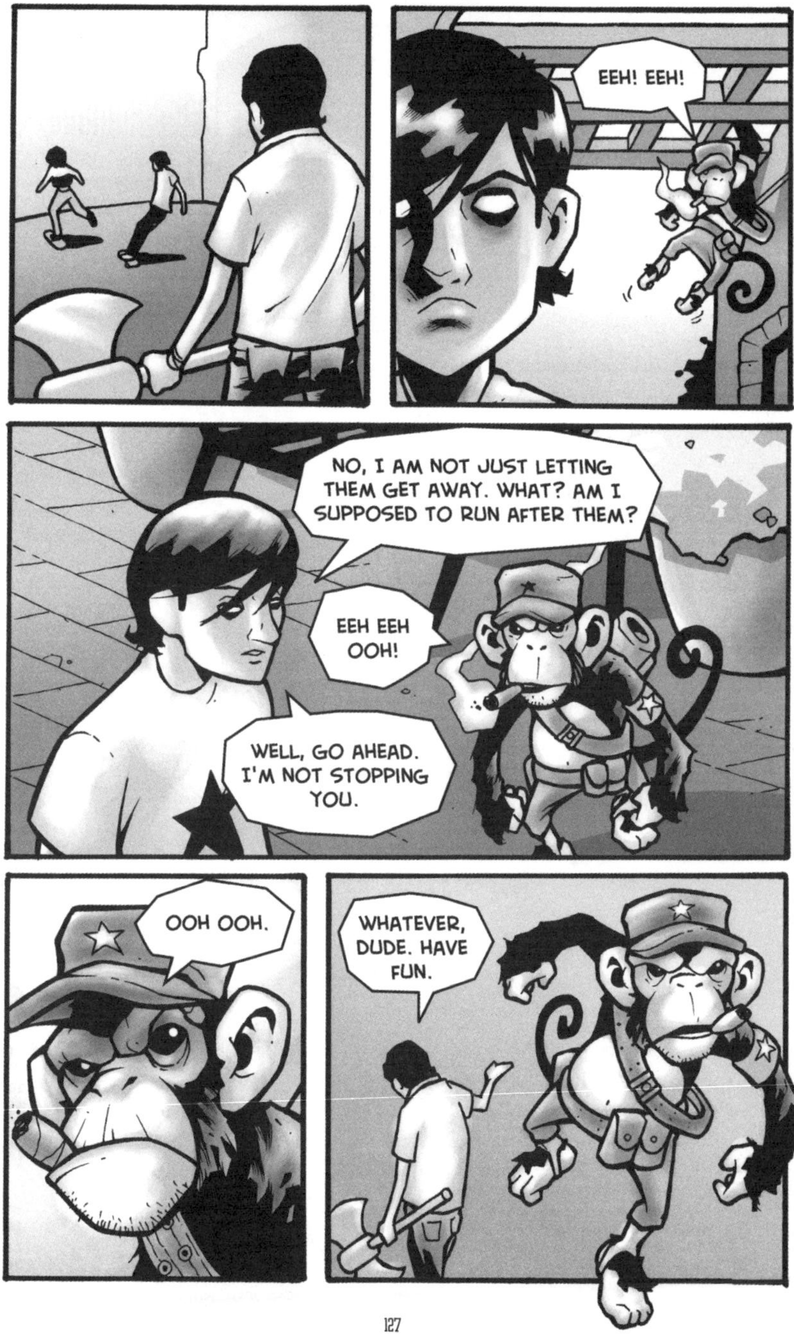
EEH! EEH!
NO, I AM NOT JUST LETTING THEM GET AWAY. WHAT? AM I SUPPOSED TO RUN AFTER THEM?
EEH EEH OOH!
WELL, GO AHEAD. I'M NOT STOPPING YOU.
OOH OOH.
WHATEVER, DUDE. HAVE FUN.

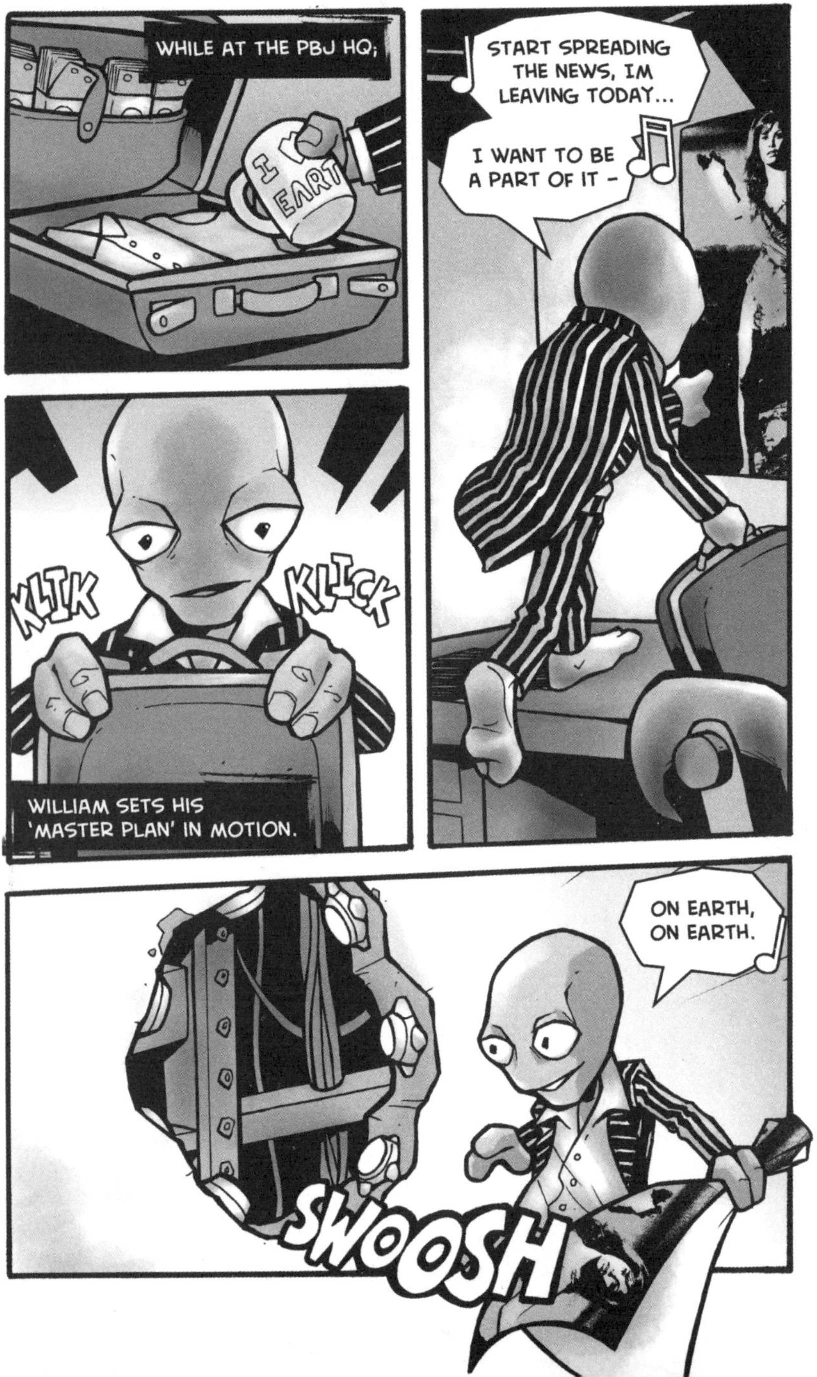
WHILE AT THE PBJ HQ;
I ♥ EARTH
START SPREADING THE NEWS, IM LEAVING TODAY...
I WANT TO BE A PART OF IT –
KLIK
KLICK
WILLIAM SETS HIS 'MASTER PLAN' IN MOTION.
ON EARTH, ON EARTH.
SWOOSH

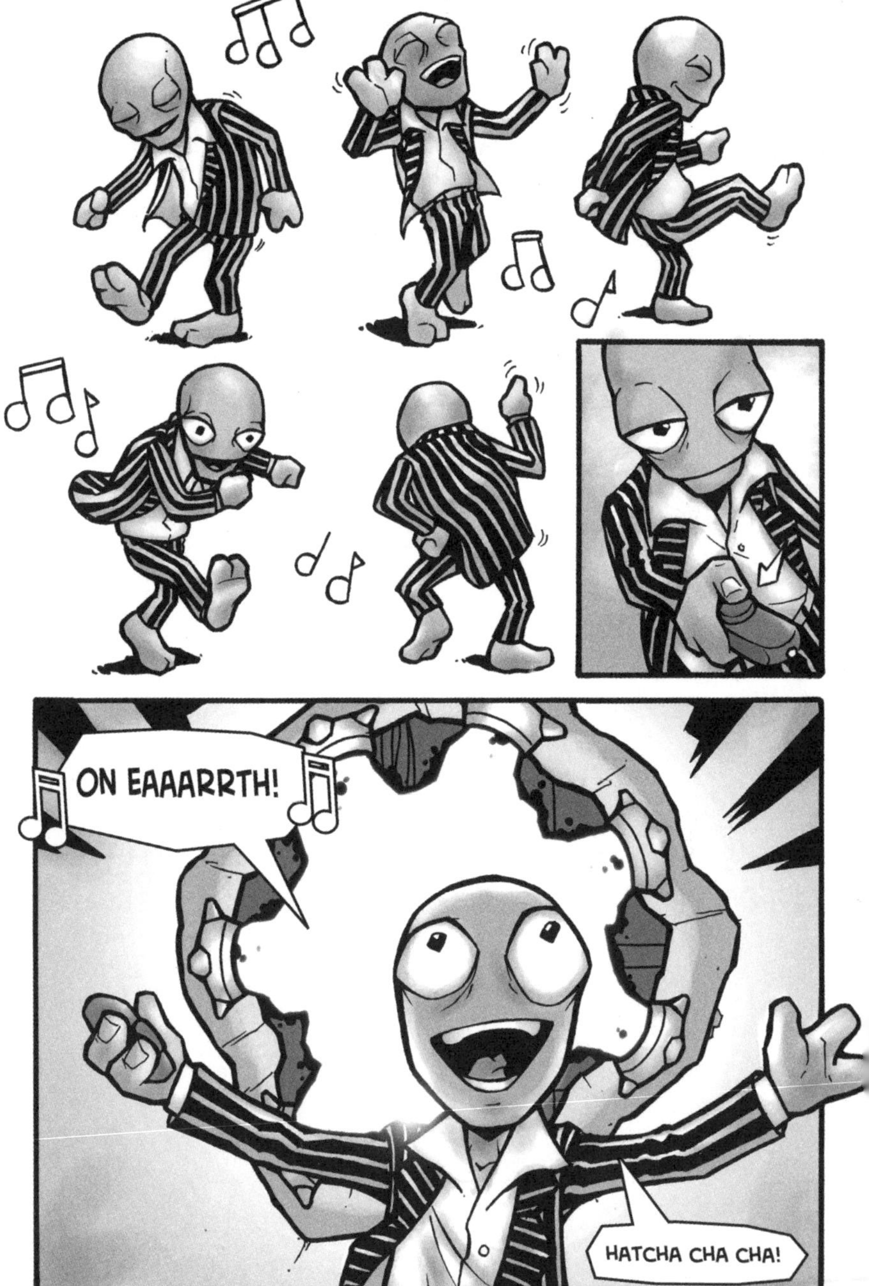
ON EAAARRTH!
HATCHA CHA CHA!

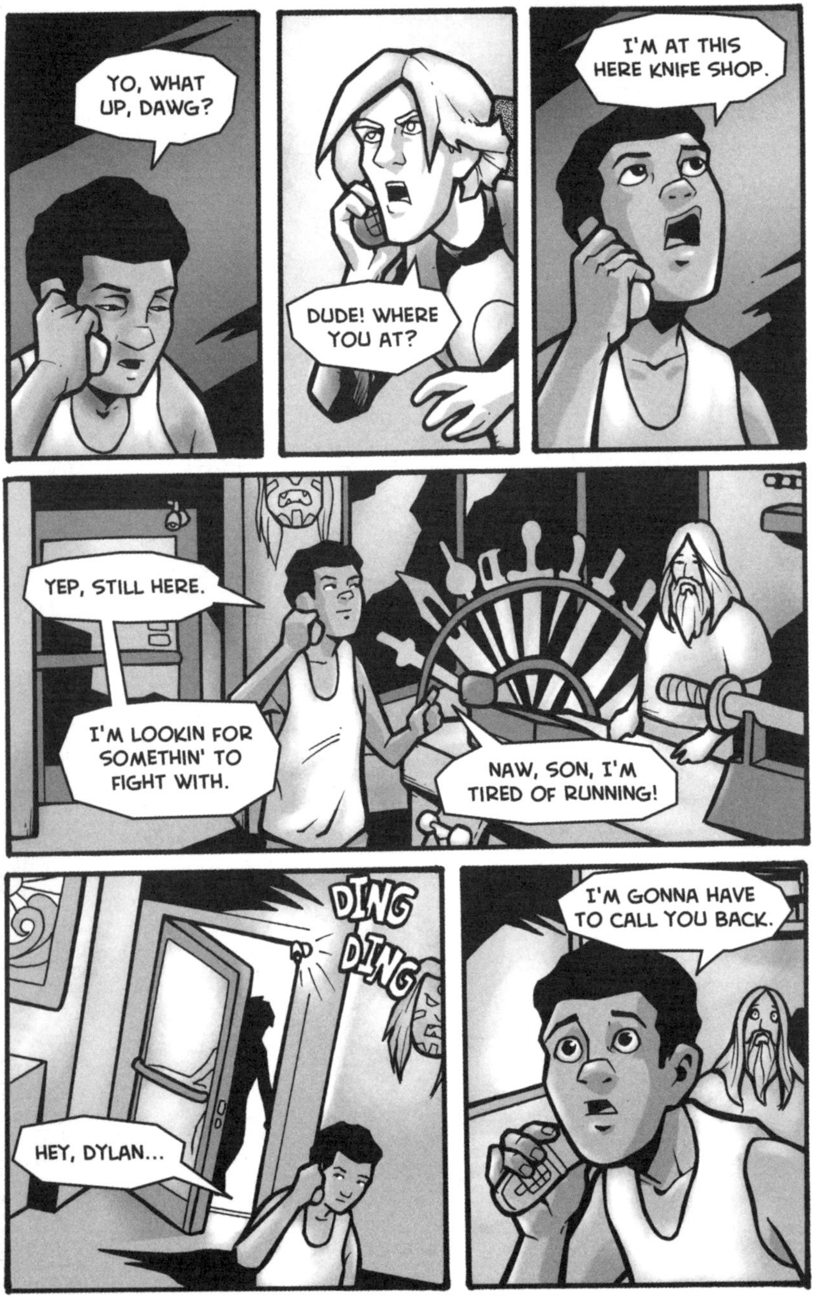

YO, WHAT UP, DAWG?
DUDE! WHERE YOU AT?
I'M AT THIS HERE KNIFE SHOP.
YEP, STILL HERE.
I'M LOOKIN FOR SOMETHIN' TO FIGHT WITH.
NAW, SON, I'M TIRED OF RUNNING!
DING
DING
HEY, DYLAN...
I'M GONNA HAVE TO CALL YOU BACK.

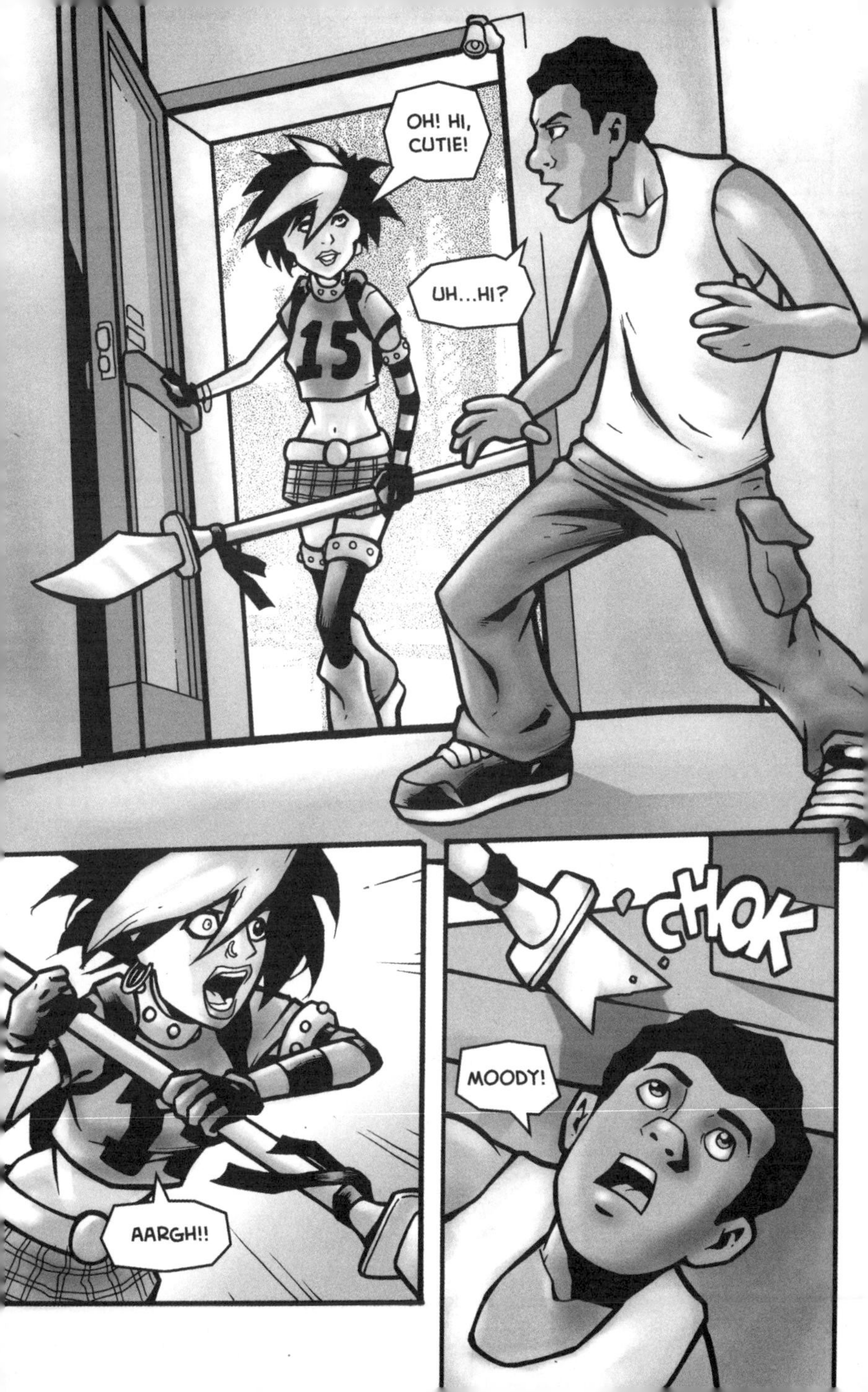
OH! HI, CUTIE!
UH...HI?
AARGH!!
CHOK
MOODY!

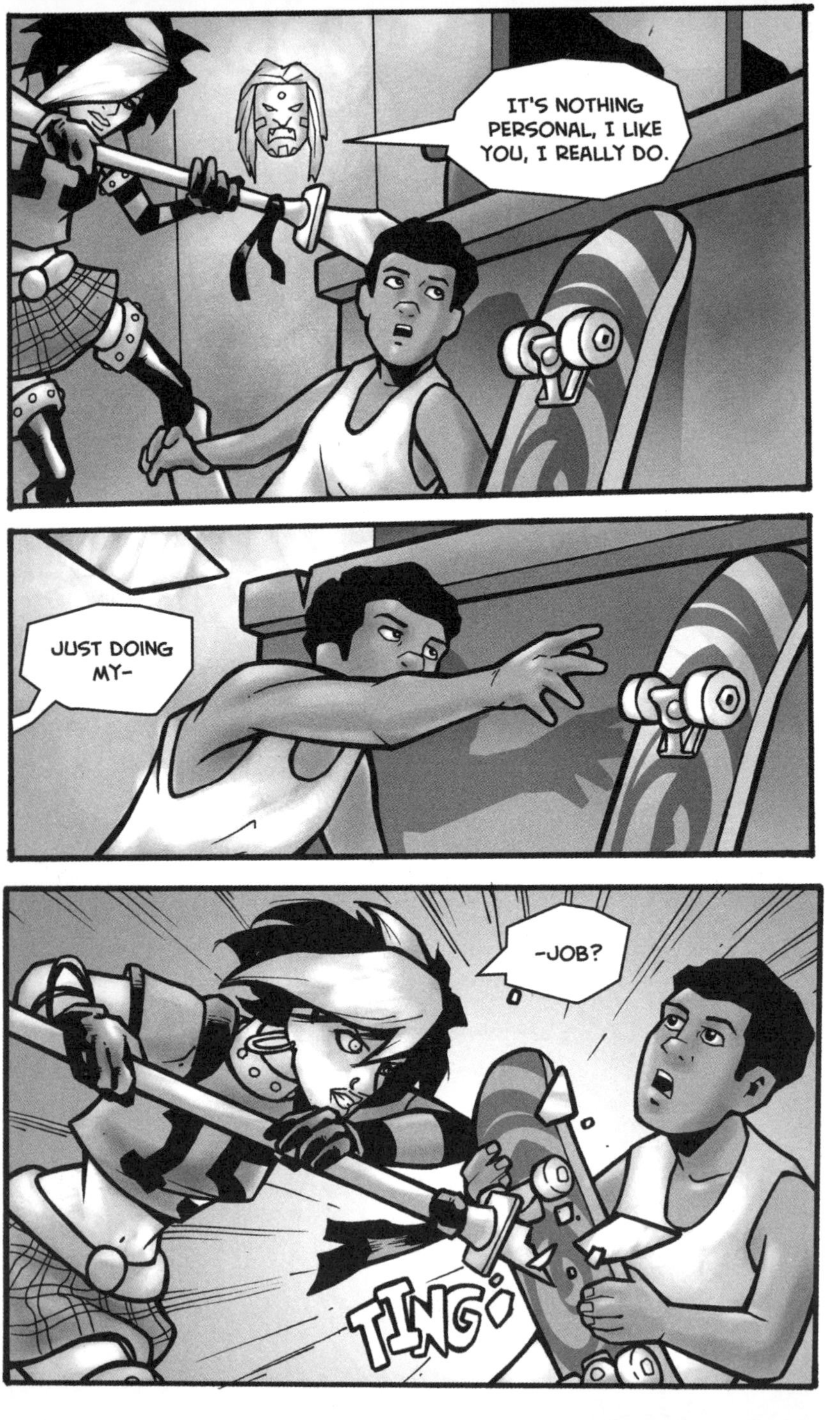
IT'S NOTHING PERSONAL, I LIKE YOU, I REALLY DO.
JUST DOING MY-
-JOB?
TING

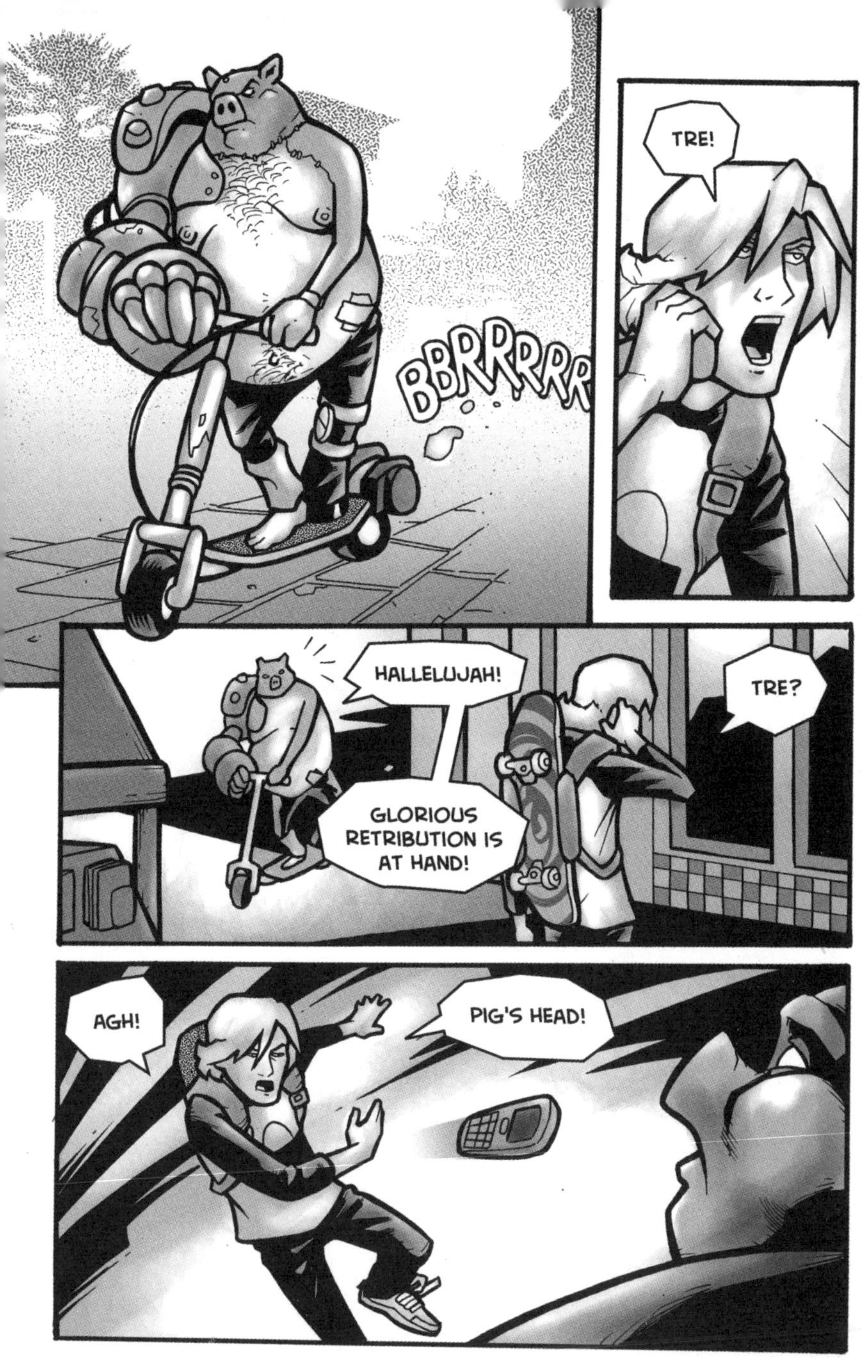
BBRRRRRR
TRE!
HALLELUJAH!
GLORIOUS RETRIBUTION IS AT HAND!
TRE?
AGH!
PIG'S HEAD!

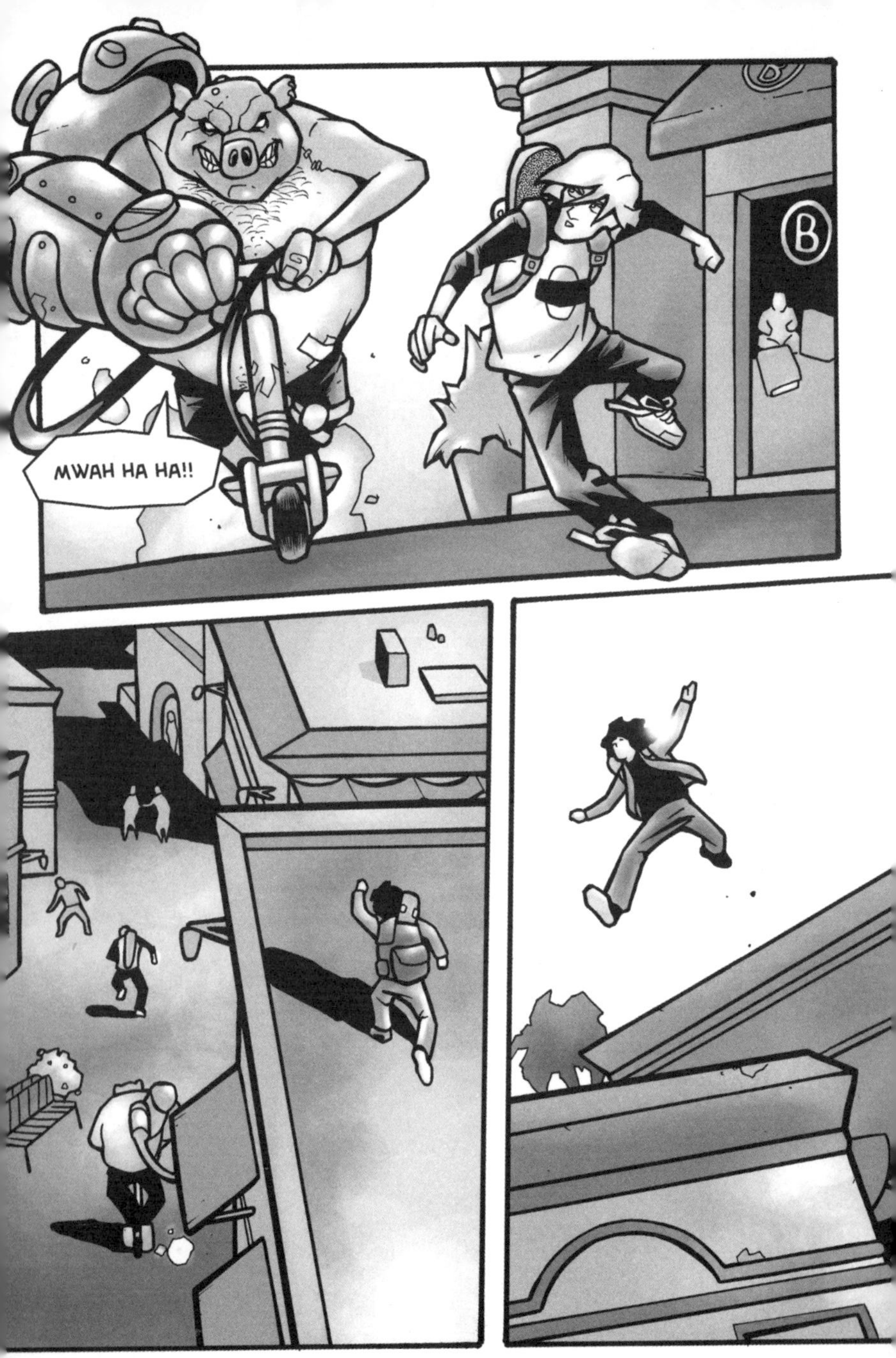
MWAH HA HA!!
B

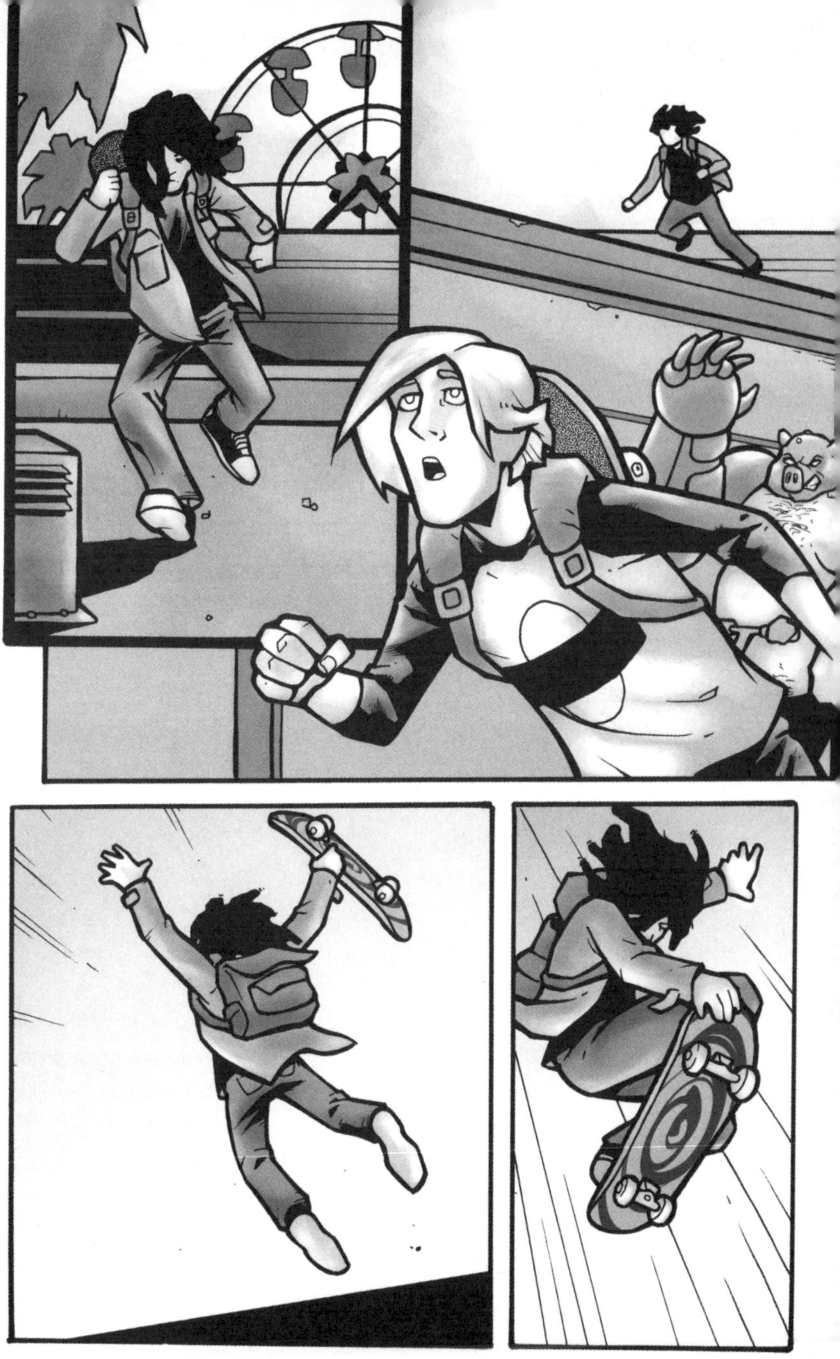

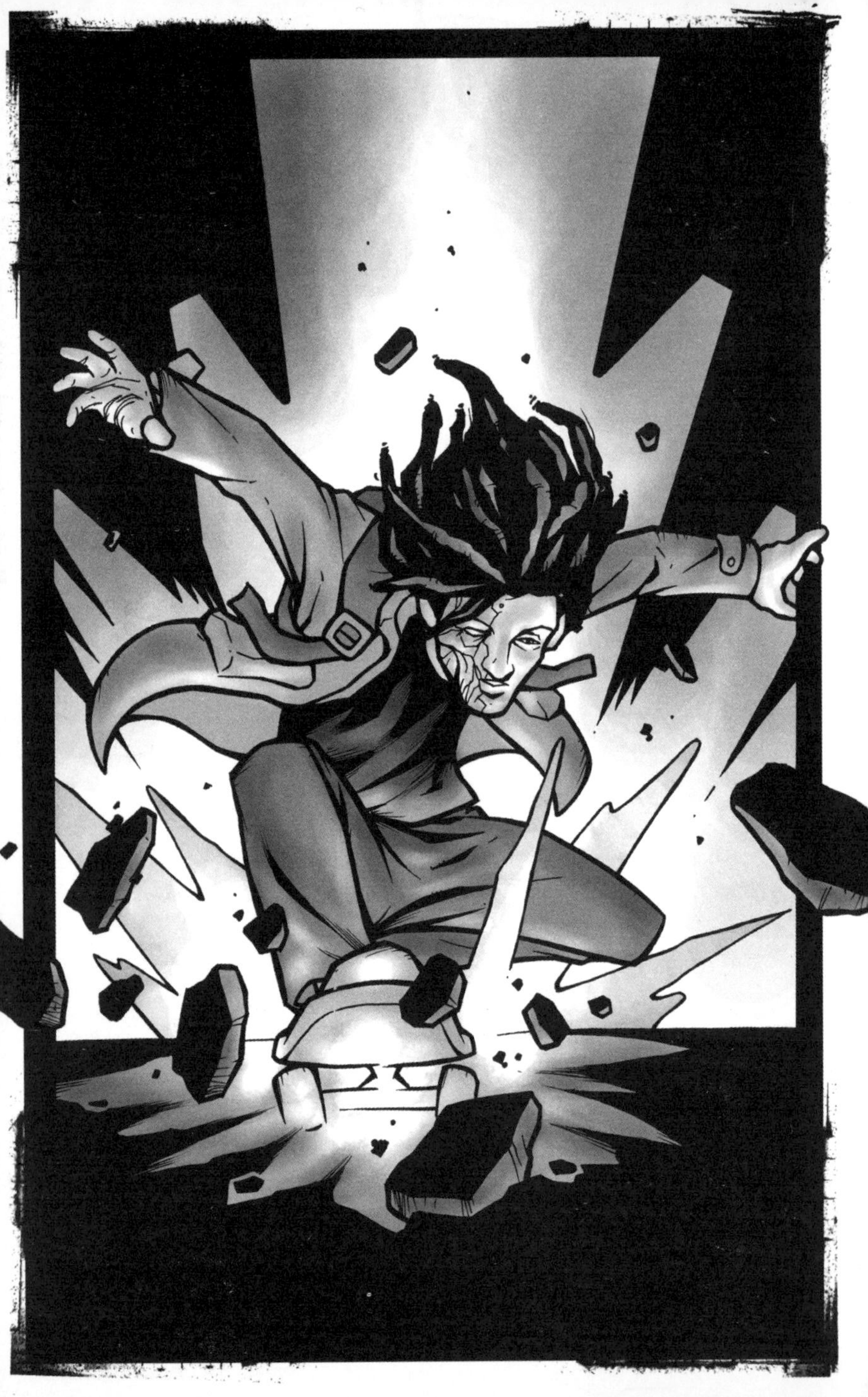

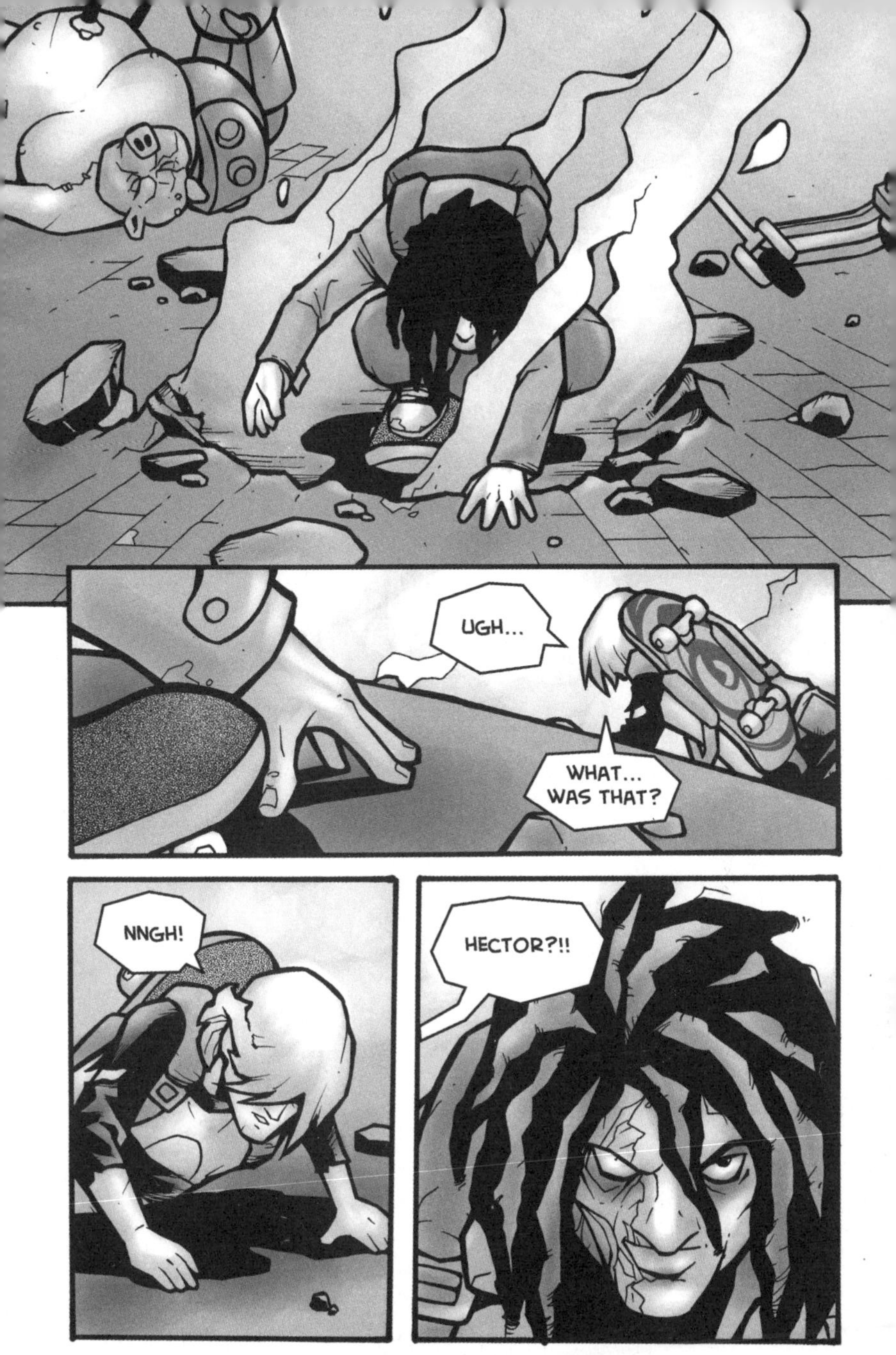
UGH...
WHAT... WAS THAT?
NNGH!
HECTOR?!!

chapter five

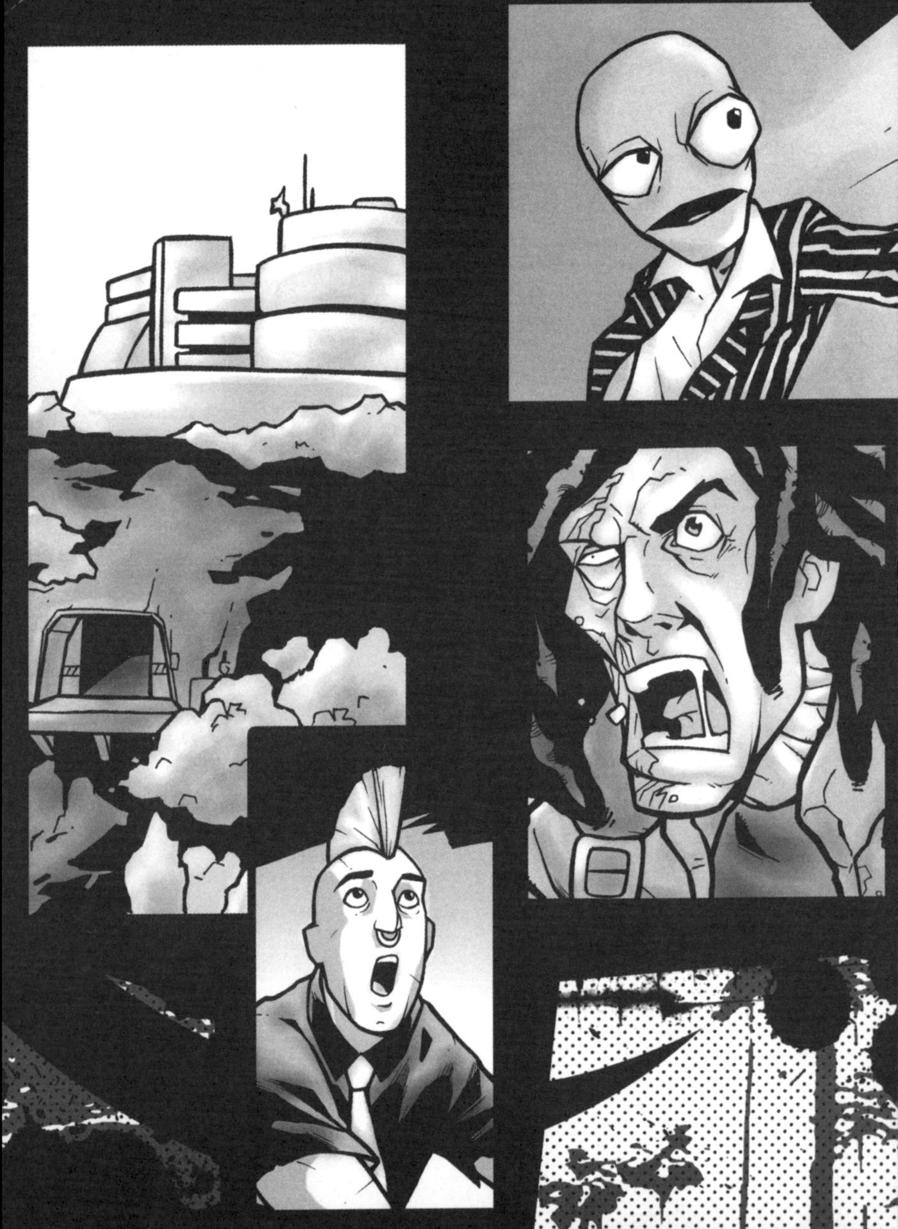

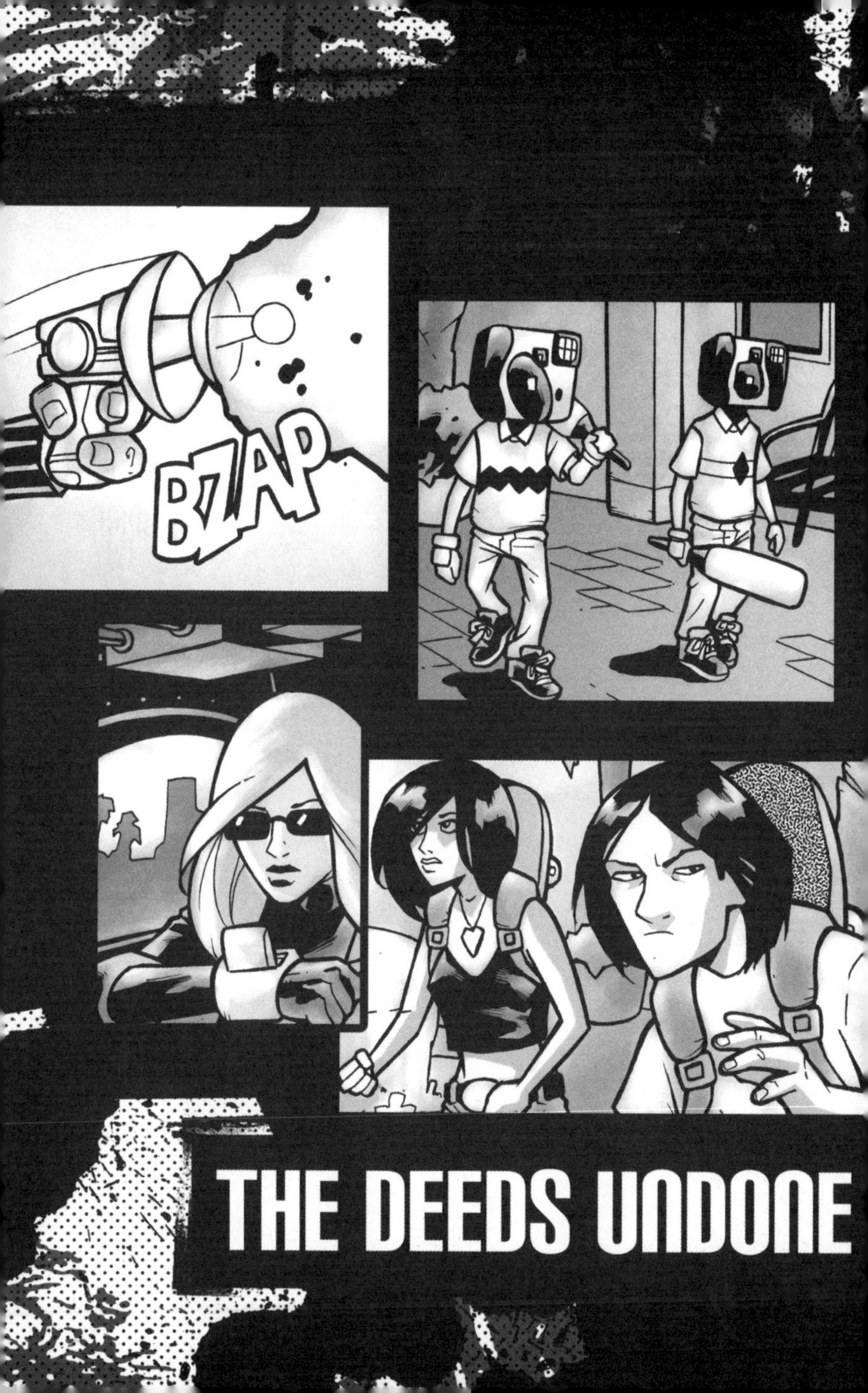
BZAP

THE DEEDS UNDONE

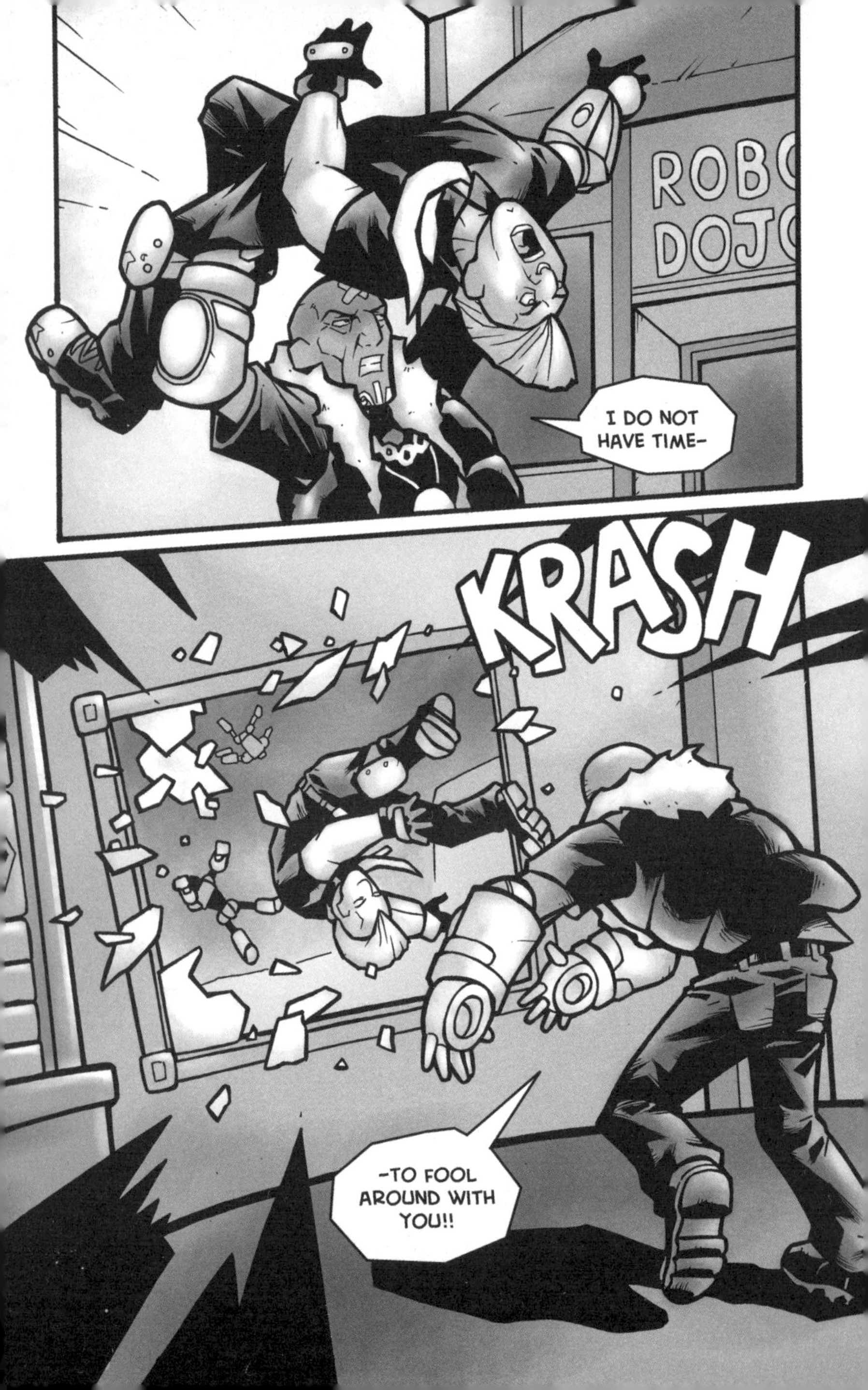
ROBO
DOJO
I DO NOT HAVE TIME-
KRASH
-TO FOOL AROUND WITH YOU!!

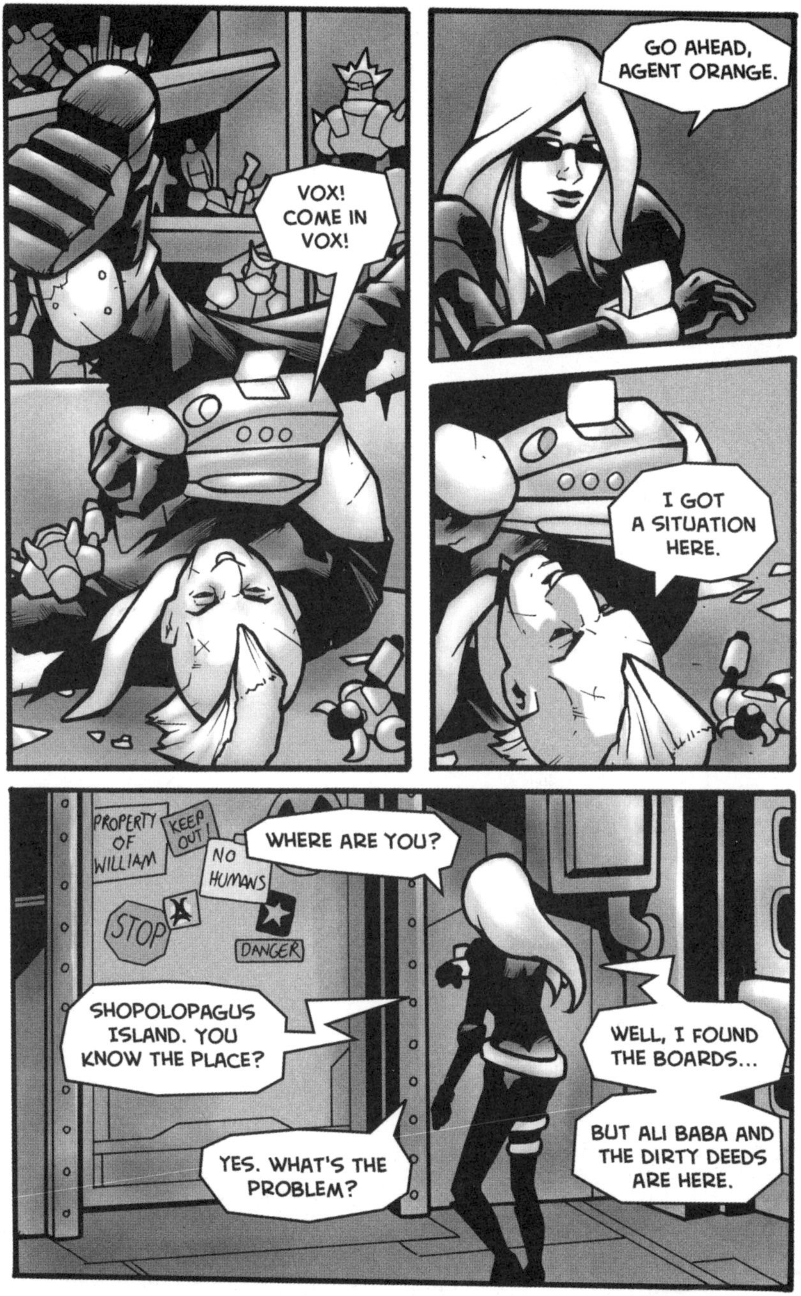
VOX! COME IN VOX!
GO AHEAD, AGENT ORANGE.
I GOT A SITUATION HERE.
PROPERTY OF WILLIAM
KEEP OUT!
NO HUMANS
STOP
DANGER
WHERE ARE YOU?
SHOPOLOPAGUS ISLAND. YOU KNOW THE PLACE?
YES. WHAT'S THE PROBLEM?
WELL, I FOUND THE BOARDS...
BUT ALI BABA AND THE DIRTY DEEDS ARE HERE.

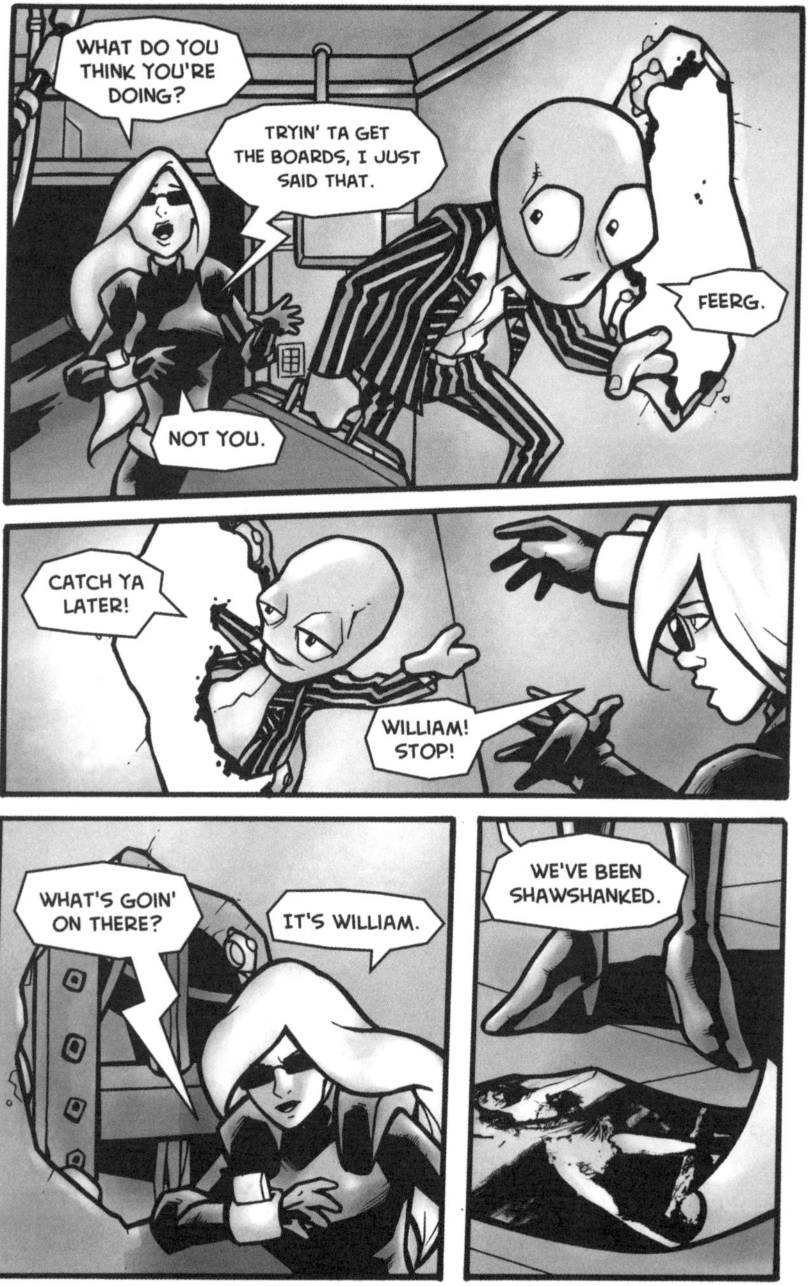
WHAT DO YOU THINK YOU'RE DOING?
TRYIN' TA GET THE BOARDS, I JUST SAID THAT.
FEERG.
NOT YOU.
CATCH YA LATER!
WILLIAM! STOP!
WHAT'S GOIN' ON THERE?
IT'S WILLIAM.
WE'VE BEEN SHAWSHANKED.

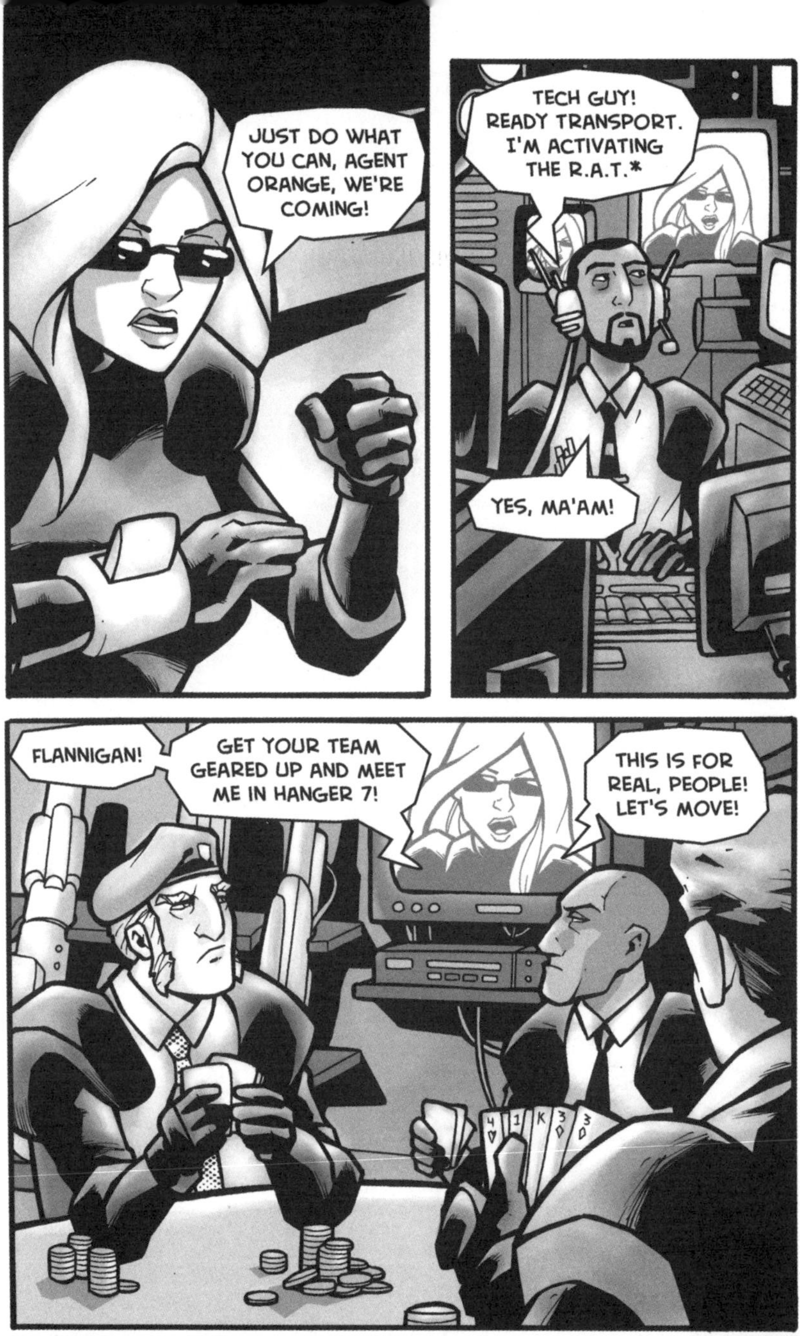
JUST DO WHAT YOU CAN, AGENT ORANGE, WE'RE COMING!
TECH GUY! READY TRANSPORT. I'M ACTIVATING THE R.A.T.*
YES, MA'AM!
FLANNIGAN!
GET YOUR TEAM GEARED UP AND MEET ME IN HANGER 7!
THIS IS FOR REAL, PEOPLE! LET'S MOVE!

* RAPID ASSAULT TEAM

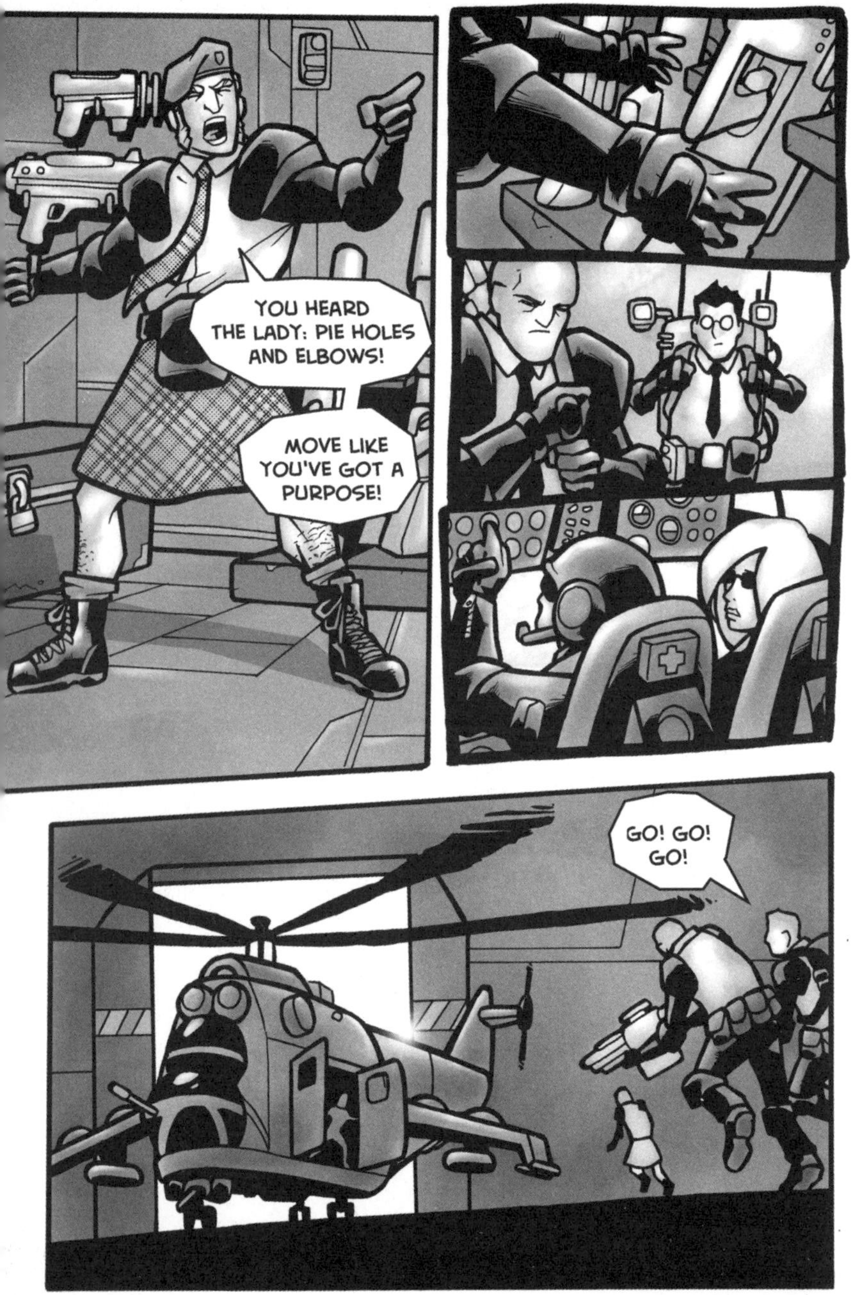
YOU HEARD THE LADY: PIE HOLES AND ELBOWS!
MOVE LIKE YOU'VE GOT A PURPOSE!
GO! GO! GO!

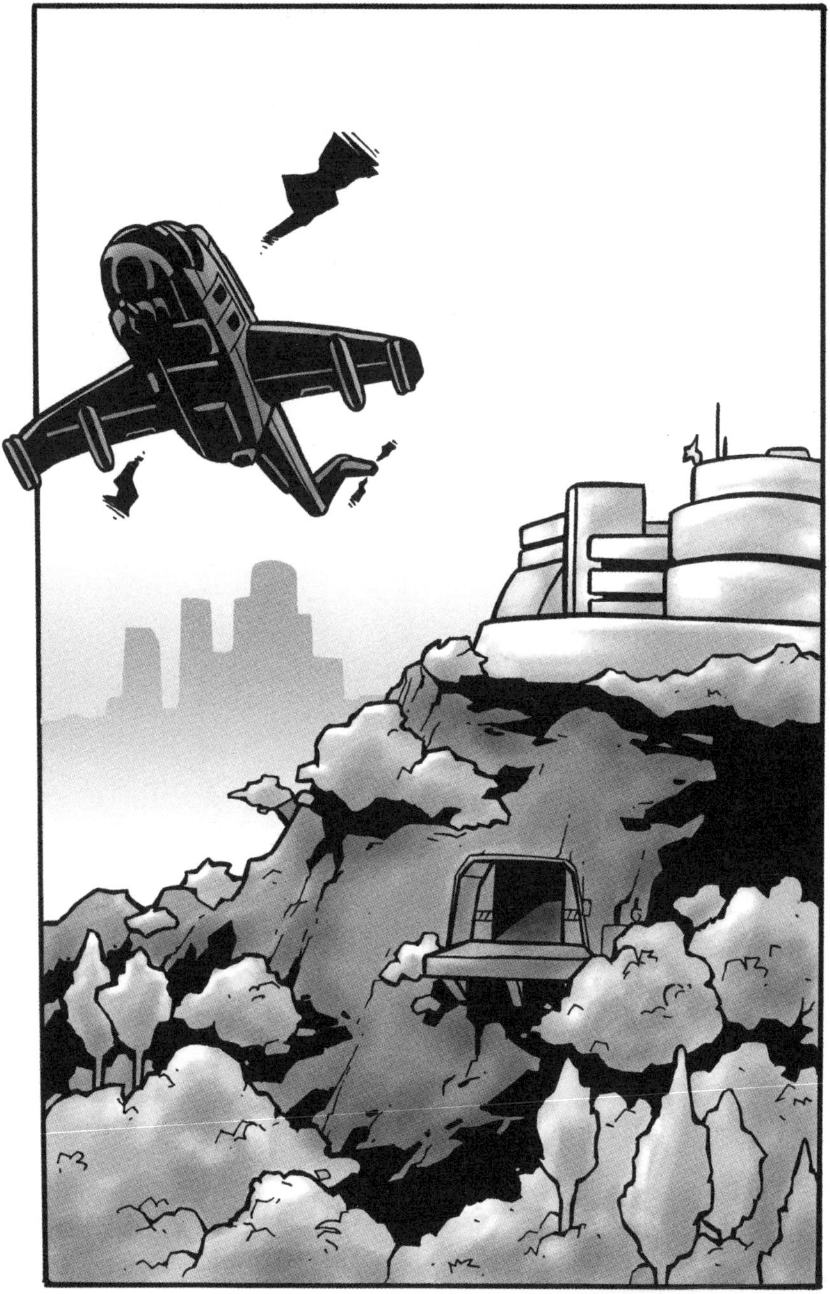

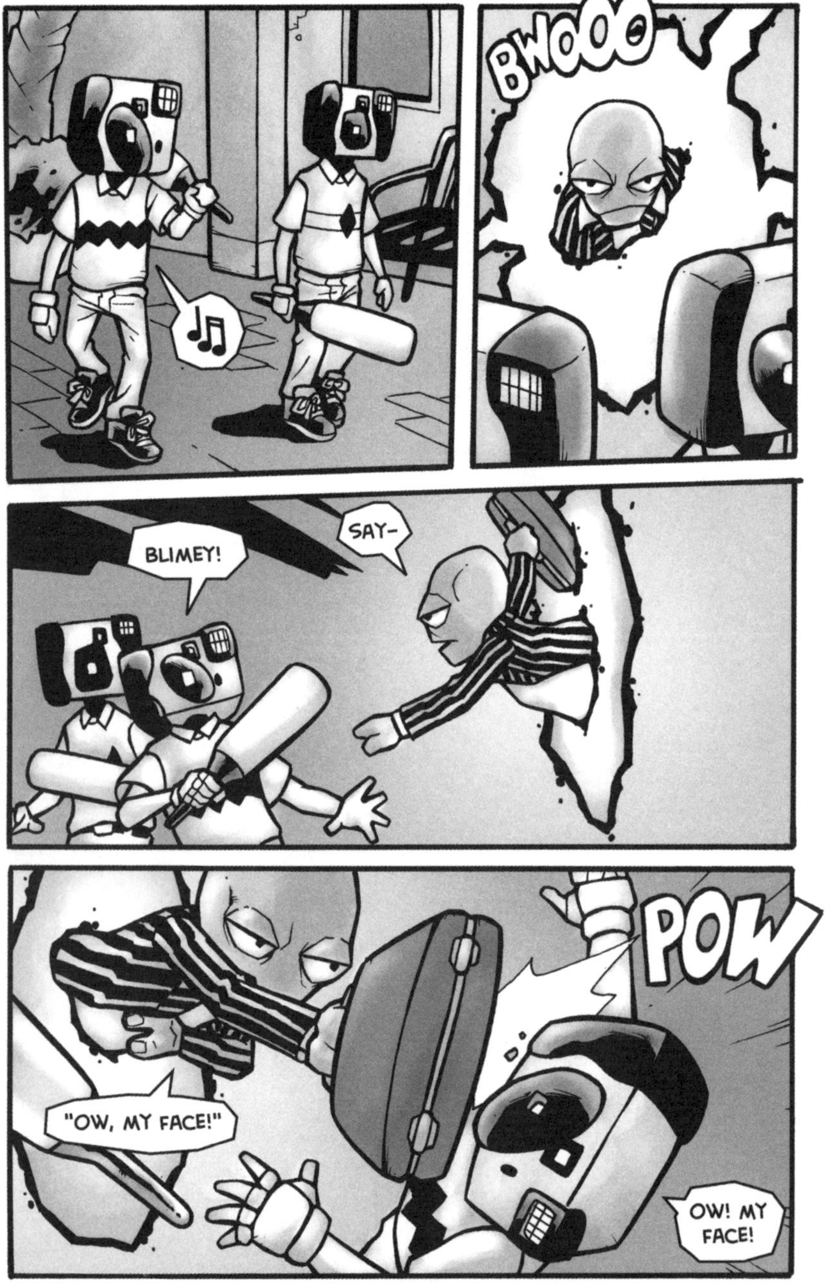
BWOOO
BLIMEY!
SAY-
POW
"OW, MY FACE!"
OW! MY FACE!

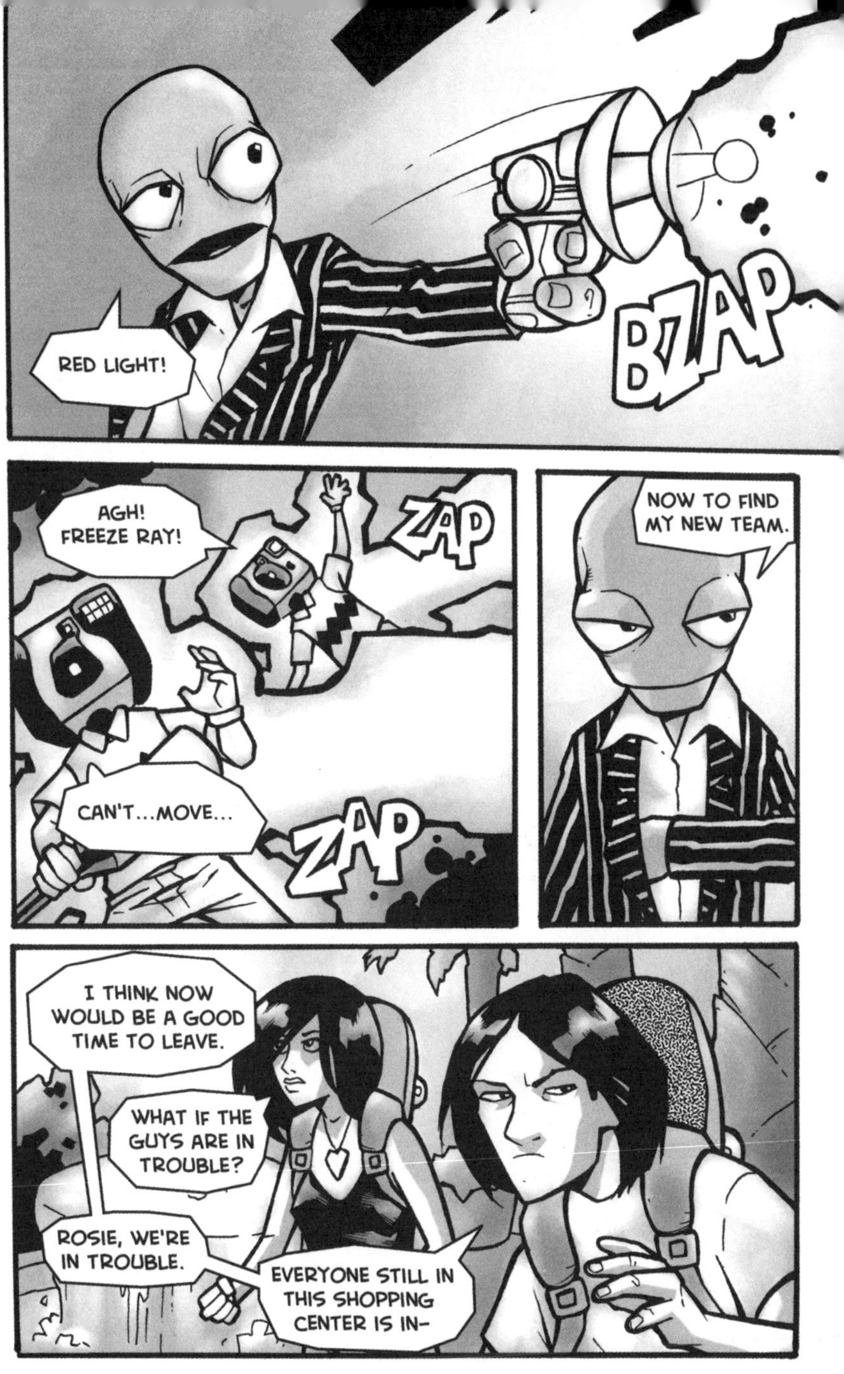
RED LIGHT!
BZAP
AGH! FREEZE RAY!
ZAP
CAN'T...MOVE...
ZAP
NOW TO FIND MY NEW TEAM.
I THINK NOW WOULD BE A GOOD TIME TO LEAVE.
WHAT IF THE GUYS ARE IN TROUBLE?
ROSIE, WE'RE IN TROUBLE.
EVERYONE STILL IN THIS SHOPPING CENTER IS IN-

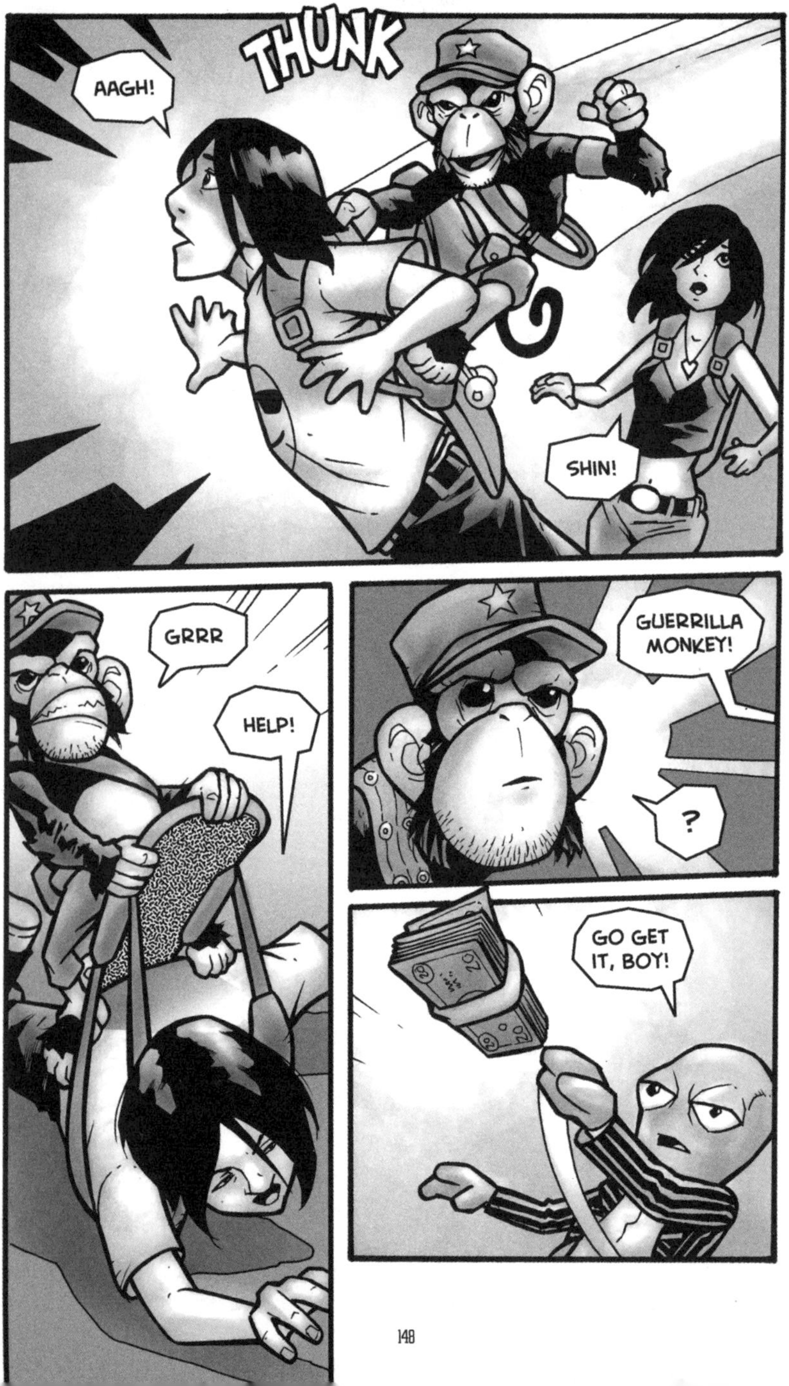
THUNK
AAGH!
SHIN!
GRRR
HELP!
GUERRILLA MONKEY!
?
GO GET IT, BOY!

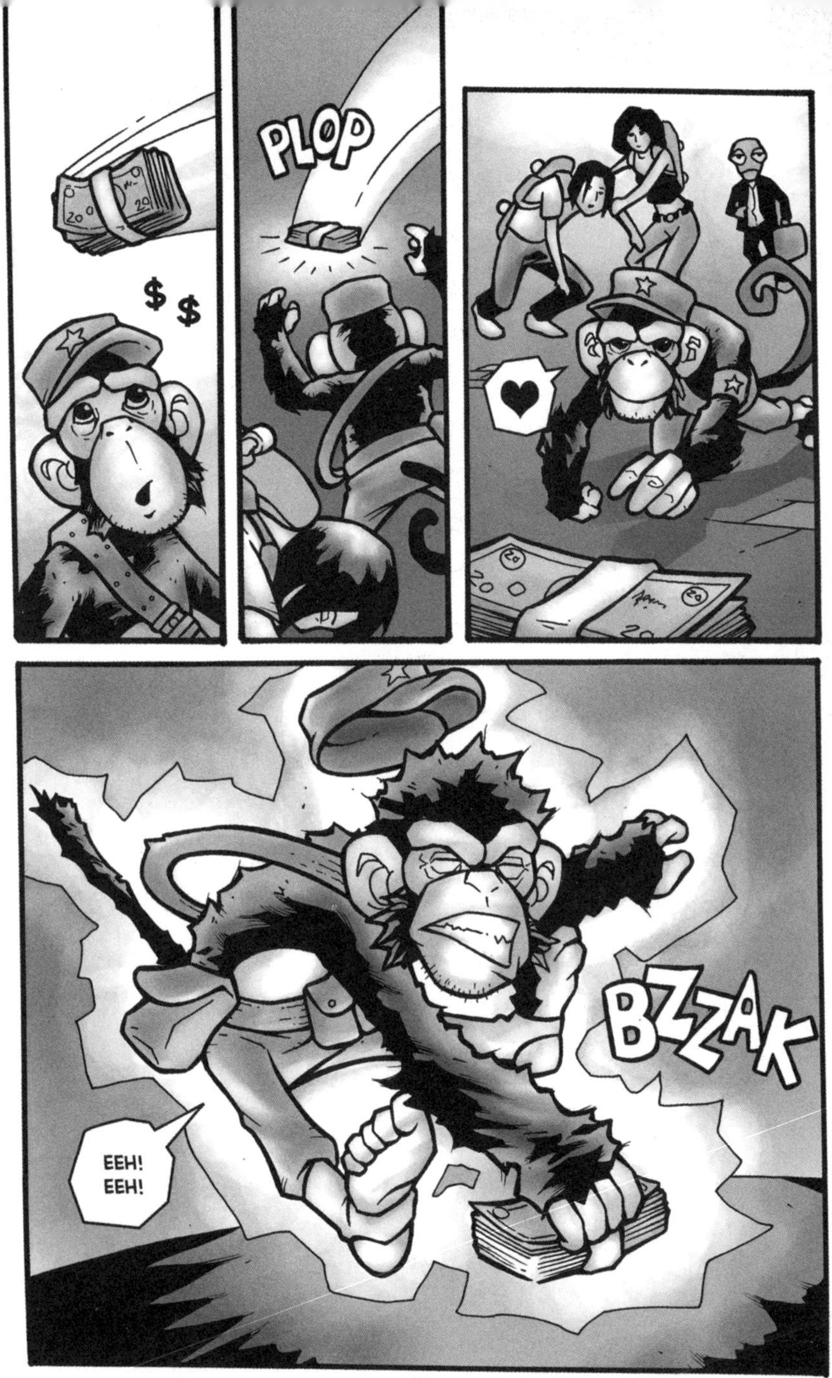
$ $
PLOP
EEH!
EEH!
BZZAK

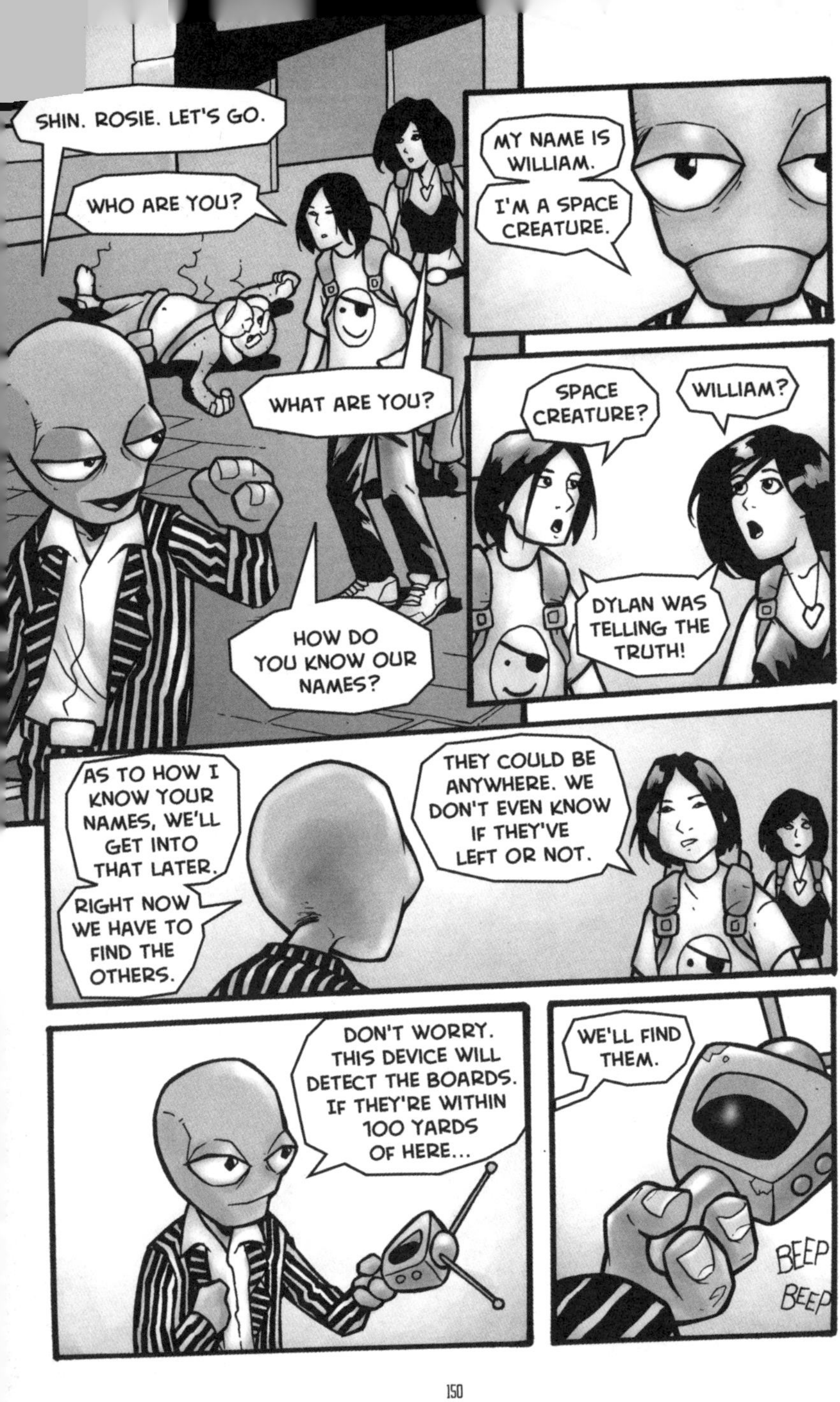

SHIN. ROSIE. LET'S GO.
WHO ARE YOU?
WHAT ARE YOU?
HOW DO YOU KNOW OUR NAMES?
MY NAME IS WILLIAM.
I'M A SPACE CREATURE.
SPACE CREATURE?
WILLIAM?
DYLAN WAS TELLING THE TRUTH!
AS TO HOW I KNOW YOUR NAMES, WE'LL GET INTO THAT LATER.
RIGHT NOW WE HAVE TO FIND THE OTHERS.
THEY COULD BE ANYWHERE. WE DON'T EVEN KNOW IF THEY'VE LEFT OR NOT.
DON'T WORRY. THIS DEVICE WILL DETECT THE BOARDS. IF THEY'RE WITHIN 100 YARDS OF HERE...
WE'LL FIND THEM.
BEEP
BEEP

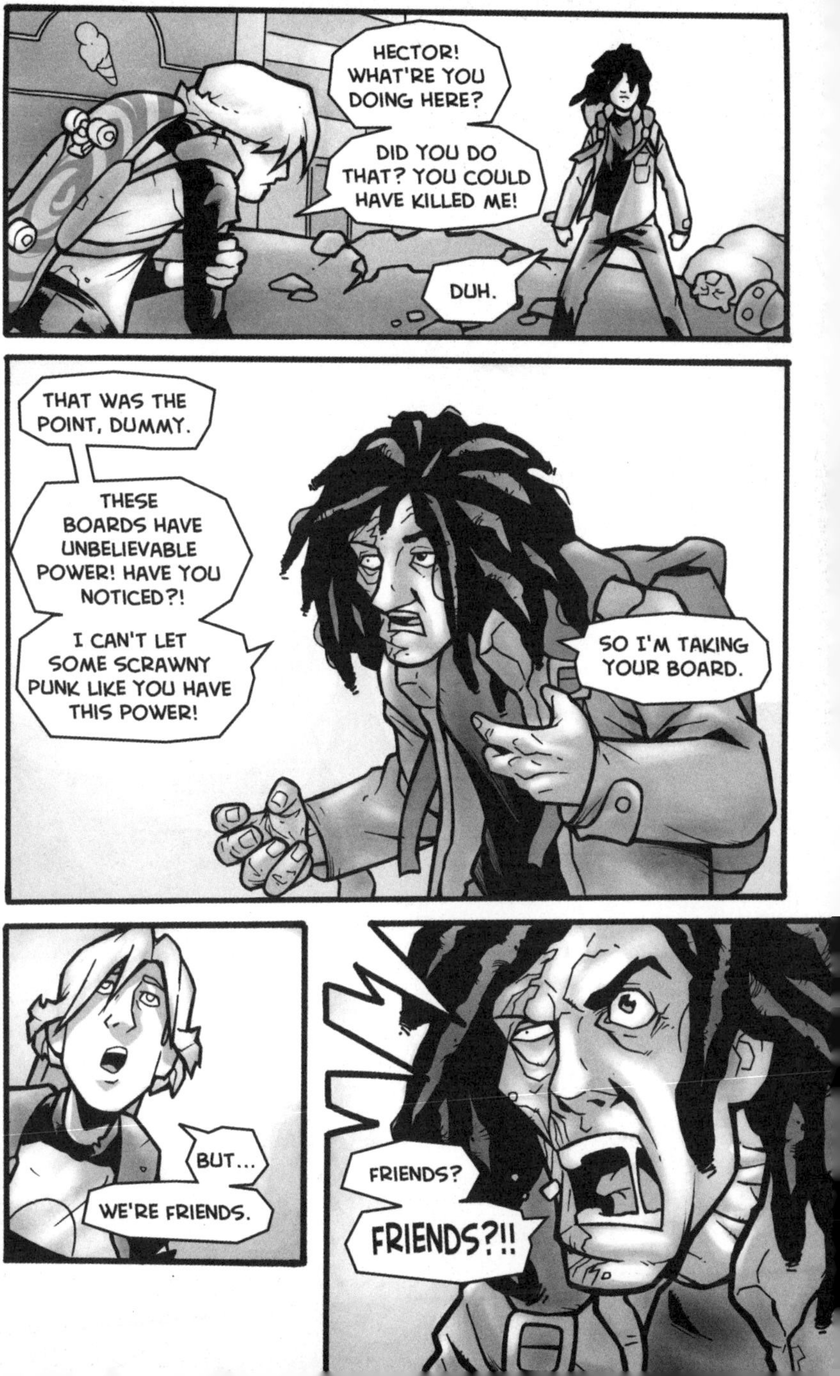
HECTOR! WHAT'RE YOU DOING HERE?
DID YOU DO THAT? YOU COULD HAVE KILLED ME!
DUH.
THAT WAS THE POINT, DUMMY.
THESE BOARDS HAVE UNBELIEVABLE POWER! HAVE YOU NOTICED?!
I CAN'T LET SOME SCRAWNY PUNK LIKE YOU HAVE THIS POWER!
SO I'M TAKING YOUR BOARD.
BUT...
WE'RE FRIENDS.
FRIENDS?
FRIENDS?!!

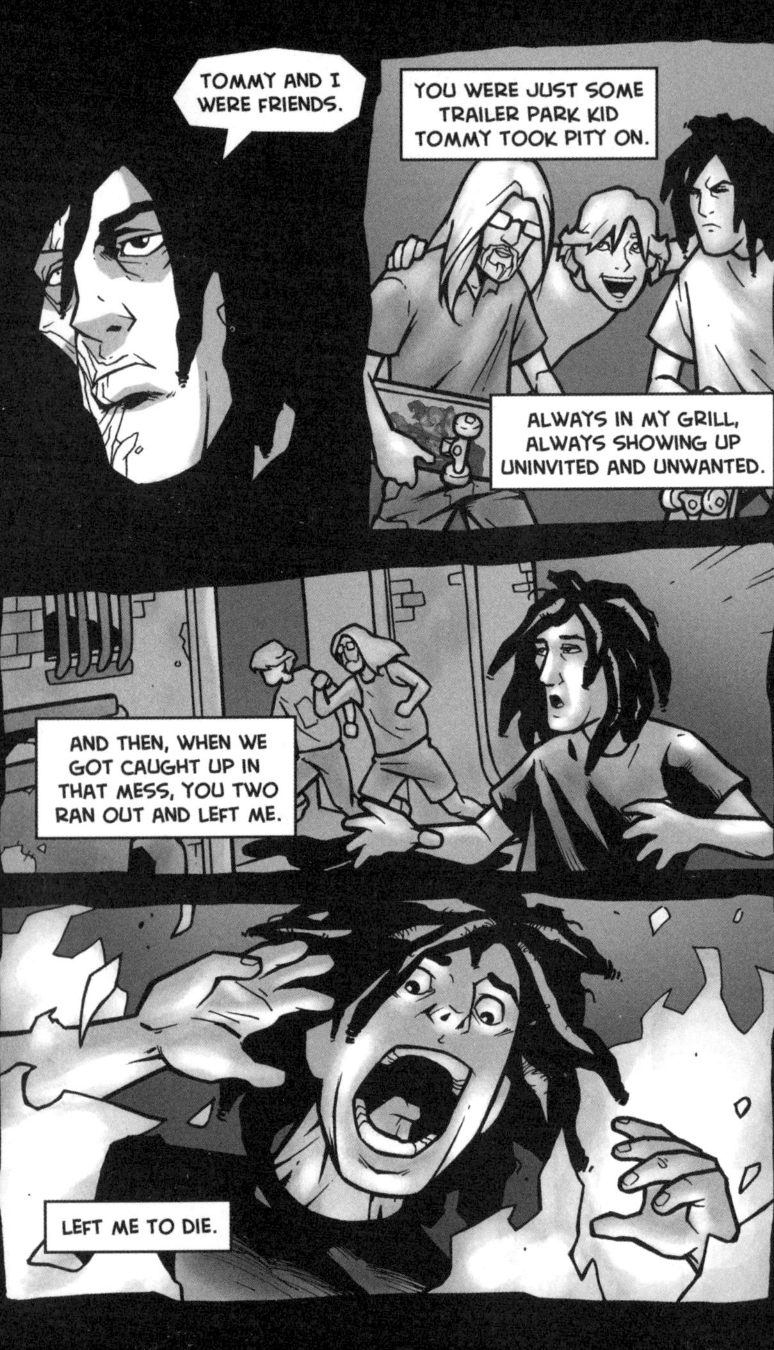
TOMMY AND I WERE FRIENDS.
YOU WERE JUST SOME TRAILER PARK KID TOMMY TOOK PITY ON.
ALWAYS IN MY GRILL, ALWAYS SHOWING UP UNINVITED AND UNWANTED.
AND THEN, WHEN WE GOT CAUGHT UP IN THAT MESS, YOU TWO RAN OUT AND LEFT ME.
LEFT ME TO DIE.

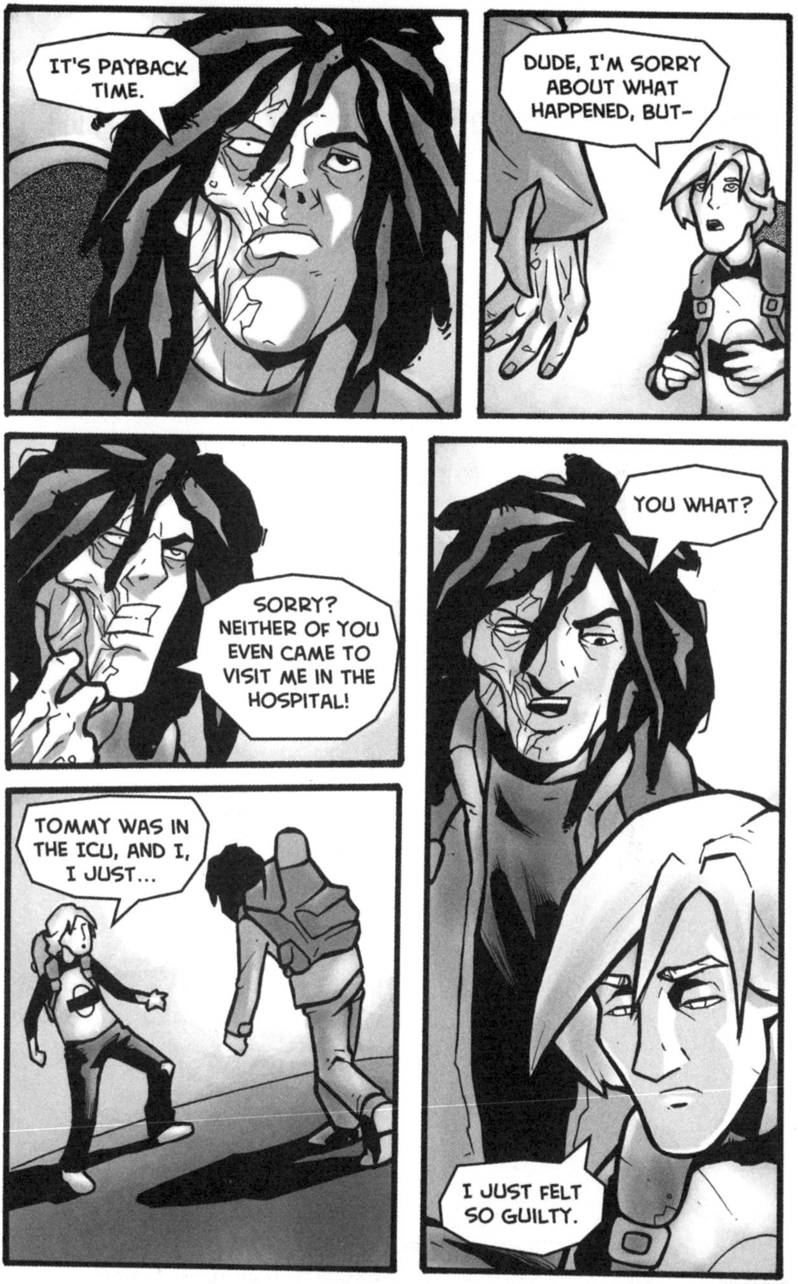
IT'S PAYBACK TIME.
DUDE, I'M SORRY ABOUT WHAT HAPPENED, BUT-
SORRY? NEITHER OF YOU EVEN CAME TO VISIT ME IN THE HOSPITAL!
YOU WHAT?
TOMMY WAS IN THE ICU, AND I, I JUST...
I JUST FELT SO GUILTY.

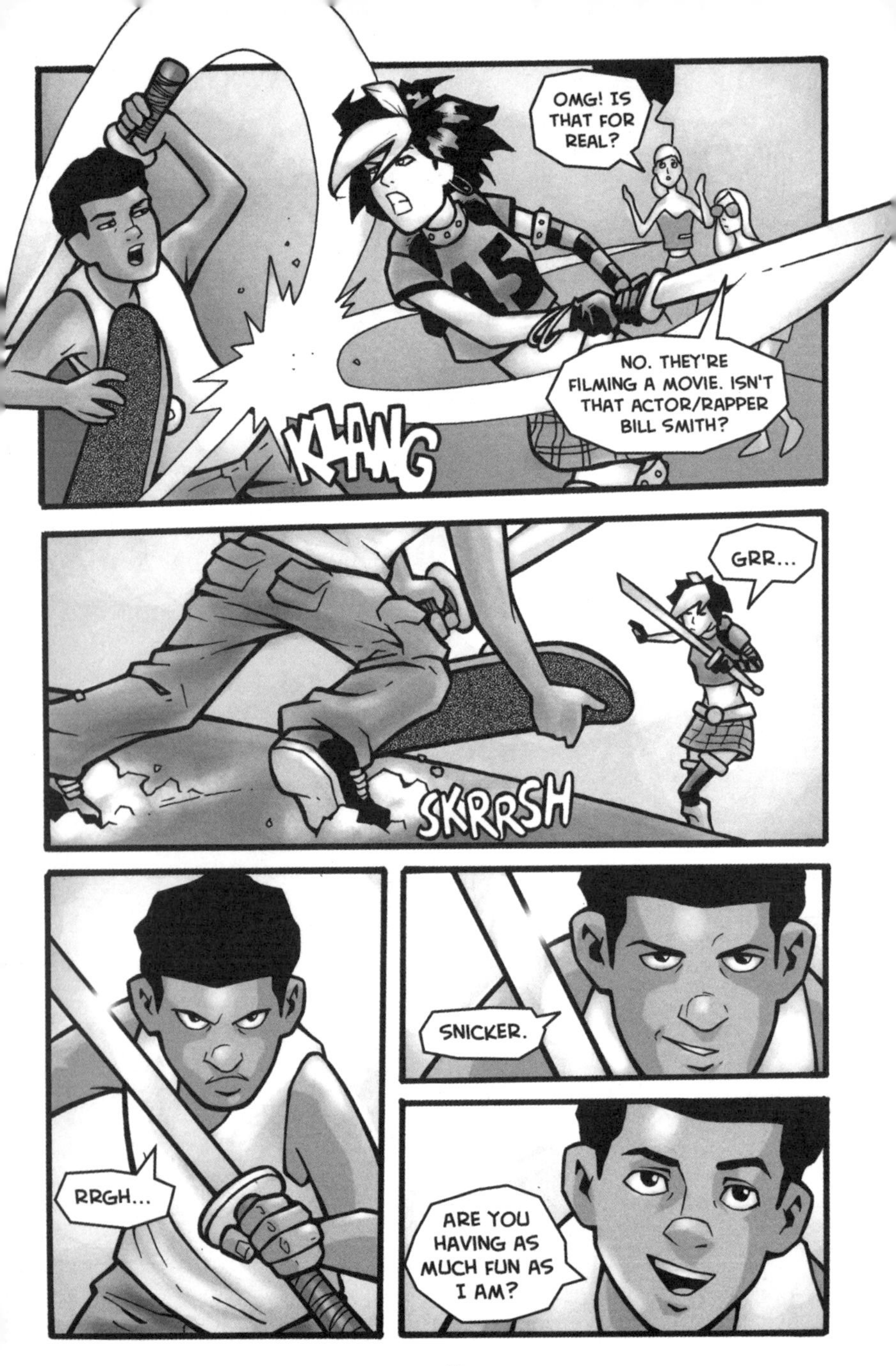
OMG! IS THAT FOR REAL?
NO. THEY'RE FILMING A MOVIE. ISN'T THAT ACTOR/RAPPER BILL SMITH?
KLANG
GRR...
SKRRSH
RRGH...
SNICKER.
ARE YOU HAVING AS MUCH FUN AS I AM?

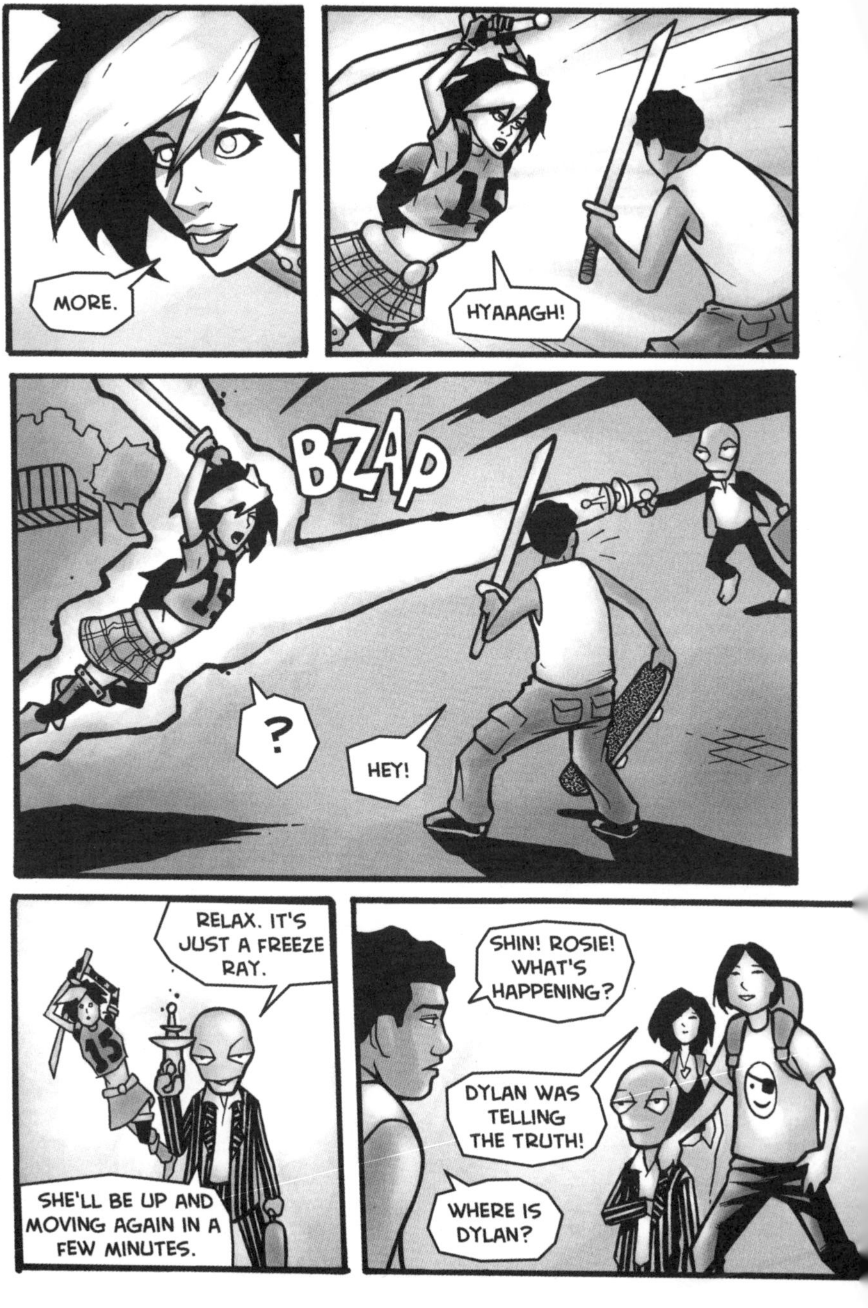
MORE.
HYAAAGH!
BZAP
?
HEY!
RELAX. IT'S JUST A FREEZE RAY.
SHE'LL BE UP AND MOVING AGAIN IN A FEW MINUTES.
SHIN! ROSIE! WHAT'S HAPPENING?
DYLAN WAS TELLING THE TRUTH!
WHERE IS DYLAN?

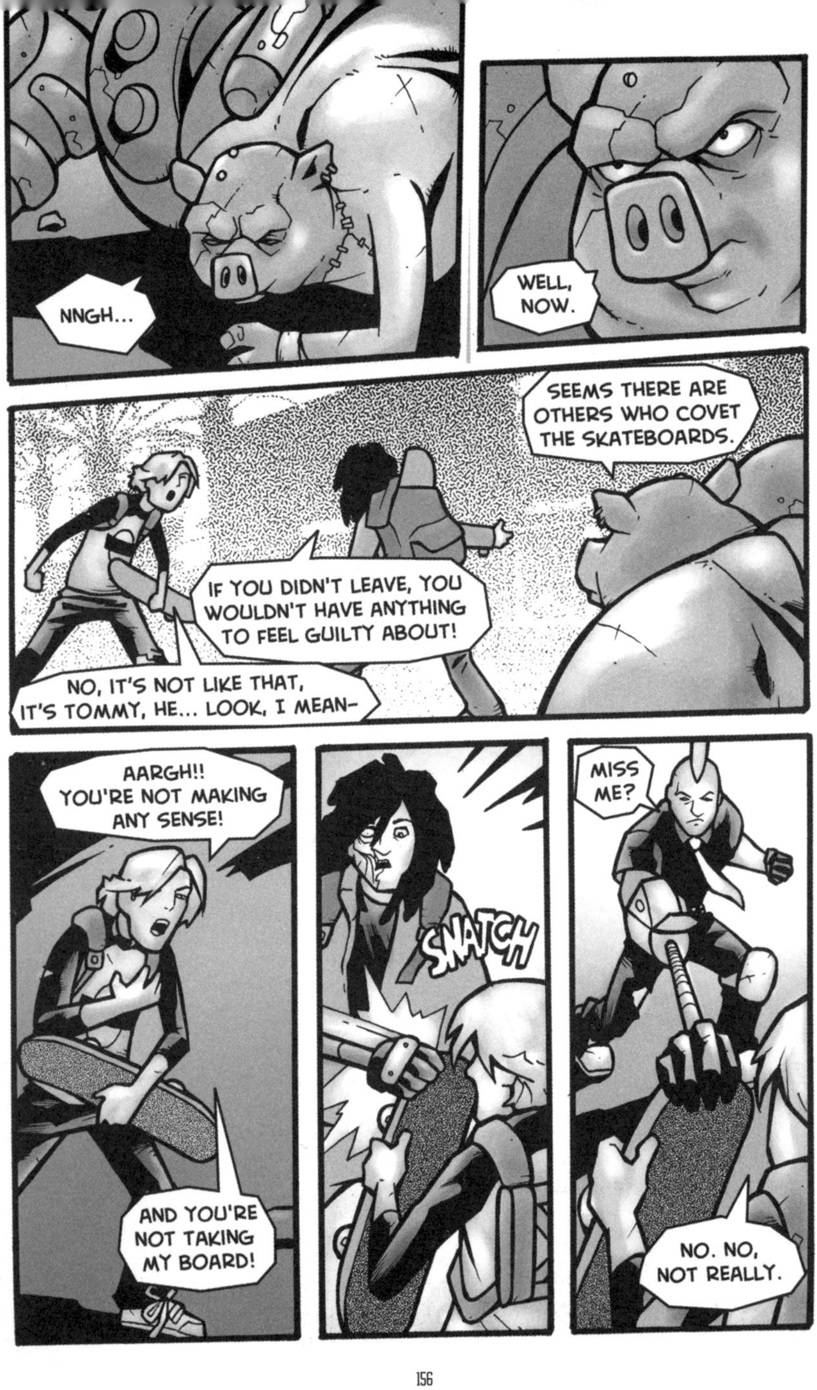
NNGH...
WELL, NOW.
SEEMS THERE ARE OTHERS WHO COVET THE SKATEBOARDS.
IF YOU DIDN'T LEAVE, YOU WOULDN'T HAVE ANYTHING TO FEEL GUILTY ABOUT!
NO, IT'S NOT LIKE THAT, IT'S TOMMY, HE... LOOK, I MEAN-
AARGH!! YOU'RE NOT MAKING ANY SENSE!
AND YOU'RE NOT TAKING MY BOARD!
SNATCH
MISS ME?
NO. NO, NOT REALLY.

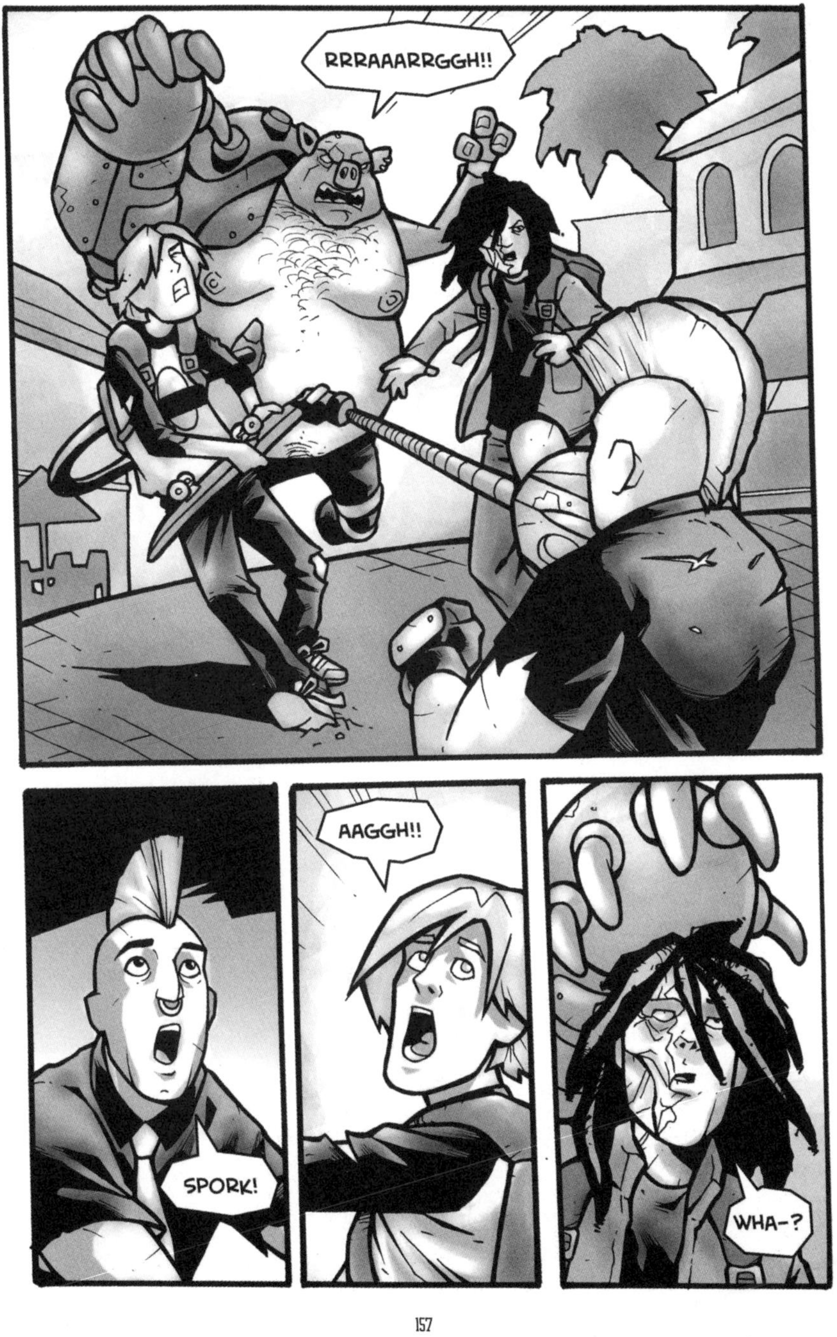
RRRAAARRGGH!!
SPORK!
AAGGH!!
WHA-?

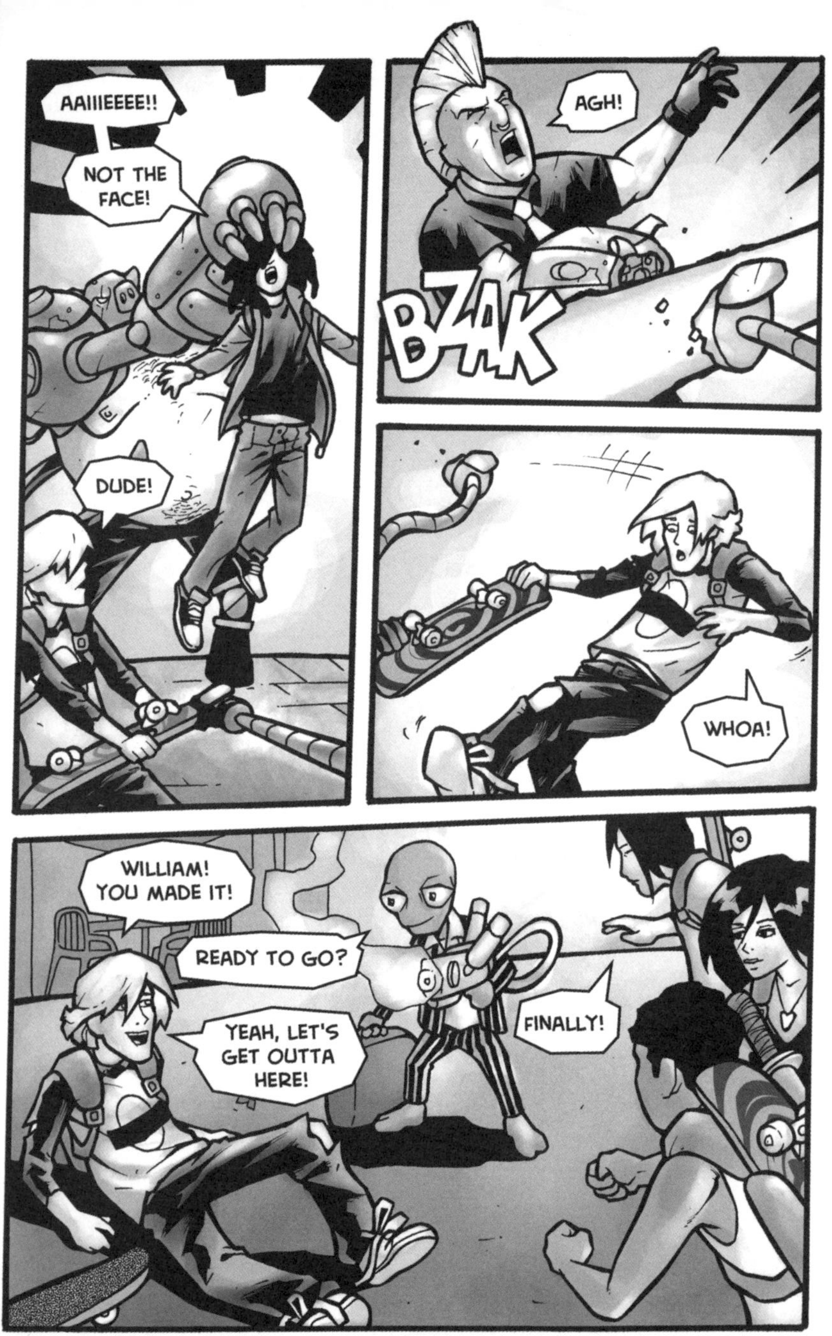
AAIIIEEEE!!
NOT THE FACE!
DUDE!
AGH!
BZAK
WHOA!
WILLIAM! YOU MADE IT!
READY TO GO?
YEAH, LET'S GET OUTTA HERE!
FINALLY!

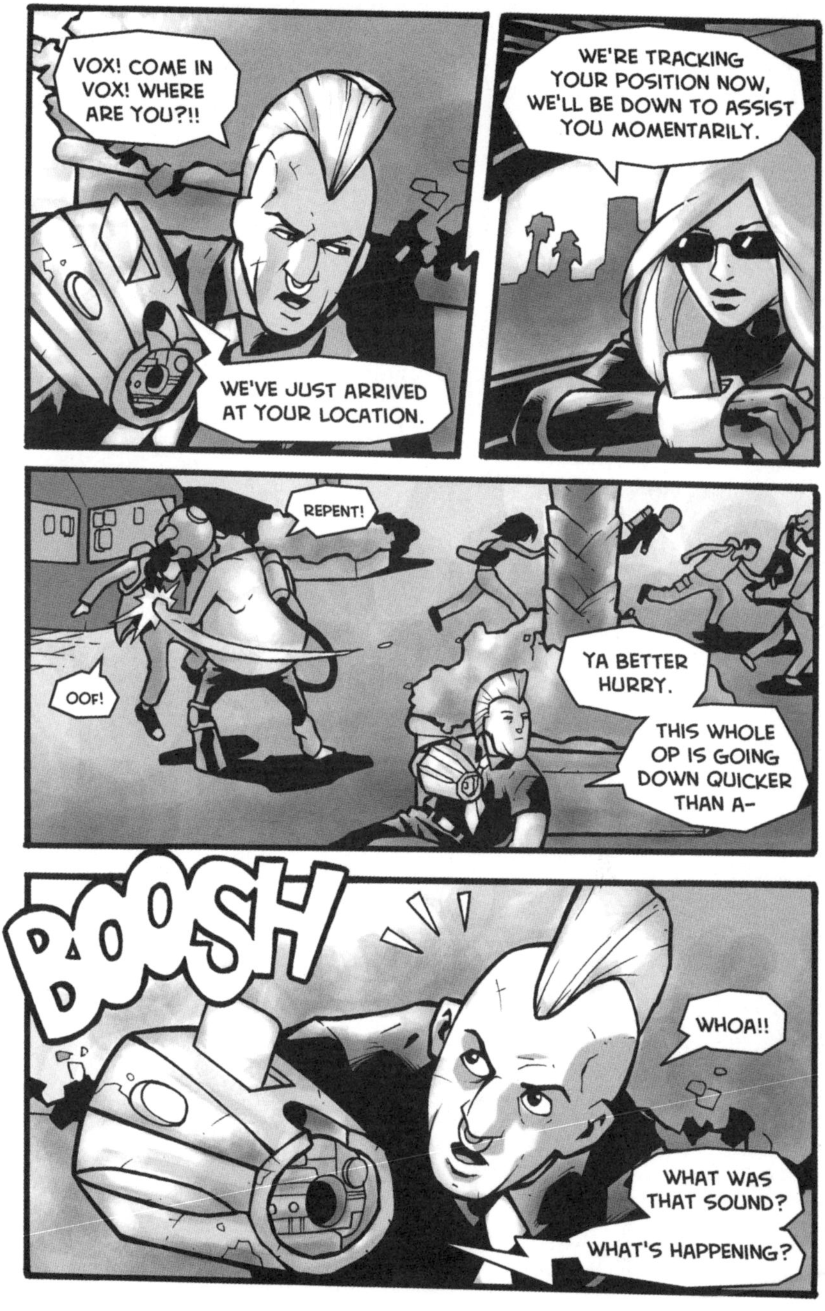
VOX! COME IN VOX! WHERE ARE YOU?!!
WE'VE JUST ARRIVED AT YOUR LOCATION.
WE'RE TRACKING YOUR POSITION NOW, WE'LL BE DOWN TO ASSIST YOU MOMENTARILY.
REPENT!
OOF!
YA BETTER HURRY.
THIS WHOLE OP IS GOING DOWN QUICKER THAN A-
BADOOSH
WHOA!!
WHAT WAS THAT SOUND?
WHAT'S HAPPENING?

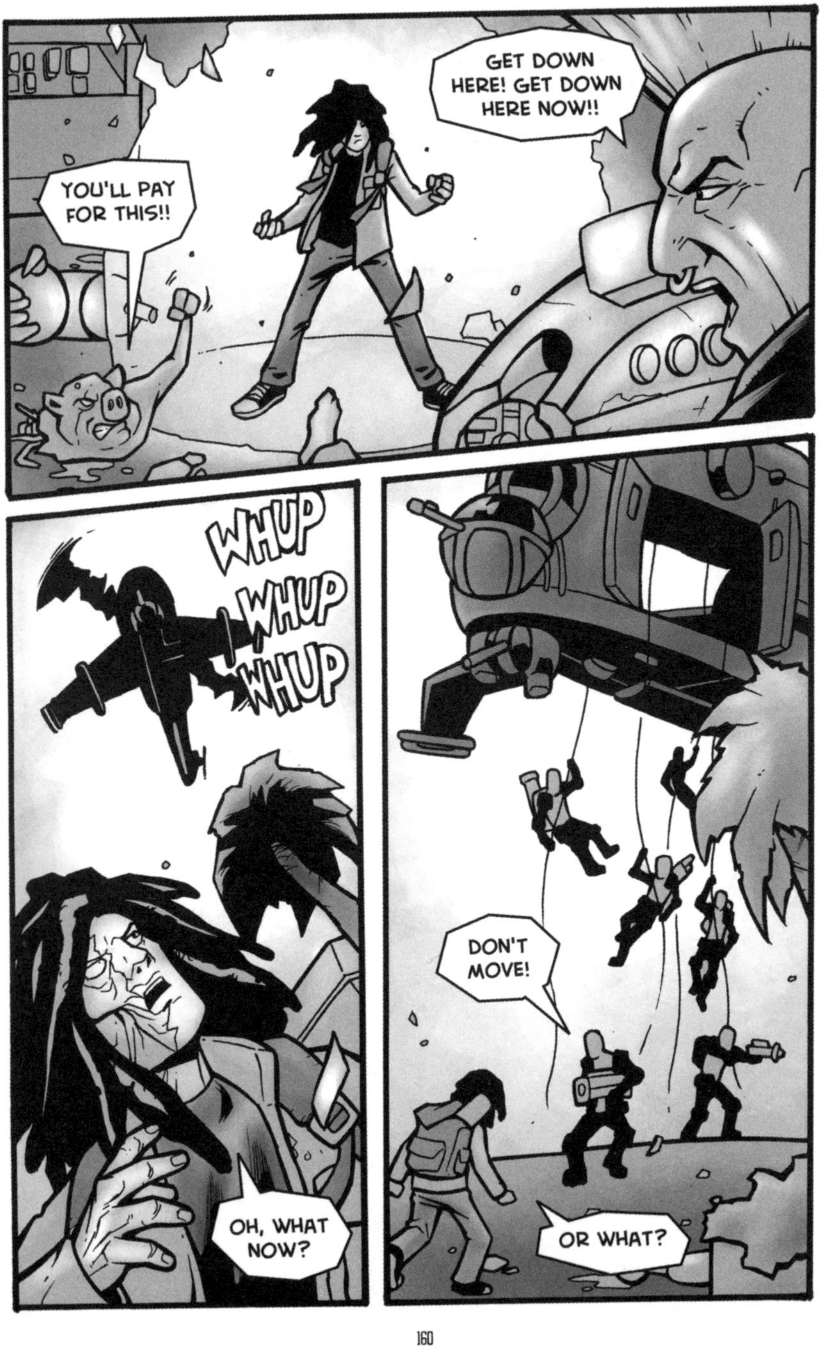
GET DOWN HERE! GET DOWN HERE NOW!!
YOU'LL PAY FOR THIS!!
WHUP
WHUP
WHUP
OH, WHAT NOW?
DON'T MOVE!
OR WHAT?

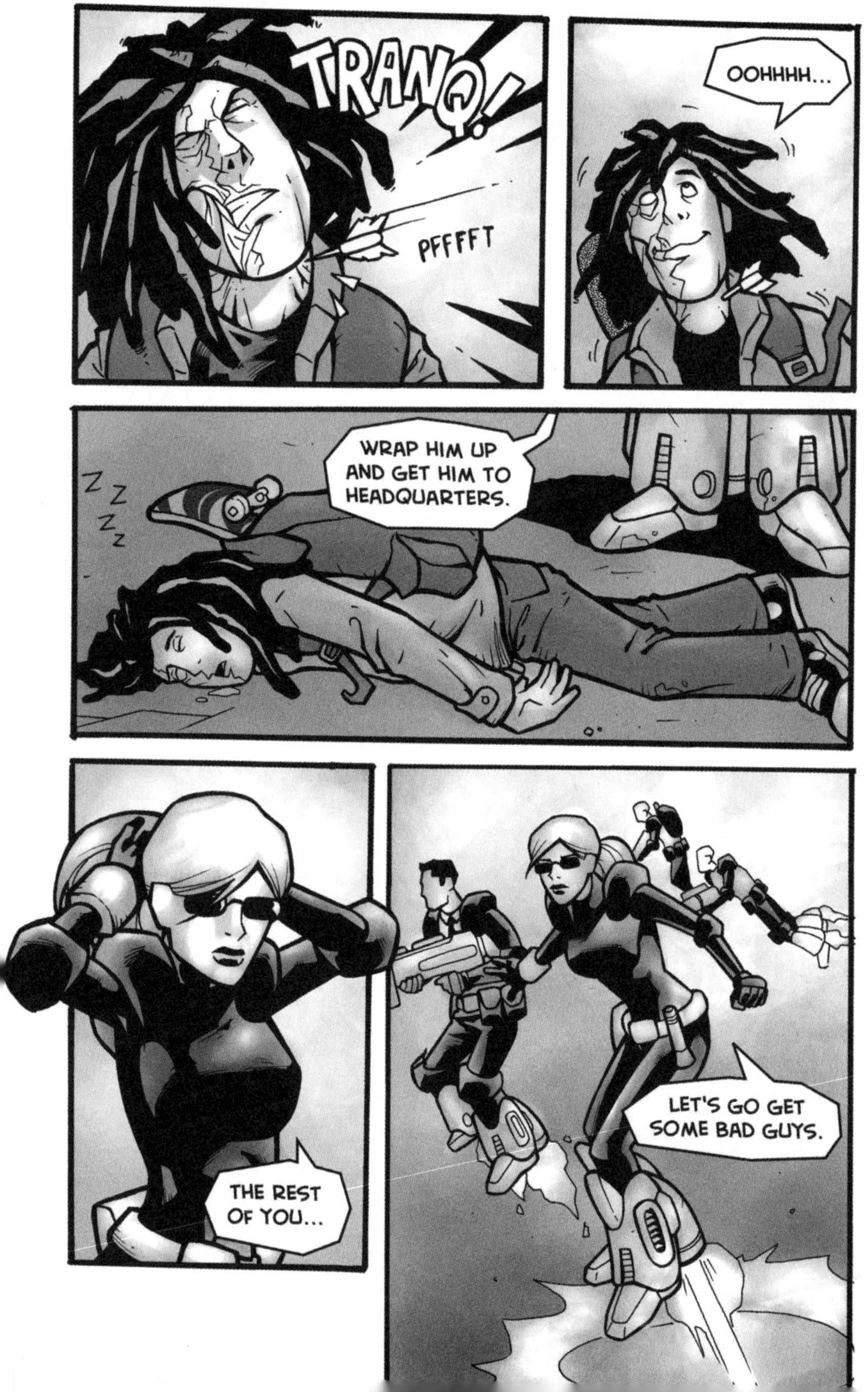
TRANQ!
PFFFFT
OOHHHH...
Z Z Z Z
WRAP HIM UP AND GET HIM TO HEADQUARTERS.
THE REST OF YOU...
LET'S GO GET SOME BAD GUYS.

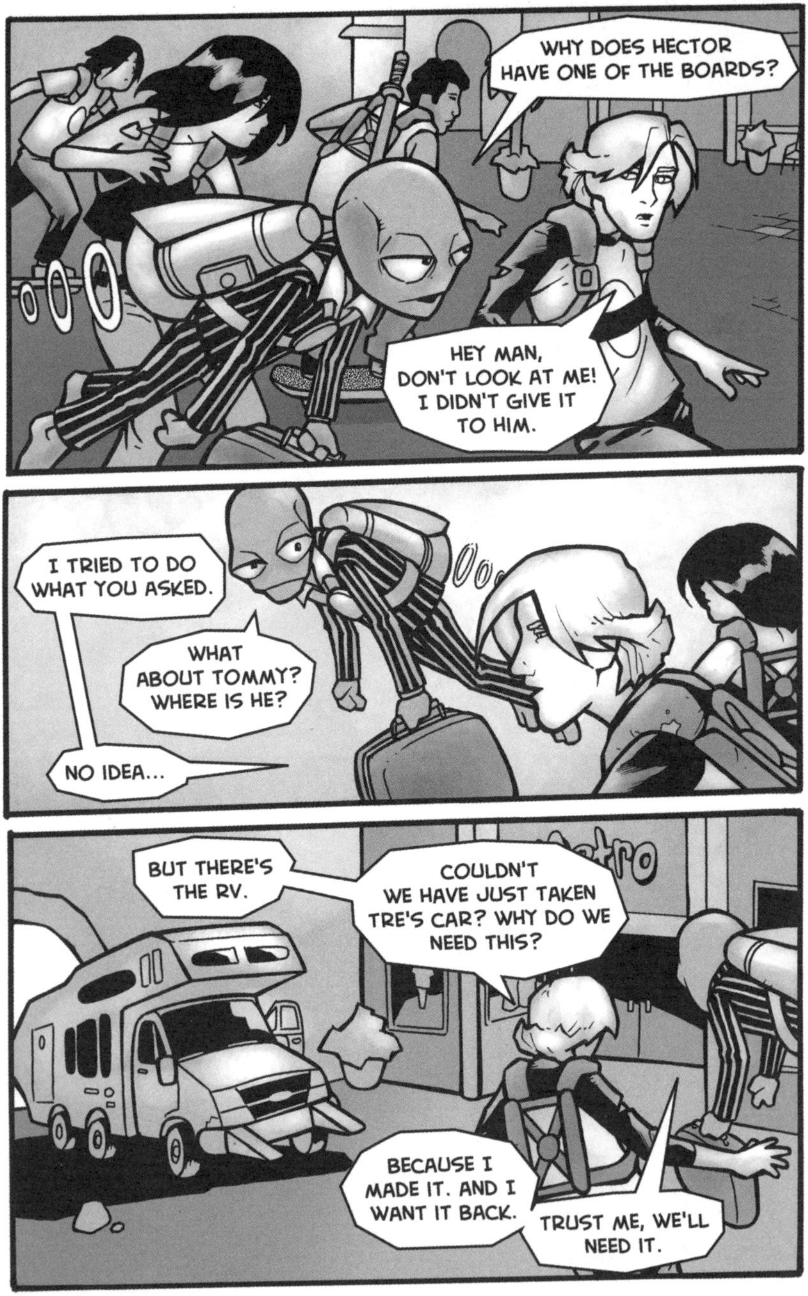
WHY DOES HECTOR HAVE ONE OF THE BOARDS?
HEY MAN, DON'T LOOK AT ME! I DIDN'T GIVE IT TO HIM.
I TRIED TO DO WHAT YOU ASKED.
WHAT ABOUT TOMMY? WHERE IS HE?
NO IDEA...
BUT THERE'S THE RV.
COULDN'T WE HAVE JUST TAKEN TRE'S CAR? WHY DO WE NEED THIS?
BECAUSE I MADE IT. AND I WANT IT BACK.
TRUST ME, WE'LL NEED IT.

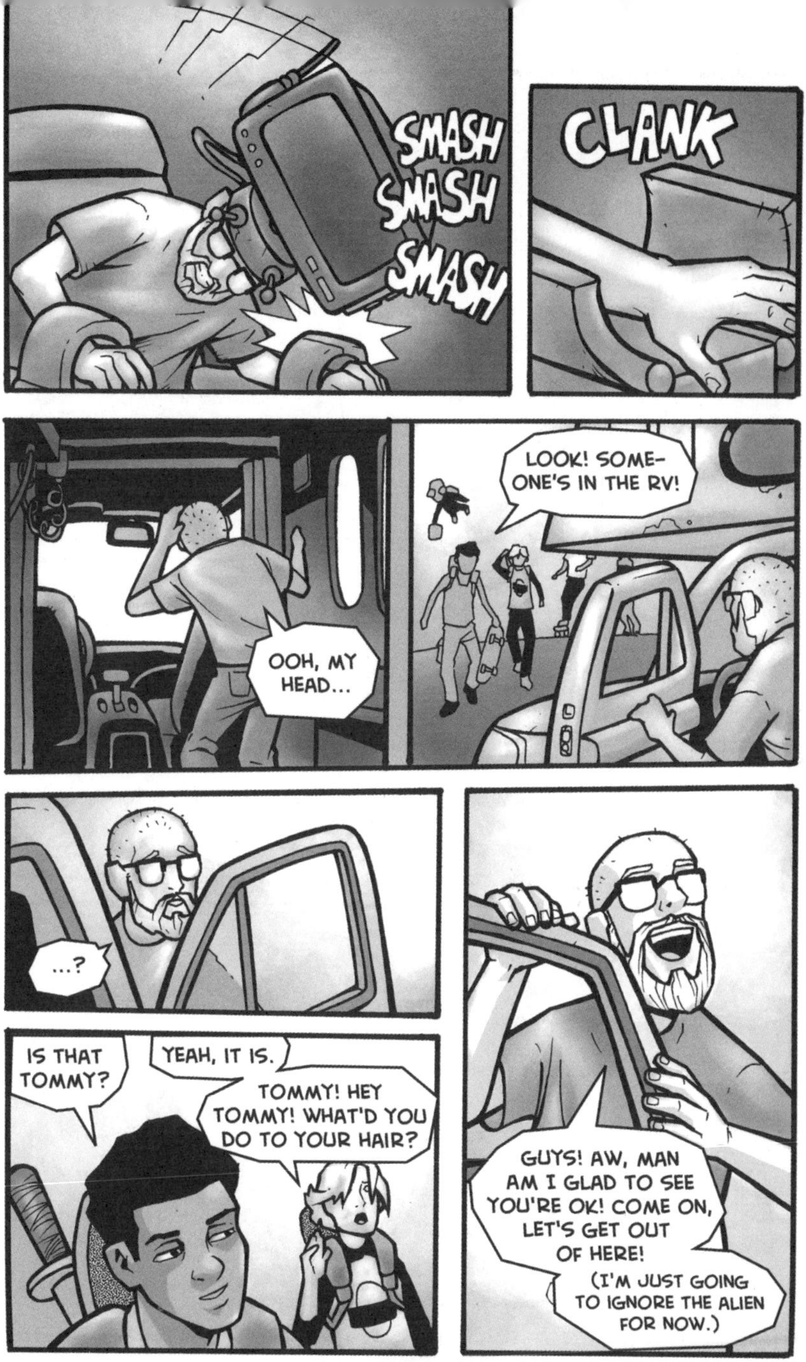
SMASH
SMASH
SMASH
CLANK
OOH, MY HEAD...
LOOK! SOME-ONE'S IN THE RV!
...?
GUYS! AW, MAN AM I GLAD TO SEE YOU'RE OK! COME ON, LET'S GET OUT OF HERE!
(I'M JUST GOING TO IGNORE THE ALIEN FOR NOW.)
IS THAT TOMMY?
YEAH, IT IS.
TOMMY! HEY TOMMY! WHAT'D YOU DO TO YOUR HAIR?

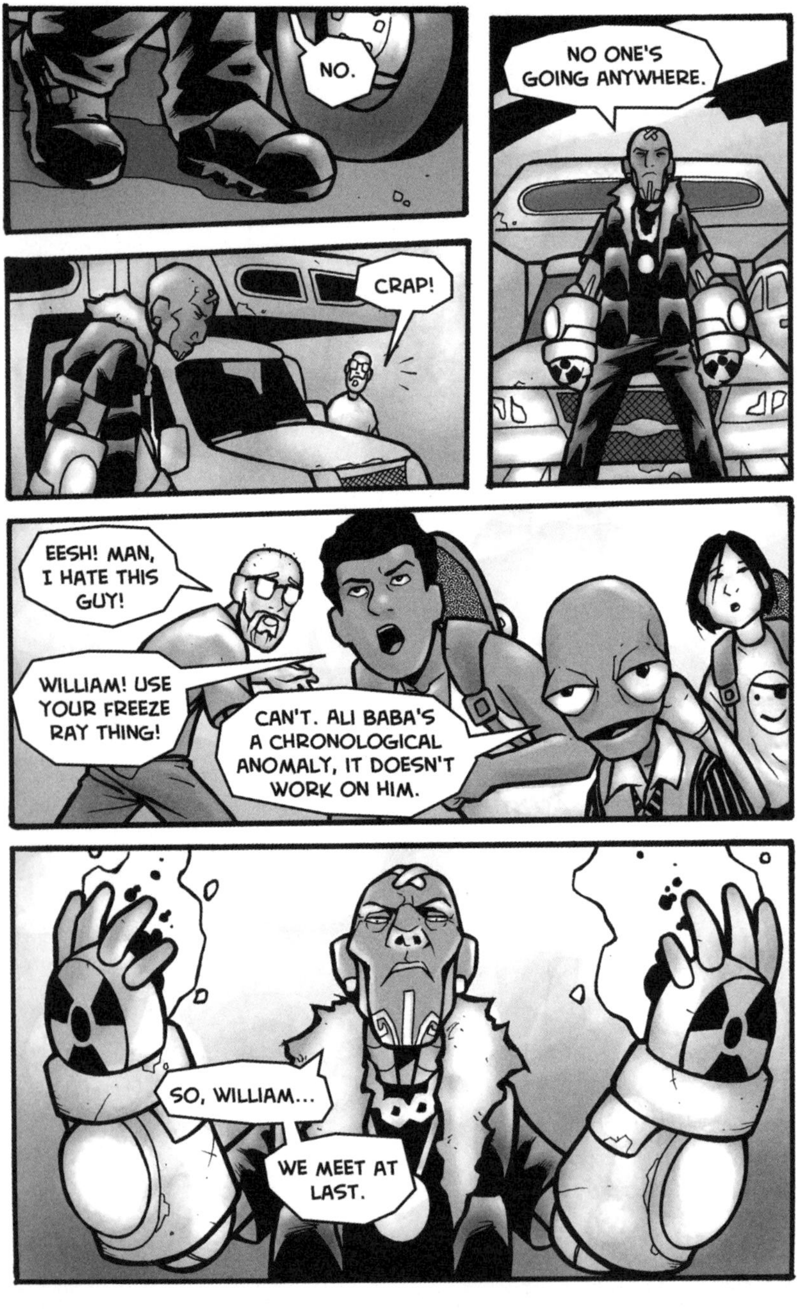
NO.
NO ONE'S GOING ANYWHERE.
CRAP!
EESH! MAN, I HATE THIS GUY!
WILLIAM! USE YOUR FREEZE RAY THING!
CAN'T. ALI BABA'S A CHRONOLOGICAL ANOMALY, IT DOESN'T WORK ON HIM.
SO, WILLIAM...
WE MEET AT LAST.

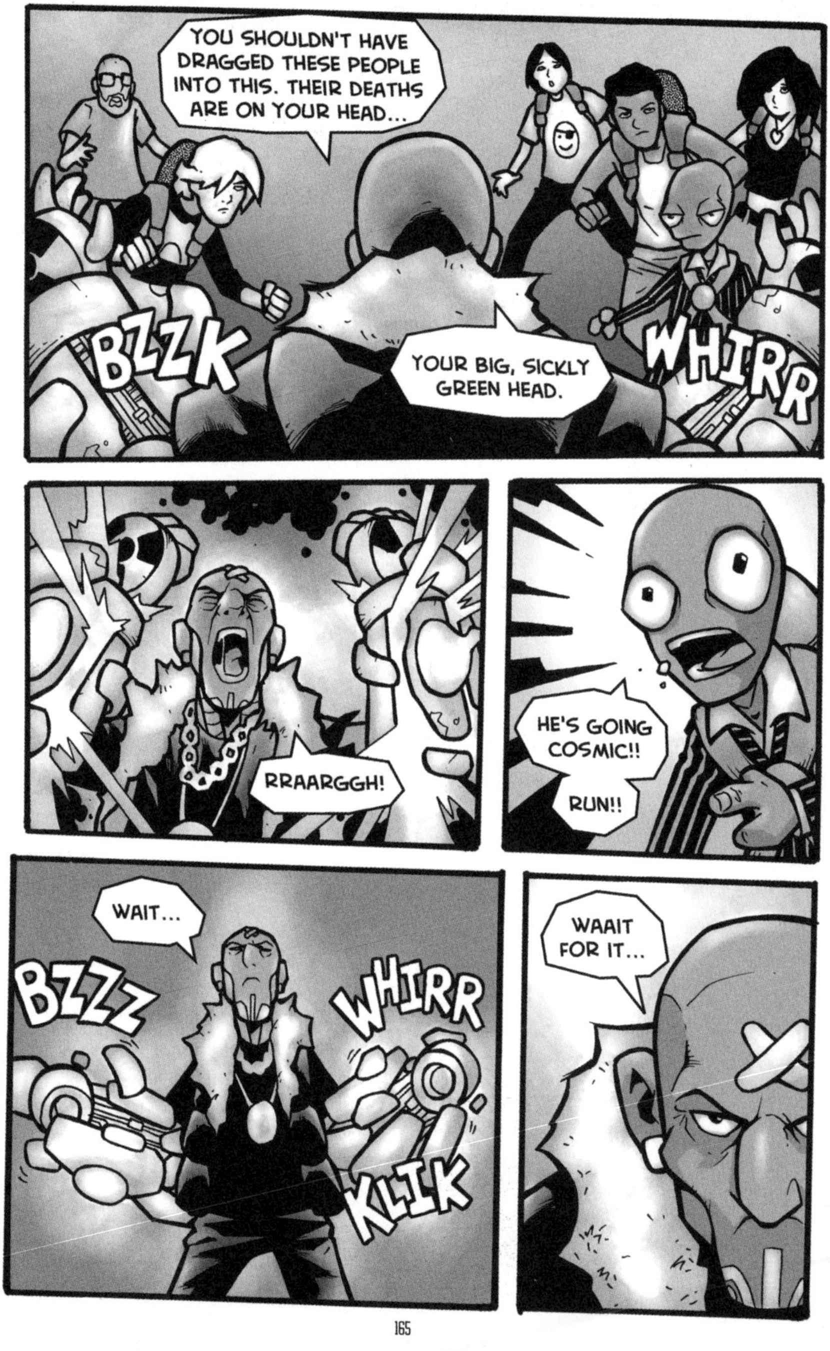
YOU SHOULDN'T HAVE DRAGGED THESE PEOPLE INTO THIS. THEIR DEATHS ARE ON YOUR HEAD...
BZZK
YOUR BIG, SICKLY GREEN HEAD.
WHIRR
RRAARGGH!
HE'S GOING COSMIC!!
RUN!!
WAIT...
BZZZ
WHIRR
KLIK
WAAIT FOR IT...

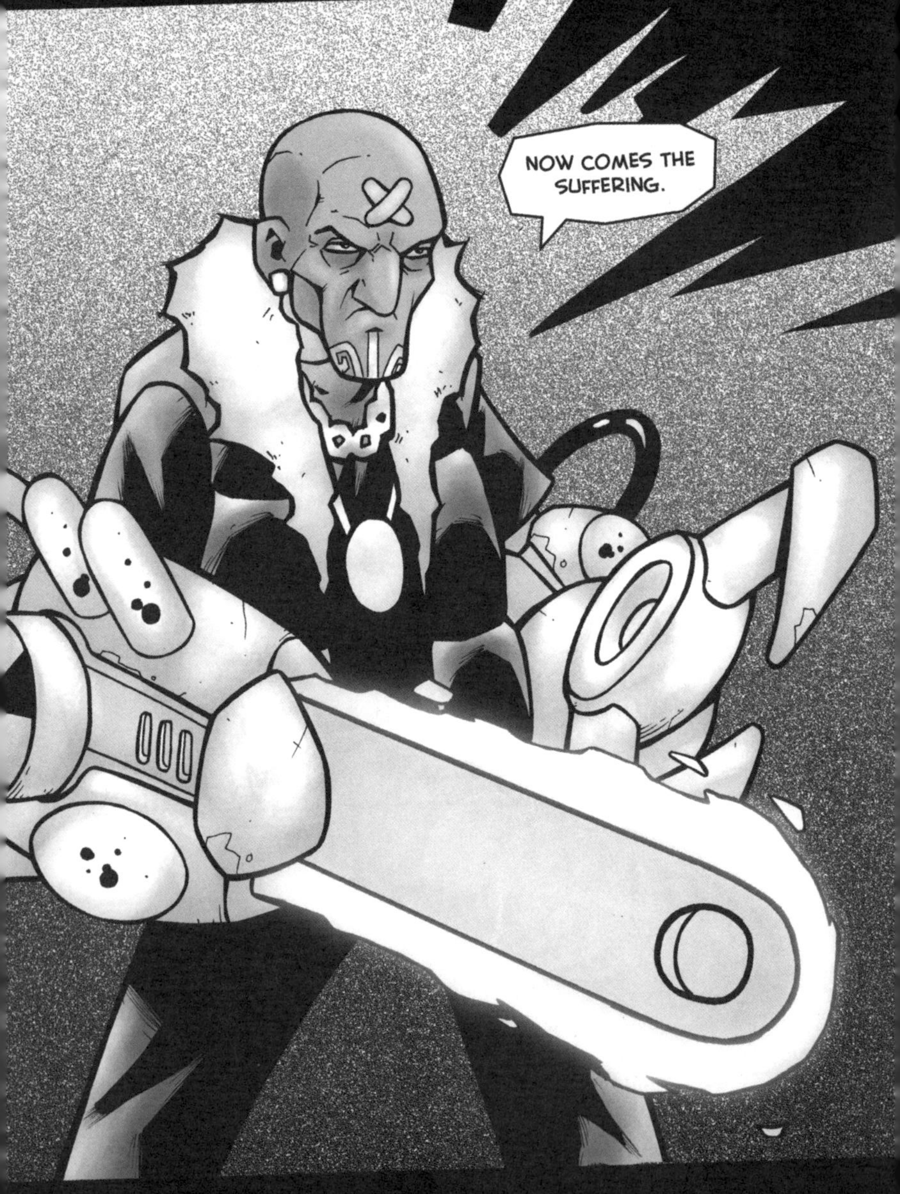
NOW COMES THE SUFFERING.

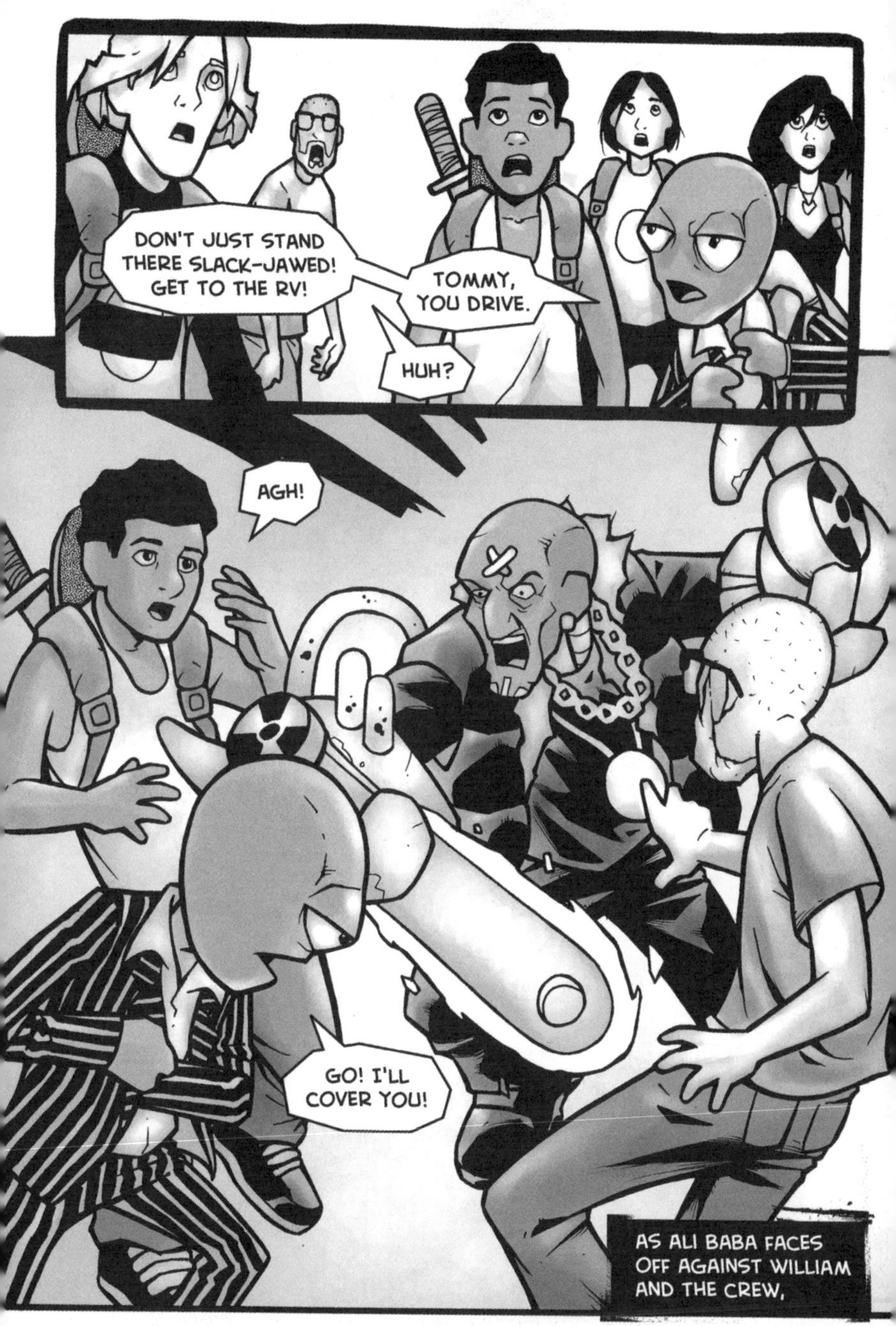
DON'T JUST STAND THERE SLACK-JAWED! GET TO THE RV!
TOMMY, YOU DRIVE.
HUH?
AGH!
GO! I'LL COVER YOU!
AS ALI BABA FACES OFF AGAINST WILLIAM AND THE CREW,

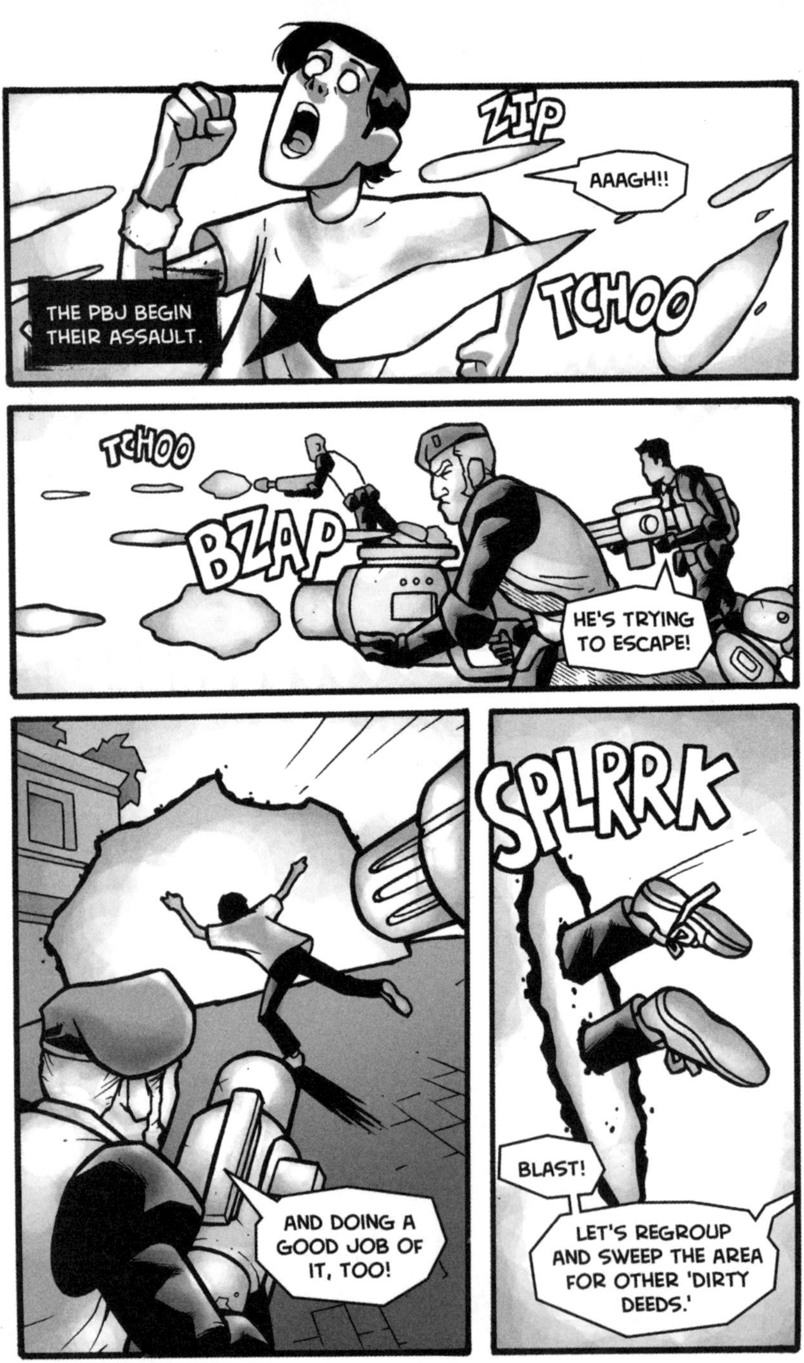
ZIP
AAAGH!!
THE PBJ BEGIN THEIR ASSAULT.
TCHOO
TCHOO
BZAP
HE'S TRYING TO ESCAPE!
AND DOING A GOOD JOB OF IT, TOO!
SPLRRK
BLAST!
LET'S REGROUP AND SWEEP THE AREA FOR OTHER 'DIRTY DEEDS.'

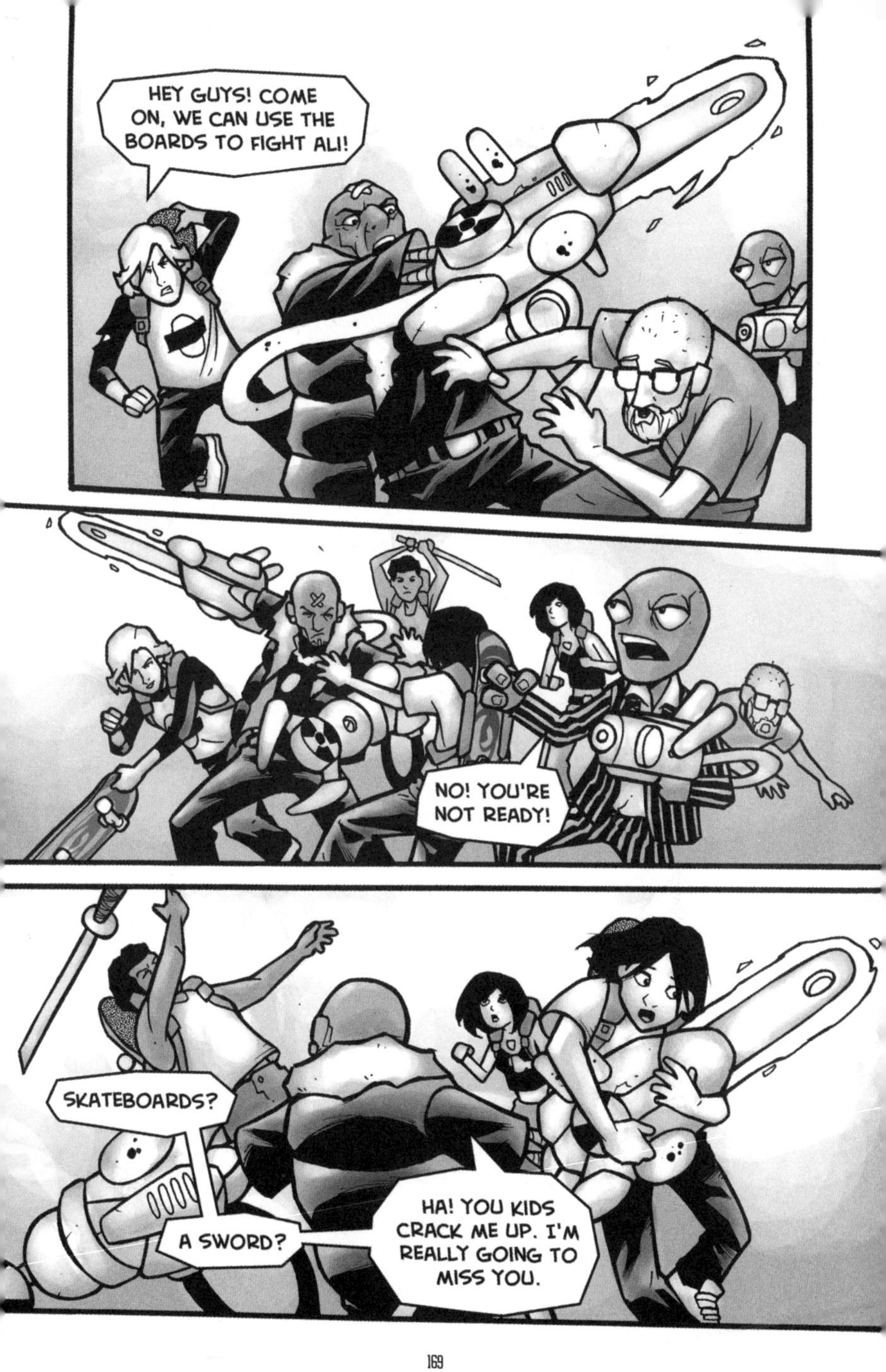
HEY GUYS! COME ON, WE CAN USE THE BOARDS TO FIGHT ALI!
NO! YOU'RE NOT READY!
SKATEBOARDS?
A SWORD?
HA! YOU KIDS CRACK ME UP. I'M REALLY GOING TO MISS YOU.

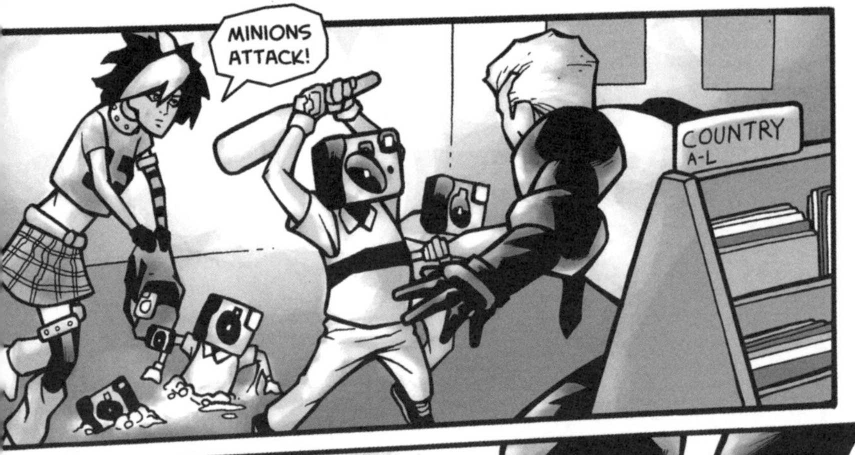
MINIONS ATTACK!
COUNTRY A-L

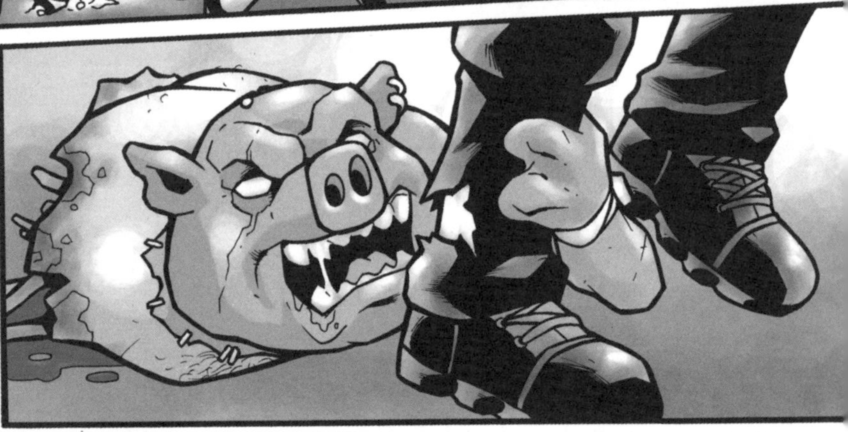

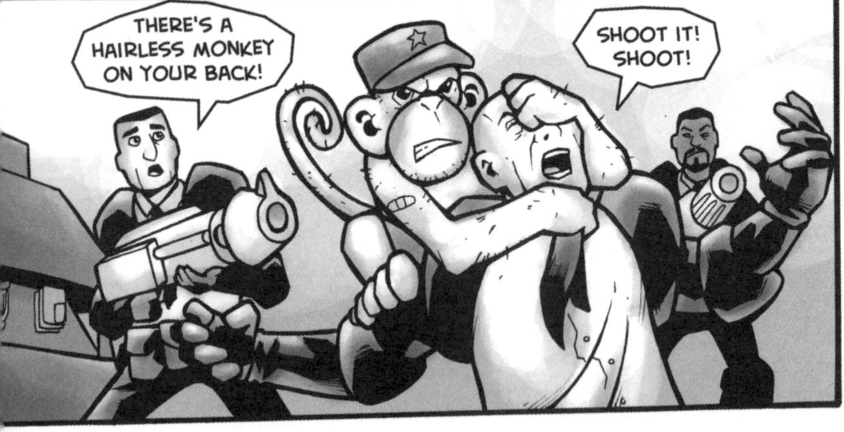
THERE'S A HAIRLESS MONKEY ON YOUR BACK!
SHOOT IT! SHOOT!

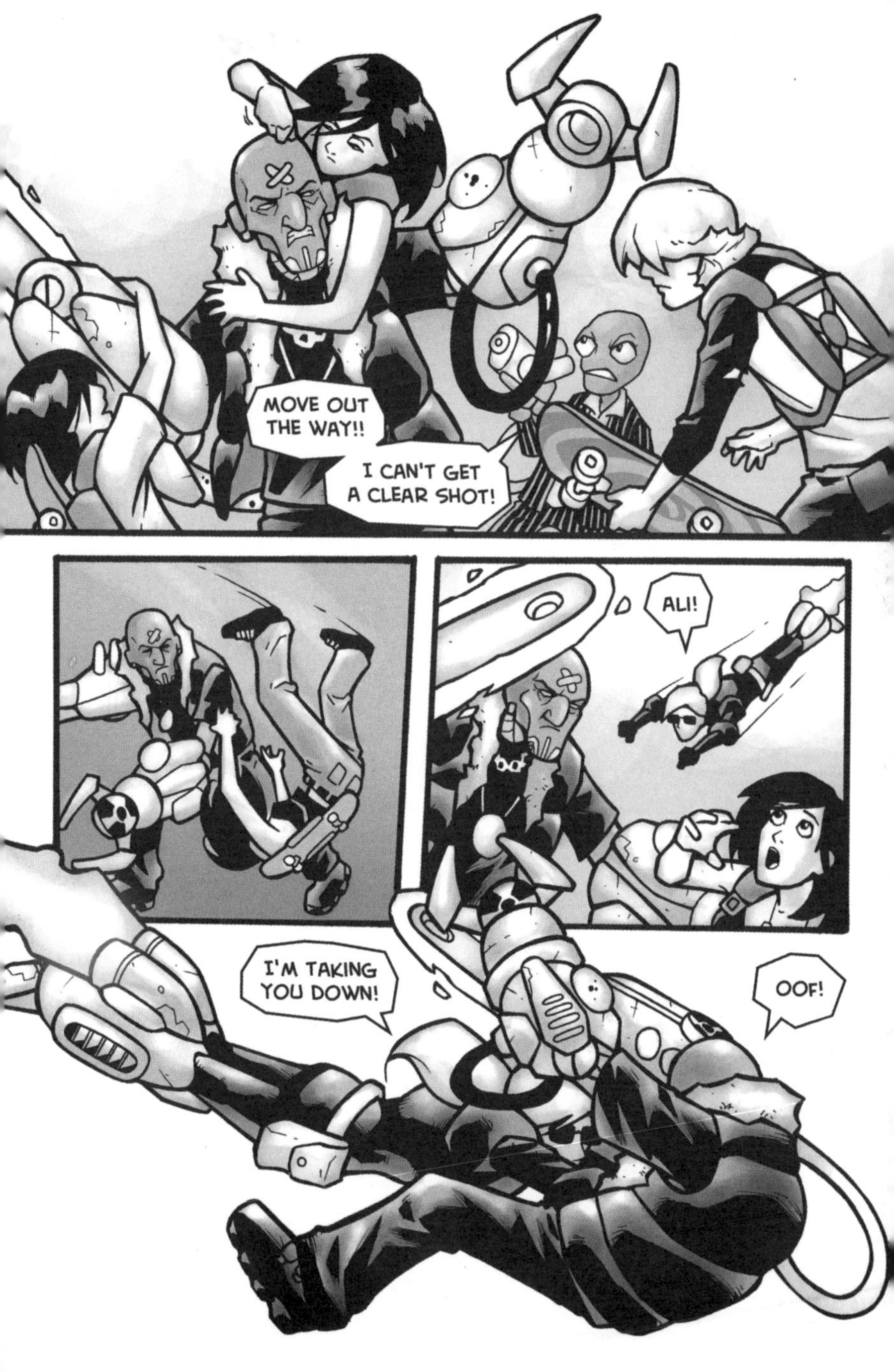
MOVE OUT THE WAY!!
I CAN'T GET A CLEAR SHOT!
ALI!
I'M TAKING YOU DOWN!
OOF!

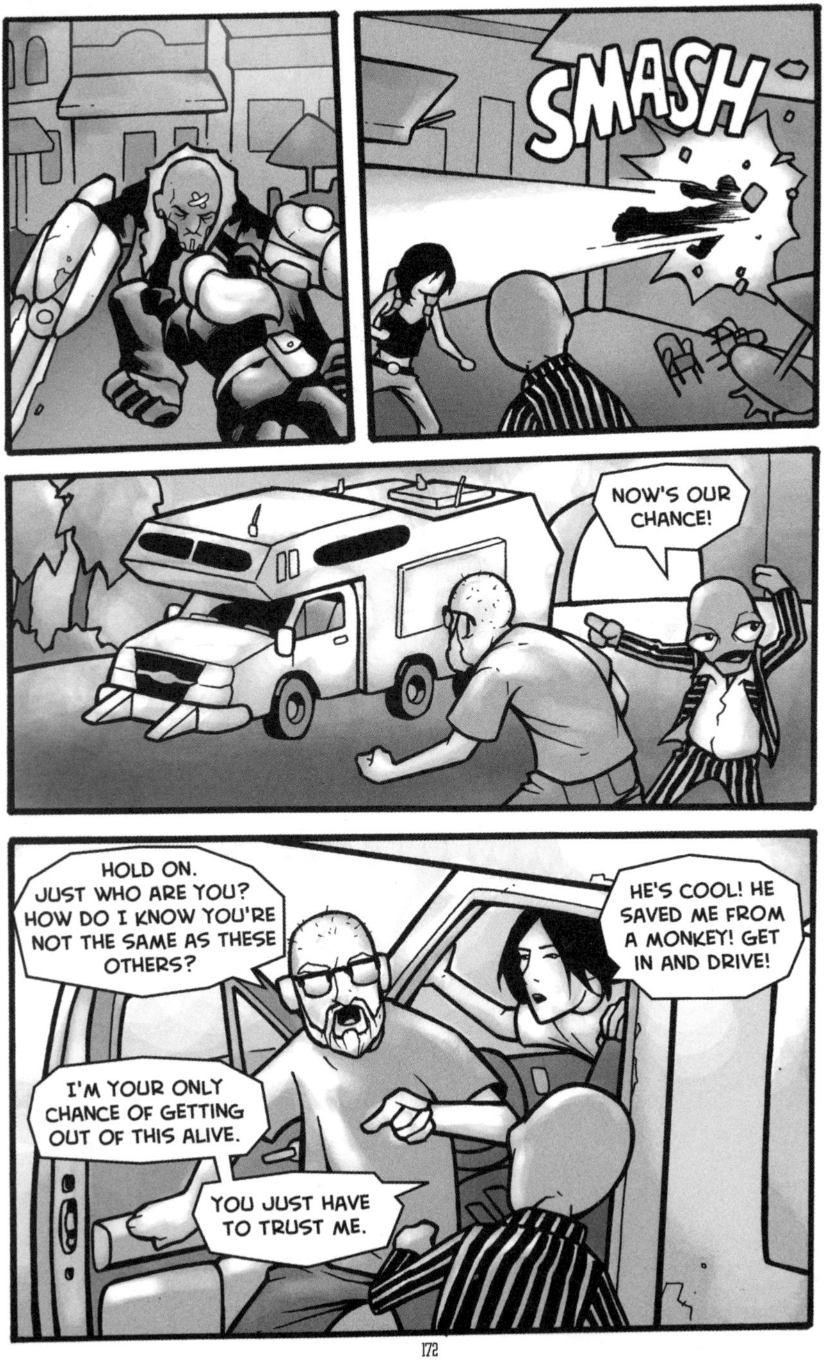
SMASH
NOW'S OUR CHANCE!
HOLD ON. JUST WHO ARE YOU? HOW DO I KNOW YOU'RE NOT THE SAME AS THESE OTHERS?
HE'S COOL! HE SAVED ME FROM A MONKEY! GET IN AND DRIVE!
I'M YOUR ONLY CHANCE OF GETTING OUT OF THIS ALIVE.
YOU JUST HAVE TO TRUST ME.

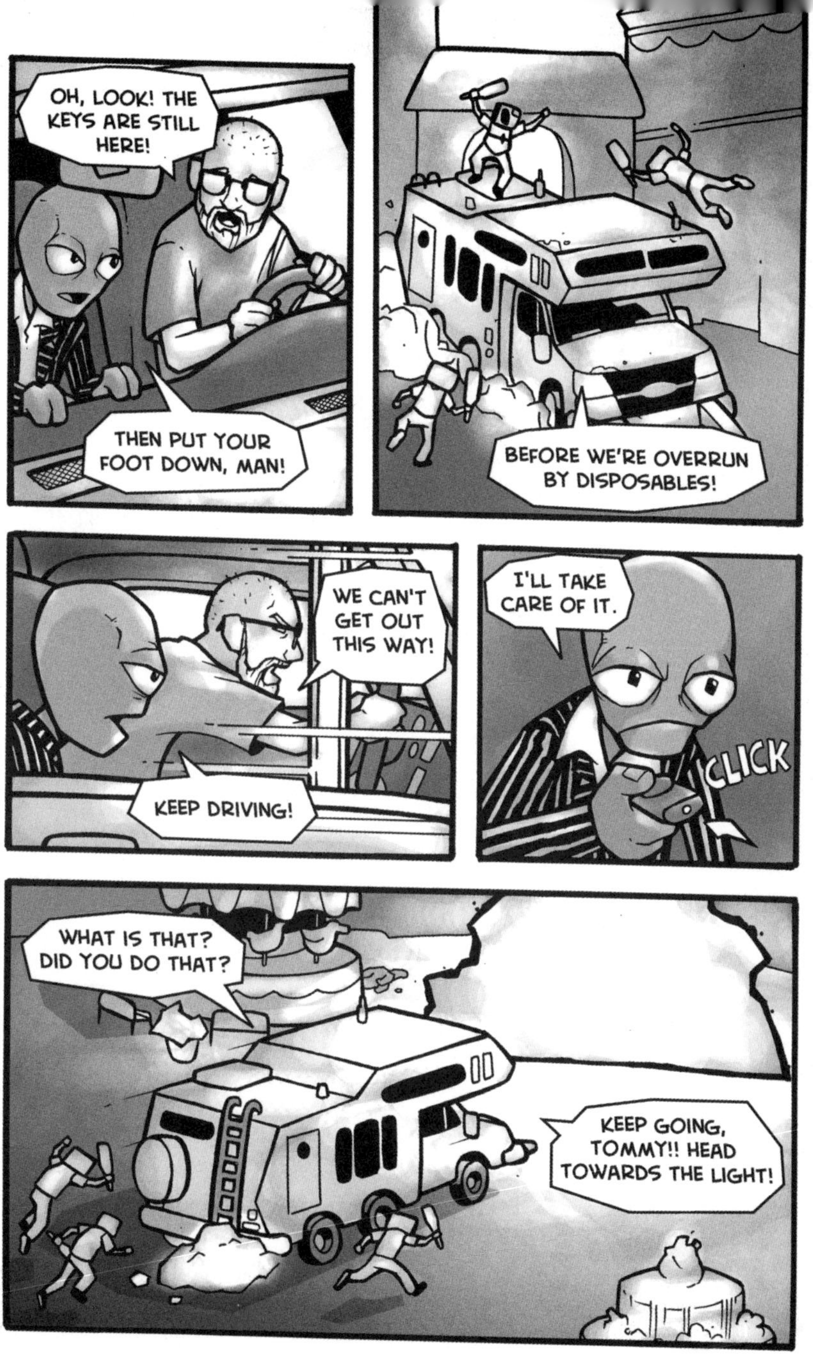
OH, LOOK! THE KEYS ARE STILL HERE!
THEN PUT YOUR FOOT DOWN, MAN!
BEFORE WE'RE OVERRUN BY DISPOSABLES!
WE CAN'T GET OUT THIS WAY!
KEEP DRIVING!
I'LL TAKE CARE OF IT.
CLICK
WHAT IS THAT? DID YOU DO THAT?
KEEP GOING, TOMMY!! HEAD TOWARDS THE LIGHT!

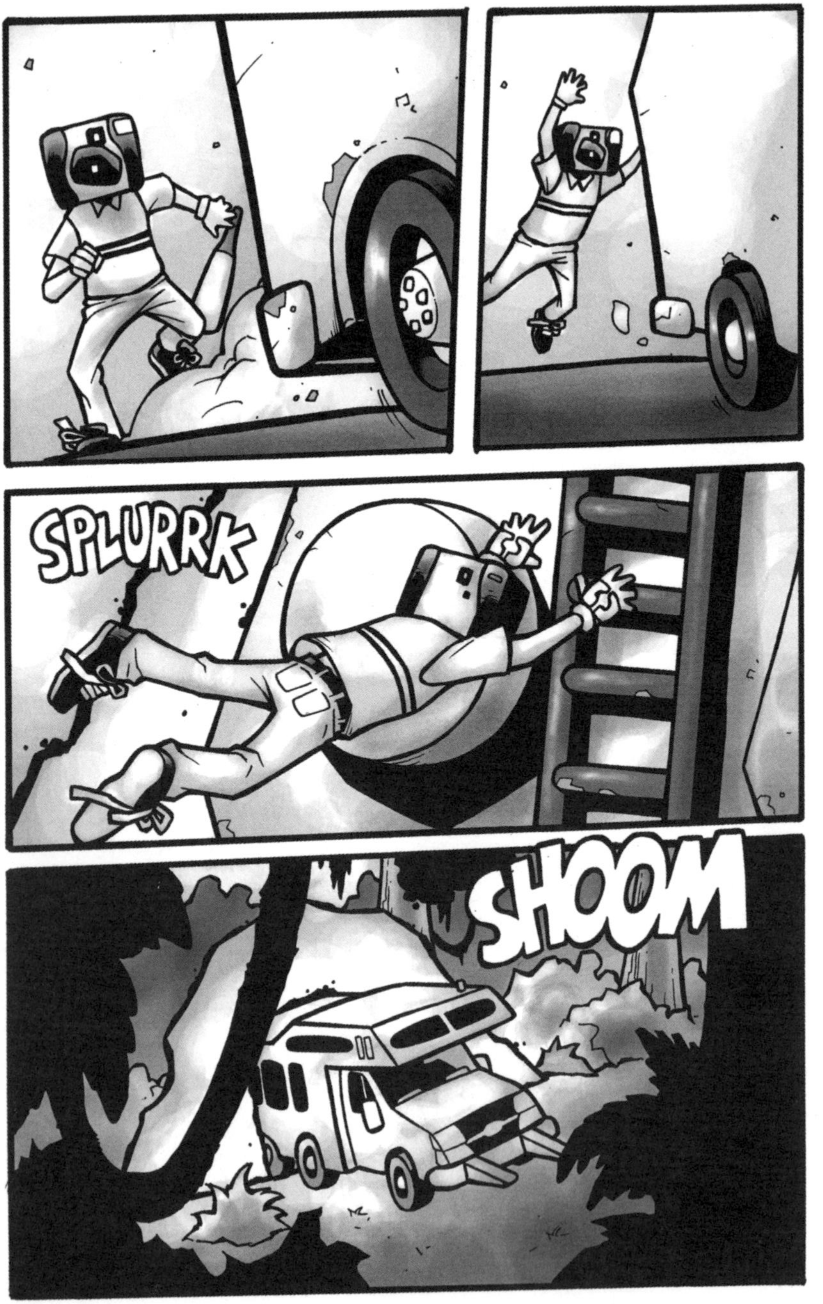
SPLURRK
SHOOM

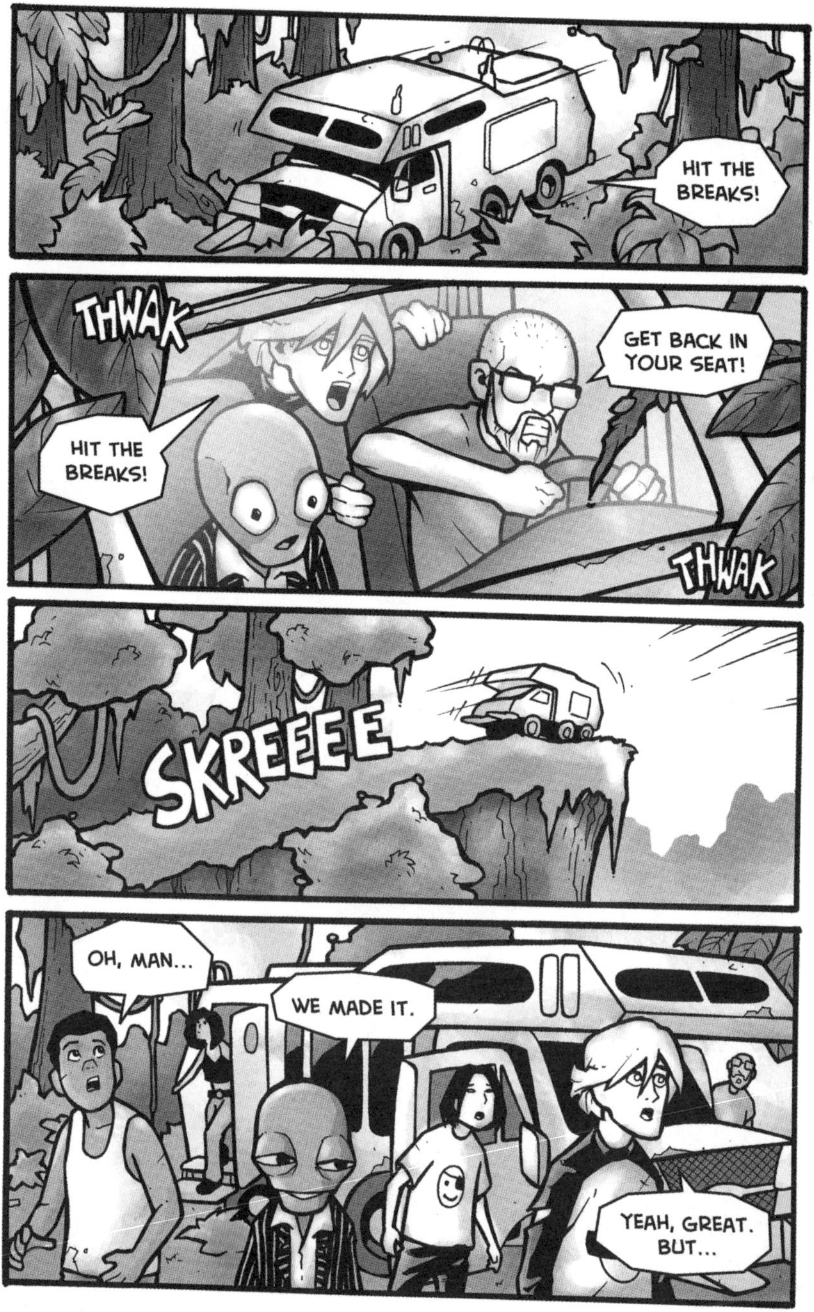
HIT THE BREAKS!
THWAK
GET BACK IN YOUR SEAT!
HIT THE BREAKS!
THWAK
SKREEEE
OH, MAN...
WE MADE IT.
YEAH, GREAT. BUT...

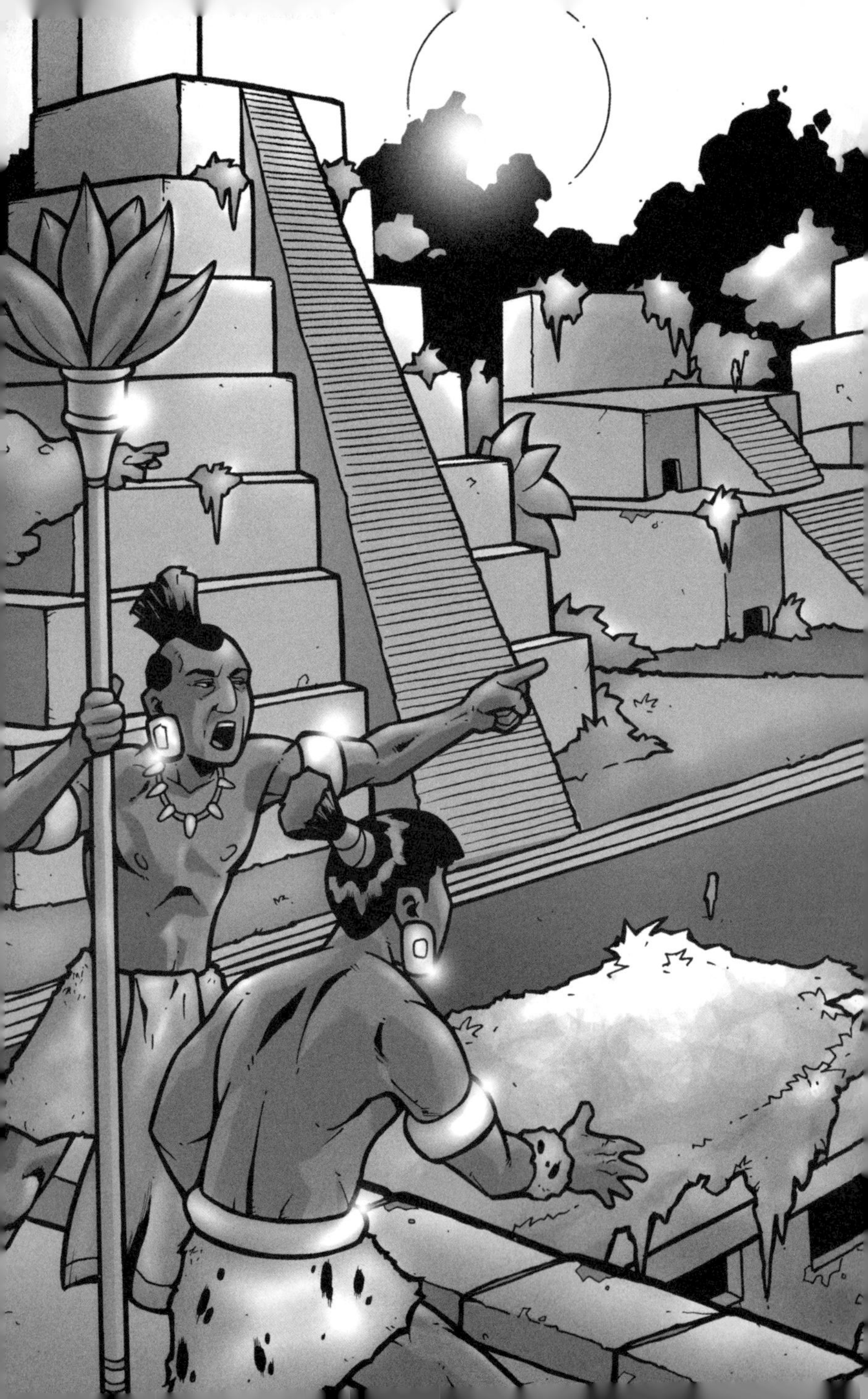

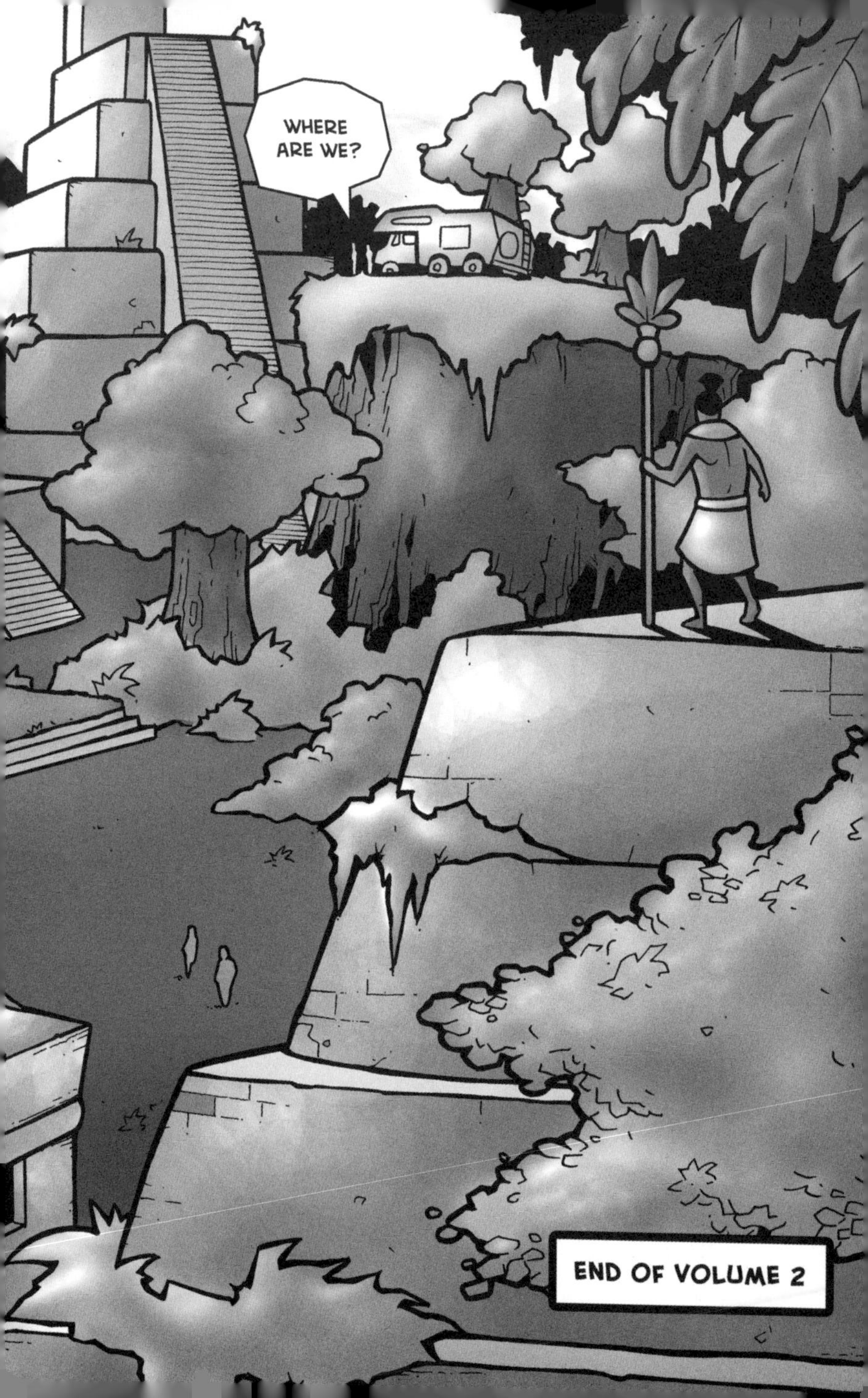
WHERE ARE WE?
END OF VOLUME 2

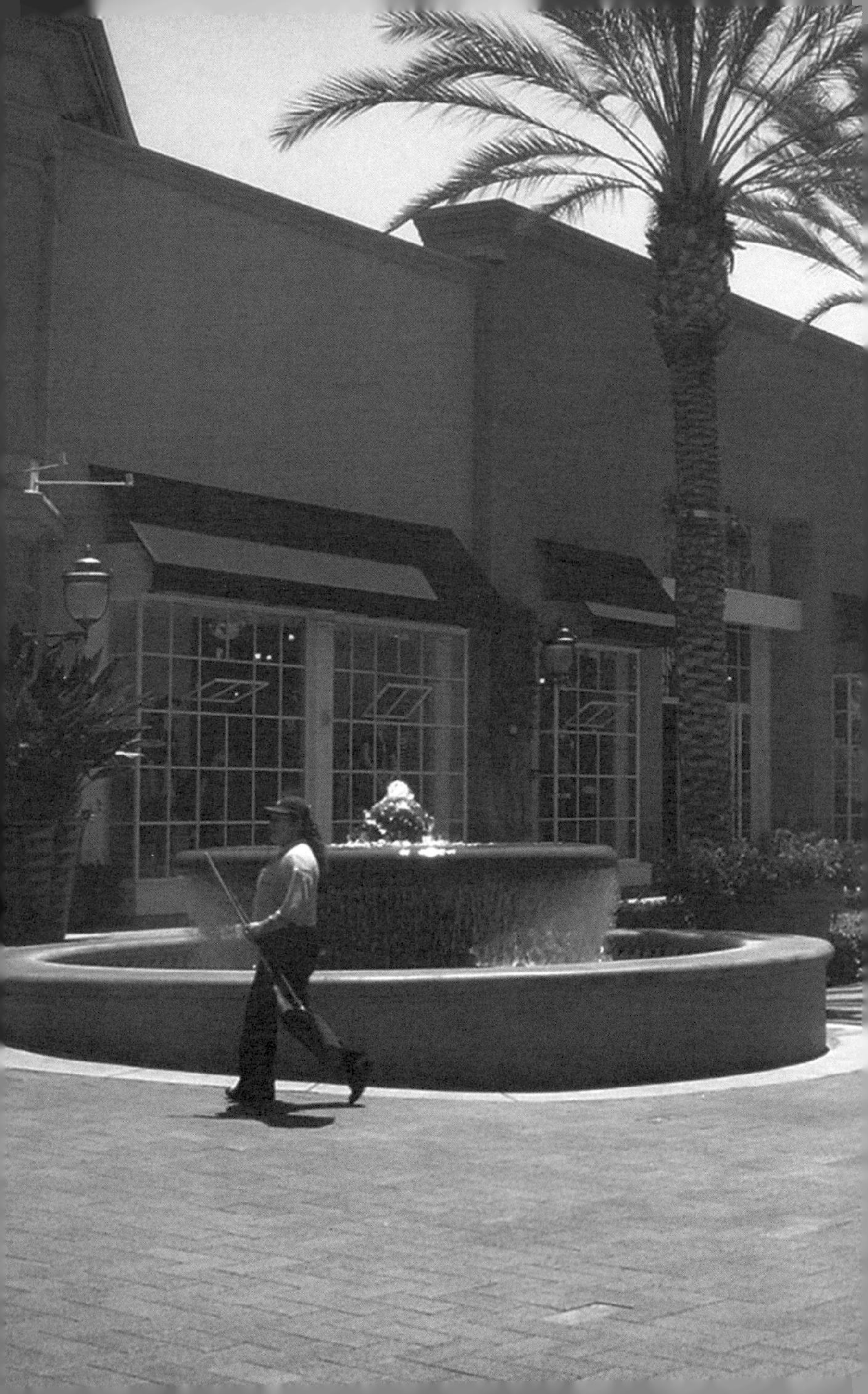

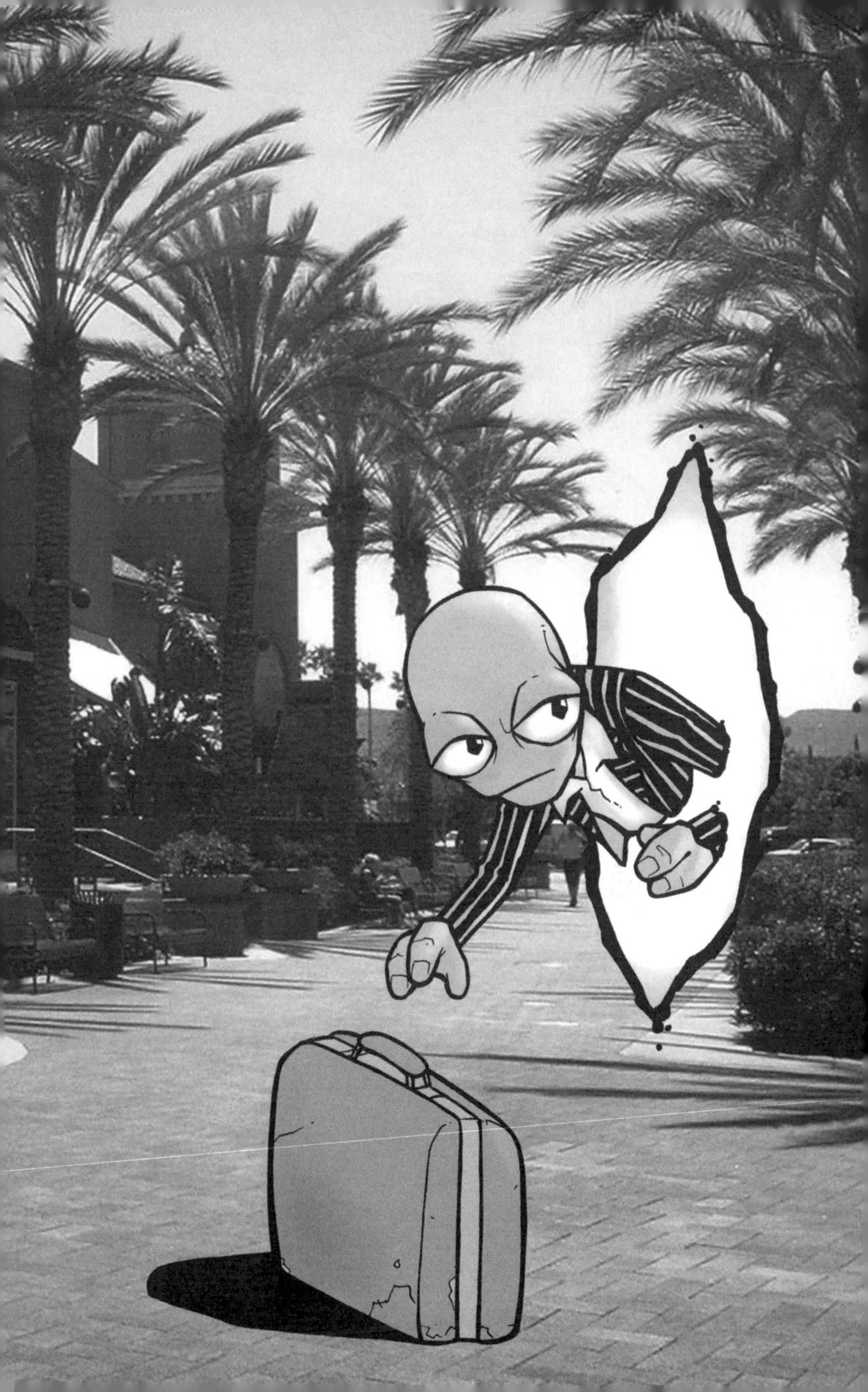

NEXT TIME IN:

Skate Farm

THE SERIES

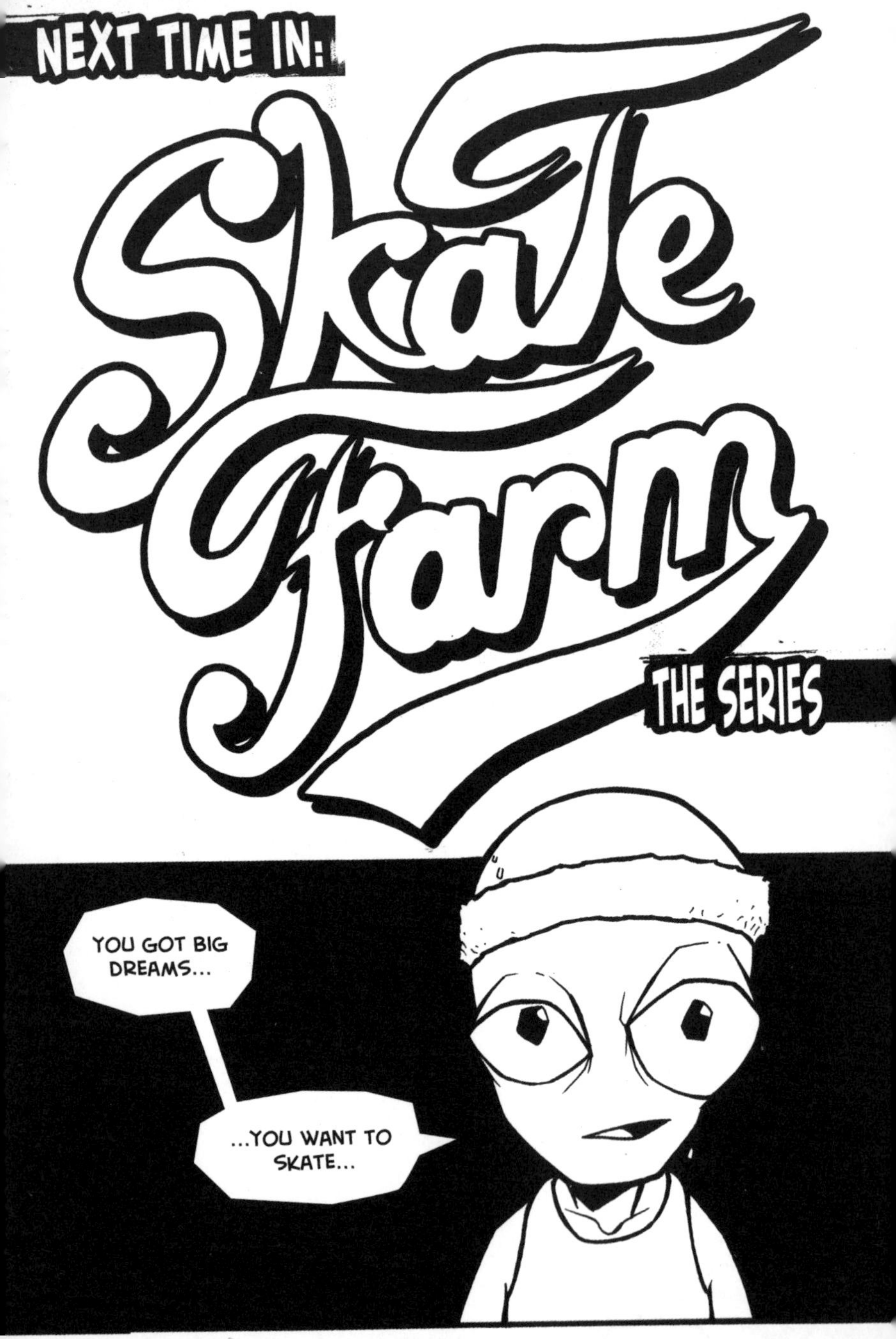
YOU GOT BIG DREAMS...
...YOU WANT TO SKATE...

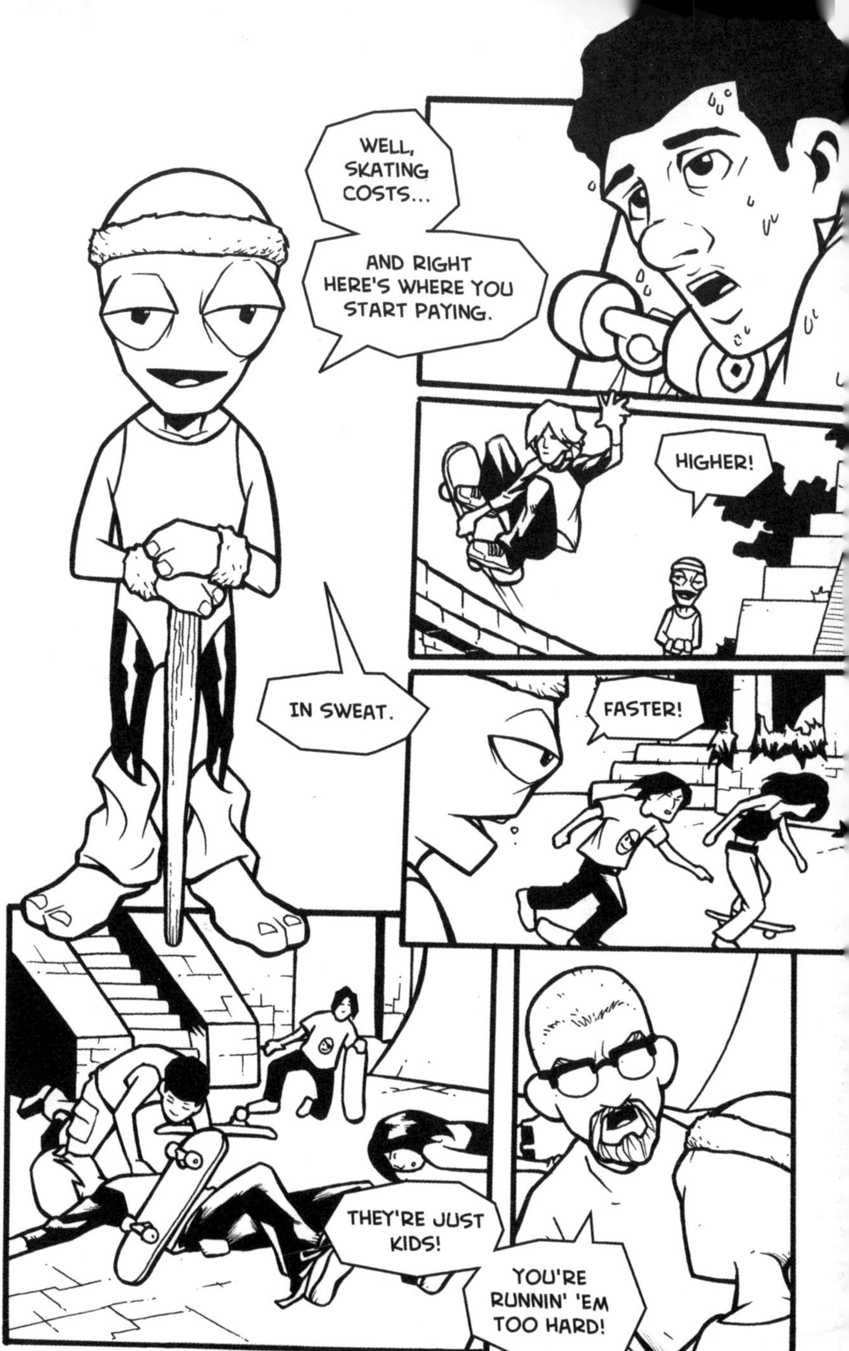
WELL, SKATING COSTS...
AND RIGHT HERE'S WHERE YOU START PAYING.
IN SWEAT.
HIGHER!
FASTER!
THEY'RE JUST KIDS!
YOU'RE RUNNIN' 'EM TOO HARD!

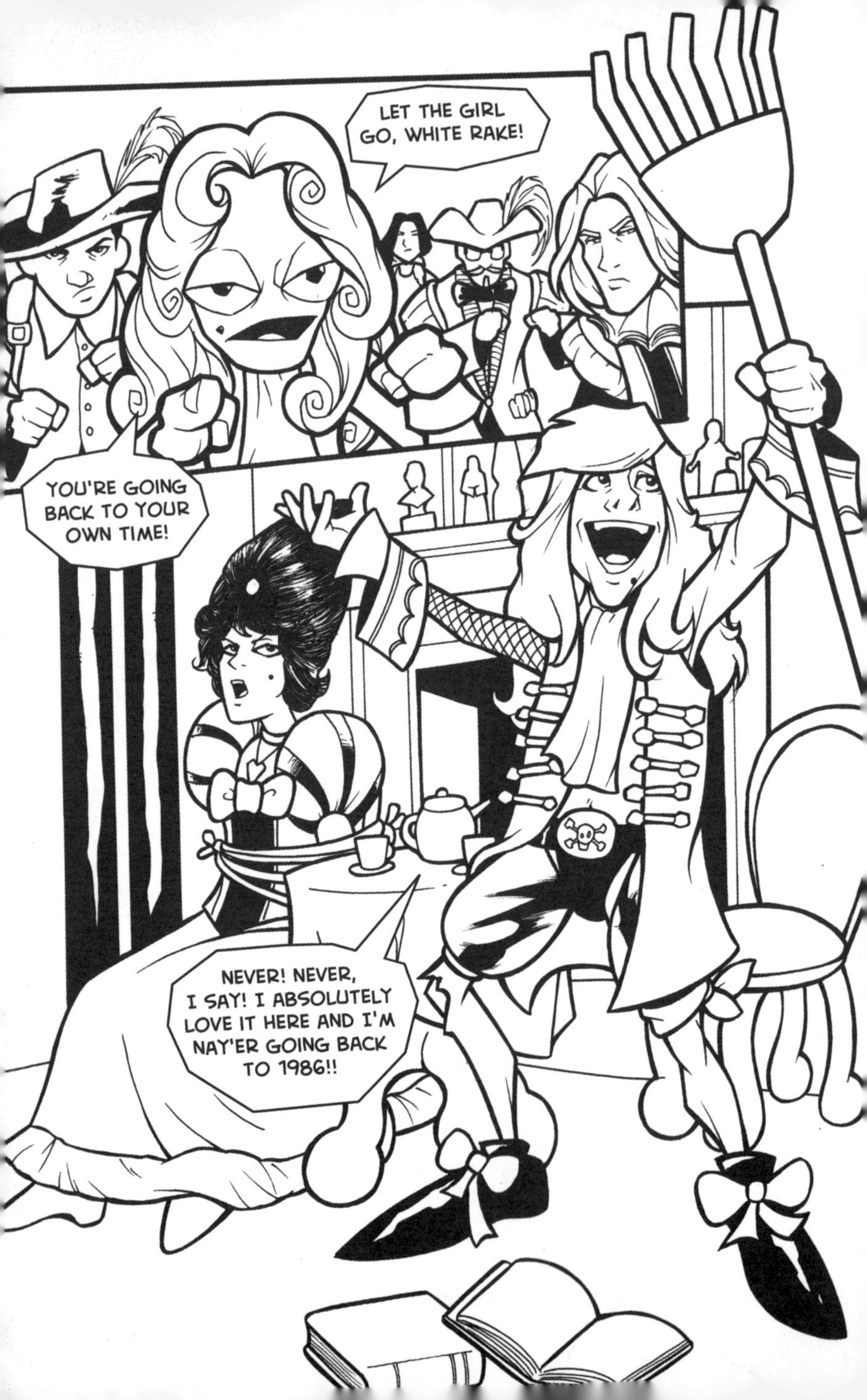
LET THE GIRL GO, WHITE RAKE!
YOU'RE GOING BACK TO YOUR OWN TIME!
NEVER! NEVER, I SAY! I ABSOLUTELY LOVE IT HERE AND I'M NAY'ER GOING BACK TO 1986!!

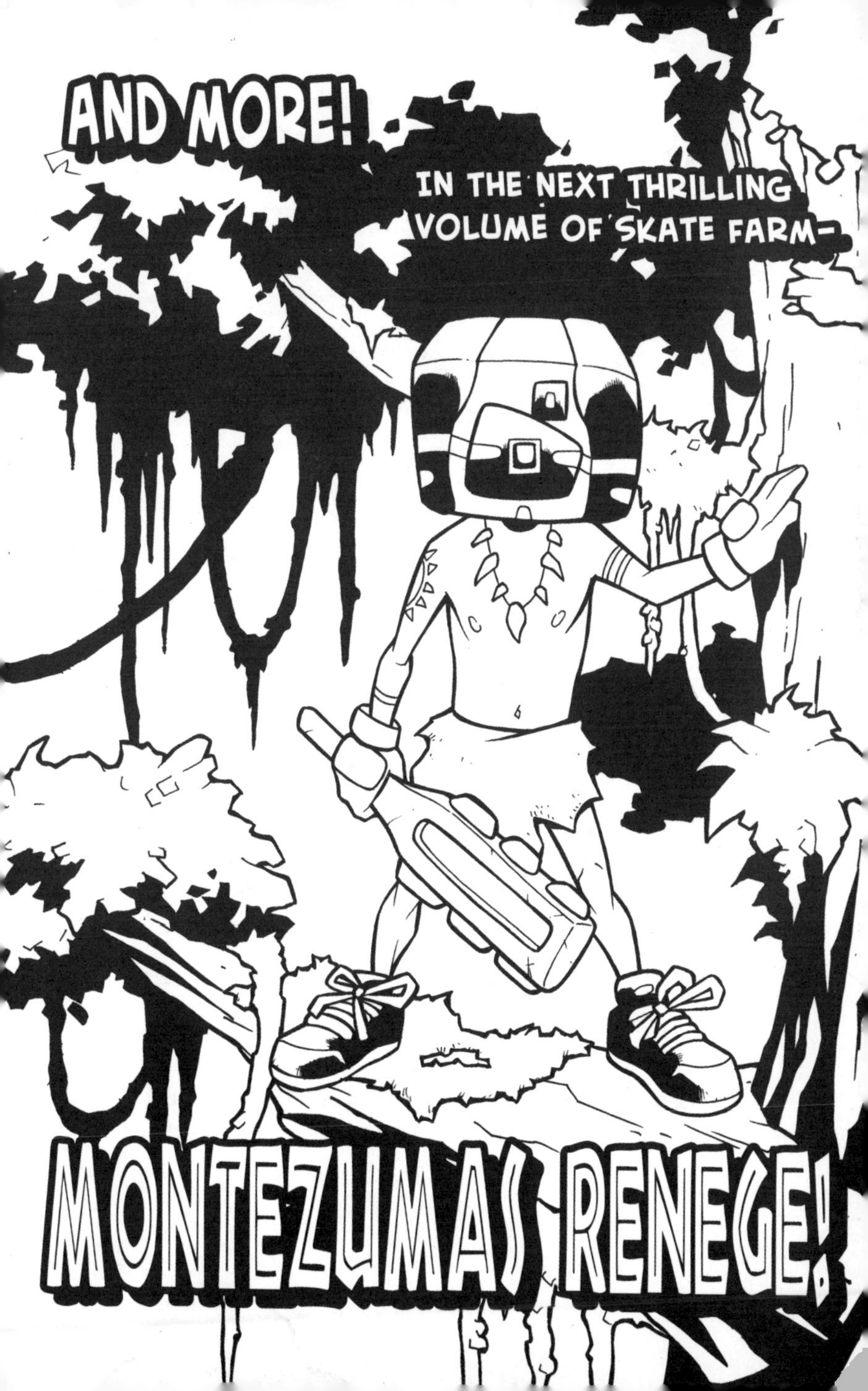
AND MORE!
IN THE NEXT THRILLING VOLUME OF SKATE FARM-
MONTEZUMAS RENEGE!

BONUS!!

ACTIVITY PAGES!

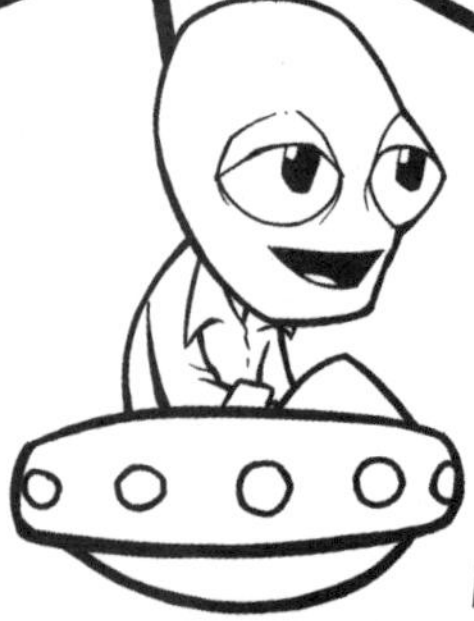

HEY KIDS!

HELP WILLIAM GET THROUGH THE MAZE AND TO HIS HOME GALAXY!!

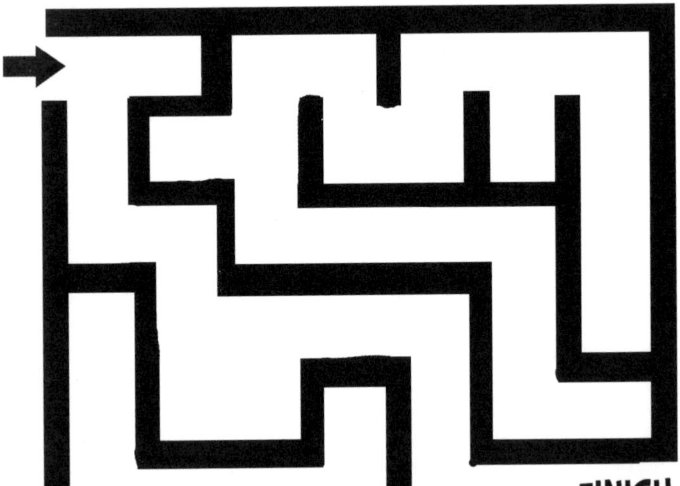
FINISH

YOU DID IT!

AREN'T YOU SPECIAL?

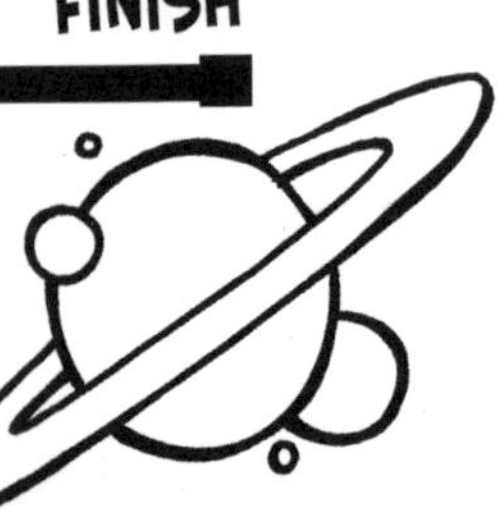

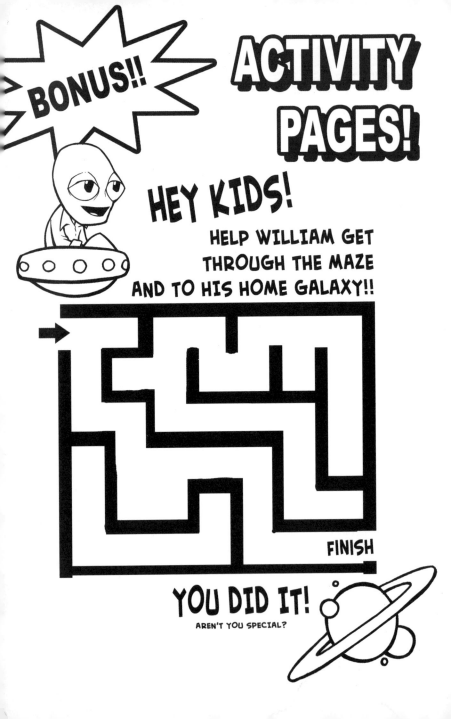

THERE'S A SUBTLE DIFFERENCE BETWEEN THESE TWO PICTURES.

CAN YOU GUESS WHAT IT IS?

DESIGN YOUR OWN SKATE DECK!*

USE THE TEMPLATE HERE
TO DRAW YOUR OWN
ORIGINAL SKATEBOARD
DECK ART! THEN CUT
IT OUT AND SHOW IT
TO YOUR MOM! OR VISIT
WWW.SKATEFARMCOMICS.COM
AND SHOW IT TO THE WORLD!!

*NOT TO SCALE

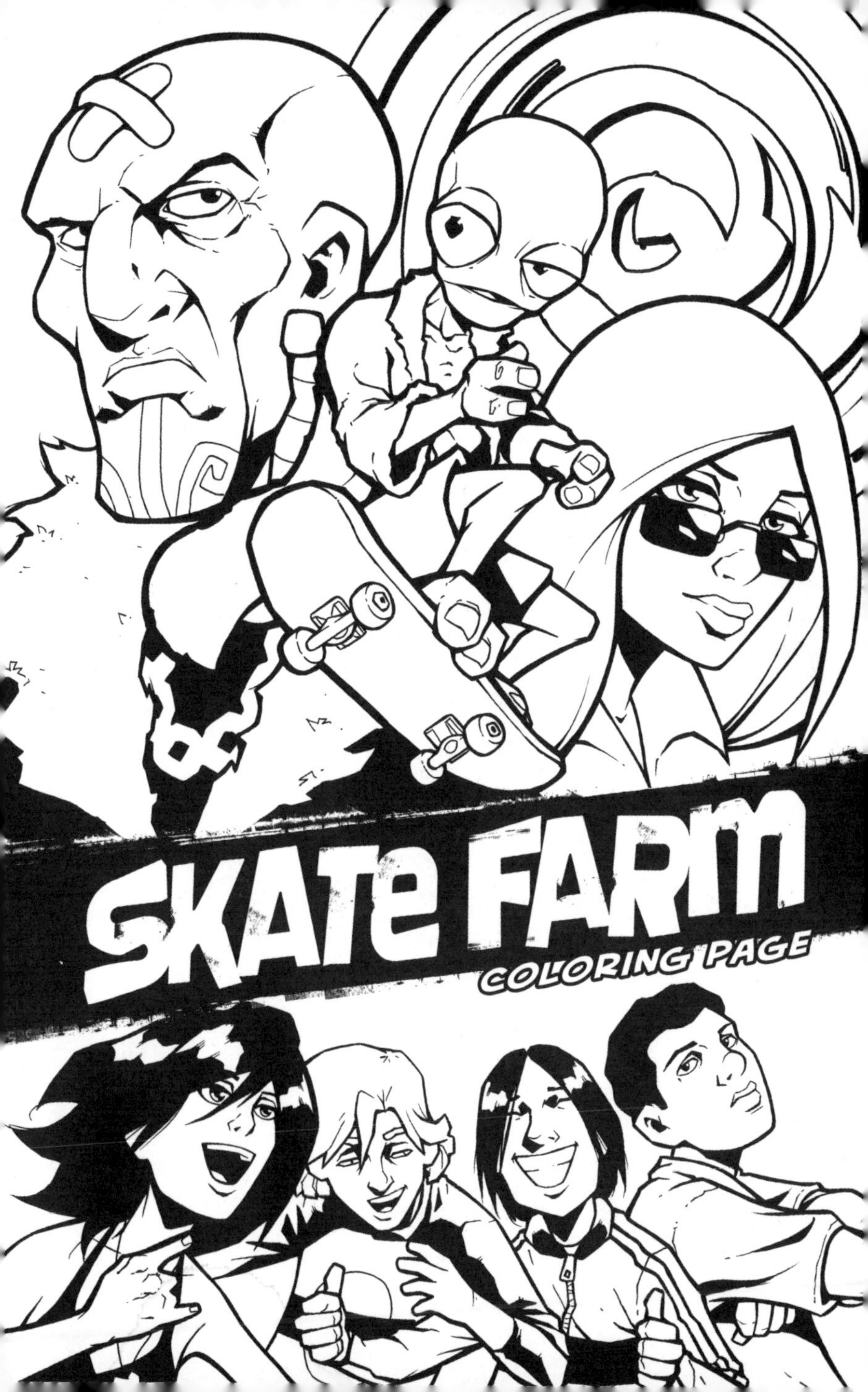
SKATE FARM
COLORING PAGE

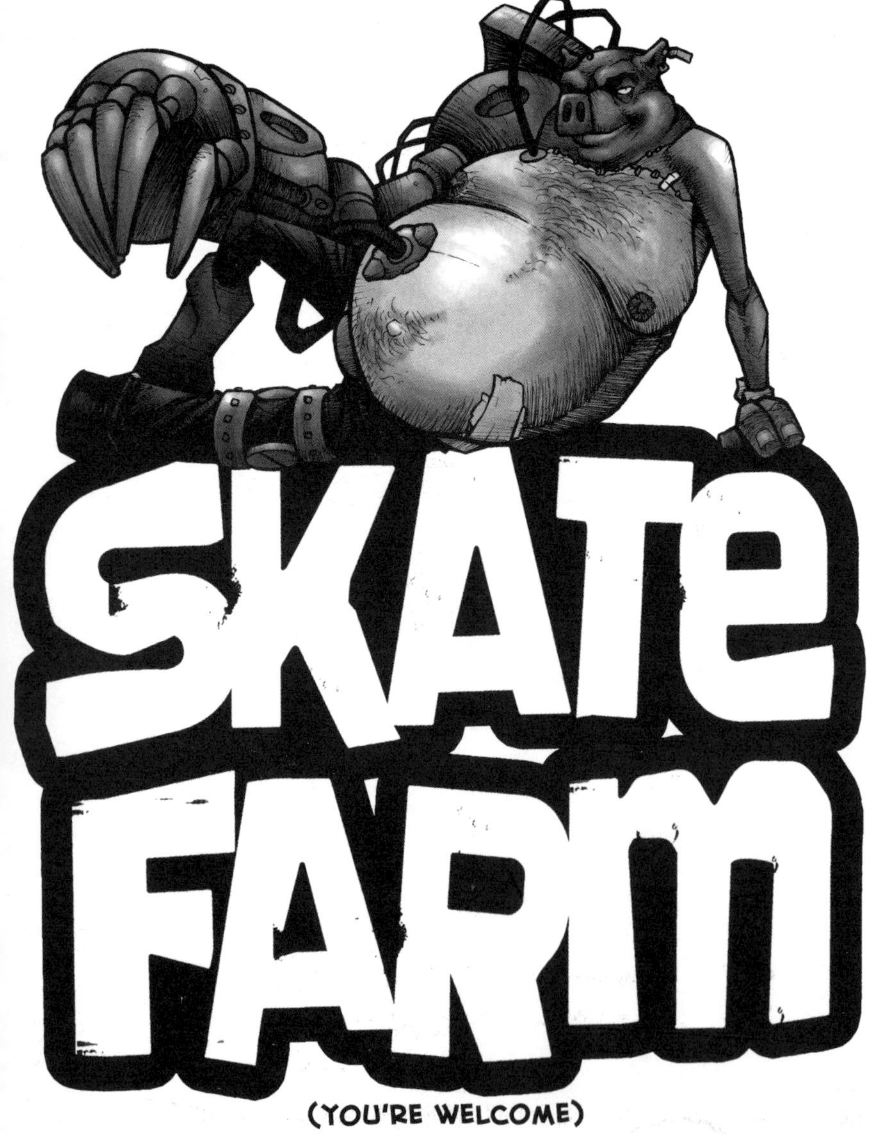
SKATE
FARM

(YOU'RE WELCOME)